CULTURAL HISTORY AF

CULTURAL HISTORY AFTER FOUCAULT

John Neubauer

Editor

ALDINE DE GRUYTER
New York

About the Editor

John Neubauer is Professor of Comparative Literature at the University of Amsterdam. Apart from coediting the semiannual journal *Arcadia*, he is the author *inter alia* of *The Fin-de-Siècle Culture of Adolescence; The Emancipation of Music from Language; Symbolismus und symbolische Logik;* and *Bifocal Vision.*

ALDINE DE GRUYTER
A division of Walter de Gruyter, Inc.
200 Saw Mill River Road
Hawthorne, New York 10532
This publication is printed on acid free paper ∞

Library of Congress Cataloging-in-Publication Data

Cultural history after Foucault / John Neubauer, editor.
    p.   cm.
    Includes bibliographical references and index.
    ISBN 0-202-30585-6 (pbk. : alk. paper)
    1. Culture—History.   2. Foucault, Michel.   I. Neubauer, John.
  1933– .
  HM621.C85   1999
  306'.09—dc21
                                        99-22892
                                        CIP

Manufactured in the United States of America
10 9 8 7 6 5 4 3 2 1

Contents

Part I. Modes of the Subject in Cultural History

Part II. Modes of Doing Cultural History

List of Contributors

Prof. Vladimir Biti
Department of Language and Literature
Faculty of Philosophy
University of Zagreb
Ivana Lucica 3, 1000 Zagreb
Croatia

Prof. Willem Frijhoff
Department of History
Free University of Amsterdam
De Boelelaan 1105, 1081 HV
Amsterdam, NL

Prof. Jan Goldstein
Department of History
University of Chicago
1126 East 59th Street
Chicago, IL 60637

Dr. Frans-Willem Korsten
Department of General Literature
University of Leiden
2300 RA
Leiden, NL

Dr. Michiel Leezenberg
Department of Philosophy
University of Amsterdam
Nieuwe Doelenstraat 15, 1012 CP
Amsterdam, NL

Prof. Ian Maclean
All Souls College
Oxford University,
Oxford Ox1 4AL
United Kingdom

Prof. Paul Allen Miller
Comparative Literature
University of South Carolina
Columbia, SC 29208

Dr. Sarah Roff
Department of Germanic Languages
and Literatures
Princeton University
Princeton, NJ 08544

Prof. George Rousseau
Leverhulme Trust Fellow
Oxford University (until 2001)
Research Professor of the Humanities
De Montfort University
Leicester LE1 9BH
United Kingdom

Dr. William Scott
Cultural History Group
Department of Philosophy
University of Aberdeen
Old Brewery, Aberdeen, AB24 3UB
United Kingdom

Saul Tobias
Department of Philosophy
Emory University
Atlanta, GA 30322

Prof. Mario J. Valdés
Comparative Literature Program
University of Toronto
Toronto, M5S 1A1
Canada

Prof. David Van Leer
Department of English,
University of California, Davis
Davis CA 95616, USA

Introduction

Michel Foucault was both a historian and a maker of culture. Not unlike Nietzsche, his adopted predecessor, he has been severely scrutinized by scholars of the disciplines in which he worked, yet the real significance of his personality and work transcend disciplinary boundaries and it transcends even the question whether in specific instances he was right or wrong. Like Nietzsche, he will probably be remembered most vividly as a great gadfly that questioned central assumptions in Western culture.

The contributors to this volume—scholars of history, literature and philosophy from the United States, the United Kingdom, and the Netherlands—were asked to address themselves to problems in cultural history at the end of the twentieth century in view of Foucault's contributions as well as the inevitable movement to go beyond them. We asked also, how Foucault's ideas functioned in the research they themselves were conducting in the late 1990s. In order to keep the discussion as broad as possible, we did not attempt to define cultural history but allowed it to cover several forms of cultural scholarship, including traditional and contemporary cultural history, cultural analysis, and the newly emerging, politically engaged cultural studies. The locution "overcoming the Foucauldian heritage" was designed as a challenge both to those who disregard Foucault's impact on studies of cultural history and to those who assume that a Foucauldian earthquake permanently transformed not only historiography but also the landscape of culture itself. In a Hegelian and (since Foucault's concept of history knows no "overcoming") very un-Foucauldian manner, we conceived of "overcoming" as an *Aufheben*, a preservation as well as cancellation.

It came as no surprise that the contributing historians, literary scholars, and philosophers addressed these issues from different angles and came to different answers. Surprising was perhaps only that the faultlines ran right through the disciplines rather than between them: each of the represented discipline produced defenders and critics of Foucault and his heritage. As Maclean suggests, one reason for this diversity is that "there is more than one Foucault": the "multiple receptions" reflect the "many-sidedness of his oeuvre" (p. 176). To this we may add that the diversity is partly due also to the differences in the national cultures in which Foucault's ideas were received. As Rousseau's and Van Leer's chapters show, Foucault's impact in the United States was deeply rooted in features of the American cultural tradition. Finally, as Goldstein notes with respect to cultural history, the cleavages within traditional disciplines were code-termined by a challenge to disciplinarity in Foucault's own work. It is this contemporary tension between disciplinary and interdisciplinary, internalist and externalist methods, which is a key topic in Goldstein's and Korsten's chapters.

In order to foreground this blurring of disciplinary boundaries, we do not group the chapters according to the disciplinary homes of the authors or their topics. The essays gathered here seem to fall rather naturally into the transdisciplinary domains: Part I, "Modes of the Subject in Cultural History," Part II, "Modes of Doing Cultural History," and Part III, "Modes of Conceptualizing Cultural History." What this implies we attempt to sketch in the remainder of this introduction.

Among the chapters pursuing the problematic status of the subject in Foucault's work and beyond, is most keen to explore possibilities opened but not fully worked out by Foucault himself. Goldstein puts flesh and blood on Foucault's "technologies of the self" by showing that the concept can be made operational to interpret the nineteenth-century French institutionalization of Victor Cousin's psychology, and, relying on Mary Carruther's work on memory in medieval culture and Roger Chartier's on Gracián, she goes beyond this by suggestively indicating how the concept may be applied to a wide variety of practices in the history of Western culture.

Goldstein's use of a new, personal, and autobiographical academic style has an analogue in George Rousseau's chapter, though the latter pushes the discourse towards more radical purposes. Rousseau deals with the subject problematics in terms of Foucault's personality and impact on the "erotophobia" in American academia and in American society at large - an impact that is unique and may well be among Foucault's most important legacies. Rousseau's cultural critique and his account of Foucault's impact on the American "mindset" has, however, a second, less visible agenda embedded in his methodology. For Rousseau's manner of narrating, his autobiographical, even confessional style in talking about the emergence of gay perspectives in studies of literature and culture "enacts" an autobiographical mode that Foucault's impact on the American scene made possible but which Foucault's "ascetic," even "monkish," attitude never permitted him to adopt in writing about history. In this sense, the chapter both outlines Foucault's heritage in America and enacts a mode of "overcoming" Foucault.

Foucault did, however, adopt a personal and engaged style in his interviews and in his journalism, most notably in the pieces he wrote on the Iranian revolution, which are the subject of Leezenberg's chapter. These apparently marginal pieces raise, as Leezenberg shows, fundamental questions about Foucault's method as well as his notion of the (vanishing) subject. In contrast, it is precisely Foucault's practical engagement (in his early work on clinics) that Korsten considers as exemplary for the "rhetorical consciousness" of critical theory. He finds a similarly informed internalist critical theory at work in the writings of Evelyn Fox Keller on biology.

Among the chapters dealing with the writing of cultural history, Frijhoff faces most squarely the problem of disciplinarity by observing that "the mainstream of history, as historians practice it nowadays" has been barely touched by [Foucault's] work, and professional historians "have seldom recognized his work as an appropriate form of cultural history," even if cultural constructions of the past, discourse analysis, and the rhetorics of historical writing, so central in the new cultural history advocated by Natalie Zemon Davis, Lynn Hunt, and others, "lean heavily on Foucault's methods and are inspired by his conceptual models" (p. 83). Frijhoff himself chooses the more controversial route of leaving American new cultural history aside and concentrating on the more antagonistic French reactions to Foucault. In the end, however, he finds a concept of "appropriation" in the work of Michel de Certeau (as well as in Frijhoff's own studies) that makes use of Foucault rather than rejecting him wholesale.

Valdés and Scott outline specific post-Foucauldian histories. The latter sketches a cultural history of the French Revolution that would rely (in contrast to Foucauldian practices) on material "from below," including provincial archives and traces of orality; Valdés, in turn, outlines a history of the Latin American literatures that builds on Foucault by embedding those literatures into their complex cultural settings but goes beyond him by replacing the impersonal and individual voice of the historian with the voice of a collaborative collective and by injecting a conspicuous hermeneutic element into Foucault's positivistically tinted approach. Making use of Paul Ricoeur's work, Valdés postulates that the meanings of historical events are constructed and that historical agents and later historians may construct widely differing meanings. Furthermore, the project of Latin American literary history intends to go beyond Foucault by giving attention to the quotidian and quotidian time and by examining "plural uses of discourse as well as multiple and diverse readings of texts which are not inscribed in the text" (p. 104). Valdés clearly agrees here with critiques of Foucault by Frijhoff and Scott.

Roff takes an interesting alternative, for her step "beyond" Foucault is at the same time a step back to one of Foucault's earliest works, the *Folie et déraison*, which she defends even against Foucault's own later critique. Showing that Foucault's treatment of the abandonment of the leprosariums and their later reuse as asylums is structurally analogous to Freud's analysis of repression, Roff persuasively suggests that the work's conception of history may be fruitful for developing psychoanalytic conceptions of cultural history.

Biti's chapter is placed in Part III, "Modes of Conceptualizing Cultural History" but actually thematizes the relationship between this group and the one just discussed, by noting a discrepancy between contemporary theories and practices of history. Biti shows that Foucault and Derrida negate modes of periodization in a problematic way, whereas the practice of history writing insistently sticks to the existing period patterns "as if obliged by the 'generic memory' of its own tradition" (p. 183). Both disciplinary fields, theory as well as practice, seem to claim specific standards and norms. Biti suggests, however, that both must respond to the same set of questions concerning a "periodizational grid," namely "who undertook it, for which purposes, faced with which problems, under which historical, situational, institutional and intertextual circumstances, and followed by which particular consequences" (184).

Focusing on the Achilles heel of periodization in Foucault's *Les mots et les choses* and *L'archeologie du savoir*, the mechanism of changeover, Maclean suggests that Foucault's epistemic conception should be revised by appealing to Weber's ideal type, Husserl's notion of disciplinary sedimentation, Collingwood's constellations of absolute presuppositions and Kuhn's paradigm" (p. 166). What this would imply in practical terms is exemplified when Maclean confronts Foucault's treatment of the Renaissance with his own, showing that "Foucault has egregiously set aside evidence for the flexibility and vitality of Renaissance thought" (p. 173). A fuller consideration of the material would allow for a more flexible notion of paradigm and paradigm shift.

Miller gives a similarly critical reading of the periodization in Foucault's *History of Sexuality*, particularly Foucault's description of a transition from classical self-mastery in fourth-century Greece to a "care of the self" in the Roman world. He accepts Foucault's critique of earlier scholarship that the growth of individualism had no teleological goal, and that "the 'care of the self' as a form of ethical self-relation can never be understood as a mere reflection of an ontologically prior sociopolitical infrastructure, but must be perceived as an original response to a complex and overdetermined practical and discursive situation" (p. 186). But Miller's paradigmatic discussion of Catullan poetry indicates that Foucault's criteria for the period lead to a reductive image, and, more importantly, that a fuller consideration of Catullus' lyric subjectivity reveals elements that negate the hegemonic mode in Foucault's model of subjectivity so that transition is subsequently motivated.

Miller's concern with Foucault's "suppression of the negative moment" in the History of Sexuality thus parallels Maclean's critique that Foucault's *Order of Things* has no human agents to bring about processes of intellectual change. Interestingly enough, Tobias' apparently different concerns touch on the same issue, even though they point towards different solutions. For if Tobias is in search of a space for philosophy in Foucault's system, this too means seeking for an agency with a modicum of independence in the hegemonic power structure: "locating within Foucault's analysis of power a space for philosophy, or for a particular notion of philosophy, which despite its interrogation and deflation (most notably by deconstruction) still bears the hallmark of the classical Kantian formulation of philosophy as the inquiry into the transcendental conditions of phenomena" (p. 221). But whereas Maclean criticizes "a quasi-Kantian categorialism[sic]" (p. 166) in Foucault's notion of epistemes, and sees Collingwood, Husserl, Kuhn, Weber, and Popper as ways of overcoming "categorial" thinking, for Tobias the contemporary interest in Kantian principles indicates precisely that the possibilities of immanent critique are limited. Criticizing Foucault, but finding in his work a slim and unimplemented proposal as well, Tobias concludes that a critical cultural history would "call for the articulation of conditions which are not reducible to visible structure or legible discourses, it calls for the thinking of transcendental limits to what can be articulated in empirical, scientific or rational language" (p. 228).

Van Leer, finally, raises questions about post-Foucauldian positions in contemporary American cultural criticism by focusing on a colonial case, William Bradford's account of Thomas Granger's execution for "unnatural" sexual activities with barnyard animals and a turkey, which in American gay scholarship has recently become "a test case not only for pre-nineteenth-century discourse of sexuality but for the convergences of sexuality with other minority discourses of gender, ethnicity, and race" (p. 211). Starting with a passage in Foucault's *History of Sexuality*, which describes the nineteenth-century birth of the homosexual as a "species," and which many regard as a founding text in American academic gay studies today, Van Leer raises the question, whether one commits the sin of "transhistoricity" by employing terms like "homosexuality" for periods that precede their discursive usage. He deconstructs Bradford's passage by suggesting that its silence about the trial and his lengthy description of the execution of the animals makes Granger into something of an "authority figure." The point is not that Bradford was "progressive," but that the most interesting reading of his text will "not merely flatter modern sensibilities" by rehearsing Granger's martyrdom (p. 219) and Bradford's Puritan prejudices. Although Foucault himself explicitly argues that one should not apply later concepts to earlier phenomena, Van Leer thinks he did not rigidly adhere to this and was less dogmatic about it than his rigorous American constructionist followers. Consciously and deliberately recasting the issues in Bradford's text in presentist terminology on the assumption that this will make its implicit prejudices explicit will not only resuscitate a suspect tradition of Puritan bashing (which is just another form of Puritanism) but disagree also, Van Leer suggests, with Foucault's strategies to come to terms with the past.

In sum, the contributors to this volume indicate Foucault's achievements and the suggestive power of his work, as well as his methodological weaknesses, historical inaccuracies, and ambiguities. Above all, they attempt to show how one can use Foucault to go beyond him in opening new approaches to cultural history. Though comprehensiveness was not attempted, their essays broach the major controversial aspects of Foucauldian cultural history—the position of the subject, the fusion of power and knowledge, sexuality, the historical structures and changes—and they explicitly analyze them with respect to antiquity, the Renaissance, and the nineteenth century. We hope that they will stimulate further discussion and reflection on Foucault, his legacy, and the cultural-institutional conditions in which they continue to function.[1]

---

[1] Indeed, the chapters in this book are part of a continuing discussion. Most of them were first read and discussed as papers on June 6–7 1997, at a two-day conference in Amsterdam, the Netherlands. The second conference on the topic took place at the University of Aberdeen a year later, on June 26-28, 1998. That second set of conference papers will be published in the journal *Configurations*. A third conference is planned for March 2000 at the University of South Carolina.

I

Modes of the Subject in Cultural History

1

No Sex Please, We're American:
Erotophobia, Liberation, and Cultural History

GEORGE ROUSSEAU

> "We are therefore in an impossible situation, unable to
> dream either of a past or a future state of affairs"
>
> (Baudrillard, *Hystericizing the Millennium*)[1]

I. Erotophobia

Thus Baudrillard on the toll our Western hysterias have taken as we approach
2000. My "we" is American: the Americans, past and future, who participate in
this attempt to fashion a post-Foucaldian discourse: not as parody or imitation
but in my own voice and inflection and about a subject that has preoccupied
me for two decades. The "dream" is erotic: the forms of sexual expression that
have been intrinsic facets of human cultures from time immemorial. The syndrome of regulation to which I refer has been discussed under other rubrics
and pondered in the media but rarely in this coinage.

Erotophobia then: approximate to Europhobia, xenophobia, homophobia,
and the many other phobias clamping down on our regulatory generation. The
force of the word lies in the second root – *phobia*: an unnatural fear, a repulsion,
not merely a benign dislike or gentle recoil. Erotophobia: in the *longue durée,* no
culturally sanctioned mass hysteria developing over several centuries, despite
cyclical peaks and valleys, based on the terror of sexual involvement. Hence the
phobic basis of the hysteria. Some might praise this fear as an internal censor;
even so, its recent consequences have been dire for almost every aspect of
American life and culture except the economic. These resonances and their
implications form the heart of my subject here.

Erotophobia: fear of Eros. Recoil from sex. Eros as state of mind, Eros
as body act. A phobia and persistent fear. A construction without lexical or
sociolinguistic profile. Without discourse or literature. The *longue durée* of erotophobia rather than its quondam appearances or the pattern of its cycles in
history. Hardly a Foucaldian term, despite Greek roots, and neither a fixture of

---

[1] Baudrillard, *L'Illusion de la fin* (1992), portions of which appeared in English as "Hystericizing
the Millennium."

our contemporary mindsets or something on the tips of our imagination. Most of us have never heard of erotophobia, let alone invoked it.[2]

More locally in diverse America, the national desexualization within our collective fear of sexuality. The empty label — erotophobia — stares us in the face: inherent in our Puritan tradition (in H. L. Mencken's constructed sense rather than the seventeenth-century historical version), revived throughout our American history, reinvigorated after two world wars, especially the Second with its contingent aftermath of McCarthyism (the inquisitions of all those who might have any ties to Communists, Jews, gays), San Francisco's Haight Ashberry (the drugs and sex revolution at grass roots), and now, most fiercely, in the new proliferating mass hysterias of post-AIDS.

Erotophobia: the xenophobic insignia par excellence, because it brandishes all those whose customs and practices are "foreign" as sexual deviants of one type or another, as well as the form of cultural hysteria and popular delusion that assumes the individual in society is perpetually being exposed to sexual opportunity and encounter. But also collective paranoia or medical malady that even accounts in part for America's legendary obesity? After all, one of the dominant explanations for the difference between the chic Parisian or Milanese woman decked out in designer clothing and the gross overweight of American women has been sexual expression and repression; especially the American woman's inability to be sexually comfortable and sexually appealing. But erotophobia as the millennium's silent epidemic? In millennial America can it lie among its worst transgressions? — in which case what kind of sexual transgression is erotophobia anyway? In an age of fierce regulation the curbing of sexual license appears legitimate, even predictable. Or is erotophobia a metonymy for American sexual history itself? — the repressive nightshade of its social arrangements. Unlike those hysterias to which women and other marginalized groups are said to be prone, erotophobia also afflicts men in large numbers, *American men*.[3]

Whatever erotophobia's aetiology, it seems intrinsic to America's puritan civilization itself. But who has sustained it — who colluded in its cycles? Are America's fundamentalist anti-sex churchmen not its devotees and proselytizers? Or the Alfred Kinsey of the famed "Kinsey Report" (*Sexual Behavior in the Human Male*), now retrieved by his revisionary biographers who claim he was a "repressed homosexual" who inflated his statistics to render American sexuality less paltry and pallid than it actually was? Erotophobia derives not from Dr. Charcot and his histrionic Hedda Gablers, but flourishes from Atlanta to Anchorage, from Salem to Sausalito, as a native, if eclectic, form of the native

[2] Composed from Greek roots (eros and phobia: the fear of body contact), the word is ambiguous in relation to the domain and boundary of Eros.
[3] Perceptive analysis of some of these developments is found in Corber (1997).

culture of sexual repression. It is not the product of one American generation or past era. Its Golden Age seems to be *now*. Postmodern popular culture affirms it everywhere despite the silence of the scholars.[4] Proof abounds in the new American cults of "appropriate" behavior and "appropriate" language (almost all reducible to sex, gender and race) but nowhere stronger than in the invigorated American "political correctness" and the massive amount of litigation tightening virtually every aspect of the definition of sexual encounter, sexual innuendo, sexual implication, from the mildest hug to the accidental pat.

From at least the Renaissance to Freud, men have occasionally been hysterical, although erotophobic is not a term Freud ever used to describe them. Men have developed nervous illnesses, however disguised, long before neurasthenia became fashionable among the Marcel Prousts and Théophile Gautiers. But the hysteria of *don't touch me, don't breathe on me, don't drink out of this glass* — differs from this lassitude. This is not neurasthenia in another key but full-blown social erotophobia, the subject of this essay.[5]

In the Netherlands, where a remarkable tradition of toleration — especially *sexual* toleration — has survived the centuries, this urgent message about the conjunction of erotophobia, hysteria, and post-Foucaldian discourse seems especially germane. But there is also another sense in which erotophobia is the post-

---

4 Even a totalizing discourse such as Luedtke (1992) is silent on the matter.

5 Since 1992 the political Left has filled many of the highest posts in America's greatest research universities: their chairs and six figure salaries. The Right has either been satisfied, or has had no choice but to remain in the lower rank universities making lower salaries, and many have fled academia for politics, business, and the military-industrial complex. By any survey the Left has won the ideological struggle in America's leading research universities while remaining a small fraction of the total population of academics in American higher education. Without this unassailable fact that sustains the development of an entire profession, I see no way of discussing Foucault or cultural history in the aftermath of his revolution. The Age of Foucault is surely dead but its legacy, its beneficiaries, its effects hardly are, and the influence of those heirs among the political Left who constitute Foucault's securest progeny will continue to determine the fate of, and use the financial resources of, America's greatest research universities until they retire or some Foucaldian episteme — discontinuity — occurs to change this state of affairs. I would not, however, be mistaken in my portrayal of the context. I am not attacking the radical Left, however sharp or straightforward these contexts, nor even questioning its motives, although I am the first to concede that my own politic has always been somewhere in the liberal middle. More importantly, I continue to believe that the threat from the fundamental conservative Right exceeds that from the Left in America. Inflexible and superstitious, irrational and supremacist, it is the one more prone to fascism. But this position should not imply approbation of their platforms or congratulation that they have turned the profession of the humanities in America into the Leviathan it has become. Theory is surely not the culprit: theory is merely one symptom of the much larger malaise. It is this death of discovery within the humanities and its particular relevance for the cultural history of the next generation that I want briefly to address, especially within the political zone that lies between the radical Left and the fundamental conservative Right: the old "liberal middle" that until the 1960s had formed the heart and soul and intestines of liberal education in North America.

Foucaldian mindset that would have engaged Foucault himself as part of the ethos of *American* self-care. Erotophobia: the word almost no one can pronounce, yet whose ethos every American has experienced in one way or another, especially in its homophobic versions. The suspicion is that the historians who might chronicle this phenomenon have fabricated or imagined it.[6] But I think not, despite those far-flung John Wayne "masculinists" who accuse us of prejudice or derogate us as "masculine feminists." Besides, the testimony of Europeans in America, and Americans returning to the *heimat*, constitutes ample evidence, for perspective counts for much in gauging the comparative ethos of a culture of erotophobia. And the fact that we Americans have been unable, or unwilling, to document this cultural syndrome, speaks volumes in itself.[7]

Discussion of postmodern erotophobia cannot be accomplished outside the orbit of America's proliferating hysterias: its disjunctions between acts and the language used to account for them. Continental America approaching 2000 is still a psychoanalytic age despite all the partisan protests and anti-psychiatry movements. And it is the case that most psychiatrists will not go on record as agreeing that sexual deprivation actually *converts* to, that is *causes,* physical symptoms within illness. Doctors have always wanted sickness to be physiological. But erotophobia now flourishes mightily in politically-correct America precisely because hysteria remains its (America's) base-root insignia. All are subsumed within the realms of the appropriate: the new yardstick for human behavior.

We Americans have, of course, our fierce intellectual critics, from Noam Chomsky to Edward Said; from Polish producer Roman Polanski to the dozens of expat Americans who will not go home. Part of the reason (not all, of course) entails the domain of erotophobia, although it is never called by this pathological sounding label. American feminist Elaine Showalter believes that Gulf War Syndrome and chronic fatigue exist in the mind rather than in viruses or genes, as do recovered memory loss, satanic ritual abuse, multiple personality disorder, and alien abduction.[8] Where did these hysterias originate, and for what do they compensate? In a puritan nation (which America remains despite its diverse populations who will soon outnumber its WASPS) there is little toleration for, nor threshold of, sexuality.[9] Thus the loop comes full circle: from puritan anti-

---

[6] Any serious historical approach would of course chronicle and document its versions with the greatest possible precision.

[7] I refer to it as a syndrome, phobia, threshold, collective hysteria and popular delusion less out of inconsistency or vacillation than from my own uncertainty about its precise taxonomy. Eventually, one would have to decide for oneself about its status as a stable category and classification in the DSM sense.

[8] Showalter *Hystories* (1996).

[9] Postmodernism implies the radical fragmentation of populations and geographical entities, and in many parts of America, especially the South and the West, Caucasians are now in a minority; it remains, however, to be seen whether their statistical diminution has affected the status of the dominant discourse as predominantly white, Protestant, and puritan; see Baudrillard *America*.

sex to proliferating postmodern hysteria, as in the current fashion to find child abuse rampant. When Marcia Clark, the O. J. Simpson prosecutor, announced relatively recently, first, that she too was raped at seventeen, and secondly, that by the time the trial ended she and Christopher Darden, her co-counsel, were "closer than lovers" despite their relationship *never* having been physical, she perfected her no-sex, virtual reality persona before American cameras, for the screen was the only place most Americans had ever seen her.[10] Only in racially and sexually diverse America can such multifarious hysterias coexist: we invent them and export them, like Coca-Cola, to the rest of the world.

The desexualization of America struck social scientists in the aftermath of the Sixties. The great wave of free love and drugs had come and gone: what had been its determinants? Charles Winick, an American social scientist, wrote about *Desexualization in American Life* at the end of the Sixties. He was followed by others attributing America's hysterias over abuse, crime, random murder, and violence to *repressed sexuality* – the same suppressions to which illnesses from cancer to road rage are now sometimes attributed. But *is* erotophobia a form of illness rather than a moral condition or social category? – especially if it makes people sick. That is sexually sick. Historically speaking, sexual repression never became a topic in polite discourse in America, and it barely is now. But the HIV that was carried across our borders in 1980 was an accident waiting to happen; and to some of us this form of historical psychoanalysis based on sexual repression seemed Foucaldian before Foucault was widely read in America.[11]

II. America, Puritanism, Erotophobia

It may appear a gross exaggeration but a *sexual* history of our generation in America omitting erotophobia is like the history of Germany without Auschwitz or Italy without Fascism. That is, the sexual consequences of "Puritan nation" (in the phrase of this major school of American history) cannot be shunted away. The only difference in valence is its relative impoliteness. Compare us with any previous American generation, or even with the buttoned-up English Victorians, and we Americans outperform all others in the mass-hysteria-based-on-sexual-fear that erotophobia is. It is not that we are silent about what we do, but what every study shows we have actually been (or not been) *doing*; and if the studies of all manner of social scientists are valid, our attitudes to the body are so phobic they hardly compensate for whatever intimate pelvic thrust has endured in American life with impunity. America: the Puritan soil for erotophobia; it seems to reside in our blood cells; in our native antipathy to "body

---

10 Clark (1997); see also Chomsky (1969).
11 For one response to the reading of Foucault in America see Gross (1994).

intercourse" (the summation of body language and physical contact) as indigenous to our Puritan heritage as the new proliferating hysterias themselves. A
nation intent from the start on breaking away from Europe and its Mediterranean center in this primary phobic response to natural human sexuality. Yet
American Puritanism should also be viewed through foreign eyes as a fundamentally anti-erotic dominant Wasp discourse. Perhaps this is what the historians
of the American novel (for example, classical American novel critic Leslie
Fiedler) have meant when claiming that the American male, despite alleged
machismo, fears for his virginity more than anything. Hence the passive heterosexual male of our native American literature who Fiedler configured as a clo-
seted passive homosexual. Fiedler's heirs in literary criticism — especially the
queer theorists — have pried open the epistemology of this closet.[12]

Erotophobia is also the night-time opposite of *erotomania*: the condition of
lust about which Foucault has written so eloquently in the *History of Sexuality*
(*HS*, II, 50). Yet even the medical history of erotomania is not what we would
imagine: in the ancient world, the Renaissance, and even in Foucault's *L'age
classique,* when another mania — nymphomania — will be born (1771).[13] The

---

[12] Sedgwick (1990). Hofstadter (1963), the historian of American anti-intellectualism, has also
connected this sexual terror to religious origins: "Very commonly a sexual fundamentalism —
thoroughgoing in its fear both of normal sex and of deviation — is linked with the other two.
One frequently gets the feeling from later fundamentalist sermons that they were composed
for audiences terrified of their own sexuality" (119). Bercovitch (1975) focuses on the spiritual
rather than sexual sides of Puritanism.

[13] Bienville (1775). The discourses of erotomania commenced in the sixteenth century, although
no works then were exclusively devoted to it; a partial chronological outline of exclusive works
includes Kunadus (1681); Backhauss, (1686); Heintze (1719). These were replaced in the 1720s
by medical treatises on an equivalent "metromania," and in 1771 by Bienville's newly coined
"nymphomania." For Foucault on erotomania see *HS*, II, 50. Of the Shakespearean version,
Elaine Showalter has commented in "Representing Ophelia: women, madness, and the responsibilities of feminist criticism," that "clinically speaking, Ophelia's behavior and appearance are
characteristic of the malady the Elizabethans would have diagnosed as female love-melancholy,
or erotomania . . . On the stage, Ophelia's madness was presented as the predictable outcome
of erotomania. From 1660, when women first appeared on the public stage, to the beginnings
of the eighteenth century, the most celebrated of the actresses who played Ophelia were those
whom rumor credited with disappointments in love. The greatest triumph was reserved for
Susan Mountfort, a former actress at Lincoln's Inn Fields who had gone mad after her lover's
betrayal. One night in 1720 she escaped her keeper, rushed to the theater, and just as the
Ophelia of the evening was to enter for her mad scene, 'sprang forward in her place . . . with
wild eyes and wavering motion'" (Parker and Hartman, 81−82). Gideon Harvey, the marginalized English Restoration physician, medicalized "erotomania" in his *Morbus Anglicus* (1672),
52−61, specifically locating it in the animal spirits and classifying it as an "amorous consumption." Such classifications later included the subspecies metromania and eventually Bienville's
nymphomania. An anonymous work of 1730 entitled *Onania* paints a picture of compulsively
masturbating females as "erotomaniacs." More generally on erotomania see Skultans (1979) and
MacDonald (1981).

abbreviated early modern "history of sexuality" has been a tale about freedom replaced and repressed by constraints that were labelled and medicalized. Vis-à-vis sexuality, the story is that unhindered Catholic (almost pagan) license was replaced by a repressive Protestantism that in the long eighteenth century was medicalized into the manias some of whose labels endure: erotomania (Ferrand), metromania (which replaced the old wandering and rampaging uterus), nympho-mania (Bienville). Early Modern doctors who medicalized female sexuality were searching for names and characteristics to mark out this behavior of lust gone out of control. As such, their endeavor resembled other early attempts in the history of sexuality to chart the paths of deviation, however fraught with error and prejudice they may have been. The doctors suspected the matter to be more complex than they could account for in their learned treatises, but this lapse in itself did not deter them from writing. Yet if constraint and repression were already in place in Protestant lands ca. 1750, why the need for erotophobia? What was this version of response? I am suggesting that erotophobia was *not* part and parcel of that (northern) European mindset but something indigenous to the peoples across the ocean in the colonies; and that although it was seeded then, in the structures of the early colonies, it did not appear in America with any palpable force (just as erotomania did not appear in Europe until the cults of sexual repression were medicalized) until certain social conditions could co-alesce: in the evolution of the American workplace into the litigious precinct it has become; in the development of America's vast legal profession; and in medi-cine under the burden of the new "plague" which was misunderstood and feared throughout the Eighties. Hence the convergence of conditions rather than any single factor is the requirement for erotophobia: a phobic reaction caused by heightened fear engendering mass hysteria. The metaphor of temperature may be best to explain the genesis of these convergences. Erotophobia arises only when the thermometer reaches a certain temperature, as it did in America in the 1980s under the stress of all the above conditions, especially the so-called "Gay Plague" occurring in the midst of a sexual revolution already unbearable to so many segments of America society.

Furthermore, in that early modern world erotomania was tempered by a medical model privileging the retention and waste of female seed: the withhold-ing of which led to so many female *maladies d'amour*, as described in seventeenth-century French physician Jacques Ferrand's *De la maladie d'amour* which Edward Chilmead translated in 1640 as *Erotomania or a treatise discoursing of the essence, causes, symptoms, prognosticks, and cure of erotique melancholy.*[14] Male seed was regulated

---

[14] Ferrand. For commentary on the origins of the tradition see Rose. Sander Gilman notes that the changing representations of Ophelia over the centuries chronicle the shifting definitions of female insanity, from the erotomania of the Elizabethans and the hysteria of the nineteenth century (126).

by other conventions and prescriptions than female. A century later, Dr. Tissot's Swiss Protestant milieu became riddled with moral considerations further reinforcing patriarchal gender empowerments. Men assumed more, not less, control over the medicalization of sexual conditions: in collecting, classifying, and describing them; so much so that a condition such as erotomania was medicalized as were so many other "melancholies" of the day. Further back, Plato's lust, or erotomania (the Greeks used this word but without the thick medicalizing function of the seventeenth-century doctors), always permeated the body rather than the soul (*HS*, II, 45). The soul was said to be immune – unavailable to the pollution. Down through the ancient and Renaissance worlds, erotomania was conceptualized as a fever of the mind interacting solely with the diseased body; the whole fabric of the body could be infected except the soul. Thus erotomania and erotophobia are opposites: the former a fever *for* sexual coitus, the latter a gesture of perpetual *recoil*, but with this twist: that in Europe the post-Tissotian moralists sentimentalized erotomania and then medically transformed it into madness. Ophelia and her sisters were afflicted by its fever. Like its child, nymphomania, it left the realm of spirits and fibres and nerves for loftier regions of mind and became a moral defect. By 1874 the now obscure Dutch physician W. H. van Buren claimed in consonance with the medicine of his time that "erotomania is a species of insanity" (464). Three years later, British physicians Woodman and Tidy defined "extreme sexual passion" as "erotomania in *both* sexes"(726). In 1882 the English Sydenham Society revived the old distinction claiming that: "by some authors this term is restricted to those cases in which the imagination alone is affected" (Power and Sedgwick, Vol. II, entry under "erotomania"). All agreed on its pathology, except that they could practice its culture in Europe as well as we do in Puritan America. This is the heritage Elaine Showalter describes in *The Female Malady* and, as mentioned above, in *Hystories: [with hys] Hysterical Epidemics and Modern Culture.*[15]

III. Child of the Sixties

Autobiographical disclosure may appear sentimental in scholarly analysis and doubtlessly represents the inverse of Foucault's own method *sans* the subject: the discourses of sexuality. But America's enduring love affair with erotophobia

---

[15] Erotomania since the 1830s also possessed an historiography albeit under different nomenclature than this; see Laycock (1840); E. Showalter, comments with soutces in *The Female Malady: women, madness, and English culture, 1830–1980* (1985), 21, that in the 1920s Dr Alexander Morison invited artists to come to the Surrey County Asylum, in England, where he was resident superintendent of the female department and used drawings in a series of lectures, e. g. "Miss A. A. . . . was an 'erotomaniac,' a domestic servant who had developed a passion for the clergyman of her parish, and who was 'generally disposed to kiss'"(21).

struck me in college early in the 1960s, although I didn't conceptualize it at all in these terms. Those were allegedly the salad days of the sexual revolution when sex and drugs were the daily pabulum of the young. But reality seemed to me just the *opposite*. Indeed I still remember wondering then (ca. 1960, when I was nineteen) how the notion that *sexual pleasure belongs to the dangerous domain of evil* got liberated, for if it was liberated it wasn't evident in my all-male surroundings.[16] Was this liberation a history or a genealogy in Foucault's sense? One episode stuck. While I was an undergraduate at (a still all-male) Amherst College in 1958 to 1962, our most famous classicist was busted for drinking with male undergraduates in his home. The alleged transgression was multifaced: luring undergraduates home, pumping them with drink as a prelude to . . . Although drinking in itself was hardly an offense unless the drinker was underage, viewed in these contexts it could seem to be. We undergraduates were slow to grasp the dire consequences but we were suddenly afraid. A new terror, absent just weeks before, overtook us. Canadian writer Michael Ignatieff has described collective fear (not irrelevant to the concerns of recent erotophobia as a mass hysteria) in *Scar Tissue*:

> In any event, what strikes me most is how poorly we grasped what was actually happening, how incompletely we must grasp it even now. That is why I call this [story] a time capsule. If someone digs it up in the future, they are bound to say, "Look at what they didn't know. Look at how they failed to understand. Look at these curious creatures. Why are they so afraid?" (9)

These transgressions, small and great, form a large part of my interest in the recent fates of erotophobia. Transgression, however, also possesses an historical silhouette, à la Stallybrass and White: the fraction of its historical contexts in America set out below. But sexual transgression always appears in paradoxical contexts: on the one hand . . . on the other. Contexts made more troubling if race and social class are factored in. Today in America, every erotophobic trace is countered with a contrary cultural force: the oppositions of addictive sex throughout the realms of Hollywood and the sexless cults of purity in America's hinterlands. Which is the *true* America? Henry Louis Gates Jr., one of our shrewdest cultural commentators, construes the development cyclically: "As the Eighties began, social progressives and reactionaries alike joined a new crusade against license in the name of liberty [...] With sex, as with the savings-and-loan industry, a period of deregulation has been followed by one of regulation"(115–16). Whether cyclic or not, the phenomenon itself appears riddled with internal contradictions: simultaneous regulation *and* deregulation. Even so, there is no doubt in Foucault's epistemic sense that some type of break occurred in the Seventies, as the new puritanism gradually eroded and

---

16 See Foucault's explanation of the dynamics of repression-liberation in the light of Greek self-care (*HS*, II, 251).

vanquished an earlier sexual license. Foucault himself, Cassandra-like, heard
rumblings late in the Seventies about anti-sex movements. In his interview "On
the End of the Monarchy of Sex" he claimed: "I have an impression of hearing
today an 'anti-sex' grumbling (I'm not a prophet, at most a diagnostician), as if
a thorough effort were being made to shake this great 'sexography' which makes
us decipher sex as the universal secret" (*Foucault Live*, 144). Some of the shakeoff
was the culmination of anti-Freud waves, other an embracing of the new, developing postmodernism more attuned to the empire of materialism and technology's effects than to sexual mystery. But Foucault knew he was being prescient
despite his disclaimer and recorded these prognostications in an interview of
1977 as the first contagion of HIV was about to be carried into America (*Foucault Live*, 144 – 45).

To continue chronologically. While in graduate school at Princeton University
after 1962 another gay faculty ring was busted, and everyone – straight and gay
– seemed to be dreaming of sex but doing nothing about it, except paying the
Swedish au pair girls on Nassau Street a couple of bucks to sleep with them.
But they were Swedes. Drugs were plentiful, as were trips to Manhattan's underworld, but anyone even *suspected* of illicit sexual intercourse, let alone deviant
genital sex, was a candidate for expulsion and the psychiatrist's couch. These
were the (allegedly) swinging Sixties, we its children, except that I – and I was
not alone here – never knew, or never figured out, that sexual intercourse could
be a regular part of it. By the time of Vietnam and Kent-Cambodia (named for
an incident at Kent State University in Ohio, where students were brutally hurt
and even killed by the National Guard's force challenging them over their stand
on the war), I had left Princeton for Harvard, as had gay American historian
Martin Duberman for New York. He has also written in these confessional
tropes about himself in *Cures*, and revealed the degree to which erotophobia
was commensurate with that alleged heyday of sexual libertinism.

When I left Princeton in 1965 I had never heard of Michel Foucault; by the
time I left Harvard just a few years later I had read *Les Mots et les choses* in French
and English and everything else Foucaldian I could get my hands on, and began
to glimpse the personal and professional liberation he afforded me. But it was
not until I had integrated myself into Los Angeles subcultures early in the 1970s
and witnessed its versions of the post-Mrs. Robinson Sexual Revolution (the
film *The Graduate* of 1968), that I could construe what Foucault would mean for
my professional life and intellectual liberation. The fabrication of simulacrum
or "virtual sex" – the copy or fake of sex – was extraordinary everywhere in
LA. Sex on the screen, sex in videos, sex in books, sex in photography: sex
everywhere except between two living and consenting breathing bodies. Visitors
to Los Angeles learn that LA is a graveyard after six; it is also a sexual void.
Foucault's writings forced me to wonder about LA's double-bind: how sex had
been paradoxically both liberated and repressed so successfully in hedonistic

LA. LA was puritanism's worst case scenario. That was just as Paris students were burning the Boulevard St. Germain in May 1968, the sacking whose fallout has had such ripple effects for post-Foucaldian cultural history. If Paris '68 brought French theory to prominence as America's largest intellectual import since von Humboldt's model of the German universities, it also persuaded some of us Children of the Sixties that there was no such thing (perhaps there had *never* been) as interest-free research and scholarship. All was ideological: one story adjudged better than another according to the listener.

Theory's toll vis-à-vis erotophobia is a story that cannot be told here, except to mention in passing what has become of that American generation of the Sixties: now in their upper fifties, widely seen, for example, on TV selling enemas and advertising retirement time shares in the Sun Belt for the geriatric set. Treacherous as it is to claim, the professional women are the least erotic of all: buttoned-up administrators like University of Wisconsin President Donna Shalala (who was given a post in the Clinton administration) and Madeline Albright who hardly exude French glamor or the gaze that kills. The Sixties radicals are now de-eroticized, teetotaling workaholics perfectly in concert with the newly invigorated erotophobia reacting against the excesses of their own youth. It is therefore hardly surprising that North Americans now commonly list health at the top of their preoccupations, ahead of love, work or money. Furthermore, as Paris burned in May 1968 I knew as yet nothing of the autobiographical Foucault behind the ingenious epistemes and tessellated discourses whose disjunctive breaks he was chronicling with such frisson and brilliance, if also such factual inaccuracies. I knew nothing about the Monk of Paris.[17]

---

17 These facets have influenced the development of Foucault studies in our time, and any rigorous survey of those calling or considering themselves Foucaldians, or among those who have compiled collections about him, his followers, and his influence, would show that few, if any, have come from the fundamentalist conservative right. This is hardly a revelation considering Foucault's erotic and penal preoccupations. The academic legacy of Foucault lies primarily within the corridors of the radical Left, even if by now everyone nods at Foucault in prefaces and introductions to books merely as the signpost of modernity or thoroughness. Serious Foucaldian cultural history is even more emphatically derivative from the ranks of the radical Left, as any rigorous survey would demonstrate, although labeling is always offensive to the labeled who rebel against it and deny its taxonomies. See Patricia O'Brien (Gould, 45) on the legacy of Foucaldian sex, power, the author and the self. O'Brien is persuasive but neglects several eminent domains, especially Foucault as a cultural diagnostician – as the academic barometer or symptom of something rather than its cause – and the "Nietzsche rots your mind" syndrome, the latter an Anglo-American *arrière pensée* that the German philosopher's logic, epistemology, and view of history were so defective that his influence poisons and pollutes even the purest intellect through contagion. Foucault is now cited everywhere by professional academics, of course, but not by journalists and social commentators, some of whom remain the most vigorous intellectuals of the age. My point here is that American social critics such as Bill Bennett, Geoffrey Will and company hold the present position of "the Intellectual," communicating at large with the public, in contrast to the specialized, narrow academics writing monographs and articles in outlets rarely seen by the educated public.

IV. Cultural History and the Sixties

That was 1968, 1969, 1970, 1971: the years of my own academic liberation. My professional move from Cambridge Massachusetts to Los Angeles was another brand of cultural history: the most discontinuous I have experienced in my life. It wasn't just that pre-AIDS LA really was all the things best-selling California historian Mike Davis has described in *City of Quartz* – a postmodern jungle, an ecology of fear, the greatest instability on earth: socially, politically, economically, geologically – but that its erotophobia was amazingly just as pronounced as in the rest of America. This sexual intimacy, even in LA, is the one of the worlds we have lost; perhaps, if the Puritan historians are right, the world we never had. Just read American novelist Brett Ellis' *Less than Zero*. For all its hedonistic reputation LA, as its inhabitants know, retires earlier than most other large cities. Purity and puritanism coexist there in a version I have never seen anywhere else in the world.

Where was Foucault now, except in his tessellated discourses on my shelves? Not yet in his chair at the Collège de France, but already a neoclassicist historian immersed in the view that Europe circa 1750 – 1820 had been the transformative moment in Western culture; and deeply enmeshed in the belief that medicine was the most accurate barometer of this Nietzschean Apollonian-Dionysian struggle for power. That historical era – the long eighteenth century – had been my own ever since graduate school. During those early years at UCLA, when I was trying to publish or perish in the tenure rat-race and amass everything new I could conjure about eighteenth-century literature, it became clear what terrains Foucault could open up to us erotophobic Americans; and this was before the histories of sexuality: just from his archeologies of thought, no matter how factually controversial they were, and epistemic births before we knew who the "Monk of Paris" actually was: a phrase that will become clearer (below) but which for now merely indicates the image he cultivated in Paris versus the later one in America. (The faculty in Berkeley adjudged his reason for wanting to sign on as their unrivalled academic excellence – little did they suspect his other motives).

V. Panic and Liberation

In time I came to see that the European Enlightenment is a perfect case in point for teasing out the hysterias and panics that continue to afflict us in desexualized America. As we approach the millennium and concur that the Age of Foucault is dead it seems appealing to dance around Foucault's tomb with glee; but it was Foucault, more than anyone else in his generation, who alerted

us to early modern panics, the petits hysterias, and, more significantly, made
them academically respectable. Take this one, for example, the antistrophe of
erotophobia, recorded in the 1975 essay on "Body/Power:"

> Let's take a precise example, that of autoeroticism. The restrictions on masturbation hardly
> start in Europe until the eighteenth century. Suddenly, a panic-theme appears; an appalling
> sickness develops in the Western world. Children masturbate. Via the medium of families,
> though not at their initiative, a system of control of sexuality, an objectivization of sexuality
> allied to corporal persecution, is established over the bodies of children. But sexuality,
> through thus becoming an object of analysis and concern, surveillance and control, engen-
> ders at the same time an intensification of each individual's desire, for, in, and over his
> body. (56−57)

Panic themes and appalling sicknesses, not the sexual body as a site of conflict between parents and children. It is the panic of the American fundamentalist conservative Right pumping millions of dollars into the new anti-homosex-
ual hysteria. The rest of America, especially the radical Left with its democratic
fringe and vast academic population, generally eschews the panic, although it
has been known to join forces with the conservative Right when such explosive
issues as homosexual rights are being decided. The panic of being outed has
resulted in still another hysteria: military suicide. The latest case is the US Air-
force's revelation that Captain Craig Button flew eight hundred miles off course
during a training mission and crashed his A10 Warthog aircraft into a mountain
in the Colorado Rockies in April 1997.[18] Craig Button's suicide, like those of
other homosexual victims before him, does not possess the sublimity of philosophical theory but represents a subset of erotophobia at America's military
grass roots: stigma as ignorance. History is permeated with these personal panics
and popular delusions; in America they now pass unnoticed, as if the ordinary
course of daily life.

Panic and relief-liberation are historically incommensurate: the more of the
former, the less the latter. But the academic sexual Enlightenment circa 1970
had not yet been opened up, so to speak: that would come later, in the Eighties,
especially under the weight of Foucault's archaeological approach to "the sediments of history" and American feminism. The "Enlightenment" I inherited at
Princeton was old historicist − an archival one: if you cannot cite the manuscript
source, the point is not worth making. Not only was generalization or − God
forbid − recourse to the first-person pronoun impermissible, but there existed
whole ranges of unlawful questions that were neither polite nor to be discussed
publicly. It was impolitic to do so in British classicist F. M. Cornford's advance-
your-career sense. This was the old historicism: erudition without a high thresh-

---

[18] *The Times* 5 May 1995, 7. The news report continues: "The dead pilot was homosexual and
dreaded being 'outed' by a former lover. Under the current 'don't ask, don't tell' regime, had
Captain Button been revealed as a homosexual he could have been discharged."

old of, or interest in, the Other. Gary Tomlinson, a leading American musicologist, has explained why in his own confessional chapter called "Approaching Others (Thoughts Before Writing)" in *Music in Renaissance Magic*. Here, in a personal mode, Tomlinson aligns himself with Anthony Pagden's *Fall of Natural Man* and Bernard McGrane's *Beyond Anthropology*, both of which insist on tracing the shifts in the construction of the Other:[19]

> The Enlightenment thinker, in McGrane's view, divested the other of its demonic quality, placing it in a position of ignorance rather than one of lack. Now the other was the victim and pitiable possessor of untruth, but was at the same time at least an entity of some sort, defined by what it could possess. This shift from nonentity to possessor (if of untrue and ignorant ideas) raised for Enlightenment thinkers large questions of cultural diversity that had been absent from Renaissance thought. (7)

Through Romantic, modernist and now postmodernist epistemic shifts, the "outed-and-panicking Other" has become a creature of pity; someone melancholic, potentially suicidal, to be medically treated and genetically explained rather than feared, as in the other abuse-and-depletion syndromes (all those in our culture of blame charging some one with sexual abuse or physical or psychical depletion through sexual misuse). The notion that people in various panic states become *seriously* sick has not yet had its day. In the Seventies we had not yet understood the archaeology of this Other any better than the erotophobia that would develop in the Decade of AIDS.[20]

VI. The Enlightenment and the Other

I could see that these sexual Others profoundly touched on our lives in Los Angeles' flagship university in the early Seventies: just as it became clear what the power structures of the eighteenth-century academic Establishment were, and how you had to play the game to succeed and climb to the top. Take, for example, two of its primary literary figures and their New Critical destinies before and after the Sixties: canonical English poets Alexander Pope and Thomas Gray. The first a homosocial bachelor whose couplet craft had been a phenomenon in the history of poetry itself, yet who could not yet be discussed autobiographically as a human being, as a creature of flesh and blood and consumed by psychosexual drives outside circles of propriety. The second —

---

[19] Tomlinson's passage continues with a revealing parenthesis: "(Pagden's closer reading of sixteenth-century sources leads him to a view more n   ed than McGrane's, in which Renaissance writers like Bartolomé de Las Casas and José de Acosta already posed questions of diversity more common in the eighteenth century);" see McGrane and Pagden chaps. 6 and 7.

[20] Some discussion is found in E. Showalter, *Hystories*; remarkable accounts of homosexual panic are found in Barthes (1992).

Thomas Gray — like Foucault hardly heterosexual, who had been said to have composed the finest and most perfect lines of poetry in the language:

> Full many a gem of purest ray serene,
> The dark unfathomed caves of ocean bear;
> (*Elegy in a Country Churchyard*, lines 53–54)

and to have been technically among the most consummate of melodious English poets — except that (and this was the oddity) he had never been the subject of a modern full-length biography: a curious state of affairs considering that the most minor figures, Grub Street hacks like Colley Cibber and John Dennis, had been the subject of many. Teaching Pope and Gray by day, and reading Foucault by night (*not* by candlelight), it became all too clear what was personally at stake in these developments. For Gray I checked everything archival over two summers only to discover there was nothing to find: nothing had been restricted or hidden, no protective families, no unknown diaries.[21]

Rather it was Gray's sexual otherness. Pope represented a rather more delicate situation: in territorial terms lorded over by a protective Yale brigade, Pope was practically the private fiefdom of Yale's Sterling Professor of English Literature, Maynard Mack, who was both Pope's modern arbiter of taste and chief power broker. A nod at Maynard Mack and his permission to publish, were *de rigueur*, certainly before anything differential or daring could be pronounced about this leonine figure of the English Enlightenment. This state of affairs was just. Mack was (and now in his late eighties, long may he remain!) the most erudite student Pope has ever had. But Foucault-Mack permits a remarkable contrast, and any caveats expressed here must be tempered in advance by my admiration for, and gratitude to, this greatest of Pope scholars. In brief, my claim is that Mack could not break loose from the Old Historicism, which had been fettered by the combined manacles of an inflexible pedantic philology and the sheer inability to construct adequate psychosocial contexts; not that there was any inherent bias or failing in his understanding of Pope's life and works. Nor can anyone reasonable expect that a heterosexual scholar born in the first decade of the twentieth century (Mack was born in 1909) would take out precious time to re-educate himself in depth about male homosocial bonding and homosexual liminality — Pope's basic mindset. That had to await Foucault and the next generation. It constituted much of the liberation of myself and my academic colleagues: "the children of Mack," as I once referred to ourselves.[22]

---

21 The exception, in German, were the letters of Victor von Bonstetten to German physiologist-anthropologist Johannes Müller commenting on his intimate friendship with Thomas Gray.

22 Much more needs to be written without nostalgia or discontent about the flaws of the Old Historicism; for all the fluff and pitfalls of the New Historicism, I would still never return to the Old.

VII. Alexander Pope and Cultural History

By the early Seventies Mack had long been at work on his magisterial biography
of Pope that would eventually contain some 500,000 words: still the longest
biography of any eighteenth-century English literary figure except Jonathan
Swift. It appeared in 1985, by which time Paris had long since burned and
the American universities had for the most part all become "theorized" and
"Foucaultized" under the weight of their new sociological ethos. Not so Maynard Mack and most of his Connecticut Yankees at Yale. Even when under
stress Mack declined to use the word homosocial,[23] and instead resorted to the
less sexually charged trope about wear and tear on Pope's *heterosexual* heart: how
it had been starved of love by women, almost as if the deformed and dwarfish
poet had been driven into homosociality by willful female dereliction.

In the concession lay at least some progress, if not a semblance of theory,
though hardly a Foucaldian liberation. No one in the 1980's sought to claim
that Pope had abused women, or gay historians sought to turn Pope queer. But
it is one thing to invoke the word − *homosocial* − and quite another to be brave
enough to tackle the large issues it implies. Pope was probably not homosexual
in any proleptic way we today could call gay. Yet his homosociality was a particularly fierce version of male romance, in the early 1980s still undefined or described; it was the obligation of the biographer of the eighteenth century's finest
poet (nothing in scholarship or criticism changed that view) to expend energy
defining it for his subject. Such lavish attention had been poured over every
great heterosexual poet; why not its homosocial masters? Foucault could have
told us why, Mack could not. Despite the American Norton Publisher's half-
million words, Mack would not ask them. Besides, Mack didn't configure the
world in these categories, so he couldn't invoke it. Power and its ideologies as
constructed rather than given precincts of authority, were not in his mindset.
Mack was surely the most consummate Pope scholar of the century, but in
realms psychological and sexual, he would not break away from the old refrain:
no sex please, we're American.

VIII. Thomas Gray and the Politics of Erotophobic American Scholarship

The situation enveloping Thomas Gray was rather more pathetic, an Anglo-
American tragedy. Gray's only biographer had been a latter-day Victorian Nor-
folk gentleman-scholar (Ketton-Cremer) in whose vocabulary the word sex

---

[23] Mack (1985): see index under all relevant sections.

hardly existed. He could not even bring himself to discuss Gray's women, let alone his men. The result was a biography of 1955 that completely misgauges its subject's pulse. You can't omit your biographee's sexual identity and hope to produce the definitive biography. At least he could have said that Gray was homoplatonic. In America, the state of affairs vis-à-vis Gray was even more erotophobic. There had been rumors that several English Department faculty members at Yale (in the Mack eighteenth-century group) were secretly linked to Washington's CIA during and after the Second World War. The CIA itself had no interest in the methods of literary analysis or the literary interpretation of poets, let alone dead English poets, and certainly not on the remote chance that such criticism could indoctrinate American college students with dangerous political or social notions. Nevertheless, the Thomas Gray they wrote about was heavily policed — so goes this line of argument — in just the way Foucault has described in *Discipline and Punish*. Whether the policing was consciously articulated and explicit is hard to know. The evidence is too scant for certainty. But these scholars accorded Gray no personal life, their interest in him being entirely New Critical (New Criticism being the leading form of literary analysis of the time at Yale), and limited to the classroom as an exponent of the pure English melodious line. Gray then was hardly a candidate for psychosexual analysis, or the prototype of the reclusive and eccentric English bachelor whose erotic fantasies thrive on Shropshire lads with flaxen hair à la Housman.

A few American scholars outside America's erotophobic orbits blew off the lid of this apparent absurdity. The fact is that Gray, unlike Pope, really *was* homosexual, and homosexual by any historical construct and in our modern sense. The most discriminating subtleties for historical veracity must configure his sexual proclivity that way. No amount of dodging will camouflage the truth. From early youth, he fell in and out of romantic love affairs with young men, even if Richard West, the poet, remained the love of his life. When West died, something died in Gray, never again to be reborn, not even through the flame burning when Victor von Bonstetten, a twenty-two year old Swiss aristocrat became his student at Pembroke College, Cambridge. Gray and his friend Nicholls frequented London clubs and young men there. Nicholls was introduced to Bonstetten and thought Gray would like him. The three met in London, Gray was whisked off his feet, brought Bonstetten to Cambridge, and three months later — was dead. The cause of death? No answer has been given that makes much medical sense. Some life-force seems to have died, taking Gray with it.

But — and this is the point about American erotophobia and its toll on historical scholarship — there still exists no reliable biography of Gray.[24] Other

---

24 Foucault was the type of *mentalité* who would have pondered the different contexts (as below), not least as "research agendas in relation to professional advancement and power arrangements within the dominant discourse of these professions;" our post-Foucaldian academic milieu has grown larger than it was in Foucault's Paris of the 1960–70s, but it remains unclear whether

subjects have been exhausted and repeated to the point of absurdity: another edition of Henry Fielding, another reading of Swift's major works, another contextualist approach to Jane Austen, but not a single biography of England's purest melodist just because of his sexual Otherness. One can claim, of course, that the lack occurs by chance: no one has been interested. Or that it is the random result of an old-styled and old-fashioned biography that resists entering the subject's bedroom. Why repress Gray when there has been so much other "gay writing" to the point of clutter? The point is not clutter but "outing." Gray must be "outed" before he can be presented and discussed in these open ways. The act of "outing" rather than the discursive one (i. e., writing a biography once he has been outed) is the brave one in its academic contexts. For culture is holistic: a mosaic of tiles that shapes the agenda of research programs. And it is by now clear that the feminists' gains have been the masculinists' losses, for Gray and Pope are not the only eighteenth-century figures whose sexual histories have been distorted or repressed: the list extends from Beckford and Cumberland to Frederick the Great and Lord Hervey. Even Robert Gleckner's 1996 study of Gray is camouflaged as Gray's debt to Milton and *Paradise Lost*: hence "Gray Agonistes" rather than "Gray and his Ganymedes," a gesture apparently still too explosive and sexually explicit within the Establishment despite the Gleckner's presence at Duke University in the same English Department as the driving force behind "the epistemology of the closet." Would it have been like this thirty years ago in the Left-Bank Paris where "Saint Foucault" joined students when they rioted and marched in the Boulevard St. Germain because their educational rights had been denied?[25]

IX. Foucault and the Map of Enlightenment

Saint Foucault — if I may now refer to him as such for his liberation of my own predicament — transformed my map as the result of the range and threshold of questions that could be asked, rather than through any empirical insight. He was, of course, in one sense the most *defective* of historians, possessing a post-Nietzschean philosophy of history without *actual history*; an organism without insides. But in his progression of sex-power-repression — the sex *in* power, and

---

we have developed adequate discourses to take stock of these relationships. For one historical approach, grounded in the Renaissance, see Etlin (1996).

[25] In the late 1970s Foucault felt compelled to describe the world of hermaphrodite Herculine Barbin: see Barbin (1980), by detailing her anatomical parts and the responses to them by her doctors (Ambroise Tardieu and company); yet all through the great expansive period of biographical research after the 1950s, Anglo-Saxon scholarship could not rouse itself to decode the sexualities of its leading Georgian male figures unless they were robust Fieldings or ailing Smolletts.

the power *of* sex — he had few peers since Nietzsche and Freud. Fear, a grand Charcotian fear, is the beacon of Foucault's history: the *grande peur* rarely inscribed into cultural history.

In 1968, as the vicinity of the Sorbonne and the Boulevard St. Germain burned, I was still too timid to ask why, for example, the campaigns against masturbation — *contra onania* — hardly began until the eighteenth century; after reading Foucault I could see why (*Power/knowledge*, 56). Childhood was another academic wasteland before Foucault. Consult its pre-1970 historiography and view its dead valleys. Foucault opened up the field. For the first time one could see how the human body had become a force of production from the time of the seventeenth and eighteenth centuries (*Power/knowledge*, 100). Foucault showed how all the forms of its expenditure which did not lend themselves to the constitution of productive forces were exposed as redundant, banned and repressed. The consequences for erotophobia were historically vast. Transposed from Europe to America one sees not the long eighteenth century but the rise of repression, and — across the ocean — the evolution of erotophobia. Wilhelm Reich, the popular psychologist, may earlier have adumbrated some of these sexual repressions, but he was hardly consulted in the bourgeois groves of academe. Yet everything Foucault touched was drenched in the dye of a sexuality that dared not speak its name, as in the conjunction of schools, military camps, asylums and prisons. Not merely the proverbial Foucaldian power and margins, but the choice of agenda, forms of subjective mediation, and, of course, the histories of sexuality (*Power/knowledge*, 150).

Foucault resurrected these sex arrangements into their historiographies of surveillance, especially in the terms of its all-male relations, prison walls, and architecture of repression. Most of us do not associate Foucault with the nineteenth century, yet there he changed my map of the historiography of erotophobia even *more* fundamentally. Consult the modern history of pornography and the sex *behind* madness. Before Foucault (and one must concede before Yale historian Peter Gay documented the broadly canvassed world of the Victorians shaping the culture Freud inherited in Germanic Europe) there was little sense of nineteenth-century sexual fabrications: of the way sex underlies so much rational awareness. Nietzsche and Freud were eloquent on the reality hidden behind rational consciousness, but it was Foucault who aligned their common modalities in the *history* of sex and madness (*Power/knowledge*, 185). The difference was sex *in* history, not sex itself. That is, history's silences and history's figures without their subjectivity. Freud wrote, of course, the customized "sexual lives" of Michelangelo, Shakespeare, and Da Vinci, but never against a contextual backdrop composed of the *historical* discourses of power and repression. It is this same *history* that endows erotophobia with meaning; sans context and *history* (especially *American* history) it is an empty label into whose orbit nothing meaningful can be swept. What erotophobia? Where precisely in America? In which camps, given America's immense diversity? But America was not always so diverse, and its origins — religious, economic, racial, social — have counted for much even by the time it liberated itself from the mother country in the 1780s. Omit this Puritan heritage, particularly the Puritan discourses in precisely Foucault's tessellated sense since the 1620s, and erotophobia signifies nothing concrete — an empty and abstract label. Puritanism and AIDS, 1680s to 1980s, form an arc of meaning only when *history* in all its complexity is brought into the debate. Yet, again and again, ignorance with respect to sex in history has been the culprit — the same ignorance that hysterically drives eroto-phobia in America, and permits it to reign there as one of its mass hysterias. The whole point of Freud's middle-class women was that he removed them from history — took them *out* of their social milieu — and enlarged their sub-jectivity by placing them on his couch; Foucault clothed their denuded sexual subjectivity, so to speak, and returned them, anonymously, to the historical can-vas. He unraveled their subjectivity by weaving them, anonymously, into his historical-sexual tapestries. His conception of the history of modern sexuality amounts to Foucault *contra* the middle-class family — the same middle-class American families who celebrate erotophobia (without naming it, of course) as their chief interpersonal ethos and on which their newest fascistic forms of political correctness are based.

"Saint Foucault," however, read little English and omitted most Anglo-Amer-ican scholarship; and he wasn't the first to suggest that science and medicine were the *most* fundamental barometers (religion was another, but for so long primitive science and medicine *were* religion) of cultural organization. Even in the Franco-German tradition in which Foucault worked, the major figures of Nietzsche, Bergson, Claude Bernard, Georges Canguilhem (Foucault's teacher and mentor), as well as the late Paris historian of science Jacques Roger, had done that before.[26] Foucault's was not a new map but a new mindset for the age, and, especially, the example of his *own* biographical liberation. A mindset is akin to a philosophy, and Foucault will not be the first philosopher (for that is what he was) on whom the historians during his life and in the first generation afterwards declared war. Liberation, however, is more subjective; what liberates one psyche, enslaves another. The Foucault declared by Princeton historian of England Lawrence Stone to amount to "a crime against humanity" was not Foucault-the-liberator but Foucault-the-mindset. The offending engine was Fou-cault's way of thinking: at once rational, rhetorical, eclectic, idiosyncratic, pre-sented entirely without a philosophy of history or adequate historicism: every-thing anathema to empirical British historicism.

Stone had no interest of which I am aware in erotophobia: not even eroto-phobia in history. The Enlightenment in which both thinkers — Foucault and

---

[26] Especially influential on Foucault was Georges Canguilhem's *The Normal and the Pathological*.

Stone — preoccupied themselves naturally had its erotophobic pockets, each scholar touched on them in his work; but it was Foucault-the-liberator far more than Foucault-the-mindset — discursive, epistemic, or otherwise — who set an example others followed. Consequently, his ephebes are rather different from Stone's, even in the aftermath of Foucault when it is now so perfectly clear that the Age of Foucault is dead. The 1980s are not 2000. We are now in a new paradigm.

X. Philosophies of "Camp"

Turning elsewhere, our American critic Susan Sontag still holds title as the "Queen of Camp," that American gay science of the chic within the nouveau named for her 1962 essay ("Notes on Camp"), which reveals her own agenda in relation to the doctrines and ethos of erotophobia I am trying to describe. But it must indicate something that references to Sontag in secondary literature constitute a fraction of those to Foucault: a miniscule number.[27] This is the revelatory diagnostic. Foucault, in contrast, is omnipresent in American scholarship, even among his deadliest foes. What can this mean given his trope as liberator as well as mindset? Foucault represented more, of course, than a new approach to the body, mind, sex, disease, insanity, *derangement*, as the philosopher of power and its complex versions of marginalization. Contrast him with his French male contemporaries — Bachelard, Barthes, Baudrillard, Deleuze, Derrida, Guattari — and one realizes what these differences amount to.

The matter is not one of choosing favorites: how does (Belgian) Paul de Man's death or Deleuze's suicide speak to you? But rather placing the mindset and the liberating energy together, and asking what it adds up to. Derrida may well be the cleverest of the French theorists of the late twentieth century, but I know few Derridean ephebes anywhere, or even ordinary readers and students, who worship in (dare one say) Saint Derrida's Temple as the result of any *liberation* other than the linguistic one.

Roland Barthes is the contender to Foucault. His own life, however, all the way to his death in 1980, five years before Foucault's, was so empty of erotic intimacy as to render discussion of Barthes and erotophobia defective. Sickly from the start; stuck in the passive grid of a shyness and post-adolescent tuberculosis that made sex impossible; Barthes was recessive and suicidal in ways Foucault never was. Nor was he a model for academics in the same vein, nor — by the end — a cult figure to the same extent. "Barthes and camp" retrospectively now appears almost to be an oxymoron, despite his remarkable insights

---

[27] A count of approximately one hundred random secondary works published 1990–96 revealed a ratio of fourteen for Foucault to each one for Sontag.

into language and its representations. Foucault's "camp," like Sontag's and Barthes', is predicated on the knowledge that sexual *difference* lies at its heart. Scholars, like their works, take on a life of their own once they have passed into the public domain. Foucault's public image was not limited to his books, even if his projected *History of Sexuality* amounted to something rather more than an event in the history of publishing. The beacon he set for lost souls lay in his embodiment of a particular *kind* of liberated life that outed the puritan sham in "no sex please, we're American." That is why there have been so many biographies in just a decade since 1985.[28]

XI. Saint Genet/Saint Foucault

One biography was titled *Saint Foucault,* named after Sartre's commemoration of French writer Jean Genet.[29] Their similarities existed for this biographer in realms political rather than discursive; that is, for Foucault the man rather than Foucault the theorist of classical discourse or histories of sexuality. Genet the liberator for Sartre; Foucault the liberator for American classicist David Halperin; even Wilde the liberator for Terry Eagleton in his play "Saint Oscar," after Oscar Wilde. Genet and Foucault also shared an almost fanatic fascination in the penal-pedophilic world. Each had paid his real debt to the penitentiary: Genet confined to them, Foucault rehabilitating their youths. Imaginary sainthood, Sartrean and Genetean, was conferred, so to speak, for service to the marginalized underworld rather than for Professor Lawrence Stone's alleged "crimes against humanity," by which Stone intended methodological crimes in the writing of academic history rather than for lived experience.[30] Others than Sartre were also liberated. *Foucault's Pendulum* concerns itself with another Foucault altogether, not Michel, but it still capitalizes on Michel through its gesture of naming and, moreover, emerges from San Marino, not Salem Massachusetts. And America today is still permeated with colleges and universities in which Saint Genet's works can barely be found. And if the American students had known about the biographical Genet behind those balconies, or − in Foucault's case − behind the tessellated Renaissance discourses, they too may have been more ambivalent. AIDS has made them all the more so, in a milieu whose puritanism has only slightly let up.

---

[28] The interpretation given, not merely the number, counts; can the male cult of Foucault already approximate the female of Jung? No female has yet written a biography of Foucault.

[29] The twin pair is J. P. Sartre, *Saint Genet* and D. Halperin, *Saint Foucault.*

[30] I was more forgiving, if less dramatic than Stone, in charging Foucault with a defective historiography camouflaged under a veil of rhetoric; see Rousseau "Whose Enlightenment?" and the late J. G. Merquior, who found my strictures substantial (63−64).

Foucault wrote, of course, long before AIDS — the AIDS that prematurely killed him in June 1984 through a compromised immune system in a medically diagnosed septicemia. Here Foucault's life gains from biographical perspective, best performed through close comparison. Barthes, his contemporary, rather than Genet, no academician, would appear the natural equivalent. Near contemporaries, friends, similarly educated and from the same social class, both homosexual, their great difference was temperamental. Foucault wrote about illness, Barthes lived it. Neither had much following in Paris despite small academic entourages (although Foucault's grew to sizable proportions in the Collège de France in the 1970s). But the liberal academics within Puritan America discovered and vigorously promoted them. Down through the Sixties and Seventies, American academics (like me) were reading both men without this biographical knowledge, certainly unaware of Foucault's relation to camp. If Susan Sontag's essay on camp has been called the single most influential essay of her generation (with justification), the one most directly explaining cultural history as sexual lifestyle, Foucault was living its twelve tenets in daily life.

David Macey, one of Foucault's biographers, is therefore right to call his biography "the lives of Foucault:" part scholar, part libertine, part liberationist, part penal reformer; in Macey's words, "Foucault lived many lives, as an academic, as a political activist, as a child, and as a lover of men"(vi). Deleuze proceeded further. He called Foucault "the cartographer of discourse," echoing his own triadic description of writing as "struggle, becoming, and the drawing of a new map" (*Foucault*, 44). The new map could have included the discourses of sexual repression, of the medicalization of sexuality, even the psychiatrization of sex. It was not at all the "map of boys," in which others have been so much more explicit, that Foucault was the new navigator. It was rather chapters like "Erotics" in *The Use of Pleasure* (*HS*, II: pt.4, chaps. 1–3), which deal with boys within the cults of self care.

This "new map" is the one I have been attempting to fill out autobiographically, not because it is Foucaldian but because it represents just the opposite. That is, one can pursue discourse à la Foucault without being Foucaldian himself. One need not think and write in the categories of *Discipline and Punish* to recognize the importance of its content. Discourse *sans* the personal constitutes, of course, the very heartland of the Foucaldian program; and in this sense my approach is entirely *anti*-Foucaldian: it violates the very post-Hegelian spirit of history towards which he toiled. My romantic subjectivity (the remembering autobiographical self) inscribes the very authority of self against which Foucault rebelled, and for which reason, in part, he never disclosed himself. Hence Deleuze in one of the strangest notes he ever appended to a Foucaldian work. Foucault, in his 1975 essay on desire in language reprinted in English in 1980 as *Theatrum Philosophicum* in Donald Bouchard's collection *Language, Counter Memory, Practice*, had speculated on the mind's alterations by drugs. The passage is unusually autobiographical for Foucault, suggesting that he and Deleuze, and perhaps the rest of their Paris circle, were routinely steeped in drugs. Bouchard submitted the whole volume's English translation to Deleuze for comments and approval. Foucault was still alive. With one red stroke Deleuze could have excised the offending passage. Instead he retained it, presumably with Foucault's ultimate approval, and added this note written and signed by himself: "What will people think of us?" (191).

The consequences of American erotophobia are much stranger than Foucault's quondam autobiographical disclosure or Deleuze's note about drugs. The Foucault who lived like an exegetical monk in Paris but who, in the last decade of his life, taught at Berkeley and enjoyed the hedonistic pleasures of San Francisco — especially their gay saunas — encountered the profound disparities of America's Puritan heritage and the erotophobia that had already been reinvigorated by 1983; the last time he came to Berkeley California before his death in June 1984. If he was a role model, exemplar, a diagnostic barometer of the intellectual mindsets of the age, he was also, by turns, a monk and a hedonist. All this against the backdrop of an America weeping under the strain of handsome Rock Hudson's coming out a year after Foucault's death.

But even by 1982 or 1983 it was clear that some type of gay plague was afoot, even if no one knew exactly what it was, and it was precipitating the most terrific *avoidance* of body contact the nation had known since McCarthyism. Erotophobia was not new on American soil in the 1950s: like America's ingrained anti-intellectualism, about which American historian Richard Hofstadter has written so lucidly, it had been woven over time into the nation's social fabric. Both its heterosexual and homosexual varieties had developed over long segments of time along different patterns and in different rhythms. Its homosexual versions — anxiety and trauma over the idea of homosexual body contact, as if the merest suggestion caused infection and pollution, plague and miasma — had always been of a fiercer strain than the heterosexual one except in times of war, when the sexes became blurred and the threat of a wolf at the door altered gender relations. The early modern European medical doctors, as I have suggested, discriminated among the varieties of erotomania;[31] so too had it been for erotophobia since revolutionary America, as the new historians have recently been demonstrating. But a new and more virulent type of erotophobia emerged in the Era of AIDS, buttressed by all sorts of new laws and political institutions in American life. This is a story not yet told. At its center lay the erotophobia that was to crescendo and erupt into full-blown AIDS hysteria by 1987 and blossom throughout the rest of the decade into the Nineties — to such a boiling

---

[31] Bienville's treatise began life as a subspecies of erotomania and metromania, in Bienville's effort to generate a new variety in which the imagination looms larger. Where would life for the new erotophobia begin?

point in the early Nineties that biological siblings, for example, would not drink out of the same glass. (I know, because I was one of them.) Yet paradoxically – and the paradoxes of history, like the counterpoint of erotomania and eroto- phobia, has been my salient point throughout this essay – it was this French thinker rather than any other who the left wing of American academia pro- moted. This virtually anonymous *philosophe* (before his notoriety in the late 1970s) who touched a nerve in American academic life. This philosopher of power and the margins who liberated us when no one else, it seemed, could. Except that we Americans were largely ignorant of his own marginalization in France and Europe. He may have held a Chair in the prestigious Collège de France but everywhere else in Europe, and especially among the professional historians, Foucault before his death was viewed with the greatest suspicion. The fact that he was liberating leftist liberal American academics (like me) counted for nothing; even counted *against* him. Finally, the Foucault who gradually coalesced into the liberal American academic's alter ego – like them, a Child of the Sixties, radical chic, ultra liberal, possessed by causes, morally and inherently relativistic, already interdisciplinary before it was fashionable, except for the arrangements of his personal ethics of sex on the two sides of the Atlantic.

XII. 1984 and the Death of Foucault

It can be argued there is nothing paradoxical at all about these developments. The cultivation of Foucault is precisely what one would have expected from liberal American academicians. If it had been the Right that would be different, but American academia is composed of the same diversities that function in larger national groups. If the Left has triumphed over the Right in academia – a big if – this is not so different from its political triumphs in the larger scene in Washington. Orwell's "Big Brother" world commenced on January 1 1984. Foucault died on June 24. Rock Hudson had not yet come out (that was a year later). But everyone in America knew there was some kind of gay plague out there that was already killing people. Europe lagged, as it does in so many mass hysterias. American students already began to display the hysterical signs of erotophobia that college counselors would find easy to treat (just say no) and sociologists glib to pronounce on (the new hysteria). I remember a male student in my class in California who would not enter the seminar room because he had heard some girl who had come to class had the flu. By early 1985 the secret about Foucault was out. Entire camps in Paris and Berkeley knew, of course, about the monastic versus the hedonistic Foucault but not the general literate public. When I was invited shortly after his death to write a piece for the *London Literary Review,* I tried to tell the truth as I knew it. But the family lawyer in- formed me I would be sued if I used any word other than medical septicemia.

So I went the way of all flesh and wrote septicemia, to the disgust of the Dutch Gay movement, for example, which chided me (rightly) for perverting history as truth. Back in LA, my graduate students who were now reading Foucault prolifically and enthusiastically did not want to hear about the hedonistic Foucault. It violated their own care of the self too ferociously and interrupted the new erotophobic hysteria they had begun to practice. It will be years before we have empirical studies of these trends, but eventually they too will form an intrinsic part of post-Foucaldian cultural history.

Foucault's hagiography was superimposed on to the cult status he had already achieved by 1984, but he would not have become the Foucault we now have – *Saint* Foucault – apart from his moment. For his public "outing" after his death occurred just at the moment of another and even larger outing: what Dennis Altman called "The Gaying of America."

XIII. Cultural History at the Millennium

What then is precisely post-Foucaldian in these matters? Where will we be viz. these concerns as we approach 2000? After departmental borders become open zones and the disciplines have been liberated beyond administrative buzz, where will we be? – for there is no doubt we are at the beginning of a new paradigm in the sense Foucault mapped at the end of *Les mots et les choses*.

The dispersion of world wide webs and virtual realities is too obvious to labor: the idea that post-Foucaldian sex will again be liberated in virtual reality. Sherry Turkle has already demonstrated how IT-sex has altered human social relations, and others are following suit by pronouncing that the toll on sex in virtual reality may be one of the largest paradigm shifts of the next generation. Virtual reality's liberation-repression sexual dynamic is fundamentally paradoxical: its professes to liberate inhibition while enslaving other energies through repression, in this case especially the physical contact between two bodies who meet and form their impressions face to face. Virtual reality paves the way to such an extended degree that sexual relations themselves become latter-day events with altered symbolic significance. I have no doubt that if Foucault had lived another decade (and here I attempt to resist the impulse to idealize a dead figure), he would have acknowledged the IT world within his constellation of language and power.[32] Jean Baudrillard has told us to "Forget Foucault" – even the title of one of his books – and the transformations of the decade 1985–95 prove him right. Foucault's epistemes and what I have crudely been calling his liberating sainthood are nothing to the new speed with which information is

---

[32] The published interviews do not pronounce on the subject except within the context of information exchange.

now being collected and disseminated. Foucault's dyad of power-knowledge implied much, of course, about IT, as did his colleagues Deleuze and Lyotard. But Foucault himself was too concerned with history's marginalizations to cultivate presentism to this postmodern Baudrillardian degree.

All those interested in the shapes of cultural history after Foucault may wonder about the connections between erotophobia and IT; yet they are present and pervasive. For computers and WWWs cannot be viewed apart from language and power, and in America, especially southern and middle western America, erotophobia, paranoia and mass hysteria are intrinsic parts of the same late capitalistic culture promoting them. The microchip is doubtlessly the most transformative agent of our generation (despite its roots in the worlds of seventeenth-century polymath Athanasius Kircher and nineteenth-century mathematician Charles Babbage);[33] even so, its Foucaldian dimensions in language and power and sex are omnipresent. The concerns of the old neoclassical medical erotomanias and erotophobias are not unrelated. They (the concerns) are merely couched in another language: Greek, technical, pathological, semiological, seemingly newfangled and thereby original but actually nostalgic and derivative from an older world.

There is, of course, no pragmatic solution to America's enduring versions of puritanism if solution is the yardstick. What could "solution" even mean to a diverse national history? Yet enduring American puritanisms (in the plural) also bring parochialism to our scholarship, as the rest of the Western world distinguishes between our unrivalled North American funding and the scholarship we produce. *Quant-à-moi* I would work hard against the Right; but now the equally ominous Left wants to control not only scholarship but our human bodies. That is, in the name of an opposite impulse ("political correctness") it seeks to legislate appropriate and inappropriate scholarship by new recourse to charges against the body (i. e. the new sexual harassment). It would be silly to claim connections between an enduring cultural erotophobia and the new harassment of the workplace; yet the net effect at the end of the day amounts to a still further post-AIDS crescendo of mass fear about body contact. For harassment, despite its focus on power relations, fares less well where there is no body contact and in the current hysterical climate every touch is potentially "sexual." The academic ripple of this new relation of Right and Left is that cultural history in America in the generation after AIDS has succumbed to both sides. The Era of the Body may be over, the Age of Foucault dead, and it is a neutral fact that our generation has felt itself collectively obliged to nod to Foucault in every preface, introduction, of almost every book. But the physical body within mundane life lives on, as does the healthy and sick body as the unsullied integer of

---

[33] The origins of the computer are not irrelevant to this argument, but I do not have the space to comment on the connections; for further reading see Barrett, Hyman, Landow, and Waldrop.

family values. The hysterias, all of which depend on a disjunction of *body and language*, are alive and well: Gulf War Syndrome, chronic fatigue, recovered memory loss, multiple personality disorder, alien abduction, satanic ritual abuse, and the widespread anorexia nervosas and bulimias of America's vast puritanical middle classes. Class issues doubtlessly loom much larger, even in classless America, than I have indicated here. But I do not believe they would alter the fundamental paradoxical point about erotophobia and history: that it *is* a Foucaldian type of category, that it has taken many Protean shapes in American life, that it still resists all sorts of polite academic discourse, that the ability to discuss it publicly in a forum is liberating, just as Foucault's own histories were in decades when the history of sexuality had not yet come of age.[34]

XIV. Erotophobia's Symptomologies

In conclusion I would like to select one new domain of post-Foucaldian interpretative work that makes these points — the new musicology — and I select a sufficiently remote field (musicology) to make them instantly, as well as one in which the sexual dimension is self-evident. Music history claims to be breaking out of the fetters in which it has been enslaved for more than two generations. I do not mean the new musicology of such scholars as Maynard Solomon, the American musicologist at Columbia University and author of books about Mozart and Beethoven, whose work on "Schubert's Peacocks of Cellini" as evidence

---

[34] It is easy now to overlook the academic taboos of those decades when, for example, Ivan Bloch (1872–1922) could not be mentioned because he was allegedly a bad scholar — an ellipsis for indicating that his subject matter was unacceptable; and whose book could not be cited (*Sexual Life in England: past and present*, originally published in 1938 but written during World War I). The generation after ours will not resemble Foucault's (c. 1954–84) in its agendas for, or analyses of, cultural history, its main concerns lying in the obtaining and maintaining of jobs rather than sexual revolutions; in applied technologies and computer skills rather than scientific discourses and interdisciplinary revolutions. A rigorous biostatistical survey would prove the point beyond any shadow of doubt, but none is needed: we know intuitively what these glances and homages amount to. Even among the opponents of Foucault — all those who disapprove of his methodology or refute his historiography — the nods are there: uniform, totemic, ritualistic, as if it were *de rigueur* to worship in the Temple of Foucault or be banished without status. Those who have refused to participate, who have come forward to name the enemy and refute his work, are few and far between. Comparison with earlier thinkers and similar shrines is useful: from Darwin and Nietzsche to Freud and Jung. Perhaps this is because Foucault's is not a "theory" in the way Darwin's (evolution) or Freud's (sex) was but an angle of vision, a way of gazing; not a method or approach but a silhouette of postmodern woman herself. There can be no certainty yet because too little time has elapsed but it is an avenue in itself worthy of exploration. The question is not merely whither cultural history after Foucault but where is this new history in the light of new strong theories?

of Schubert's homosexuality has so stirred the traditionalists.[35] So far has it now gone that the Viennese tourist industry, which thrives on promoting Mozart and Schubert as the Austrian Coca-Cola, claims it can be destroyed. Maynard Solomon is, of course, part of the new, post-Foucaldian musicology and has perhaps won his case because his scholarship is otherwise so authoritative. But I specifically refer to the new opera criticism gathered around Wayne Koestenbaum's *The Queen's Throat*, the new musicology called by one prominent group of scholars in the title of their book *Queering the Pitch* (1994)[36] and, more substantially, the Columbia University Press series called *Between Men — Between Women*, which has already produced about two dozen books, all of which share assumptions I want to anatomize here *en bref* and in conclusion within the context of post-Foucaldian cultural history.[37]

This new American musicology focuses on opera because it is in opera that its gay and lesbian bent flourishes. Opera, more than any other form, acts as the mirror reflecting its own collective plight. It proceeds by discovering traces of *travesti* everywhere; that is, gender ambiguity, gender reversals, cross-dressing, drag, and — of course — tragic love among its Traviatas and Mimis. It is not merely ideological in its bisexual and homosexual affinities, but ferrets out the strains of opera's libretti, musical scores, and, perhaps most of all, its directors, producers, and performers: the Fassbinders and Marilyn Hornes, as well as Puccinis, Strausses and Benjamin Brittens. It lures us to ask: what is opera anyway if these are its sexualities? Its practitioners are widely read, bibliographically virtuoso, and rarely obscure. They are infrequently hermeticists or obscurantists, even if their prose clarity varies. The pleasure of reading them derives from making connections with the traditional sphere: a kind of *inter legato*, or interconnectedness among disparate realms in which the reader separates wheat from chaff but where plenty of wheat exists. In this group Wayne Koestenbaum writes in his own voice, like the diva Maria Callas he so reveres, but the others thrive on collaboration.[38] The collaborative act is essential: from inception of projects to celebrations at completions, these collaborations bond, insure visibility, expunge the old loneliness that kept workers in the chains of solitude, and even encourage scholars to fall in love. An example is the 1995 volume *En Travesti: Women, Gender, Subversion, Opera*, edited by Corinne Blackmer and Pat Smith.[39] Of the fifteen contributors, only two are male; their part as "masculine femi-

---

35 See Solomon and also McKay.

36 See Brett et al.

37 See Koestenbaum (1994). The subjectivity Foucault removed from discourse is now returning to it, especially in the new historical scholarship about real biographical women, much of which excavates and documents forgotten figures and celebrates their lives.

38 Koestenbaum sensed this crucial importance of the collaborative act viewed within the contexts of sexual desire and the erotics of scholarship (*Double Talk*).

39 Blackmer and Smith. A significant caveat is that this new post-Foucaldian musicology overlooks social class: what do opera and the working class, even in America, share?

nists" within the collaboration is clear. The confessional dimension of *all* the essays is its most salient feature.

The new American musicology and especially the new opera criticism is ritually confessional. It begins with the self, and its "I" − its subjectivity − is omnipresent. Its self-revelations amount to an eternal "coming out." Almost every essay opens by dramatizing some self-confession, as in Stanford University's Terry Castle's opening essay: "I must begin with this confession." Even the introduction dramatizes a confession about an anonymous friend the editors knew who discovered her lesbianism through opera CDs. Names are explicitly named without the ellipticism of the old historicism because the whole point is the preformative act of "coming out" in collaborative writing. Publishing is itself an exhilarating form for discovering new referents for self and extinguishing former pain, as well, of course, of reconstructing anew the tradition of opera. Straight heterosexual scholarship (if one can refer to it in this crude way for the point of contrast) required no such position. For all one might say about equivalency in both gendered groups, the "straights" had no illicit or covert sexual arrangements to fear or painful loneliness to expunge. By virtue of this lack of recognition, straight academics may wonder why the confessionalism is necessary, as the biographical non-heterosexual Foucault knew all too well by the end of his life. For gays everything lies in the pain of coming out. It is precisely the "pariah phenomenon" of declaring oneself as part of this new musicology I am trying to describe.[40]

Like most criticism, the bulk of this work will not be read in thirty years. The next generation will only read the most brilliant part of it, but as a diagnostic I think some will survive, especially as an emblem of the new post-Foucaldian cultural history. For this new opera criticism exceeds the aim of rectifying incompleteness: reifying the sexual arrangements that have been overlooked. Its preformative act is more complex by virtue of permitting a "coming out" while actually performing a new gay reading that is unabashedly presentist, unfazed by anachronism, committed to discover the inherent gayness of almost every human relationship, and dedicated to a homology of holism by interpreting all representations as pieces within a large mosaic. Despite its blatant solecism to historical mindsets, there is a native pragmatism to such a temporal switch for the way it privileges the self. The difference with "straight interpretation" is apparent when this work is compared with Catherine Clément's *Opera, or the Undoing of Women* or Linda and Michael Hutcheon's *Opera: Desire, Disease, Death*. These "straight" feminists view women *apart* from their lesbian contexts, although they dutifully acknowledge and are generous to those contexts. For the

---

[40] The tradition of the Oscar Wilde-Montgomery Hyde "hiding the love that dares not speak its name" has broken down in the late twentieth century; post-Foucault analysis can explain why in the terms of power/marginalization structures within government.

former, lesbianism is everything: from self-confession to preformative inter-pretative act to final critical reading.

The choice of opera is not fortuitous: the plight of the fallen woman virtually emulates the gay's ritual plight more than any other modern genre. Only a genre inscribing — for example — the biblical Cain and the St. Sebastians of Medieval and Renaissance painting could vie with opera. Moreover, the new practitioners such as Wayne Koestenbaum, playwright Terence McNally in his *Lisbon Traviata* and *Master Class*, and the new opera academics, want an *explicit* discourse naming the thing itself: same-sex love is insufficient. Archival historians signing on to the new self-confessionalism might reconstitute, for example, the history of gay opera audiences, difficult as it is to discover the evidence.[41] Most extraordinary is the new American opera criticism's replacement of the old as the dominant discourse gaining institutionalization.

Its professionalization reconstitutes gender arrangements and collapses the ancient battle between the sexes. The contributors to *En Travesti* are biographi-cally gay, and those who are not — especially among the males — are "feminist masculinists" who might as well be. Sexual orientation, or mental sex, is what counts here, not one's biological gender. And this orientation is what will be professionally transformed through the new filiation. For the new American opera critics what counts is adherence to the dominant discourse — the funda-mental incursion of homosexuality into every aspect of modern opera — not anything so mundane as biological gender or genital disposition.

It hardly requires evidence to claim that thirty years ago the "love that dared not speak its name" was *terra interdicta* in American academia. Today Gay Studies and Queer Theory is an integral part of the academy, with formal programs everywhere and newly developing degrees. The practitioners of the new Ameri-can opera criticism I am discussing all have academic posts, and I predict their stock, so to speak, will rise because it has now been made so explicit. Queer theory is now entirely overt rather than encoded within something else. Any attempt to "encode" — to "mythologize" — it by concealing it, is in fact so politically incorrect that only the unsavvy would attempt to do so. It is post-Foucaldian insofar as it admits the subject into discourse and augurs the new landscape of academic study. It is not a phase and it will not disappear after the millennium.[42] It is quickly being exported to Europe, like everything else Ameri-can, five or ten years after the fact.

Just a few months ago I met a group of Italian musicologists at a conference in Bologna Italy who knew all about the new American gay opera criticism and

---

41 Apparently nothing whatever has been researched or written about the changing constitution of opera audiences since homosexual men began appearing there in droves in the mid-eighteenth century. Such scholarship would be a difficult piece of detective work for the new opera critics.
42 On the persistence of these concerns into the new millennium see Bloom (1996); Thomson; Murray; and Horton.

were avidly reading it. One of them was a middle-age female professor in an Italian conservatory of music; the happily married Catholic mother of four daughters, with a heavily annotated paperback copy of *En Travesti* stashed in her tote case. When I sought her opinion, she professed no contradiction. She liked the new opera criticism despite its fundamental anachronism and radical presentism. She judged its value by its bravura in ferreting out the unseen in gender relations, and the *sprezzatura* that spoke to her as an Italian feminist. She claimed to be fundamentally post-Foucaldian in an Italian key, and stated she could never live in America because of its cults of savage puritanism.

XV. Apocalyptic Fantasies

In conclusion, if my premise has any validity whatever, the irony of the new American musicology is that it issues from an erotophobic and paranoid America mired in new hybrid forms of cultural hysteria. If the romantic French or the luscious Italians had invented the new musicology, that would be something else. But coming from Waspland, which now exports it to the rest of the world, there is a tension and paradox, and also a fundamental contradiction: this academic opera discourse of lascivious castrati and crossed-dressed same-sex lovers issues from a newly puritanical post-AIDS America. And it emerges in a dominant cultural discourse at once autobiographical, confessional, explicit, brazen, and contemptuous of those incapable of appreciating its revelations. Its authors − still primarily female − are "coming out" with a vengeance.

It may be that the new American musicology − merely my concrete example, among many, of a post-Foucaldian gesture and practice − was entirely predictable. After all, we dream of what we do not have: if puritanical, fundamentalist, hysterical, politically correct and conservative America continues to legislate what is lawful and unlawful in matters of love, as it has done in state after state,[43] we can at least live through our new musicology. But whether predictable or not, it has caused a stir in the international academic scene and appears to be the only opera criticism people are genuinely excited about. In the sense that its practitioners are almost all under forty, the children of the war babies, the result of a generation raised on the daily pabulum of Foucault's writings, who openly acknowledge him and profess to have been liberated by his histories − this brand of new musicology seems to me fundamentally post-Foucaldian.

My heuristic erotophobic trope then amounts to a paradox, predictable or not. It has a profile but not a name. It is thoroughly problematic and virtually antiquarian. It requires a profound sense of the history of *both* female and male hysteria from the Greeks forward to fathom its internal contradictions. It re-

---

[43] I refer to the proliferating new anti-sodomy laws in Georgia, Arizona and Oregon.

quires too much concentration and proof to be brought to the forefront of the conscious imagination. Viewed from the *inside* — from within sexually and racially diverse America — it appears to be unsupported by case evidence; a phantasmagoria rather than any type of medical epidemic. Moreover, liberated Americans in the richest and most powerful country in the world will not accede to be called puritan, hysterical, erotophobic on mere anecdotal evidence without hard *DSM* authority. Finally, America is even more diverse than I suggest, if now also growing less, rather than more, homophobic. Thus, homophobic erotophobia deserves to be treated as well; as does the (again paradoxical) coexistence of an erotophobic conservative Right and an apparently sex-driven, even sex-obsessed, Hollywood. But where is middle America in all this calibration?

Erotophobia exists, admittedly, in a circle of inconsistencies and incommensurabilities spelling trouble, if not doom, for the thesis. I have conceded erotophobia's predicaments and have been suggesting that it is a larger class of response, as it were, than homophobia, but I have not adumbrated the interrelations, nor the probabilities, of a more drastic homo-erotophobia despite an intuitive sense that they lurk everywhere. Even more problematic for concrete proof about erotophobia as something existing beyond the personal and anecdotal realm, is the fact that opera in America (in light of the example I chose from the new musicology) remains classbound. The poor cannot afford to attend it even if they wished, nor am I claiming they are banging on its doors. Argue, if one wishes, that opera's poignant fables have trickled down to the poorer classes in America: still, the average American gay laborer or gay construction worker probably still knows nothing about Mimi's or Madame Butterfly's tragic world. Moreover, my erotophobia possesses no developed discourse of its own, old or new, and — moving from the representational to the factual — few would therefore be foolish enough to try to cure it. Despite all my protests, the word itself (like its cousin erotomania) still seems misconstrued or misguided: a malapropism for something else. All these caveats and desiderata are true — yet there is still matter in the subject. Diverse America is growing *more*, not less, hysterical as a mass society. The defect lies in my inability to clothe erotophobia in a proper discourse, not in the lack of sufficient historical material or adequate proof.

I am no prophet but I think Foucault would have listened, fiercely critical yet without contempt — even the late Foucault who himself heard voices crying anti-sex: "I have the impression of currently hearing an 'anti-sex' grumbling (I am not a prophet, at most a diagnostician), as if an effort were being made, in depth, to shake this great 'sexography' which makes us try to decipher sex as the universal secret" (*Foucault Live*, 144). Whether he would have judged my sally into sexual discourse pre- or post-Foucaldian I do not know, nor whether he would have concurred with my sense of erotophobia's historical origins and insistence that, in America at least, it cannot be understood apart from other versions of puritan mass hysteria. Radical critiques of American Puritanism are not topics with which Foucault is ever associated, and seem ironically remote from the visitor who, at the end of his life, tasted America's subterranean hedonism more daringly, if perhaps also more tragically, than the natives. Still, if Foucault had responded, his metacommentary would have been in a language different from mine and in other categories; perhaps proving, yet again, that discourse, even the old-styled rhetoric, is everything in these matters. But Foucault in Berkeley was fascinated by the endless paradoxes suggested by my trope no sex please, we're American, although my Ivy League teachers could not and did not face them (the paradoxes). For them the subject was not liberating but explosive, treacherous, off limits – an erotophobia of the present not to be pondered. Liberation for us lay in this disjunction, long before the Clinton debacle.

2

Foucault's Technologies of the Self and the Cultural History of Identity

JAN GOLDSTEIN

Let me begin with an autobiographical reminiscence, one that concerns, appropriately, theory and its relation to practice. While I was writing my dissertation as a history graduate student at Columbia University, I also attended classes at the Columbia Psychoanalytic Institute. Although my status was that of a so-called special candidate, someone who was learning psychoanalytic theory solely for the purpose of applying it to scholarly research, the instruction I received was geared to the needs of the regular candidates, who were being trained to conduct psychoanalysis with patients. I have a vivid memory of the day in the basic theory course when we discussed Freud's transition from his topographical model, in which he divided the mind into conscious, preconscious and unconscious spaces, to his structural model, in which he postulated the relatively stable and persistent organizational entities of ego, id and superego. The shift occurred around 1920, by which time Freud had been spinning out psychoanalytic theory for over two decades. But, according to my teacher, Freud never went back to his earlier work to recast it in terms of the ego-id-superego triad; nor did he ever repudiate that earlier work, couched though it was in now-outmoded categories. Rather, within his corpus, the topographical and structural models simply coexisted.

After the requisite, joking reference to Freud's anal retentiveness, the teacher noted that this overlap posed not real problem to the practicing analyst; indeed it represented a resource. The analyst should, we were told, keep both models in free-floating and evenly hovering attention (that tool of the trade) and, when listening to a patient, interpret the material according to whichever model its own particular content evoked. Thus the teacher said that he personally relied more on the structural model in his daily practice, but that there were circumstances in which he was glad to have the topographical model in his repertory, too, for it sometimes allowed him to make better sense of what the patient was telling him.

I cannot remember what my reaction to this methodological pronouncement was at the time, although I suspect I was surprised that anyone would admit unapologetically to such an informal, ad hoc deployment of theory. Over the years, however, as I became a practicing historian, I have from time to time thought back to this episode in my education and have realized that my relationship to theory is now remarkably similar to the one the analyst described. While I always come to my material with the questions that *I* have asked of it (rather than its seeking me out in my office and dumping its problems in my lap), I come equipped with a small company of theories that I regard as smart, astute, insightful by dint of the interpretive work that they have been able to do in other settings as well as their heuristic value in helping to pose interesting historical questions to begin with. I then pick and choose among my theoretical repertory as the material seems to dictate. Thus for example in my current project, which concerns the competing conceptions of self and the politics of selfhood in France in the century following the 1789 Revolution, I have drawn from time to time both on Foucault's concept of technologies of the self and on Habermas' account of the reciprocal creation of the bourgeois public and private spheres and its bearing on the nearly simultaneous constitution of the sciences of political economy and psychology (Habermas, *Structural Transformation*). It does not trouble me that, on the meta-level of their evaluations of the Enlightenment, Habermas and Foucault disagree. I am not after all treating either as a total theory capable of illuminating everything but treating both as local theories with specific competences.

Hence the question to which our June 1997 conference in Amsterdam was devoted strikes me as either well-posed or not so well-posed depending upon where the accent is placed − or, more specifically, how the deliberately (and provocatively) ambiguous phrase "after Foucault" is understood. For a group of literary and cultural historians to discuss how, why, and where they have found Foucault useful or of little value, to map out, as it were the terrain of competence of Foucauldian theory as it appears from our vantage point in the late 1990s (and I am here paraphrasing, very loosely, the letter inviting me to this conference), seems like an eminently sound and sensible idea. On the other hand, to entertain the proposition that (and I am here quoting from the poster for our conference) "however much [we] have gained from Foucault [we] are now moving further by overcoming our Foucauldian heritage," seems like an odd and uncongenial exercise. The first formulation posits "after Foucault" as a temporal position in need of further definition and acknowledges the likelihood that the work of Foucault will continue to exert a fertile influence on historical and literary scholarship. The second formulation also posits "after Foucault" as a temporal position in need of further definition, but it assumes that Foucault's influence has dried up and poses as a question only what new wellspring of theory will come to take its place.

What is the basis of the slippage between these two statements of purpose, each linked to a particular interpretation of the rubric "after Foucault"? The first appears to correspond to the term "cultural history," featured in the title of the conference, and the second to the term "cultural studies," featured in the smaller print on the poster. Cultural history and cultural studies usually stand in quite different relationships to Foucault.

As I have pointed out before (Goldstein, "Introduction," 15), cultural historians can and do draw important inspiration from Foucault *without* accepting the strong claim of certain Foucauldians that the academic disciplines, as they are practiced in the late twentieth century, are unself-consciously enmeshed in and therefore irredeemably tainted by structures of power, that they are, in other words, basically no different from those nineteenth-century bodies of enlightened scientific knowledge that Foucault so brilliantly analyzed in *Surveiller et punir* and that he called the disciplines. To be sure, Foucault himself sometimes lent support to that strong claim – for example, when in the late 1970s, at the end of his reply to the historian of medicine Jacques Léonard, he spoke of the possibility of a future collaboration between historians and philosophers that would be not the standard anodyne "'interdisciplinary encounter'" but "a work in common of people who seek to 'de-discipline' themselves" (Foucault, "Poussière et nuage" 39). This watchword of "de-disciplinization," largely ignored by cultural historians, has been taken up by the practitioners of cultural studies, who invented a new field in the hope of freeing themselves from the distasteful baggage of the older disciplinary formations and who sought in Foucault a theory that could undergird a new form of intellectual endeavor that would serve as a dissent from power. It is, I would suggest, only if one expected so much from Foucault to begin with, that one might now want to leave him behind as an empty husk. Cultural history, whose ties to Foucault were always less binding, has by contrast not exhausted what Foucault has to offer.

Determining the precise relationship of a "disciplinary" cultural history to a "de-disciplinary" cultural studies is, of course, a thorny problem, and I do not wish to imply that a facile dividing line between the two can be drawn. In thinking about the problem, I looked at the essay by Michael Steinberg in a recent collection devoted to the theme of disciplinarity and dissent. Steinberg numbers himself among the cultural historians and, as it turned out, I sympathized with his position on this matter. "Should the farmer and the cowhand be friends?" Steinberg asks, recalling the song from the 1942 Rogers and Hammerstein musical *Oklahoma*. Is there, in other words, any possibility for a truce and even a collaboration between the worker in the disciplinary vineyards and the post-disciplinary cowhand bent on subversion and disruption? Steinberg wants to give a positive answer to that question for several, overlapping reasons: he rejects as inapplicable to himself the caricature of disciplinary historians offered by cultural studies – that is, "antiquarians and/or ideologues who hide a vicious form of presentism, instrumental reason and indeed neo-colonialism under their antiquarian innocence"; he finds that the definition of cultural studies advanced by certain of its practitioners aptly characterizes what most cultural historians think they, too, are doing – for example, an "examination of the symbolic orders in which intrasubjective meanings and social practices are constituted and contested"; and finally he does not want to relinquish his identity as a historian because he cannot let go of a certain disciplinary allegiance that he describes as "hold[ing] myself responsible to the existence and exigencies of an object-world that is morally, materially, linguistically and culturally constituted," the positing of which "has nothing to do with the claim of its empirical epistemological availability" (105). That is, without adhering to some naive positivist concept of "objectivity," Steinberg wants to retain the belief in "something out there" that must guide historians' investigations, holding them to standards of care and scrupulosity in their handling of sources, even though they have long since given up the idea that they can straightforwardly reconstruct the past or that there is a single way of "getting it right" (103, 105, 11).

I am not sure that I follow every part of Steinberg's dense argument or that I would embrace the "syncretism of cultural history and cultural studies" for which he eventually pleads and that he depicts as "the understanding of modern subjectivities as instantiations of multiple consciousness," in which "multiplicity does not contradict coherence" (Ibid., 127). But I completely sympathize with his sense of being caught in an unpleasant dilemma between dissent and disciplinarity, wanting — and indeed believing himself able — to practice a history that is unsettling in its effects and at the same time responsible in its methods to something stubborn and resistant, not infinitely malleable, that emerges when one consults in abundance the written and other remains of the past. Or, at least, that is how I read the underlying drift of Steinberg's essay because that is what I want to do. In fact, I went into intellectual and cultural history after having concentrated primarily in English literature in college precisely because I wanted to encounter that external resistance, because I felt that, cheered on by approving literature professors, I had become too adroit as an analyst of texts and could bend a text into saying almost anything. I needed recourse to factors outside the text in order to supply more stringent rules for the game, to serve as a check on my pyrotechnical and, I suspected, increasingly solipsistic feats of reading.

I. The Brief

With this methodological introduction *cum* autobiographical confession as background, let me turn to the substance of this essay, which is to argue for the continued usefulness to cultural history of one of Foucault's concepts, that of technologies of the self. My current work on the constitution of selfhood in nineteenth-century France[1] will provide me with my initial examples, but my

---

[1] That research will appear as a book tentatively titled The Post-Revolutionary Self: Competing Psychologies in Nineteenth-Century France to be published by Harvard University Press. Several portions of the project are already in print or in press: "Foucault and the Post-Revolutionary

remarks, as I will show in the penultimate section of the essay, have a more extended reference. I began my project on selfhood nearly a decade ago, before the now ubiquitous interest in "identity" had swept the humanities and social sciences. But that interest in identity is also well-served (though not, of course, completely satisfied) by the Foucauldian concept.

The current vogue of identity scholarship is noteworthy for, among other things, the fact that it has few theoretical moorings, with most scholars using the keyword in an intuitive, commonsensical manner. In this, it is quite different from an earlier vogue of identity scholarship, the one inspired by Erik Erikson in the United States in the 1960s. Whatever one might think of Erikson's concept of identity (and it is surely imprinted with the American liberal optimism of its era), it was at least *relatively* explicit, grounded in a neo-Freudian developmental schema in which the psychosocial stages beginning in infancy culminated in an adolescent crisis which, if successfully weathered, resulted in the individual's autonomous forging of his or her identity. The very paucity of theoretical conceptions informing today's fascination with identity would seem to argue strongly for pursuing and elaborating Foucault's concept of technologies of the self. Though no more value-neutral than Erikson's, this concept has the advantage of being more finely historically attuned, capable of adjustment according to the different intellectual, institutional, social and political environments in which selfhood is embedded at different historical moments.

In making my argument, I will of necessity be going over ground that I covered in my earlier essay, "Foucault and the Post-Revolutionary Self." But the point, as well as the endpoint, of the two contributions differ. In the first, I wanted to show that Foucault's theories might be applied, without stress or strain, to the "ordinary" practice of history. My strategy was to establish that, at least with respect to one historical phenomenon – the dissemination of the philosophy of Victor Cousin in nineteenth-century France – Foucauldian categories could quite elegantly subsume the bevy of empirical detail turned up by my research in archival and printed primary sources. That essay ended by focusing on an aspect of Foucault's theory that my data belied and that struck me as revealing attitudes more culturally specific to France than its author realized. I thus concluded by cautioning historians to be sensitive to the potentially misleading inflections that Foucault's French context might introduce into his theories. In the present contribution I review what I said before about applicability of the Foucauldian concept of the technology of the self to the trajectory of Victor Cousin's philosophy. But I go beyond the earlier essay and make a stronger case for the continued vitality of Foucauldian theory ("after Foucault") by rifling through some recent historiography and mounting a retrospective argument for the application of that concept to other scholars' work.

Self," "Saying 'I,'" "The Advent of Psychological Modernism in France," and "Eclectic Subjectivity and the Impossibility of Female Beauty."

II. Technologies of the Self

Foucault first articulated the concept of a technology of the self in "Subjectivity and Truth," the 1980–81 lecture course at the Collège de France in which he sketched out the plan for what would later become Volumes 2 and 3 of his *History of Sexuality*. "I have begun an inquiry," he wrote in the obligatory end-of-the-year summary,

> into the modes of self-knowledge that have been put into use and their history: How has the subject been established at different moments and in different institutional contexts as an object of knowledge that is possible, desirable, or even indispensable? How has the experience that one can have of oneself, as well as the knowledge that one can form from that experience, been organized by certain schemas? How have these schemas been defined, valorized, recommended, imposed?

He went on to say that he would take as the "guiding thread" of this inquiry something he called "technologies of the self." By this he meant "the procedures, which have doubtless existed in all civilizations, that are proposed or prescribed to individuals in order to fix, maintain or transform their identities with particular ends in view" and which operate by means either of "a mastery of the self by the self or a knowledge of the self by the self" (*Résumé des cours* 133–34).

The 1980–81 lectures were, of course, far from the first time that Foucault had addressed the constitution of the subject; that topic, or something closely approximating it, had already loomed large in *Discipline and Punish* and in the introductory volume of the *History of Sexuality*; and hence understanding the concept of technologies of the self requires that we articulate it with respect to that earlier work. As Hubert Dreyfus and Paul Rabinow have pointed out, *Discipline and Punish* and vol. 1 of *The History of Sexuality* represent a perspectival division of labor, the first offering a genealogy of the modern individual as object, the second a genealogy of the modern individual as subject (Dreyfus and Rabinow 126 and chapter titles on 143, 168). Thus, in a stunning denouement in *Discipline and Punish*, Foucault announced that the disciplinary examination and the data-filled dossiers that it amassed made possible "the everyday individuality of everybody," which he glossed as "the constitution of the individual as a describable, analyzable *object*" (190–91, my italics). In *The History of Sexuality*, by contrast, he depicted confession in its religious and scientific guises as "an immense labor to which the West has submitted generations in order to produce [...] men's subjection: their constitution as *subjects* in both senses of the word" (60, my italics). Both books depicted the individual as an effect of power, brought into being either by the observations and written notations of the disciplinary expert or by the provocations and definitive interpretations of the confessional expert. Yet if, in Foucault's play on words, subjection (*assujetissement* in the French) to sexual confession produces a subject, the disciplinary examination, he tells us, "functions as a procedure of *objectivation* and subjection" (*Disci-*

pline and Punish, 192, my italics). As I have argued elsewhere, the distinction between these two constitutions is to some degree defensible, but ultimately individual-as-object and individual-as-subject effectively interpenetrate one another ("Foucault and the Post-Revolutionary Self" 108 – 10). Foucault implicitly acknowledged this himself when, by the early 1980s, he had homogenized his vocabulary and adopted the term "subject" to refer to *both* those individuals produced by disciplinary procedures and those produced by confessional ones ("The Subject and Power" 208).

In *The Use of Pleasure*, where Foucault highlights the problem of the subject and attempts a schematic integration of the approaches to it dispersed throughout his earlier work, the plot thickens. Foucault now viewed the historical specificity of human experience at any given moment as constructed along three axes: "the sciences (*savoirs*) that refer to it; the systems of power that regulate its practice; the forms within which individuals are able, are obliged, to recognize themselves as subjects..." (4). Analysis of the first two, *savoir* and *pouvoir*, had comprised the bulk of his earlier work; analysis of the forms of subjectivity would occupy him in his current project. Unfortunately for my concerns here, Foucault never spelled out the implications of this tripartite mapping. In particular, he never indicated what, if anything, the regimens of power/knowledge (the first two axes) had to do with the various historical experiences of subjectivity (the third axis). His vocabulary in *The Use of Pleasure* sometimes echoed the arresting double entendre on "subject" that had figured in his earlier work. He spoke of the "mode of subjection" to the moral code as an aspect of the formation of the subject (27), thus suggesting that subjects still remained for him power-effects. But he now also employed a new term, "subjectivation," which by dint of its novelty in his prose, suggested that Foucault might no longer simply equate subject-making with subjection. In fact, in *The Use of Pleasure* "subjectivation" functions as the governing rubric in Foucault's system of classification: the "mode of subjection" to the moral code is subsumed under it as one of its possible types (32).

Foucault left, however, most of the freight carried by the term "subjectivation" unpacked. He indicated that subjectivation was subject-making in the reflexive mode; that its special domain was the relationship that the self establishes to the self; that its privileged modus operandi was the so-called technology of the self. But the tantalizing possibility that the term contained a hint of human agency that Foucault's earlier work had categorically rejected remained just that – a tantalizing possibility.

Hence for purposes of this essay, let me adopt a provisional resolution to the problem of the third axis. I will assume that a technology of the self is necessary linked, be it weakly or strongly, to a regimen of power/knowledge. Without such a linkage, it is difficult for me to conceive how such a technology could become sufficiently generalized among a given population as to acquire historical significance; nor can I readily imagine a *subjectivation* in a Foucauldian universe that is not in some measure also an *assujetissement*. Foucault implicitly acknowledges this linkage in the 1981 passage I quoted above when he speaks of technologies of the self as schemas for the organization of self-knowledge that are, in a particular setting, "valorized, recommended, *imposed*." And he implicitly acknowledges the linkage once again in the just-cited passage from *The Use of Pleasure*, where he offers as his initial depiction of the third axis "the forms within which individuals are able, *are obliged*, to recognize themselves as subjects."

Once the three axes are aligned in this fashion, the concept of a technology of the self seems to refer to the subject's own, intimate elaboration of a subjectivity that was in the first instance founded or constituted through interpersonal mechanisms of power/knowledge necessarily involving an element of coercion. Subjectivation then refers to the individual's conviction − ultimately an illusory conviction − that he or she is acting autonomously and is engaged in a "purely" reflexive act of self-fashioning on the basis of values freely assented to. Through its linkage to a power/knowledge regimen, the concept of the technology of the self thus shares in the great advantage of Foucauldian historical logic: it bridges theory and practice, completely and forcefully elides sophisticated intellectual systems and routinized social practices (Goldstein, "Foucault among the Sociologists," 177−84).

III. The Example of Cousinianism

My research on competing psychologies in France after the Revolution has drawn my attention to a practice that might well be called a hegemonic technology of the self in nineteenth-century France. That research began with the premise that, by destroying the guilds and other corporate bodies that had served as the matrix of individual life under the Old Regime, the Revolution reproblematized the self. In keeping with the Enlightenment credo that reliable, scientific knowledge about human beings was attainable, the post-Revolutionary solution to that reproblematization was to seek to define and stabilize the self by developing a science of psychology. In fact not one such "objective" science but three emerged and competed during the period, roughly, 1780−1850: *Idéologie*, the latter-day version of the sensationalism of Locke and Condillac, with its tabula rasa mind impressed by sensations originating in the outside world and entering through the sense receptors; phrenology, with its cranial bumps revealing in any given individual the relative size of the different brain organs, each controlling an intellectual or affective trait; and the philosophical psychology of Victor Cousin. The contestation among the three never took place solely at the level of ideas because, in the hyper-politicized environment created by the incomplete resolution of the Revolutionary upheavals, each psychology rapidly acquired a strong political coloration and, moreover, because proponents of all three made strenuous efforts to institutionalize their theory in the state-run educational system established during the Revolution. I obviously cannot go into the details of this competition here. Suffice it say that Cousinianism, which postulated a priori a unified, holistic self, emerged as the winner and that the most tangible mark of its victory was educational monopoly.

A derivative thinker but an academic entrepreneur of real genius, Cousin had "psychology" − meaning, of course, his own brand of psychology − officially declared the first substantive part of the philosophy taught in the state school system. Not only did he gain full control over philosophy instruction at the university level but, even more important, he installed his philosophical psychology in the curriculum of every lycée in France, where it remained with few fundamental alterations from 1832 until nearly the end of the century. To staff the multitude of lycées with competent philosophy teachers, he trained a "regiment" (as they were called at the time) of loyal disciples and arranged for their expeditious job placement.

Cousin succeeded in this endeavor not only because of his consummate skills in administrative maneuvering but also because his psychology had the advantage of being closely allied with an acceptably middle-of-the-road political ideology: the constitutional monarchism of the *juste milieu*, which rose to power with the July Monarchy (1830−48) and stood for a cautious and conservative liberalism, the dominance of the bourgeoisie, and a determination to avoid renewed revolution at all costs. Indeed the Cousinian fetishism of the unified self, or *moi*, was intimately tied to these political goals, especially the last one. Cousin believed that sensationalism had vitiated the self both by rooting it ultimately in human biology and by building it up through an accumulation of discrete, passively received sensations that could never be melded into an integral whole. In his view, the widespread eighteenth-century acceptance of sensationalism, and of the flimsy, tenuous self that came along with it, held no small measure of blame for the radical excesses of the Revolution; a whole generation of Frenchmen had grown up without a moral backbone or sense of ultimate responsibility for their actions, with no internal brakes preventing them from yielding to revolutionary fantasies. Cousin thus assigned to the a priori self an urgent remedial role, which in turn led to its absolute pedagogical centrality and hence to the sudden popularization of the word *moi* among lycée graduates. As one of his disciples wrote in the article "Moi" in a contemporary encyclopedia that found its way into many bourgeois households:

> This word [*moi*], which in the past belonged only to the domain of grammar and which was nothing more than the most notable of pronouns, has become, after the word "God," the substantive noun *par excellence* (Matter, 259).

Let me indicate how Cousin's psychology functioned in nineteenth-century France as both a technology of the self and as a regimen of power/knowledge and how these two, linked Foucauldian concepts can help us understand the mechanisms of self-making in that historical context.

Cousinianism was a technology of the self because it emphasized and aimed at imparting skill in introspection. According to the personal myth that Cousin propagated, it was during a heroic phase of introspection that he had as a young man refuted sensationalism, observing his own inner spaces and satisfying himself that they contained not only the residues of sensation but also a pure spontaneous activity, a will which he named the *moi*. Autobiography was subsequently translated into pedagogy, so that making direct contact with one's volitional force through introspection became a major lesson of the philosophy classroom in the nineteenth-century lycée. Thus a Cousinian pedagogical manual of 1838 enumerated the difficulties the teacher might encounter in his efforts to lead his charges to grasp the "interior reality" (*fait intérieur*), and the national administrative decree of 1832 establishing the new philosophy curriculum even stipulated that students be able to "*describe* the phenomenon of the will" (Gatien-Arnoult, *Cours*, 81 note 1; "Procès-verbaux"). As Cousin characterized his introspective method it had, in the self's arduous attainment of knowledge of itself, all the requisite marks of a Foucauldian technology of the self. Here are some relevant passages from his famous 1828 lectures:

> What is psychological analysis? It is the slow, patient, and meticulous observation, with the aid of consciousness, of phenomena hidden in the depths of human nature. These phenomena are complicated, fleeting, obscure, rendered almost imperceptible by their very closeness. The consciousness which applies itself to them is an instrument of extreme delicacy (*Introduction*, Lesson 2, p. 6).
>
> There is, Gentlemen, a psychological art, for reflection is, so to speak, against nature, and this art is not learned in a day. One does not fold back upon oneself easily without long practice, sustained habit, and a laborious apprenticeship (Ibid., Lesson 5, p. 35).

In addition to providing a technology of the self, Cousinian psychology functioned in nineteenth-century France as a regimen of power/knowledge in Foucault's sense. It was, in the first place, officially prescribed as a form of pedagogy throughout the state system of secondary education and also given maximum impact by its strategic location in that part of the lycée curriculum regarded as its summit or crown: the *classe de philosophie* of the third and last year. Second, as an emanation of bureaucratic power – and in keeping with the meaning that Foucault gave to "power" – Cousinian pedagogy both constrained its recipients and created them. In the interest of socio-political stability, it exacted their assent to a set of allegedly fixed, immutable principles about "the true, the beautiful and the good"[2] – metaphysical principles that the students were said to appre-

---

[2] Cousin's lectures on that subject, first delivered in 1817 and later published under the title Du vrai, du beau et du bien, became the official French philosophy textbook for much of the nineteenth century. See Zeldin 2: 409.

hend as the direct consequence of their introspection (since psychology formed the "vestibule" to ontology) and which were, furthermore, homologous to the structure of consciousness (since will corresponded to mankind, sensation to nature, and reason to God). But at the same time, Cousinian pedagogy conferred on them a literal gift of selfhood: the knowledge that each was the possessor of a *moi* — a source of will and willed activity in the world that could be known and talked about.

Third and finally, by conferring this gift only on the elite segment of the population which attended the lycées — that is, the male bourgeoisie — Cousinian psychology implicated itself still more deeply in power relations. Cousin made quite clear that everyone had a *moi* in principle, but he tempered this stance of psychological democracy by his unquestioned assumption that in the majority of people the *moi* would remain more or less fused in a "primitive synthesis" of the elements of consciousness, rather than becoming detached, scrutinized and appropriated through reflection. He even went so far as to specify that the degree to which these elements of consciousness became disaggregated formed the sole basis of the difference among people (*Introduction*, Lesson 5, pp. 39–40). Thus, like instruction in Greek and Latin, but more intimately tied to an individual's interior landscape, instruction in eclectic psychology became a marker, a criterion for distinguishing socially dominant from marginal groups. Bourgeois males learned psychology, but workers did not and women did not. The significance of these exclusions was underscored by their longevity. For example, even after the Third Republic founded lycées for girls in the 1880s, women still did not learn psychology. Republican educators omitted it from the female philosophy curriculum in all but the most watered down form at the very same moment that they were retaining it full strength in the newly overhauled philosophy curriculum of the boys' lycées (Goldstein, "Saying 'I'" 331–33).

In saying that Cousinian psychology supplied the nineteenth-century male bourgeoisie with a technology of the self, I do not wish to imply that it singlehandedly gave them what, in ordinary parlance, is referred to as a sense of self. Clearly the bourgeois sense of self was the result of a host of social practices that constituted members of that class as persons worthy of deference, as men to be reckoned with. What Cousinian psychology gave them uniquely was a language that enabled them to conceptualize the particular stuff of their "selves" in a way that could never have been accomplished simply through the unmediated experience of having money and possessions or being treated with respect. That language, which pinpointed the active, volitional and utterly unified character of the self, received concrete support from the introspective method. The specificity and limitations of Cousinian introspection, and hence of the kind of self it supported, need to be emphasized. Cousinian introspection was *not* used to lavish attention on feelings or to validate their nuances (tellingly, Cousinianism did not, for all its loquaciousness, conduce to autobiographical writing of the confessional sort) but was used instead to gain factual certainty that one had an active principle of assertion stirring within and hence was equipped if not destined to be a doer in society. Nor did Cousinian introspection encounter an unruly self that needed to be mastered by itself in an Augustinian-style struggle: the self's essential harmony with the metaphysical structure of the universe had been posited in advance; its constraints were in-built; it had, in a word, already received the go-ahead signal.

And, I would submit, it is the Foucauldian concept of the technology of the self that helps the historian to perceive the role played by Cousinianism in forming bourgeois identity. Cousinianism is not a new topic for historians; but it has been generally treated as a narrowly academic phenomenon, a chapter in the history of French philosophy and especially the professionalization of that philosophy.[3] It is by asking new questions of this old material – questions honed with a Foucauldian sensibility – that the material can be made to yield new results and to shed light on the politics of selfhood and the socio-political parameters of self-fashioning at a critical juncture in history: that of the triumph of the bourgeoisie.

IV. Other Technologies of the Self: A Historiographical Sample

It is evident, too, that phrenology, a loser in the three-way competition of psychologies in France, furnished its own, quite different technology of the self. One would have one's cranium read by a phrenological aficionado, or do the job oneself with the aid of an illustrated manual, and thereby learn one's dominant intellectual and affective traits, be they positive (e. g., benevolence, conscientiousness, ability to perceive form) or negative (e. g., destructiveness, secretiveness). Then, depending upon one's real-life opportunities, one could deliberately train one's positive brain organs – the theory held that education would increase their physiological magnitude – with a particular occupation in view. The purpose of self-knowledge in the phrenological framework was thus to select rationally one's niche in the division of labor and thereby to maximize one's chances of economic success and ascension of the social ladder. If the dominant metaphor of Cousinianism was depth, or the privileged introspection into dark and hidden places that would provide assurance of one's voluntaristic dynamism, the dominant metaphor of phrenology was superficiality, a visual assessment of

---

[3] I say this, of course, not to disparage the Cousin historiography but only to indicate that it has been written with a different scholarly agenda in mind. For important examples, see Bolgar, Doris S. Goldstein, and, most recently, the monograph of Patrice Vermeren. A different and equally important approach to Cousin, one that aptly sees him as the "guru" of a Romantic youth culture, is ch. 3 in Alan B. Spitzer's book.

cranial contours accessible to everyone that would aid in the management of a career. Nineteenth-century Frenchmen could readily translate themselves into phrenological terms. To cite just one example that I recently came across, here is a medical doctor arguing in a pamphlet in 1828 that he and his colleagues ought to be accorded more esteem in society: "Let us dare say that medicine requires the strongest of abilities and, to use the language that the admirable writings of Monsieur Gall [the founder of phrenology] have made comprehensible to all, that there is no profession that simultaneously occupies a larger number of brain regions" (Salle 46–7).

But, despite promising signs in the 1830s, phrenology never received in France the blessings of the official establishment that were bestowed on Cousinian psychology; it never became a part of the regimen of power/knowledge and was never generalized on a large scale as a technology of the self. But it did apparently achieve that status in Britain, even though, in the absence of a strong centralized bureaucracy, regimens of power/knowledge across the Channel typically worked through more informal structures. As an excellent 1984 book by the historian of science Roger Cooter has shown, phrenology was, in a two-stage process, widely adopted by members of both the middle and working classes of nineteenth-century Britain. It reached the former through the vehicle of savant societies and served them as a mode of self-assertion against the gentlemanly elite who made up the professional cadres at the beginning of the century. It then reached the latter by means of mechanics' institutes and furnished them with an ideology of self-help, of individual rather than collective solutions, that engineered their consent to bourgeois dominance. (Cooter, esp. chs. 2, 5, 8) While Cooter never employs the Foucauldian category of technology of the self, it is clear that the category readily applies to the story he recounts and that it would, moreover, provide a way to exploit that story to theorize about the constitution of class identity.

Let me cite an example from much farther afield. In ancient Greece and Rome and in medieval and early modern Europe an art of memory, quite foreign to us today, was widely practiced by educated people (Yates, *Art of Memory*). Following this art, one improved one's mental retrieval system by imagining one's mind as a vast storehouse whose particular architectural features became the setting for various bits of data, themselves sometimes embodied to render them more striking and hence more memorable. The fine 1990 work of the literary historian Mary Carruthers on memory in medieval culture does not make use of the Foucauldian category of a technology of the self any more than Cooter does. But for someone familiar with that category, it indicates how the art of memory could serve as the scaffolding for a particular technology of the medieval self.

According to Carruthers, medieval culture enjoined a mode of ethically responsible reading that included: (1) marking key passages in the margins; (2)

writing them down in the personal notebook called a florilegium and committing them to memory; (3) ruminating on a text in the literal sense of a cow chewing its cud — a metaphor enacted in the monastic custom of reading during meals — and thereby "making it one's own." In this morally serious activity, the reader was not asked to interpret the text from an objective, scientific standpoint or to attempt to seize the author's intention but was instead encouraged to view the text in a manner he or she found personally meaningful. The reader thus re-authored the text; there was no clear demarcation between "my experience" and "what I read in a book" (*Book of Memory*, 162–69, 174).

From this approved mode of reading Carruthers derives the medieval conception of a self as that entity founded on the memory of significant, flagged passages in texts. The medieval self, she writes, is a "subject-who-remembers" — and remembers not his or her own first-hand experience of the world but rather those texts on which he or she had placed a personal stamp and had systematically committed to memory. Carruthers offers as an example of such a self an anecdote told by Abelard about Héloïse. The unhappy young woman justifies her decision to enter a convent to the many people urging her not to submit to so harsh a penance by reciting through her tears the lament of Cornelia in Lucan's poem *Pharsalia*. From a modern, individualistic standpoint, the use of someone else's words to express so personal a decision seems inappropriate. But the medieval self is not given to radically personal expression; it is rather a character constructed of memorized and personally imprinted bits and pieces of text found in the public domain (Ibid., 179–82). The medieval mode of reading, which gave rise to this specific and singular form of selfhood, therefore qualifies as a technology of the self.

It is, to return to the distinction I established earlier in my discussion of the problem of the third axis, a technology of the self more weakly tied to a regimen of power/knowledge than is, for example, Cousinian philosophical psychology, which would seem to occupy the strong end of that spectrum. The latitude of interpretation of texts allowed the medieval reader would certainly loosen the tie. But, on the other hand, the injunction to memorize and the specification of the florilegium as a requisite mode of writing prior to memorization would contribute the properly Foucauldian elements of "technological" constraint. Indeed, Carruthers' description of this medieval reading practice and its written auxiliaries is decidedly similar to Foucault's own description of a classical Greek practice that he labeled a technology of the self — the keeping of notebooks called *hypomnemata* that "constituted a material memory of things read, heard, or thought, thus offering these as an accumulated treasure for rereading and later meditation"(Foucault, "On the Genealogy of Ethics," 364).

Yet another example of a technology of the self that has not been labeled as such can be found in Roger Chartier's astute analysis of Old Regime French court society and its rituals of courtesy. Following the lead of Norbert Elias,

Chartier views the court as the institutionalized interpersonal environment that, throughout Europe, underpinned the absolute monarchical state. In order to monopolize power in his own hands, this argument runs, the absolute sovereign had to produce and continually reproduce rivalry between power-seeking elites; he thus designed and used the court, most famously the one at Versailles, to achieve that end (Chartier, "Social Figuration and Habitus"). As a stylized locus of intense rivalry, the French court, in Chartier's view, fostered a particular set of psychological traits. These were both recommended and anatomized in a treatise of the Spanish Jesuit Gracián on "the art of prudence," which became something of a classic when it was published in French translation in 1684 under the significantly altered title, *L'homme de cour.* Chartier contends that the courtesy described by Gracián and exacted at court was no superficial behavioral pattern but was rather, for the court's habitués, the organizing principle of a total personality ("Trajectoires" 315 – 16)

Couched in military vocabulary and portraying a world starkly divided between allies and enemies, Gracián's text delineated a personal identity tailored as much to its entourage as to its possessor. In Chartier's formulation, "the construction of each individual's identity [was] situated at the intersection between the self-representation that he propose[d] and the credence accorded or refused to that representation" (Ibid. 315). Since what counted was not the inner authenticity of this identity but rather its exterior, social validation, identity resided first and foremost in the capacity to influence others. Such fundamental other-directedness did not, however, entirely denude the self of an interior dimension. Indeed a certain training in interiority was explicitly enjoined as the first stage of the courtier's identity formation.

"The passions are the breaches (*brèches*) of the spirit," said Gracián's French translator, employing the military vocabulary that ran through the treatise (quoted by Chartier, ibid. 319). Hence, in the hostile world of the court, an appropriately prudent and defensive self would shore up those "breaches" or, in other words, keep its passions hidden. But to carry out such a project of concealment effectively, the self had first to know its passions. "The first step," said Gracián, "is to become aware that one is passionate. It is by that means that one enters the lists with full power over oneself." Or, later, "To be master of oneself, one must reflect on oneself" (quoted by Chartier, ibid. 317, 321).

Self-control, self-containment, and mastery of the passions were the hallmarks of the courteous man, but these exercises in interiority had an ultimately active aim. Only by controlling his passions could a courtier practice the much-recommended arts of ruse and dissimulation. Only by studiously masking his true emotions and intentions could he rationally calculate his conduct so as to induce people to feel and act as he wished them to feel and act. Self-mastery was, according to Gracián, the key to manipulating others, and manipulating others was the key to the "polite" warfare, the jockeying for place and power, that was the stuff of life at court (Ibid. 319–21).

Many times reprinted, the French translation of Gracián was thus a widely accessible how-to book, a codification of a particular technology of the self – though Chartier does not invoke that concept – that enabled its readers to mold themselves to the requirements of a royal court under a system of political absolutism. But Chartier makes even broader claims for the psychological mechanisms detailed by Gracián. Uniquely among European nations, he suggests, Old Regime France experienced a *curialisation* of its culture – that is, an adoption of the modalities of the royal court, including even its cooking and its sports, by members of other social strata (Ibid. 328–30). On the psychological plane, this *curialisation* entailed a generalization of the basic rule of court-based courtesy: the self-censorship of spontaneous impulses. (Chartier does not specify whether self-mastery was, outside the court, routinely harnessed to the typical courtly effort to manipulate others for competitive advantage.) The generalization of some form of the courtly technology of the self was achieved in different ways for different classes. Bent on upward social mobility, the bourgeoisie imitated their aristocratic betters on their own initiative. The children of the lower orders had courtesy inculcated in them in the schools run in many cities and towns by charitable religious orders, where the writings of Jean-Baptiste de La Salle served as a pedagogical and plebeian version of Gracián (Ibid., 331–32).

V. By Way of Conclusion

This essay has examined four dissimilar and chronologically dispersed sets of practices that qualify as Foucauldian technologies of the self: introspective apprehension of a spontaneous activity of will; reading cranial bumps to make informed educational and occupational decisions; a bricolage of memorized passages from literary texts that guides emotional response; and strict control of the passions aimed at dissimulation and a calculated manipulation of others. As it emerges from this brief inquiry, the methodological advantage of the Foucauldian designation "technology of the self" is threefold. In the first place, this designation provides theoretical anchoring to the current vogue of identity scholarship and does so in a way that includes within the purview of identity formation practices that do not seem immediately relevant to it and might otherwise escape the researcher's net – for example, the medieval art of memory or nineteenth-century cranial inspection. Like all good concepts, in other words, Foucault's technologies of the self enables us to discern less than obvious affinities among particulars, to form groupings where none existed before.

Second, by dint of its link to a regimen of power/knowledge, a technology of the self collapses the distinction between theory and practice. It is by definition a combined theory-and-practice, one whose widespread use is ensured by an institutional connection. Thus at least three of the four examples I have discussed has its corresponding institution. In the early modern and modern French examples, institutions of the state not surprisingly preponderate: the centralized system of secondary education was responsible for disseminating the Cousinian *moi*, the court of the absolute monarch for producing and reproducing the courteous, rigorously self-controlled self in tactical pursuit of insincerity. In the case of phrenological self-analysis in Britain, the work of dissemination fell not to the British state, classically laissez-faire during the nineteenth century, but to voluntary associations: the savant societies and mechanics' institutes. (Carruthers, a literary historian, is not explicit about the institutional locus of training in the ethically responsible mode of medieval reading. But she tells us enough to suggest that the practice was associated with the Catholic Church and perhaps more specifically with its monasteries.) The institutional connections of a technology of the self provide a guarantee of its historical significance. Rather than being isolated or idiosyncratic, a practice deserving of that label was certainly familiar to and taken seriously by a consequential number of people.[4]

The final advantage of the technology of the self concerns what might be called the rhetorical force of that Foucauldian category. As an application of knowledge, a "technology" (and Foucault no doubt chose the term advisedly) is capable of being set out for potential users in the form of an instructional manual; indeed each of the four practices I have discussed here actually appeared in something resembling that form. From the vantage point of present-day readers, this "how-to" format serves powerfully as a point of imaginative entry into a different and historically specific experience of being a self. It helps to persuade us that our own "selves," too, are historically mutable entities and hence that our way of experiencing and thinking about the world could be different from what it is. Defamiliarization occupied a salient place in all of Foucault's work (Goldstein, "Foucault among the Sociologists," 170–74, 183). But his last work, which gave rise to the concept of a technology of the self, was especially strongly marked by the quest for alternative ways of thinking about the world, a quest that Foucault described as both "the true historian's search for truth," (referring to the work of his colleague Paul Veyne) and as the

---

[4] In my insistence on the importance for the intellectual and cultural historian of the nexus between ideas and institutions, I am in agreement with the essay in this collection by Ian Maclean, "The Process of Intellectual Change: A Post-Foucauldian Analysis." But Maclean and I differ quite sharply in our assessments of Foucault's performance in this area. Focusing on the early works *Les mots et les choses* (1966) and *L'Archéologie du savoir* (1969), Maclean faults Foucault for his inattention to institutions. Focusing on the works from the mid-1970s on, which rely on the concept of power/knowledge, I by contrast praise Foucault for a theoretical tour de force that renders institutions thoroughly integral to ideas.

purpose of "philosophy today" (referring to his own undertaking). In the same 1984 text in which he coined the term "subjectivation," he wrote:

> After all, what would be the value of the passion for knowledge if it resulted only in a certain amount of knowledgeableness and not, in one way or another and to the extent possible, in the knower's straying afield of himself? [...] [W]hat is philosophy today — philosophical activity, I mean — if it is not the critical work that thought brings to bear on itself? In what does it consist, if not in the endeavor to know how and to what extent it might be possible to think differently, instead of legitimating what is already known? (*Use of Pleasure* 8−9)

To use the category of a "technology of the self" is thus to participate in the Foucauldian project of prying oneself and one's readers loose of rigid certitudes, of inserting human beings into truly contingent, historical time — in short, of putting possibility into play.

3

Foucault's Rhetorical Consciousness and the Possibilities of Acting upon a Regime of Truth

FRANS-WILLEM KORSTEN

I. Language and Action

In the light of Foucault's objects of study it seems a bit absurd to delimit his own work to discursive texts. If we study Foucault, we should ask what the scope of his "body" of texts is, and whether this does not include the way in which he arranged his life in a practical sense. He was trained as a philosopher, for instance, but also earned a license in clinical psychology, and in his twenties actually worked in a clinic for some time (Eribon). Generally we do not feel the need to interpret such biographical information, at least not in the way we interpret Foucault's texts. Still, Foucault's work in the clinic hints at what shall be the central issue of this paper: how — instead of analyzing a regime of truth — we can act directly in and upon it. In this respect, I shall argue that in terms of theory we find ourselves after Foucault. In terms of practice we may wonder if Foucault is not a spectre in front of us.

The issue I want to address can be traced on another plane as well. There is a tension between the form or style of Foucault's texts and the sometimes crude, but always concrete institutional practices that are the object of his studies. This tension can be seen, semiotically, as a sign for the rhetorical chargedness of Foucault's object of study. Language is foregrounded through his style, as something you cannot get around, over, or under. Indeed, Foucault's work has contributed enormously to the idea that style or form and content are not to be considered as separate, but as a linked couple. While admitting, however, that form and content are two sides of a coin, I find it relevant to ask whether writing eloquently about crude, concrete practices is not in effect diverting our attention from concreteness. To put it in other words, the awareness that language is a matter of practice can remain a relatively isolated practice of awareness. In my rhetorical focus on language, I recognize that language has its own materiality. Yet, it may also produce material effects on other planes. This difference has implications for the scope of what is called critical theory, which is greatly indebted to Foucault's work.

If one wants to be critical, one should not be just critically aware. The idea is to change something. The possibilities of action in this respect become a delicate subject when I confront critical rhetorical theory with an object of its analyses that has changed our daily lives considerably and very concretely: the sciences. The sentiment has rightly been discarded that the humanities are about spiritual matters and the sciences about material ones. In fact, the last decades have produced a variety of studies that explore the intricate relation between the two, among them David Locke's *Science as Writing* (1–22), and Stephen Jay Gould's *Mismeasure of Man*, *Wonderful Life*, and *Full House*, which are good examples of showing the relation in practice. In this respect, George Levine's title for the volume that started a Science and Literature series is a telling sign: *One Culture*. I admit that in some ways one can speak of one culture, but the frame of my thoughts in this paper is provided by the worries expressed by philosopher of science Evelyn Fox Keller. Keller expresses a "growing preoccupation with the material consequences of science, nowhere more dramatically in evidence than in the successes of nuclear physics and molecular biology" (*Secrets* 9). Keller herself has demonstrated in *Refiguring Life* how the research and discourse on genes in the course of this century was evidently culturally charged, specifically how it was gender-biased. Meanwhile that research has been productive. Its effects may reflect our – "one" – culture. It has also confronted us with basic, hitherto non-existing questions, which are the result of new material phenomena such as gene-manipulation. Foucault's ideas about language and criticism can still provide a useful frame, here. Such a frame is at the same time too limited for the current lop-sided relation between critical rhetorical studies and the sciences.

After Foucault, the rhetorical analyst who studies the relation between language and science can choose between two major possibilities. S/he can choose to reconstruct rhetorical interaction in the past, as John Neubauer already sketched in 1983. Or s/he can critically assess present rhetorical interactions. In both fields important contributions have been made. A third possibility relates more to Foucault's practical clinical work, however trivial that may seem due to the short time that Foucault worked professionally in this field. This third possibility amounts to an attempt to strategically influence the actual use of social and scientific language and, accordingly, to influence their engineering force. The three approaches may be intertwined, their directions are distinct. Rhetoric – largely confined to politics in classical theory – has been studied since Foucault in areas far beyond the boundaries of politics. This may have led to the diffuse idea that rhetoric is always somehow political. My contention is that the critical relevance of a rhetorical theory requires more focus. In relation to the sciences this critical relevance depends upon the concrete political operation of a text within a certain field. In this respect one should not follow scientists, as the subtitle of Bruno Latour's famous *Science in Action: How to Follow Scientists and Engineers through Society* has it. The issue is to confront scientists, or think with them in their field. Recent works of Evelyn Fox Keller provide a possible paradigm.

II. Rhetorical Consciousness

The possibilities of rhetorical criticism with regard to the sciences were marked in this century especially by Thomas Kuhn's *The Structure of Scientific Revolutions* and Michel Foucault's "The Discourse on Language" (*L'ordre du discours*). The first contended that scientific changes depend for an important part on the scientific community. Whether reality or truth exist are questions that matter, but in practice the answers to these questions need the sanction of a community of experts. This entails that any scientific result must exact, or aim at, a communal sanction. Accordingly, as Paul Hoyningen-Huene showed in an excellent study with respect to Kuhn, rhetoric becomes an intrinsic quality of scientific language. Foucault, as is well known, contended that any organized community operates ideologically; some forms of knowledge are preferred as opposed to others, some forms are simply taboo. Besides, in his view, language is not just a medium of influence, or a rhetorical vehicle, it is one prime organizer of the conceptual frame within which one can think, do research, and do other things (for overviews of what came after Foucault in this respect, see Terry Eagleton, Murray Krieger, or Jonathan Culler). The different post-Foucauldian approaches can be gathered under or connected to the heading critical rhetorical theory are ideology critique, postcolonial, feminist, ecological criticism, criticism relating to gender, or more broadly to culture (e. g. Paul de Man, Barbara Johnson, Teresa de Lauretis, Gayatri C. Spivak, Homi K. Bhabha, Mieke Bal). In all these kinds of criticism, language proved to be a major issue. Therefore, in light of what came after it, Foucault's work provided the first formulation of what I want to call rhetorical consciousness.

It will be useful for the development of my argument to consider the analogy between rhetorical and historical consciousness. Frank Ankersmit argued in *History and Tropology* that historical consciousness came into being with the notion of virtù and the harsh everyday reality of Italian political life during the Renaissance. Virtù is a complex notion which entails psychic strength, power, authority, shrewdness, and a feeling for the right moment. Especially the latter feature points to the political underpinnings of the notion. According to Ankersmit, the idea of virtù marked the difference between the modern era and the Middle Ages because it foregrounded the domain of the earthly community with its field of political forces within which a politician could act. Historians could subsequently present this field as somehow organized. Ankersmit considers this political quality of the Renaissance world as the basis of historiography, especially because it allows us to narrativize the world in different ways.

The notion of virtù was taken up prior to Ankersmit by Hannah Arendt in *The Human Condition* and *Between Past and Future* (see Dana Villa), who stated that virtuousness is the crucial notion in assessing the quality of a political action. In her view the virtue and quality of a politician depend not only upon his or her ability to appear in the political arena, but especially on our assessment of it with hindsight. Although Arendt was not concerned with historical consciousness in relation to virtù, her notion incorporated historicity since virtuousness meant for her both the appearance within a field and its assessment with hindsight.

Foucault had argued from early on that the language of the modern sciences has allowed us to reflect upon ourselves as objects of knowledge. Accordingly, this self-reflection found its basis not in philosophy or in political action, but in the action with and the action of a specific scientific language. Following Foucault, I suggest that rhetorical consciousness comes into being with the discursive practices of the social and scientific engineers of the eighteenth century. Since then, it has become possible to define rhetorical consciousness as an awareness of the discursive practices that define subject-positions and the way in which subjects are related to other entities. This viewpoint implies that a changes in scientific practices may result in another kind of rhetorical consciousness, or that a change in rhetorical consciousness may affect scientific practice. My question is what the implications of this viewpoint are for rhetorical actors who want to operate critically.

III. Plurification or Extremity

In practice, criticism has often restricted itself to analyses of what is not allowed, not done, insufficient, unjustified, and so forth. In its focus on exclusion, Foucault's *L'ordre du discours* provides an illustration of this delimitation. Of course, criticism can also focus on what ought to be allowed. Or it can probe the limits of what is allowed. In this respect, it can either provide a plurification of visions or explore the extremes of possible visions. Both modalities stretch the span of ideologically enforced limits.

Ankersmit has sketched how, for instance, historiography has a structurally built in critical component that makes for a plurification of visions. Any historical text contains a proposal to look at a historical constellation in a certain way. Such a proposal, Ankersmit argues, only acquires meaning because it differs from other proposals. As a result there is an inherent negativity, or an inherent criticism: Historical insights are produced by proposals that rejects other proposals. However, this built-in negativity leads to the positive meaning of criticism as sketched above. Any intersubjective insight into the historical past is possible only if we have a number of different interpretations. Ankersmit locates insight, here, at the intersection of different interpretations. In order to enlarge our insight, in order to broaden the field covered by these intersections, difference and diversity count, as well as the measure to which a proposal differs.

Evelyn Fox Keller provides a good example of such a plurification of visions. In *Refiguring Life*, for instance, she analyzes a series of lectures entitled "What is life"? that Erwin Schrödinger gave in 1943. By that time, Schrödinger was one of the most famous figures in searching for the smallest particle in the inanimate world. In 1943 he extended his attention to another field by asking whether one could not start looking also, technically, for the smallest animate particle, the bios. Whether or not his reflections led to them, we are now familiar with DNA and its genes, with gene-technology and -manipulation. Indeed, it would be tempting to see Schrödingers lectures as a paradigm for intentional action. Schrödinger proposed something, people got to work, and the result was the finding of the genes. Keller presents another interpretation, by focusing on the way in which this smallest particle was depicted, namely as a little "man." She constructs a historical development that starts with what Darwin in 1844 called "Being" and Maxwell, in 1870, "demon." With Schrödinger in 1943 genes had become "soldiers" of "local government stations." All of his cognitive metaphors characterize a being that willfully governs the development of cells. Keller's point is that this image is culturally charged. She contrasts the idea of a willing being with the conception that biological organisms are messages, whereby every molecule, including DNA, can be both sender and receiver. Thus she plurifies the historical vision of what happened. She is not so much interested in what happened after these lectures. Instead she emphasizes a historical continuity which is based on culturally invested core notions that do not remain exactly the same, but that transmute through time. In tracing that transmutation, Keller also differentiates the conception of what a gene is.

It is also possible to propose criticism by means of extreme or radical approaches. Historians, according to Ankersmit, should try to seek the limits of possible interpretations in order to provide maximum plurification. In this sense they should be willing to accept a "maximum risk" (*History and Tropology* 84). Likewise, Culler has argued that scholars "should apply as much interpretative pressure as they can, should carry their thinking as far as it can go." As Culler sees it, extreme visions have more chance "of bringing to light connections or implications not previously noticed or reflected on" ('Overinterpretation' 110) – a point also made by Gould. The critical component here is that extremes, per definition, deliberately eschew embodying the consensus that has been established within a community. Building forth on previous analyses, this possibility was also explored by Keller.

In *Secrets of Life* Keller presents interpretations that are theoretically innovative and that shed a new light on scientific practices. Her point of view is strategically directed by feminist choices. In the eyes of the orthodox scientific community, science develops by itself, it progresses from primitive states to more sophisticated ones; questions of gender are not considered to be intrinsically related to this development. Keller chooses the word "secret" to contend the opposite. In her analysis, "secret" becomes a thread that allows to locate a defining persistent attitude in the history of the modern sciences. Focusing on an article by Robert Boyle from 1744 about the essence of the scientific project, Keller argues convincingly that the sciences have been seen as a male profession from the start. This distribution, or exclusion, coincided with the phenomenon that men wanted to unveil the secrets of a nature metaphorized as feminine. This idea of unveiling has led to a persistent uneasiness to address issues of genesis and sexual generation.

There is no contradiction between the plurifying and extremist critical approaches. They may coincide, as Foucault noticed in *L'ordre du discours*. However, the concrete political scope of these two approaches is limited. The first — being aimed at the construction or reconstruction of historical constellations — is historical. The second — with its sometimes idiosyncratic creative potential, its tendency to seek the extreme per se, and its possibility to see or read reality differently — can be called aesthetical. Both approaches may have political implications, even though they are not taking practical, political, or material application into account. One only needs to look at the tenuous and barely existing relations between extreme critical interpretations and the course of affairs in current, concrete scientific practice. Here, a third type is called for; one that has remained sketchy in Foucault's theory, though, as I have suggested, his practice in the clinic provides a hint. Foucault himself touched on the problem in *Il faut défendre la société*, when he suggested that the civilized organisation of society is not only something to fight for, but that such a civilized form of organization is in fact the transmutation of a struggle. In light of what I am discussing, this implies for the relation between criticism and the sciences that one should try to move beyond the idea of two opposed parties. A transmuted struggle requires that one should operate within a single field.

IV. Criticism in Practice

Anyone who is familiar with the sheer amount of well funded, politically and socially supported, scientific research, also knows that critical rhetorical analyses have very little, or no influence on concrete research programs and processes. Keller feels and addresses the unease this may cause. Her work "reflects the growing preoccupation with the material consequences of science" (*Secrets of Life* 9), and it illustrates that critical theory need not be hopelessly failing in the sciences. Its relevance depends upon its ability to change itself from an outsider into a reflective insider. Instead of analyzing the virtuousness of others, it can also choose to start acting itself "virtuously," in the political sense of Ankersmit and Arendt. I mean that critical theorists should try to enter a certain field and try to influence the actual course of affairs.

The hostility between rhetorical criticism and the sciences was at the center of a recent row caused by the physicist Alan D. Sokal, who had put some deconstruction, psychoanalysis, and quantum physics in his processor and cooked it up. The result was a nervous kind of nonsense which was accepted by an important periodical promoting critical theory. Sokal's political agenda is not my concern here, rather the handicapped reactions to him. Stanly Fish, for instance, has argued that the sociology of the sciences has never pretended to move into the field of physics itself (see Dennis Dutton and Patrick Henry. Unfortunately, this implies that critical theorists could not see that the article made no sense in physics, or that psychoanalysis and deconstruction have nothing to offer to the practice and theory of physics. And what when a theory pretends to be critical; a stance Fish clearly supports? Surely criticism wants to be relevant for what happens in specialized fields, otherwise it becomes a matter of decoration at worst and at best an isolated practice that might give one a sense of superiority but that does not change much.

In Keller's *Secrets of Life/Secrets of Death* some chapters provide examples of how a critical theory can act within scientific research. Keller describes these chapters as "more technical" since she focuses on the language used in "actual research agendas" (10). In chapters 6 and 7, for instance, her central question is what makes species survive. Biologists prefer two options in answering this question. Species survive if they are most competetive or most fit. There is nothing wrong with these answers. Competition and the fight for survival are evidently observable. The point is that these answers are presented as the only ones. As such they fit in with social clichés of modern Western culture. One could, therefore criticize these ideas on the basis of strategic or ideological choices. But biologists would probably not pay much attention to such criticism, for the ideas of competition and fitness have proven to be productive. They allowed us to explain many things in the operation of evolution. Keller's choice is more daring. She traces the history and meaning of the notions of "competition" and "fitness" within biology. She then shows where biologists have left opportunities for research unused, have forgotten possibilities that where present in these concepts from the beginning, and, especially, why the current uses of the terms are methodologically unsound. This way she does not fight against them as an opponent, from the outside. The scene of the struggle is transmuted into an internal one.

Keller's movement into a field poses its own demands as to the type of rhetorical analysis and criticism, and the uses it is put to. She was trained as a bio-physicist, then for personal reasons, moved out of that field, got acquainted with feminism, and consequently with psychoanalysis and rhetoric. Only then did she move back into biology. Here, she actually took and takes part in ongoing discussions, and she influences their course. Her position within biology is solid, considering that she edited the biological standard reference book *Keywords of Evolutionary Biology*, in which she also wrote one of the chapters. Thus, instead of analyzing processes from the outside, she has become a constructor of the language that researchers actually use. She has influenced concretely the framework in which biologists tend to think. In other words, she has questioned and tested the rhetorical consciousness that influences the questions researchers pose, and the directions that interest them. The political implications do not stop here. A biology that promotes competition and the fitness of species as inherently natural, has a distinct political force, it can be used rhetorically and politically. A biology that conceptualizes cooperation and the importance of individual sexual reproduction offers distinctly different rhetorical and political possibilities. I am not saying that one should prefer the one option above the other for its political implications. But these implications make it important to note that one option has been preferred in scientific practice.

    In order to be so effective, Keller had to operate politically, wit virtù in Arendt's sense. She had to appear, indeed be, an expert in the specialized field she criticized. To remain critical in such circumstances requires a balancing act between assessment and participation, between reflection and engagement. Thus, the implication of what I suggest is partly that we are only able to influence the course of affairs in scientific practice if we belong to one of its fields. More generally, I suggest that any theory which takes the consequences of its critical quality seriously has to consider how and where it can make its mark in practice. In this respect, and rather ironically, Foucault's work in the clinic stands adverse to some of his later work, which often reveals a loose underpinning. In other words, Foucault himself has often ignored the importance of being accepted within a field according to the standards that rule there, as, for instance, Maclean's contribution in this volume shows. I think it is precisely this sloppiness that could with hindsight damage the critical potential of his work. We are after him, in the sense that our methods and tools of critical analysis have evolved since then, or have been put to other uses. But few are those that follow Foucault's example; for he had worked in a clinic before writing about it.

4

Power and Political Spirituality:
Michel Foucault on the Islamic Revolution in Iran

MICHIEL LEEZENBERG

Foucault's writings on the Islamic revolution in Iran have not received the critical attention they deserve.[1] Published in Italian and French periodicals between the autumn of 1978 and the spring of 1979, they may be seen as exercises in contemporary history or, as Foucault himself called it, 'journalism of ideas'; as such, they form an interesting complement to his other forays into cultural history, which deal with temporally more remote, but specifically European events and institutions. By and large, however, these articles have been either passed over in a slightly embarrassed silence, or taken as proof that Foucault's enthusiasm for oppositional movements led him to uncritically applaud dictatorial regimes. Both attitudes, I believe, are mistaken: I hope to show that these journalistic writings indeed have a rather problematic status within Foucault's work as a whole, but not for any such obvious reasons. I make no apologies for trying, in a perhaps rather un-Foucauldian manner, to locate them in his *oeuvre*. Further, not being a specialist on either Foucault or the Iranian revolution, I hope to avoid the two opposing risks of burying difficulties under apologetic exegesis and of merely pointing out alleged 'factual errors' at the expense of more interesting theoretical questions.

I. A Background of Revolutionary Events

Although the emphasis here is on Foucault's views on the Iranian revolution rather than the revolution itself, a brief recapitulation of events until early 1979

---

[1] These articles are now conveniently available in vol. III of Foucault's *Dits et écrits 1954–1988* (abbreviated DE), which contains almost all of his scattered writings and interviews. There are minor discrepancies between the French texts as reproduced in DE III and as quoted by Eribon, presumably due to translation differences; but these do not involve any points of importance. One 1978 article from *Corriere della Sera*, 'Taccuino persiano: Ritorno al profeta?', dated October 22 (according to Stauth) or 28 (Eribon), is not reprinted in DE III.

may serve as background information.[2] Shah Reza Pahlavi's regime had never gained a broad base in Iranian society, but had acquired a measure of legitimacy in the decennia following the CIA-backed coup that had brought him to power in 1953. By the mid-1970s, however, protests against the repressive nature of the regime and the widespread corruption started to increase dramatically. The shah reacted by simultaneously intensifying political repression and introducing half-hearted reform measures — a combination which only exacerbated tensions.

At first, demonstrations calling for reforms were led by secularized and largely left-wing urban intellectuals; but in January 1978, a demonstration by seminary students in Qom against a government-sponsored newspaper article criticizing ayatollah Khomeini led to a confrontation with security forces that left several demonstrators dead. This triggered the shi'ite Iranian clergy, which until then had remained relatively quiet, into action, and most of the subsequent protests against the shah were centered around mosques and religious gatherings. The clergy, from the highest religious scholars ('ulamâ) to the humblest village mullahs, contributed not only a highly effective mobilizing force, but also an extensive organizational network, to the protests.

On September 8, or 'Black Friday' as it came to be called, a massive demonstration on Jaleh Square in Tehran was violently crushed, and between 2,000 and 4,000 demonstrators were killed. This massacre seriously reduced the chances for reconciliation, and henceforth the popular rallying call was for the shah's departure, rather than for reforms. Despite, or perhaps precisely because of his physical absence, Khomeini was a major source of these more radical demands: he had been exiled from Iran in 1963, and had resettled in the shi'ite holy city of Najaf in Iraq, from where he could afford to be more critical of, and less compromising towards the shah than other opposition leaders. Another source of inspiration for the revolution was Ali Shariati, a Maoist-inspired (though anti-Communist) shi'ite pamphleteer who had died in 1977.

In December, the shah declared himself ready to negotiate directly with the opposition, but by then his position had already become untenable: on January 16, 1979 he left Iran, never to return. A provisional government led by Shahpour Bakhtiar tried to introduce quick reforms, but it was widely seen as too closely associated with the shah for it to have any legitimacy. Upon his arrival in Tehran on February 1, Khomeini appointed a new government, headed by the moderate opposition leader Mehdi Bazargan, and Bakhtiar's government was subsequently ousted in a three-day uprising from February 10 through 12. Among the groups that had headed the revolution, a fierce competition for supremacy now developed. Moreover, in the total anarchy following the collapse

---

[2] For more details, see the excellent political histories by Shaul Bakhash and Dilip Hiro; cf. Halliday, *Dictatorship* for an assessment of Iran right before the turbulent events of 1978 and 1979.

of the Bakhtiar government, armed *komitehs* or revolutionary committees had formed all over Iran, a powerful but uncontrolled (and probably uncontrollable), erratic and often violent new force. Khomeini managed to impose a measure of central control on these *komitehs*, increasing his own power base in the process. He did so not by trying to curb the revolutionary fervor, but by channeling it to some extent with the installation of revolutionary courts, most of which were quick to mete out capital punishment, thus satisfying the popular desire for vengeance. The courts' violence and lack of adequate standards quickly led to protests both in Iran and abroad, but Khomeini stood solidly behind them (Bakhash, *Reign* 59–63). On the whole, however, even as powerful an individual as Khomeini himself was led by events as much as he led them, and his emerging as the victor in the power struggle, let alone the eventual political shape post-revolutionary Iran was to take, was by no means a foregone conclusion (ibid. 6).

II. Foucault in Iran[3]

Foucault had long been active on behalf of Iranian dissidents and political prisoners, and – like many others – undoubtedly saw in the popular protests a chance for a change of things for the better, and perhaps even for the ousting of a repressive and unpopular, but apparently solid, regime. Taking up an invitation from the Italian daily *Corriere della Sera*, he set out to write a series of articles on the Iranian protests, based on on-the-spot observations.

He meticulously prepared his Iranian journeys. He received updates on developments and addresses for contacts from Ahmad Salamatian, a left-of-center, secularized Iranian intellectual who was to become deputy minister of Foreign Affairs in Bani-Sadr's short-lived post-revolutionary government. Further, he read Paul Vieille's sociological studies on Iran, and Henry Corbin's work on Iranian Islamic philosophy and spiritual life (cf. Corbin, *Islam Iranien*). Between the 16th and the 24th of September, 1978, one week after 'Black Friday', Foucault paid his first visit to Iran. As it was difficult to get in contact with the religious opposition, Foucault concentrated his inquiries on members of the secular opposition and the military. On September 20, however, he had a meeting in Qom with the moderate ayatollah Shariatmadari, who opposed the direct participation of the *'ulamâ*, the higher shi'ite clergy, in government. Below, it will appear how Shariatmadari colored Foucault's writings about the revolution.

---

[3] This information is largely taken from Eribon's ch. 19, and from the editorial introduction to Foucault's Iranian articles (DE III: 662). Macey's (406–11) portrait of Foucault in Iran is rather less charitable and well-informed than Eribon's.

In October, after his return to France, he had discussions with the future president of Iran, Abol-Hasan Bani Sadr, at that time still in exile; on one occasion, he and a group of journalists also met Khomeini, who had just arrived in France on October 3, after having been expelled from Najaf by the Iraqi government. What was said at this meeting is unknown, but at this time, Khomeini was still intentionally vague towards his European interlocutors on precisely what he meant by his call for an 'Islamic republic' (Bakhash, *Reign* 48). In this period, Foucault published several articles in the *Corriere della Sera*, and one in the *Nouvel Observateur*.

From the 9th to the 15th of November, Foucault was in Iran again; this time, he talked with members of the urban middle class, as well as with oil laborers in Abadan. The same month, a second series of articles appeared, but apart from an interview with Pierre Blanchet and Claire Brière (apparently held in late 1978 or early 1979), he remained silent about subsequent developments. He did not pay any further visits to Iran either, even though he maintained interest: thus, he went to Paris airport to see Khomeini's departure on February 1, 1979. Possibly, this silence is due to the many negative, if not hostile, reactions that his articles drew almost from the start; in early April 1979, Foucault was even assaulted in the street, according to some observers because of his Iranian writings.[4] Only in April and May 1979 did he return to the Iranian revolution in writing, with an open letter to the new prime minister Mehdi Bazargan and with two articles of a more general nature (DE III: 780–7, 790–4), which indeed suggest that he had been badly shaken by his Iranian experiences, and by the many hostile reactions to his writings in the French press. I will return to the significance of this silence below.

III. Journalism, Contemporary History, or Philosophy?

It should be kept in mind that Foucault's writings on the Iranian revolution are mostly of a journalistic character, and do not directly relate to his philosophical and historical work. Nevertheless, there are some clear, if rather implicit, links to his broader theoretical concerns. First, for Foucault, both journalism and philosophy investigate the nature of the present, and in particular the question of who we are at the present moment (DE III: 783). He traces this convergence of interests back to Kant, whose answer to the question "What is Enlightenment?" (1784) introduced an entirely new type of question, viz., that of the present as a philosophical event, and thus in a sense defines modern philosophy as a whole (DE IV: 562, 680). Enlightenment, as captured in Kant's famous

---

[4] *Le Monde*, April 4 1979; *Le Matin*, April 3 and 14, 1979; *Nouvelles littéraires* 2681 (1979): 16. Surprisingly, this incident is not mentioned in either Eribon's or Macey's biography.

slogan *sapere aude*, 'dare to know!', or even modernity as such, is also characterized by the public use of reason, and by a certain type of political rationality
that is free of the religious. Significantly, Foucault proceeds to link Enlightenment and revolution: Kant saw in the French revolution, regardless of whether
it would succeed, and of whether it would turn out violent and murderous, a
sign of mankind's unmistakable progress towards further emancipation and self-
determination (*Der Streit der Fakultäten*, ch. II.6), and as such, Foucault suggests,
'the revolution is precisely what completes and continues the very process of
Aufklärung' (DE IV: 685).[5] A journalistic inquiry into a revolutionary event, especially one which so centrally involves the public and political use of religion as the
uprising in Iran, thus implies a philosophical commentary on modernity itself.

Foucault tries to reach a journalistic understanding of the present by means
of what he called 'reportages des idées'. The present world, he argues, is replete
with novel ideas, especially among suppressed or hitherto ignored groups of
people:

> Some say that the great ideologies are in the course of dying. The contemporary world,
> however, is burgeoning with ideas [...]. One has to be present at the birth of ideas and at
> the explosion of their force; not in the books that pronounce them, but in the events in
> which they manifest their force, and in the struggles people wage for or against ideas. (DE
> III: 706–7)

This emphasis on the historical force of ideas is directed as much against the
first forebodings of postmodernist claims concerning the end of grand ideologies as against the Marxist dogma that ideology is secondary to economic
factors. As a reporter of ideas in Iran, Foucault himself 'would like to grasp
what is *in the course of happening*', even though he considers himself a neophyte in
journalism (DE III: 714; emph. in original).

A second major link is formed by the theme of power and resistance. Foucault was obviously fascinated – and disturbed – by the Iranian population's
readiness to risk imprisonment, torture, and even death, and tried to discover
precisely what gave them this apparently totally unified, and heroic, will. In
general, revolt may be seen as an extreme case of resistance against domination,
and would thus seem a convenient illustration of Foucault's criticism of a juridical view of power with its domination- and state-oriented perspective, a criticism
formulated in particular in the first volume of *Histoire de la sexualité* (*Volonté*
107–35).

Third, Foucault's writings on Iran may be seen as a tentative application of
his more theoretical ideas to a contemporary event in a non-Western society,
whereas his earlier studies had limited themselves to Western European, and
especially French, historical events and institutions. Some, e. g. Said (*Foucault* 9),

---

5 Politically, Foucault undoubtedly cherished the prospect of the shah's government being ousted,
  although philosophically, he could (unlike Kant) hardly describe this revolutionary enthusiasm
  in teleological terms of progress and liberation.

have accused Foucault of an implicit eurocentrism; it is indeed an open question whether the conceptual tools developed in his earlier works can be applied to rather different historical and cultural materials.

Foucault's first articles in the *Corriere della Sera* show few obvious traces of such broader concerns, as they are no more than preliminary forays into an unknown territory, informed by an inkling that something quite novel was taking place. They try to assess, for example, the role of the army, and the character of the protests against the shah's 'archaic' program of modernization (DE III: 680 – 3). The economic reforms introduced in Iran since the 1960s had, for the most part, benefited only a small part of Iranian society, and the increase in oil wealth in the 1970s had only helped to exacerbate the already serious corruption and political repression. In other words, Foucault's critique of the shah's Western-inspired modernization program as 'archaic' is less a relativistic rejection of the idea of modernity in general, than a criticism of one specific program to reach it.

Foucault also notes the apparent absence of any clear social or economical basis for the mass protests, in which both urban workers and bazaar merchants participated (DE III: 702), implying, of course, that events in Iran do not allow for a Marxist explanation. At first sight, this observation seems correct, as the Iranian economy had shown a steady growth throughout the 1970s, especially after the drastic increase in oil prices in 1974. The sudden wealth, however, had led the Pahlavi regime to engage in a reckless spending spree, which caused a serious overheating of the economy. The government then cut down on investment and stopped recruiting for the civil services sector, which in turn led to a decrease in business opportunities, mass unemployment and sudden impoverishment among the middle and lower classes (cf. Hiro, *Iran* 60 – 3; Bakhash, *Reign* 12 – 3). In other words, there was a clear economic base for the protests: for large parts of the population, the supposedly affluent 1970s had only brought new hardships and frustrated expectations – a familiar precondition for the emergence of revolutionary movements.

Foucault gradually shifts his attention towards the peculiar character of Iranian Islam, notably its potential for resistance against state power. At the time, the very idea that Islam, in whatever variety, could be revolutionary, rather than inherently reactionary, seemed anathema; but Foucault correctly saw the decisive importance of political Islam in the protests, both as an ideology for mass mobilization and as providing an institutional and organizational base for the opposition to the Pahlavi regime. This correct assessment is paired, however, with a number of seriously flawed or oversimplified remarks on shi'ism in general. Thus, Foucault believes that the shi'ite clergy knows no hierarchy; that shi'ite religious authority is given by the people; and consequently, that clerics can ill afford to ignore popular angers and aspirations (DE III: 687, 691). In fact, the shi'ite *'ulamâ* have over the last centuries shaped themselves into a highly organized and hierarchic institution that is to an important extent autonomous from both state and society. Foucault at once corrects himself by adding that the shi'ite clerics are by no means revolutionary, but that the shi'ite religion *itself* is the form taken by political struggle, especially when it involves mass mobilization. These remarks still sidestep a long history and risk attributing causal power to shi'ite ideology itself, but perhaps one cannot expect detailed historical analyses from a newspaper reportage.

Foucault also gropes at length for an explanation for the fearlessness and 'perfectly unified collective will' (DE III: 715) of the unarmed demonstrators, which he thinks characterizes not a political movement, but a revolt against the existing political order of the whole world: 'the most modern form of revolt – and the maddest' (DE III: 716). Aptly, then, it is not a politician, but the 'almost mythical personality' of Khomeini who is able to guide the protests and maintain their momentum. Foucault is well aware of the potential violence of this confrontation: 'the image [of the unarmed saint versus the king in arms] has its own captivating force, but it masks a reality in which millions of dead come to inscribe their signature' (DE III: 689–90); he adds (692) that he finds the definitions of Islamic government which he has heard 'hardly reassuring'.

Here, too, Foucault's insight is at odds with the then widespread opinion that Khomeini was merely a figurehead with no power or program of his own. He explains the intensity of the link between the ayatollah and the people from three facts: Khomeini's not being there, his not saying anything (other than "no" to every attempt at compromise), and his not being a politician. The last point even led Foucault to state: 'there won't be a party of Khomeini's, there won't be a Khomeini government' (DE III: 716). Predictions are always risky, and this one has proved wrong on both counts: on February 5, 1979, Khomeini appointed Bazargan to form a new government, and two weeks later, the strongly pro-Khomeini Islamic Republican Party was formed. Although Khomeini formally stayed outside these new political structures, they unmistakably strengthened his power base, and Foucault's remark suggests a serious underestimation of his political ambitions. Again, however, he was by no means alone in this. Before 1978, nobody outside a small circle of specialists knew of the political ideas among the Iranian shi'ite *'ulamâ*, let alone about the existence and political doctrines of Khomeini, and this circle itself was equally surprised at the course and speed of events in 1978 and 1979. Even such a well-informed observer of Iranian society as Fred Halliday (*Dictatorship* 299), writing on the eve of the revolution, considered it unlikely that the Iranian clergy was to play a major role if the shah's regime should be overthrown.

Perhaps the main shortcoming of these reportages, apart from such forgivable errors, is that they overemphasize the religious dimension of the demonstrations, at the expense of their unmistakably nationalist element: a clear demand for national sovereignty was expressed in the protest against the American presence and against alleged Zionist conspiracies to undermine the nation. The sweeping characterizations of the social role of shi'ite Islam and of Khomeini's role in the protests are perhaps inevitable for newspaper articles, but at times come dangerously close to idealist explanations.

IV. Uncritical Support for Khomeini?

Opposition to Foucault's alleged enthusiasm for the prospect of Islamic government and the person of Khomeini began to be voiced upon publication of the first *Nouvel Observateur* article. It intensified after Khomeini's arrival in February 1979 had triggered off a violent power struggle, accompanied by a wave of summary executions. Thus, in *Le Matin* (March 24, 1979), Claudie and Jacques Broyelle accused Foucault of blindly supporting Khomeini, and called on him to 'acknowledge his errors'.[6] More recently, Bernard-Henry Lévy (*Aventures* 482−3) has written that Foucault's judgment on Iran was blinded by his 'hope for a pure revolution', a hope he allegedly shared with many French intellectuals. He construes Foucault's remarks on Khomeini's 'mythical dimension' and 'mysterious link' with the people as signs of a personal admiration. He believes Foucault's main error, 'a practically obligatory stage in this spiritual journey', is an initially boundless and uncritical enthusiasm, which founders on the violence of actual events and leads to an eventual disenchantment with ideals.

Such criticisms, often made with the benefit of hindsight, are not only off the mark but also unfair. Most of them emphasize the violent turn of events from February 1979 onwards, when Foucault had ceased publishing his commentaries; but even in his earlier journalistic articles, Foucault nowhere speaks of the revolt in terms of progress or liberation. He reacted fiercely against these accusations, and forcefully rejected the antagonistic attitude they presupposed:

> The problem of Islam as a political force is an essential problem for our era and for the years to come. The first condition for addressing it with a minimum of intelligence is not to start by confronting it with hatred (DE III: 708)

Indeed, Foucault has to be credited for perceiving the historical importance of this revolution at an early stage, and for repeatedly visiting Iran in order to see for himself what was happening. He was clearly fascinated, and troubled, by this unprecedented assertion of a unified popular will. He may have underestimated Khomeini's political role, but none of his published writings express anything remotely like a blind admiration for Khomeini or an uncritical enthusiasm for the prospect of Islamic government.

More interesting, if hardly less polemical, criticisms have been voiced by non-Western intellectuals. Thus, Mohammed Arkoun, in an interview with Hashim

---

[6] Unfortunately, I could not find this article; cf. Olivier & Labbé, *Désir.* 220n4 for its main points.

Saleh (*Fikr*), argues that philosophers like Foucault and Derrida, despite their critique of eurocentrism, 'remain within the walls of the European tradition of thought'. In their archeologies of different systems of knowledge, religion — and in particular Islam — is consistently ignored, despite the presence of millions of Islamic immigrants in Europe. Moreover, when they do write about Islam, as Foucault did on the Islamic revolution, they say nothing but stupidities (*hamâqât*). Foucault, Arkoun concludes, did not understand anything of what was happening in Iran, and would have done better not to have said anything about it at all.[7] On a more moderate note, Darius Rejali argues in his *Torture and Modernity* (14—16) that Foucault cannot properly account for the persistence of torture in pre- and post-revolutionary Iran, in a state that (at least under the Pahlavi regime) 'slavishly emulated the Western regime of truth', where the need for torture has supposedly been abolished by disciplinary forms of punishing, such as imprisonment. Such criticisms have considerably more force, as they point to the fundamental question of whether and how Foucault's ideas, which derive from the study of specifically European events and institutions, can be extended to a non-European domain at all. I hope to show, however, that they do not apply to all of Foucault's Iranian writings to the same extent.

V. 'Political Spirituality' and its Ancestors

Foucault's first article for a French audience, 'A quoi rêvent les Iraniens?' (DE III: 688—94), is by no means a mere summary of the Italian reportages. It delves much more into the history of Iran and of shi'ite Islam. And it is here that things become problematic. To begin with, his explanation of the call for Islamic government is obviously colored by the restricted range of his interlocutors:

> "What do you want?" During the whole of my stay in Iran, I never once heard the word "revolution". But four times out of five, I got the answer "Islamic government" [...]. One thing should be clear: by [this], no one in Iran means a political order in which the clergy would play a role of ruler or provider of cadre (DE III: 690).

This seriously underestimates the character and background of the contemporary debate; most importantly, Foucault was apparently unaware of Khomeini's concept of *velâyat-e faqîh* ('guardianship of the jurist', i. e., government by the shi'ite clergy), as Rodinson (*Primauté* 307) notes. In his earlier writings, Khomeini had not questioned the legitimacy of the Pahlavi monarchy as such, and merely called for the clergy to play a greater role in political affairs; in the 1960s, he had developed far more radical ideas against the background of the rising Marxist-inspired student activism. But even among the main clerics involved in the revolution, there was no consensus on the nature of an eventual Islamic govern-

---

[7] I am indebted to Mariwan Kanie for drawing my attention to this interview.

ment. Bani-Sadr, for example, had come close to identifying the shi'ite idea of the *imâm* as the only legitimate ruler with a European idea of popular sovereignty, by developing a concept of *ta'mîm-e imâmat*, or 'generalized imamate' (cf. Bakhash, *Reign* 93 – 5). For him, each member of the community could become a jurist or even an *imâm* through piety and self-discipline; consequently, he saw no need for a separate class of religiously trained jurists. Ayatollah Shariatmadari, the only religious authority whom Foucault met (DE III: 691), consistently opposed any role for the clergy in worldly leadership.

Foucault's most controversial remark, however, was his suggestion that those participating in the demonstrations against the shah might be trying to introduce, or reintroduce, a spiritual dimension into political life (DE III: 693 – 4), and that this might be the ultimate motivation for their heroic and self-sacrificing behavior:

> At the dawn of history, Persia has invented the State and rendered its services to Islam […]. But of this same Islam, it has derived a religion that has given its people indefinite resources for resisting State power. Should one see in this desire for an 'Islamic Government' a reconciliation, a contradiction, or the threshold of a novelty? […] What sense, for the people, in seeking at the price of their very lives this thing, the possibility of which we have forgotten since the Renaissance and the great crises of Christianity: a political spirituality. I can already hear some Frenchmen laughing, but I know they are wrong (DE III: 694)

Although the suggestion that all participants were seeking the same spirituality may seem rather implausible, the desire for Islamic government as an alternative to the Pahlavi regime's sellout to the United States and other foreign powers was undeniably a major mobilizing force. One may wonder to what extent this desire was nationalist or populist, rather than religious in character, but at least Foucault rightly asks whether this Islamic government might in fact be something radically new, instead of assuming – as many would be tempted to do – that it simply amounts to a step back in time.[8]

In the context of Foucault's journalistic work, the notion of political spirituality should probably not be given too much philosophical weight. Elsewhere, however, it is explicitly linked to his other philosophical concerns. First and foremost, however, it obviously reflects his intense attempts to come to terms with the apparently novel logic of the early revolutionary events; as seen, he implicitly and explicitly denies the possibility of understanding the revolt in the familiar categories of class struggle and the like.

It seems, however, that Foucault's emphasis on the spiritual dimensions of the uprising derives less from what he observed on the ground than from what

---

[8] The implementation of Islamic government has indeed turned out to be something radically new, rather than a return to some 'pre-modern' political order, even if it has in part been legitimized as such. It features a constitutional court, a directly elected president and a supreme leader or 'guide' (*rahbar*), none of which is anticipated in earlier shi'ite political thought, let alone in the original community of believers headed by the prophet Mohammed (cf. Abrahamian, *Khomeinism*).

he had been reading in preparation. One major source for the notion of political spirituality, acknowledged as such by Foucault, is Ali Shariati (DE III: 693; cf. Rodinson, *Primauté* 308).[9] In his pamphlets, Shariati had developed a view of shi'ite Islam as the 'religion of the oppressed', giving the potential shi'ite opposition to any form of worldly government a more revolutionary character. Shariati, active in the 1960s and early 1970s, had been inspired by champions of Third-World liberation like Mao, Castro, and Fanon, but at the same time he emphasized shi'ite Islamic spirituality as an antidote to Marxist-inspired materialism (e. g. Shariati, *Marxism*; cf. Abrahamian, *Khomeinism*, ch. 1).

Another, and probably more important, influence is Henry Corbin. According to his editors (DE III: 662), Foucault's preparatory reading on Iran included Corbin's important works on Islamic – in particular shi'ite – philosophy and spirituality (e. g. Corbin, *Histoire*; *Islam Iranien*). Corbin, more than any Westerner, had devoted his academic life to the publication and translation of manuscripts from the philosophical traditions of Islamic Iran; his representation of Islamic thought is cast in a distinctly Heideggerian mould, but is simultaneously guided by the essentialist idea that the 'real' Islamic spirituality is to be found in the more esoteric and Gnostic branches of shi'ism in Iran.[10] Thus, he concludes his history of Islamic philosophy with an appeal to Iranian Muslims to preserve their 'traditional spiritual culture' against the Western impact (*Histoire* 497 ff.).

Corbin's hermeneutics of Islamic texts stress the distinction between the superficial exoteric (*zâhir*) meaning and the true, inner (*bâtin*) meaning. In an interview on the Islamic revolt (DE III: ch. 259), Foucault also makes much of this distinction, when he describes the Islamic Revolution as both an inner and outer experience, as both a timeless and a historical drama (DE III: 746); significantly, he also links it to his own theoretical notions when he tries to capture what he calls 'perhaps the soul of the uprising':

> Religion for them was like the promise and guarantee of something that would radically change their subjectivity. Shi'ism is precisely a form of Islam that, with its teaching and esoteric content, distinguishes between what is merely external and what is the profound spiritual life (DE: 749)

and elsewhere, as an explanation of Iranian attitudes to propaganda:

> They don't have the same regime of truth as ours, which, it has to be said, is very special, even if it has become almost universal [...]. In Iran it is largely modeled on a religion that has an exoteric form and an esoteric content. That is to say, everything that is said under the explicit form of the law also refers to another meaning (DE III: 753–4).

---

[9] Perhaps Shariati's notion of political spirituality had reached Foucault by way of Mehdi Bazargan, when the latter two met in Qom in September 1978 (cf. DE III: 781).

[10] For more on Corbin and his use of Heideggerian hermeneutics in interpreting mystically inclined Islamic philosophy, see my 'From Freiburg to Isfahan: Heidegger and the "Wisdom of the East"'.

I will return to Foucault's appeal to regimes of truth below. His other writings from this period suggest that the formation of, and changes in, subjectivity are processes in which various kinds of power relation are crucial. That political spirituality might also be seen as a form of resistance against a prevailing power with its concomitant form of political rationality is suggested by a passage from the Tanner lectures which Foucault presented at Stanford in October 1979:

> Those who resist or rebel against a form of power cannot merely be content to denounce violence or criticize an institution. Nor is it enough to cast the blame on reason in general. What has to be questioned is the form of rationality at stake (DE IV: 161).

For a European audience, then, the concept of political spirituality also suggests an alternative to a kind of political rationality that has been predominant since the Enlightenment. Such suggestions are certainly interesting and worth exploring further, but it should be noted that Foucault's case rests in part on a rather biased view of what shi'ism amounts to in doctrinal terms. His Corbin-inspired claims notwithstanding, the exoteric-esoteric opposition is not an essential part of shi'ite Islam, not even in its Iranian varieties. In shi'ite Iran, esoteric currents have always remained a minority phenomenon, and most clerics have traditionally been suspicious of such Gnostic and esoteric doctrines that might undermine the *shari'a* (Islamic law) as the basis of social order.[11]

Foucault not only presents a minority view as the 'real' shi'ite faith, he also speaks consistently of shi'ism *tout court*, as if it were a monolithic and historically stable set of doctrines, or even a 'timeless drama' which has formed a base for opposition to state power 'since the dawn of history'.[12] In fact, Islamic 'spirituality' in Iran has undergone radical transformations over the centuries, both among the population at large and among the shi'ite clergy.[13] Ever since the mysterious disappearance of the twelfth *imâm* in 873 CE, the shi'ite community had faced the problem of legitimate spiritual and worldly authority. Because just rule would only be established at the end of times, when the Hidden *Imâm* would reappear, all worldly government was in a sense illegitimate by definition; but most shi'ite scholars recommended acquiescing in this cosmic injustice as part of the shi'ites' eschatological fate. This ambivalent attitude towards state power became even more pronounced when law-based 'twelve' or *imâmi* shi'ism became the state religion of the Safavid empire in the sixteenth century. On the whole, shi'ite jurists and theologians have not developed a consistent and gen-

---

[11] Instead of appealing to the elitist *zâhir-bâtin* distinction, Foucault might as well have appealed to the much more widespread politeness principle of *ta'rof*, the Iranian equivalent of *comme il faut*, which, for example, requires one to invite visitors to stay for dinner for the sake of politeness, even if one has no real intention of actually hosting them.

[12] Stauth (15–6, 34) already noted that the concept of political spirituality implies a relapse to an Orientalist view of religion as in itself determinative of social action.

[13] I cannot trace these developments in detail here; see Mottahedeh, *Mantle*, and Abrahamian, *Khomeinism*, ch. 1, for the main points raised.

erally accepted theory of the state and of legitimate rule. Before the 1960s, however, none of these thinkers held that monarchy was in itself illegitimate; on the contrary, many of them explicitly considered a bad government better than the anarchy of revolution. The development from quietism to revolutionary Islam in this period was itself a revolutionary innovation in shi'ite thought.

Although Foucault would undoubtedly have rejected the idealist position that the shi'ite faith possesses causal historical powers of itself, he faces similar difficulties as the idealist. Thus, only by ignoring historical and other variations can he avoid the question of what, if any, is the regime of truth shared by both law-oriented and more mystically inclined Persian thinkers, not to mention the population at large.[14] He also leaves it unclear whether the allegedly sought-for change in subjectivity would amount to a return to a truth regime predating the shah's Western-inspired modernization project, or leave the existing truth regime intact. His ignorance of historical developments in shi'ism and his appeal to a presumably timeless drama or a millenarian *zâhir-bâtin* distinction, then, allow for a totally idealist, if not transcendental, reconstruction of his ideas on Iran. This opportunity was eagerly grasped by Corbin's pupil Christian Jambet, who ascribes to him a roundly essentialist and ahistorical view, disguised as a spiritual 'metahistory' which seems completely at odds with all of Foucault's other writings:

> Foucault's point is not the politics of a future state but the essence of an uprising, of the 'spiritual' politics which makes it possible [...]. He sees immediately that here history is the expression of a metahistory, or again of a hiero-history, and that the temporalisation of time is suspended in favor of messianic events, whose place is not the world of phenomena understood by science (*Subject* 234).

Here, Foucault's interest in the Iranian revolution as an unprecedented historical event has to make room for an inquiry into the supposed spiritual or transcendental essence of any uprising. The convergences that Jambet perceives between Corbin's 'meta-historical' phenomenology and the archaeology of knowledge seem less the result of any natural affinity than traces of Corbin's direct influence on Foucault's Iranian writings.

But are the essentialist ideas of shi'ism as a force, irreducibly opposed to state power, and of a specifically Iranian-Islamic regime of truth, both heavily dependent on Corbin's work, really so at odds with Foucault's more general notions, such as 'episteme' and 'regime of truth'? In a 1977 interview, Foucault suggests that 'each society has its régime of truth [...]; that is, the types of discourse which it accepts and makes function as true' (P/K 131/ DE III: 158), and that the contemporary Western European regime of truth (which is centered on a form of scientific discourse and the institutions which produce it) is by

---

[14] Significantly, he fails throughout the Brière & Blanchot interview to address the questions posed to him regarding ethnic and other cleavages among the protest movement.

and large the same regime operating in the socialist countries, but probably different from that in China (P/K 133). The concept of 'regime of truth', then, seems to play much the same structural role that such notions as 'culture' or 'world view' play in more idealistically inclined authors: it allows for a sweeping characterization of an entire historical period or geographical region. As such, it faces the risk of reducing singular historical events to static and essentialist categories, a risk implicit in any attempt at historical classification or periodization. In short, political spirituality may be quite suggestive as a journalistic notion, but as a philosophical concept it is deeply problematic, indeed indicative of more general problems that Foucault faces.

VI. Power and Power Struggle

The biggest surprises, however, lie in store for those who turn to Foucault's Iranian articles with his 'analytic of power' in mind.[15] After all, the relevance of the Islamic revolution to the concerns of *Surveiller et punir* and the first volume of *Histoire de la sexualité* is obvious. In the latter work, Foucault argues at length against the prevailing juridical view that tends to see power as a kind of institution, and instead proposes to represent power relations as at the same time intentional and non-subjective, as no individual has full control over the directedness of power relations (*Volonté* 124). The juridical view 'from above' sees power merely as domination, or as a purely negative force, thus ignoring its productive capacities: 'the representation of power has remained haunted by monarchy. In political thought, the king's head has not yet been cut' (ibid. 117). As an alternative, Foucault proposes to take the forms of resistance against different forms of power as a starting point. A systematic awareness that power inevitably calls up resistance, i. e., that resistance is internal to power relations, opens up the way for an analysis of power relations through the antagonism of strategies (Dreyfus & Rabinow 211/ DE IV: 225). Admittedly, Foucault does not intend his analytic of power as a general theory, but rather as a tool that can open insights into 'a certain form of knowledge about sex' (*Volonté* 109, 128); yet, it might equally provide new insights into power relations in rather different spheres.

The implications of this shift from a juridical to a strategic view of power do not seem to be sufficiently appreciated by all of Foucault's students.[16] Seen

---

[15] For more detailed discussion of Foucault's views on power, see especially Dreyfus & Rabinow, ch. 6, 9; Taylor, *Freedom*, esp. §III; and Cohen & Arato, *Civil Society*, pt. II, ch. 6.

[16] Thus, Taylor (168) seems to mistake Foucault's claim that 'power comes from below' for the idea that one should study power in micro-contexts of local dominators and dominated, rather than in macro-contexts like state or class; in fact, Foucault rejects the domination model at both the micro- and macro-level. Olivier& Labbé (*Désir.* 234) likewise attribute to Foucault a state-

from this novel perspective, however, the Iranian revolution, and in particular the chaotic and violent power struggle that erupted when the shah had left and the old institutions of power and government, including the army and the police forces, had collapsed (and, so to speak, the king's head had actually been chopped off) would seem to provide an ideal test case for an analytic of power. An analysis of the institutional bases and different strategies of the various actors involved would have proven a worthwhile, if by no means easy, task; in particular the ways in which Khomeini managed to accumulate political power for himself, by refusing to compromise and by encouraging and at the same time channeling popular action, would have formed an interesting challenge to Foucault's view of power as an intentional relation without an (individual) subject.

But nothing of the sort happened. Instead, Foucault hardly tried to link his initial fascination with the novelty of the protests to his more theoretical interests in power and resistance, and when he did address the violence that marked the post-revolutionary power struggle, he fell back on a universalist position that takes the rights of the individual and the rule of law as a kind of moral rock bottom. This universalist ethics appears clearly in several articles published in April and May 1979. Thus, in an open letter to Mehdi Bazargan, published in mid-April (DE III: 780–2), Foucault argues that political processes against representatives of a former regime are a touchstone regarding the 'essential obligations' of any government. His letter was addressed to precisely the wrong person, however, as Bazargan had already publicly protested against the many summary executions, and against the revolutionary trials, which he called 'shameful', in late March (editor's note, DE III: 663; cf. Bakhash, *Reign* 61). More importantly, real power at this moment lay with the revolutionary committees and courts as much as with the Bazargan government.

The same theme is picked up in 'Inutile de se soulever?' (*Le Monde*, May 11–12, 1979; DE III: 790–4), where Foucault argues that enthusiasm for the Iranian revolution is not a legitimization of (post-) revolutionary violence: 'the spirituality that those who were going to die appealed to has no common measure with the bloodthirsty government of a fundamentalist clergy' (DE III: 793).[17] The ethics he defends is not relativist, but rather 'anti-strategic' (794): it involves showing respect when a singularity arises, but being intransigent when power infringes on the universal. Foucault's ethics is clearly universalist in its stress on the rights of the individual, that is, something much like classical

and domination-oriented view, according to which revolt constitutes a limit or obstacle, but not an end, to power.

[17] In another article, 'Pour un morale de l'inconfort' (DE III: 783–7), Foucault addresses the difficulty of having to revise one's certainties without giving up one's convictions. Years of experience, he writes, lead us "not to trust any revolution", even if one can "understand every revolt". As Eribon notes, this sounds very much like an acknowledgment that his journalistic adventures in Iran had been a failure.

human rights. Being 'anti-strategic', it may be opposed to power-as-strategy almost by definition, but its appeal to laws without franchise and rights without restriction (ibid.) almost presumes that such laws and rights are themselves defined without any recourse to power. The question then arises on what *philosophical* basis Foucault can make such an appeal, given his earlier attempts to cast doubt on the universalist aspirations of reason since the Enlightenment; moreover, on earlier occasions, he had explicitly refused to condemn the possibly violent, dictatorial and even bloody power that the proletariat could exercise in 'revolutionary justice' over the vanquished classes.[18]

This problem deserves further attention, but here, the central question is why Foucault reverted to such a classical (dare I say Enlightenment-inspired?) position. Was he really so shocked and surprised at the revolution developing into a violent competition for power? Perhaps he had ignored the political power struggle hidden behind the religious slogans because of his emphasis on the spiritual dimension of the revolt that expressed its supposedly unified popular will. Rodinson (*Primauté* 309 f.) argues as much, with his remark that all cases of political spirituality have eventually submitted to the 'eternal laws of politics', that is, the struggle for power, and adds that Foucault more generally has undermined the concept of political power with his constellation of micro-powers. Or had Foucault simply lost interest in the revolution as a political struggle *for* power, once the 'spiritual' revolt *against* the shah's power had been successful? This may be suggested by his early remark that 'the phenomenon which has so fascinated us – the revolutionary experience itself – will die out' (DE III: 750), reflecting his view that his main interest, the unified popular will, was not the result of a political alliance or compromise, but something that stood outside politics, or temporarily transformed it.

Foucault's silence on the complex post-revolutionary power struggle and his subsequently reverting to a universalist ethics based on immutable laws suggest a conceptual inability to move beyond the domination-resistance dichotomy implicit in the juridical view of power which he himself had so strongly criticized. Seen in this light, his ignoring of historical developments in shi'ite Islam, and of internal divisions along lines of political outlook, class, ethnicity or denomination between those participating in the uprising, may not be an accident after all. It points to a far more general difficulty of how to account for variation and change in regimes of truth, or epistemes, or paradigms (cf. Dreyfus & Rabinow 262; Taylor, *Freedom* 182). In other words, Foucault's conceptualization of regimes of truth and political rationalities, and even his strategy-oriented analysis of power relations, may still be too static and monolithic to allow for a genuine

---

[18] Witness, for example, the discussion on popular justice as opposed to bourgeois justice, and the famous television debate with Noam Chomsky (DE II: chs. 108, 132).

explanation of such drastic changes as occur in revolutionary periods, and of power struggle in absence of the effective concentration of power in the government and state apparatus.

VII. By Way of Conclusion

Let me return to the three links between Foucault's Iranian writings and his broader concerns. First, Foucault's journalistic intuition that something radically new was occurring in Iran has certainly proved correct. He managed to put aside much fashionable prejudice and ask many interesting questions, and intelligently sought for adequate answers at a time when no one quite understood as yet what was in the course of happening. Second, however, Foucault surprisingly failed to analyze the revolution in terms of 'power from below' or his strategy-based view of power, and ultimately even reverted to a universalist ethics based on laws and rights that do not seem to allow for compromise or discussion. Third, Foucault's more philosophically loaded remarks on the revolution betray a strong influence of Henry Corbin's work. His explanation of the specifics of the revolt in terms of a distinct Iranian-shi'ite regime of truth and of a desire for a change in subjectivity and political rationality seems less a genuine application of his conceptual tools than a relapse into the conventional text-based idealism of Oriental studies – that is, into precisely the kind of idealist 'history of ideas' which his earlier writings had done much to discredit.[19] Foucault's general works thus do not display the obvious eurocentrism of which he has been accused. At the same time, however, his Iranian writings point to deeper difficulties of his work concerning power relations and intellectual change. They foreshadow the remarkable shift between *Le volonté de savoir* (1976) and the last two volumes of *Histoire de la sexualité* (1984), from the microphysics of power to the self-constitution of the individual as a desiring subject, where power is no longer a central theme.[20] The latter works read much like an exercise in conventional history of ideas – albeit with an unconventional theme – with their focus on the literate male elite of ancient Greece.

There is little point in biographical speculation as to whether Foucault's sudden reversal on the Islamic revolution is due to his revulsion at the revolutionary violence or to his dismay at the outcry among French intellectuals. His silence

---

[19] The most famous example of a Foucault-inspired critique of the philological bias and essentialism of much conventional Orientalist scholarship is, of course, Edward Said's *Orientalism* (1978).

[20] Edward Said (*Foucault* 8−9) attributes this shift to Foucault's disenchantment with the public sphere, to his pursuit of 'different kinds of pleasures', and to his 'unusual experience of excess' that was the Iranian revolution: 'it was as if for the first time Foucault's theories of impersonal, authorless activity had been visibly realized and he recoiled with understandable disillusion'.

on the power struggle and his subsequent reversal to a universalist ethics may not merely be expressive of his shock at the violent turn taken by events, but also reflect his more general intellectual problem of how to account for conceptual change and its relation to changes in power. Depending on one's perspective, then, one may either see Foucault's journalistic writings on Iran as a missed opportunity; as the conclusive proof that his conceptual tools are too static, monolithic, and idealist to allow for any practical use; or as a promise, not yet fulfilled, that a Foucauldian vision of cultural history may be extended to non-European territory. Paradoxically, however, Foucault-the-journalist showed a far greater sensitivity to the specific and novel character of the Iranian revolution as a historical event than Foucault-the-philosopher. His attempts at a journalistic understanding of the present may yet change our appreciation of modernity, with its entire political rationality inherited from the Enlightenment – and of the protagonists of the contemporary Islamic world, who, far from being 'anti-modern' as often thought, are searching different ways of being 'modern'.

II

Modes of Doing Cultural History

5

Foucault Reformed by Certeau:
Historical Strategies of Discipline and Everyday Tactics of Appropriation

WILLEM FRIJHOFF

Has cultural history really met Michel Foucault? The question may seem somewhat provocative, and, in the light of the theme of this conference, perhaps a bit superfluous. As Frédéric Gros concludes in his *Que sais-je?* on Foucault, by means of his continuous attempts to 'tell stories' that may change our lives, the philosopher has linked up in one critical movement the three accepted meanings of 'history': i. e. the narrative, the domain of knowledge, and the field of action. Yet my initial question is less rhetorical than it might appear at first sight. Of course, in one way or another all the works of Foucault deal with history and with culture. Leading French historians like Fernand Braudel and Robert Mandrou have quickly applauded *L'Histoire de la folie*, published in 1961, at the zenith of quantitative history (Eribon 142–144). The cultural construction of the past, discourse analysis, and the rhetorics of historical writing itself, so central in the new cultural history advocated, for instance, by Natalie Zemon Davis and Lynn Hunt, lean heavily on Foucault's methods and are inspired by his conceptual models (Wuthnow; Hunt, "Introduction"; O'Brien; Iggers; Hutton; Jones). But we should face it: the mainstream of history, as historians practice it nowadays, has been barely touched by his work. Indeed, professional historians themselves have seldom recognized his work as an appropriate form of cultural history.

I. Foucault and the Historians

Of course, quite a few authors have considered Foucault's *oeuvre* as a new form of history (Major-Poetzl; O'Farrell) – but in the eyes of many professional historians the generalizing form of history-writing in Foucault's style is not just genuine history, since it substitutes intellectual concepts for historical realities; nor does it answer to the basic requirements of the historians' *métier*. Some of them went so far as to qualify Foucault's writings as little more than rubbish and to reject violently his historical work (Stone "The revival"). Such bitter criticism and strong resistance may have faded away by now, but the same may be said of the awareness of Foucault's novelty. The streamlined Foucault of the European historical textbooks has been amputated of his asperities, specially those of his later works which most clearly interact with his attitude in life. Even the most empathic French historical reading of Foucault in recent years, the 1992 collection of essays edited by Luce Giard, does not cover the whole Foucault: *Surveiller et punir*, published in 1975, appears as the closing book of the 'historical' Foucault. Obviously something has gone wrong in Foucault's encounter with the professional historians (Farge; Noiriel; Prochasson).

At least so in Europe. In the most recent account of the state of the art in French historical studies, the two authors, Boutier and Julia, list his name just in the middle of a range of other theorists who have inspired historical research in Foucault's homeland after the breakdown of the global history paradigm in the 1970s: Tocqueville, Weber, Bourdieu, Habermas, and most of all Elias ("Ouverture" 45). Actually, none of these is recognized as an historian in his own right. Including Foucault, the six authorities are presented as philosophers or social theorists who provide history-writing with analytical concepts and theoretical approaches developed outside the practice of historical research. They use historical evidence mainly to test their hypotheses and to develop a line of thinking that may be fruitful for further research. The attraction they exert derives precisely from the fact that their models have been developed at a certain distance from historical evidence itself. Other researchers use them readily. On the other hand, historians who develop explanatory models in close interplay with their sources, often discover at the end that their method can only be applied to that single sequence of historical data. Outside their current research it proves to be useless – a conclusion which justifies the question whether such a unique explanation really has any explanatory force at all.

This is the problematics which forms the historical background of my theme. There is a manifest tension between the practice of history and the historian's elaboration of explanatory models. Historians tend to be eclectic, if not epistemologically naïve, in their way of analysing evidence and constructing historical narratives. The philosophy of history, so strongly developed in some countries of Europe, has in fact little direct impact on the practice of historical research or historical narrative. Most historians quite obviously trust in the self-evidence of their sources and their narrative – a positivist position which somehow contrasts with their professional discourse, eagerly stressing history's otherness. It would lead us too far to analyse here the whole evolution of historical awareness. May it suffice to ascertain that the historians themselves oscillate between a strong identification with the past considered as familiar, or similar to the present, and an equally strong estrangement facing the past as far away, alien, and irreducible to the demands of the present. Few historians had a stronger feeling of their alienation from the past than Michel de Certeau, who was one of Foucault's main interlocutors among the French historians.

II. Historical Otherness

To begin with, I would suggest – but I think that it is much more than an educated guess – that in the 1960s and 70s, when Michel Foucault published his major works, the dominant attitude towards the past was one of estrangement. The otherness of the past, related to major changes in the global society, resonates in many historical themes and in still more historical works of that period. Otherness, resistance, or obstruction with regard to the established rules were the privileged themes of social history: strikes, rebellion, revolution, magic, witchcraft, prophecy, anarchy, deviance, folly, unruly behaviour, popular culture, the world turned upside down, prenuptial sexuality, cross-dressing, crime, heresy, mysticism, and even religion itself – since religion was by then a declining factor of social cohesion.

What in this context made Foucault attractive to a wide range of younger historians was his ability to provide explanatory schemes which put historical otherness back into a familiar, or at least a recognizable structure of perception. His concepts accounted for their insertion into a proper historical reason, even if that reason – developed in *Les Mots et les choses* in terms of the *episteme* – should be radically different from ours. In this respect, one should not misunderstand the historians' attacks on Foucault. The *episteme* concept was heavily criticized on the left wing of historical scholarship (Vilar 188–189), as it was on the right wing, but in France it actually introduced Foucault into the debates of the whole historical trade (Bertels 24). Whereas his early works on the historical perception of madness and *The birth of the clinic* had confined him more or less to the small group of historians of medicine and psychiatry, and to the growing but still somewhat marginal sector of *histoire des mentalités*, this broad intellectual concept with its globalizing ambition of a 'general history' was a domain which they recognized as their own (Huppert).

In fact, the specialists of the modern period, which was so central to Foucault's own scholarship, were the last to surrender themselves. The first acknowledgements of Foucault's significance came from generalists in the other sectors of history. The classical historian Paul Veyne, who guided Foucault in his research on classical Antiquity, was in 1978 one of the first leading historians to applaud Foucault publicly in an afterthought to the second edition (1978) of his influential essay on historical epistemology (Veyne "Foucault"; Eribon 345–349). In his introduction to the ambitious dictionary of the French 'new history', published in the same year, the medievalist Jacques Le Goff recognized Foucault's importance, both as a methodologist and as an historian. Yet he mentioned at the same time the persisting doubts of many colleagues (Le Goff, "Présentation" 14). It was only from that moment on that Foucault really began to take the place of the anthropologist Claude Lévi-Strauss as the social historian's main interlocutor in historical methodology. His system thinking was better

fit for incorporating historical scholarship and respecting the essentially diachronic character of the historical narrative than Lévi-Strauss's flat structuralism.

Indeed, Foucault's works emerged during a threefold crisis of history-writing
in France. First, in the 1970s, French structural anthropology began to lose its
power of attraction for the historians. Second, social and economic history got
a powerful competitor in the emerging *histoire des mentalités* and in cultural history,
which stressed the vital importance of experience (the *vécu*) and the constructed
character of historical reality — a shift encouraged by the rapid decline of Marxist historiography (Poster). Finally, first breaches were made in the apparent self-
evidence of serial and quantitative methods in history (Furet). Doubts on the
harmony of social evolution and on the business cycles as meaningful representations of historical change destroyed the coherence which history had obtained
diachronically. They brought about an urgent need for a new harmony. Foucault
provided such harmony, synchronically. His subtle and differentiated vision of
historical transformation still participated somehow in the current paradigm of
structural history but satisfied at the same time the demands of transhistorical
explanations. His method resulted in a kind of *mutationnisme*, far from traditional
historicity and equally far from any single diachronic image of the past (Bourdé
& Martin 280–288). Yet in one way or another it accounted for historical
change.

III. Conceptual Analysis versus Historical Practice?

It was not the cultural continuity of the past which mattered to Foucault, nor
the exchanges or influences between historical persons or groups, but the internal cohesion of the different conceptual systems of which he could detect
the sediments under the face-value of historical documents. He looked for the
structural relations between these conceptual systems, for their correlations and
transformations, i. e. the crossing over from one system to another — not for
uninterrupted, sliding developments or gradual transitions, since in his view the
research for gradual change blurred the understanding of the point of reversal
between two systems. But the genealogy of the mind, the transformation of one
conceptual system into another is not really perceptible in historical fact; it
presents itself only through an analysis of the discourses involved. The voices
which really matter in Foucault's method are those of the people who articulate
the concepts of the past and translate them into a social policy, involving the
mind, the human body, or even society itself.

Hence Foucault's scepticism towards the traditional historical research of his
decades, which was directed at the construction of quantitative or qualitative
series of empirical data over a long period. Discontinuity was his starting point
for the analysis of the perceived forms of otherness, and his personal solution

to the problem of coherence in history. Indeed, for Foucault, the coherence should not be sought in the historical process itself, but in its epistemological foundations. His *Discipline and punish* is perhaps the most accomplished expression of his method. In this book, built around the contrast between two consecutive, sedimented conceptual systems of punishment, Foucault constructs a genealogy of social discipline which finally pervades all the institutions of society, including the army and the school, the latter being in itself largely a creation of the new disciplinary system. For Foucault, however, discipline is not really a historical fact but a political concept which emerges in history through the construction of specific forms of social order. It is this conceptual coherence that puts its unitary mark upon the different expressions of institutional order in society. It makes us recognize such different institutions of the 19th century as the prison, the school, the family, and the army, as pertaining to one single conceptual framework.

Discipline and punish is certainly the most recognizable book for the common historian since it deals with historical events and institutions instead of analysing the paradigms of science and of the history of the mind, as Foucault essentially did in his previous books, such as *The order of things* or the *The archeology of knowledge*. It was an eye-opener for many historians and it really made Foucault an interlocutor of social history, not only of philosophy and of history of science (Farge). Immediately though, *Discipline and punish* was heavily criticised by the social and political historians for its selective and often naïve treatment of historical evidence, its anachronisms in crucial chapters of the analysis, and the absence of the voice of the historical agents — or the victims — themselves (Léonard; Bourdé 285). Foucault's answer has clarified his position. He replied that his book must not be read as a global "study of a period but as the analysis of a problem," the problem being the question why a new mechanism of punishment had emerged around 1800. His study was not about 19th-century society but about the rationality of a new practice, i. e. the strategy of social discipline as made manifest in the 19th century (Foucault, "La poussière" 29–39). In fact, it concerned a wide range of similar practices which Foucault tried to connect between each other by defining their underlying conceptual system and the social strategy involved in their realisation.

Although Foucault's deconstruction of historical texts has certainly influenced historical research, the paradox is perhaps that his major theories, endlessly quoted but barely developed by his followers, have proved less inspiring than his case-studies. In fact, the impact of Foucault's theoretical concepts on historical research appears to have been largely confined to the particular themes which were at the core of his own research, since these themes facilitated a quick operationalization by current historical methods, both on the macro-level of state and society and on the micro-level of power relations in social life: social discipline, criminal justice, psychiatry, mental asylums, medicine (Dinges

"Foucault"). Foucault himself has called this "The microphysics of power" (*Microfisica del potere*) — 'power' being, together with 'governmentality', the two main concepts which connected him to the ongoing research in social history (Dreyfus; Burke, *History* 40−41, 79; McNay). But even here the absence of a truly developmental perspective has hindered Foucault's breakthrough in the study of social change. His theoretical reflections may have much inspired the historians of the themes and objects with which he developed and demonstrated his paradigm, but I wonder whether they have really proved fruitful for further analysis beyond Foucault's own insights. The *épistème* concept, for example, has not exceeded the status of an interesting suggestion among the historians, even in intellectual history. In a certain sense, Foucault has become a prisoner of his own books and perhaps a victim of his most zealous supporters too.

A good example of what I would call the historical perversion of his work is the once famous and much-read study of Foucault's pupil Jacques Donzelot, *The policing of families* on the social discipline of the family in the 19th and early 20th century. Relying heavily on Foucault's concept of 'biopolitics', i. e. the political power to manage life itself by conjugating political technology with social psychology, Donzelot sketches in this book the outlines of a Big-Brother-like vision of historical transformation of the family, which he calls at the same time 'queen and prisoner' of the evolution described (Minson 180−184; Hutton 94−95). In his view, the gradual but continuous policing of the family by the state did not only correspond to the emergence of a proliferating discourse but was a historical reality. Donzelot did not deny that the family sometimes resisted the ever more restrictive and policing measures of the political power, but he interpreted these forms of resistance exclusively as functions of the political game. They did not really speak to the family's own concerns but only to the degree to which the state's policing power had penetrated. Finally, his study was a claim to historical awareness. In his own eyes his method made history tell us "who we are" (Donzelot 8). For him, therefore, the construction (or the historian's reconstruction) of the policing discourse coincided perfectly with historical reality. I wonder if anything could be further removed from Foucault's own convictions in that matter.

Nevertheless, some of Foucault's concepts have resisted the damage caused by his fans and by the oblivion of time. Thus, in connection with the concept of social discipline, cultural strategy has remained a central notion for the historian. Besides, Foucault was not the only intellectual developing such concepts. Gerhard Oestreich's notion of *Sozialdisziplinierung* came up about the same time and proved to be perfectly operational, but in a very different social and political setting (Oestreich; Hsia; Dinges "Armenfürsorge"; Schilling). Though from the very beginning Oestreich's concept was loaded with a more historical meaning, both notions came together in a structured view of the ever growing regulating power of the state, the churches and the social elites since the beginning of the early modern period, expressed in analytical terms like 'elite offensives' towards citizens, against superstition or in favour of civilization.

IV. New Developments in Cultural History

Yet in the meantime cultural history has globally taken other pathways: those of the linguistic turn, of discourse analysis and narrativism, of historical anthropology and microhistory. Three main factors may be considered responsible for this evolution:

1. The shift from objectivism to a subject-oriented approach in cultural history, from the concepts and structures back to human agency, and from cognition to emotion. Foucault's own latter work on *The history of sexuality* and the technology of the self, and his courses at the Collège de France (in *Dits et écrits*, vol. IV) have much contributed to this evolution – less perhaps by means of their thematic treatments than by the particular interaction between subject, historical experience, politics, and ethics which he develops in them. This would, however, ask for a further analysis which exceeds the limits of this short synthesis (Gros 91–95).

2. The shift from the analysis of cultural forms to that of cultural meanings, from morphology to semiology, from research on the diffusion of forms to analysis of the ways of attribution of meaning.

3. The shift from the fascination for historical elites and for those invested with power, either political, economical, social or cultural, very vivid in the 1960s and 70s, to a new interest in the people, in ordinary men and women, and in those without power, whoever they are and wherever they may have lived: labourers and seamen, slaves and prostitutes, people in the countryside, in the slums of the early industrial towns, or in the colonies overseas.

Criticism against historical objectivism is not new. Some twenty years ago English social historians, such as E. P. Thompson, violently attacked structural historians, including Louis Althusser and Michel Foucault, together with the objectivist approaches of the quantitative historians (Roth). Thompson's plea went in favour of a return to anthropocentrism. In his view, history can only be understood as a product of human agency. Whereas Althusser saw history fundamentally as a process without a subject, Thompson considered history as a form of agency between subjects. History works with relationships between persons. Actually, this accent on human relations as the proper object of historical knowledge was not really contrary to the structuralist view. But whereas the structuralists were inclined to formalize these relationships and interpret them as determined by pre-established models, institutional structures, formalized ideas and fixed value-systems, Thompson and his fellow-historians made a pas-

sionate plea for contingency. In his own words: "We can see a *logic* in the responses of similar [...] groups undergoing similar experiences, but we cannot
predicate any *law*" (Thompson 9–10). This opposition between logic and law
may be considered as crucial for the development of cultural history in the past
two decades. Logic refers fundamentally to a play or a process, guided of course
by rules, figures and symbols, but always open, not closed. It leaves space for
new players who may join the party and even change the rules, provided that
they be numerous, strong or persuasive enough. More important yet, according
to the human agency-paradigm the logic of history is not rooted in some sedimentary *epistème* but in the performance of life itself. It may be elucidated by
the analysis of the elements involved.

The subject-oriented *history from below*-school of which E. P. Thompson was
a major representative, found in the same years its counterpart in France. In
fact, different new forms of interest in the ordinary people of history have
arisen simultaneously during the 1970s in many countries of Western Europe:
history from below, people's history, labour history, popular culture studies, or
Alltagsgeschichte (history of everyday life). Typical is the shift of European ethno-
logy and folklore studies from the geographical paradigm to the historical, and
hence to the social (Frijhoff *Volkskunde*). Henceforth, cultural differences were
no longer perceived as rooted in old spatial structures – the prehistoric tribes
and their presumed territories – but primarily as historically constructed or
generated by forms of social differentiation: town versus countryside, modern
versus traditional regions, elite versus people, popular or mass culture versus
intellectual culture or high esthetic values, etc.

V. Culture and Social Discipline

Seminal work has been done in this respect by the two cultural historians Peter
Burke and Robert Muchembled in their books on the people of the early modern European society, both published in 1978. They have brought the people
back unto the agenda of cultural history and have strongly advocated the social
differentiation of culture in past societies, but in different ways. Whereas Robert
Muchembled adhered strongly to the social discipline theory for which, beside
Norbert Elias, he paid probably a large though implicit tribute to Michel Foucault, Peter Burke – who equally ignored Foucault – showed how popular
culture as an autonomous cultural system was patiently fabricated, constructed
by the elites of the different countries of Europe. As for Muchembled, he used
a form of reading that tried to detect a pattern of disciplining intentions under
the repressive sources of the judicial authorities. Hence his picture of the pre-
industrial peasants, presented as victims rather than agents of history, and virtually void of any initiative other than rooted in traditional culture. Burke, however,

more open to constructivist theories of history, organized his narrative so as to
let them much more latitude for the display of some proper identity, independent of the state's views or the cultural strategies of its elites.

The interstice left open by Burke proved finally more fruitful than the
doomsday scenery of fiercely repressing authorities and unremittingly persecut-
ing elites developed by Muchembled before he returned, in his last synthetical
study of early modern France, to a more balanced image (Muchembled *L'invention*). This is not to say that Muchembled did not pay attention to the symbolical
language of the historical underdogs themselves. On the contrary, he remained
close to the face-value of his texts — very similar to the way in which Herman
Pleij in his different studies presents the cultural artefacts of the early modern
Netherlands as a coherent cultural code (Pleij, *De sneeuwpoppen*; Pleij, *Op belofte*).
But Muchembled derived the cultural system of the underdogs solely from the
language of their persecutors.

The works of Foucault, mostly published more than a decade earlier, still are
totally absent from Burke's study, as they are from that of Muchembled. This is
not to say that Burke has continued to ignore Foucault. His "bold reconceptual-
izations" are given a very favourable welcome in Burke's 1992 survey of the
relations between history and social theory (Burke, *History* 52). Other cultural
historians have been more reluctant. In the introduction to his celebrated study
The Cheese and the Worms on the world view of the 16th-century miller Menocchio, Carlo Ginzburg adopts a very critical attitude towards Michel Foucault.
His reproach concerns mainly Foucaults' conceptualism which makes him unfit,
in Ginzburg's eyes, as a guide or a tool for historical research. In the battle of
narrativism, which in historical circles started at that very moment, Ginzburg
has adopted from the very beginning, with great consistency, a moderately 'realist' attitude, in agreement with his originally Gramscian inspiration. He has even
strenghtened this 'realist' position in his later work, probably against the mainstream of historical research. According to Ginzburg, cultural differences are
not simply an effect of discourse, they exist in reality, and historical evidence is
fit to document this reality as such.

Hence Ginzburg's opposition against those who tend to consider the so-
called 'popular culture' as a mere creation of elite discourse — a narrativist
position which in his opinion is due to the influence of Michel Foucault. Indeed,
in *Madness and civilization* Foucault privileged the language of normality and the
social acts of exclusion above the cultural signs of the experience of madness.
Therefore he has, in Ginzburg's eyes, introduced a way of reasoning that by
privileging discourse floats definitely away from the research of historical evidence. Besides, his discourse shares the estheticism of language, not the contin-
gencies, the misery or glory, of history. Hence — still according to Ginzburg —
Foucault's silence on history itself.

According to Ginzburg, in Foucault's presentation of *Moi, Pierre Rivière* this silence is brought to its zenith: the murdering boy's case remains cloudy, since Foucault and his collaborators refuse to link together into one single interpretation the conflicting discourses presented by psychiatry, criminal justice and the boy himself. In Foucault's eyes, any interpretation would violate the proper logic of the texts under review. This type of discourse analysis results therefore in an estrangement, a drifting away from the historical narrative. The procedures of exclusion employed by psychiatry and criminal justice, but also the justification written by the boy himself, stress the incongruity of the boy's parricide and make him a stranger in the realm of 19th-century reason. For Ginzburg, however, historical analysis has to go the other way round. Not the discourse-bound degree of alienation from the social process and the community has to be stressed by the historian, but the retrievable data, the context-bound evidence, the 'traces' or 'facts' which link a man to his culture and his community, and which may explain, not so much the logic of his exclusion by the powerful, but that of the incriminated act itself, which in final analysis is the logic of the whole society made personal. We may add to this picture the contextual logic of the historical documents themselves, brilliantly brought forward by Natalie Zemon Davis in her *Fiction in the archives*.

In this respect there exists a curious incongruity in the evolution of the works of Carlo Ginzburg himself, one of the cultural historians who has most inspired the present-day generation. His former works – such as *The Night Battles* on the Benandanti sect, or the analysis of miller Menocchio's mind – are very much concerned with attribution of meaning. They describe historical and socially differentiated forms of attribution of new meaning to older forms of knowledge or experience. "How does culture work?" was Ginzburg's main question. His last synthesis on the diffusion of the images and legends of the witches' sabbath in Europe, *Storia notturna*, presents itself however as a certain return to formal structures. Though a fresco of tremendous erudition, it shows that in cultural history formal structures alone, and the diffusion paradigm adopted here by Ginzburg cannot account for historical meaning. They do not suffice to write history as a narrative. His central question for this last book seems to have been with what culture works, not in what way it achieves its meaning in given communities. History with the subject left out proves however to be unsatisfactory. In fact it is not history at all.

Ginzburg's comments on Michel Foucault's works may well reflect the attitude of many historians, and explain why finally the method of Foucault's earlier books – the one that established his scholarly reputation – has been hardly ever followed by professional historians. How enthusiastically they may applaud Foucault's contributions to historical debate, how much they may be interested in discourse analysis or narration, very few historians are ready to let themselves be locked up in a closed type of *épistème* or in the analysis of cognitive sediments which involve a philosophical not a historical reason. Whatever their ideological background, their theoretical premisses or their methodological standpoint, their supreme guide is in last analysis the contingency of factual evidence. In the historians' eyes, historical evolution is much less linked up with something within the existing order than due to outer factors or external influences. Their grammar of change does not privilege the syntax of discourse itself but the impact of foreign corpses on the established reality, and the forms of cultural creolisation which may derive from it.

At the same time, however, they ultimately postulate the legibility of the past in continuity with the present – either as a form of *verstehende Geschichte*, empathy, or as a constructed legibility of historical representations (narratives, images, artefacts, configurations, texts, tables or graphs that are immediately legible to us): in both cases the historical *ratio*, the narrative of history-writing, becomes directly understandable. This is not the right place for a discourse on the philosophy of history. Anyway, it is not really the philosophy of history that is at stake, but the cultural construction of the past. As such, the threefold evolution of cultural history, briefly outlined above, has tempered the strategical view of the social evolution which had been suggested by the works of Michel Foucault.

VI. A Contemporary Critic: Michel de Certeau

The most pertinent criticism of Foucault's position in cultural history is certainly due to his contemporary, Michel de Certeau (1925–1986 – Foucault lived from 1926 to 1984). Certeau was a Jesuit theologian, a trained psychoanalyst, and a historian whose research explored the edges of past systems of thought. Just like Foucault, Certeau worked on the margin of the French university with its strong hierarchy of academic power, and his late recognition has at least partially benefitted from his travels overseas. Instead of making disciples in the traditional sense, Certeau created research networks in which he engaged his rich personality.

Certeau does not really question Foucault's central views, since the cultural construction of the past is their common concern, and both refer to a particular relation between the field of practice and the conceptual order. In fact, Certeau has been one of the first close readers of Foucault among the historians, and the one who introduced Foucault into French cultural history (Ahearne, "Feux persistants" 136–138). Very early, Certeau has critically assessed the value of the conceptual analyses in Foucault's *The Order of Things* (Certeau, "Les sciences humaines") and recognized the pertinence of Foucault's image of social discipline (Ahearne, *Certeau* 143–147). Foucault is always in the background of Certeau's theoretical reflections on the historian's practice. For Certeau too, social discipline is not only a theoretical tool that knits cultural conceptions together but really a main representation of cultural agency in the past centuries. However, Foucault's analysis starts from the philosophical order and aims at a constructed and differentiated, but finally coherent global narrative. He retires — as Certeau has put it — to an in-depth analysis when the multifacetted movements at the surface resist him too much (Certeau, "Le noir soleil" 132). For Certeau, historical practice is more than mere cultural analysis, since it is rooted in a social space, a 'scientific' practice (i. e. an operation according to the rules of science), and a narrative. It claims therefore a certain relation to 'reality', its discourse having the ambition to tell a 'truth'.

In Certeau's view, Foucault's research strategy is typically that of a social scientist, much less of an historian. He wants to link things together into one single historical movement, leaving out what does not fit. His final aim is to detect the regularity of history, not its particularities — to quote a central phrase of Michel de Certeau's reflections on the historiographical operation. Cultural history, on the contrary, works with the world as it presents and constructs itself, as a whole. It tries to account for the meaning of everything, which means that it has to start from the whole field of particularities, from the tactics of everyday life. It also means that the relationship between the regularities of history and the particularities, evasive and centrifugal, of the historical reality needs to be continuously kept in mind (Certeau, L'écriture 99; Chartier, "L'histoire" 161).

Historically, the tactics of social discipline does not always achieve the pursued order; it may also prevent or even pervert it. Hence the need for a complementary vision, with additional conceptualizations, for rendering Foucault's insights truly operational in cultural history. In fact, it is above all on the notion of tactics that Foucault and Certeau differ. For Certeau sees tactics not primarily as an operation located within the prevailing power structure or as an instrument of the agencies of control, but as a basic form of human life, the way all people take up reality, including the power structures, or the way they cope with it, transforming it at the same time. Foucault's "microphysics of power" needs, one may say, to be inserted into the microphysics of human agency itself.

VII. The Rise of a Concept: Appropriation

The notion with which Certeau has enriched history-writing is an old word recharged with new meaning and forged into an analytical concept: *appropriation* (Burke, *History* 96–98; Frijhoff, "Toeëigening"). Initially, in all the languages of Western Europe appropriation (*Aneignung, toeëigening*, etc.) referred to taking possession of material goods. In the course of the past three decades 'appropriation' has become a major tool for cultural analysis — to a point that the cultural psychologist Jerome S. Bruner placed it recently in the centre of his theory on

Acts of meaning. The very first article in the very first issue of the new *Journal of Early Modern History* (1997) is precisely on 'the appropriation of culture' in the Mongol Empire. Literary theory and cultural anthropology can be identified as the two main sources for the breakthrough of 'appropriation' as an analytical concept in cultural history. Both the linguistic turn in historical writing and the rise of anthropology as a model for historical analysis account for its success.

In fact, the paradigmatic change of the historical concept of 'culture' itself has to be taken into account as well. The quick though barely perceptible process of widening the concept of culture in the 1960s and 70s, from an esthetical to an essentially anthropological notion (Frijhoff, *Cultuur*), has played a major role here. Michel Foucault certainly was one of the main agents of this conceptual change. He used culture as a society-wide parameter.

In the 1980s, 'appropriation' takes the place of 'acculturation', 'reception', 'consumption' or other traditional, one-way notions of cultural transfer in the work of cultural anthropologists such as Johannes Fabian. Indeed, 'appropriation' is an essential cross-cultural tool. It expresses how cultures or other symbolic systems that are opposed to each other amalgamate or melt together in order to form a entirely new cultural reality. New culture is in its turn deemed to change through amalgamation with other cultural impulses, artefacts or agencies. The important point here is not the exact issue of the process but the two-way approach itself. Appropriation is the way in which the intended receivers – or even the not intended receivers – make things, ideas, symbols their own, through their transformation and their adaptation to the receivers' standards, whatever these may be, and how far they might be removed from the intentions of the sender. The very terms used in this definition show that the concept of 'appropriation' enters into a communication perspective.

Central to the understanding of what has been proposed here is the notion of human agency and a bottom-up view of the historical process. One of the best historical examples of 'appropriation' is Carlo Ginzburg's book on the mental world of the 16th-century miller Menocchio, in which he shows convincingly how culture operates in a given context, both top-down and bottom-up. He analyses the way in which Menocchio deals with his own few readings and with other cultural impulses or forms of knowledge transfer in order to shape his personal interpretation of the universe around him and of human destiny, considered heretical by the Inquisition. But he shows also how the miller reacts upon the disciplinary strategy of the religious authorities who want to bring him back unto the path of orthodoxy. Finally his world picture is built up by the encounter of given forms or traditional artefacts, ideas, symbols, figures, books, made meaningful through the agency of a subject that appropriates them in contact or in conflict with others and makes them part of his personal identity by the attribution of a personal meaning.

The notion of appropriation does not eliminate that of social discipline. On the contrary, the clash between personal appropriation and the intended meanings addressed to or even imposed on the individual by political, religious or cultural authorities is precisely the interface between personal agency and social discipline, between individual tactics and collective strategy. Appropriation makes the strategy understandable – it humanizes the process of cultural transfer and restores to our historical understanding its two-way nature. In this vision, strategies of social discipline are not denied, but their relevance is tempered and their effects are subordinated to the appropriation of discipline by the intended group, and modelled by the superimposition of their own meanings on the ideas or models of behaviour dictated by the powerful.

Clashes between social discipline and individual or collective appropriation of norms find normally their way into the archives of criminal justice, of civil authorities, of the Inquisition, of church reports. People were questioned. Actually, the interrogations to which they were subjected about their deflection from orthodoxy or from the current norms of behaviour constitute a tricky source for the historian. They may be read – and so is common practice – as reflections of a disturbed relationship between the prescribed norm and the practice of life. They form a negative testimony to the observance of the norms. Yet they often conceal that positive part of behaviour which is the personal appropriation of the cluster of values in which the norm is involved. They state clearly what has not been done but most often omit to describe how the conflicting attribution of meaning really was performed outside the framework of prescribed meanings. In short, they are much easier to use for a study of social discipline and its shortcomings than for a bottom-up analysis of culture.

VIII. Strategy and Tactics in History

It is precisely on this point that the research perspective of Michel de Certeau intends to provide the historian with a complementary approach (Ahearne, *Certeau* 121–128). His central concern was to correct by the analysis of human agency the research vision of social discipline. He therefore developed the notion of the 'formality of practice', i. e. the way in which "practices operate on the objective forms of standard cultural or religious representations, and appropriate them in such a way as to transform them" (Ahearne, *Certeau* 48). Certeau has written down his views and made them operational in numerous articles and a few books, the most important one for our theme being the long essay *L'invention du quotidien*, the first part of which, entitled *Arts de faire* has been published in 1980 and translated under the title *The practice of everyday life*. In this study, Certeau describes with much subtility the tactics with which the common man or woman constructs his or her daily life as a meaningful event, linking norms, prescriptions and routines to perceptions of utility, images of power, feeling of well-being and attributions of meaning, in brief through tactics of coping with the power strategies of others. It is precisely this coping tactics, with its everyday competency, but somewhat on the margin of the prescribed order, which forms the quintessence of culture since it is the place of creation (Laermans 53–63; Boureau; Frijhoff, *Wegen*).

In the course of his analysis Certeau enters briefly but incisively in discussion with both Michel Foucault and Pierre Bourdieu. Without in the least denying the value of Foucault's analyses of the strategies of disciplinary procedure, he asks some short questions which in fact reverse the main perspective sketched by Foucault. Certeau assesses the retrospective character of Foucault's analysis: starting from the point of arrival, which is the disciplinary organisation of present-day society, Foucault goes back in history selecting precisely those procedures which have succeeded. But what about those practices which have not been organised into, for instance, a structure of social discipline? Or which have not succeeded in securing for themselves a cultural offspring? Are they simply the rebuke of history? Or do they constitute a cultural reserve from which peculiar configurations of social strategy can emerge using the special organisations of space and speech which Foucault rightly analyses?

What may seem without interest for the philosopher is on the contrary of primary importance for the cultural historian. It is not so much the organising principle of the social strategy that matters to him but the whole field of cultural conditions, opportunities and tactics which determines the range of meanings that can be attributed in the practice of everyday life – but which can also pervade and finally pervert the strategies put forward by the powerful and identified as such by Foucault. In the cultural historian's eyes, Foucault and his followers stop their analysis halfway: instead of scrutinizing, for example, the appropriation of the body by the subjects of history, they concentrate on the semiotics of the power exerted by the disciplining agencies, and ignore the ways in which its reception changes the effectiveness of the power arrangements themselves (List). The same holds for the rituals of punishment: an analysis of their forms of appropriation by the public reveals a much richer semantic field than power relations alone (Lake & Questier). Admittedly, Foucault has made a formidable contribution to cultural history when proving that writing the history of the body is a political act. His representation of the history of the body itself, however, seems far too simplistic.

But what possible creativity may be opposed in everyday life to the big, compelling movements of history? And how exactly do these everyday skills transform the old order when they formalize themselves into new rules for belief, discipline, social order, and life itself? Certeau's essential point is that particular cultural forms, acts or artefacts never have a fixed meaning once for all. Meaning is attributed through the practice of appropriation, either individually or collectively. It is valued and manifests itself formally in relations, rules, and perceptions of self and other.

Even a strict observance of the law is no guarantee whatsoever for an equally strict appropriation. On the contrary, the authorities may be totally mistaken about the sense of such a group observance, when outer obedience is counterbalanced by inner disobedience, as many examples of Nicodemism or group simulation in history have shown – consider, for instance, the way in which the French Huguenots coped during a full century with their repressive state after the Revocation of the Edict of Nantes (1685), not to speak of the English recusants, or the Christians in the Turkish Empire. Considered as such, the distinction between strategies of social discipline and tactics of appropriation is as fundamental for the understanding of the cultural ruptures and intellectual shifts in history as the reconnaissance of the tectonics of the *epistèmes*. The tactics of appropriation provide the proper historical response to the problem of the selection of a range of alternative possible meanings in a given system of classification, which has been "stated in extraordinarely illuminating fashion by Foucault", according to the microhistorian Giovanni Levi ("On microhistory", 103).

Finally, considering Certeau's position with respect to the relation between strategy and tactics, two acceptations of the notion 'appropriation' have to be distinguished. In the first, more traditional acceptation, appropriation itself may be seen as a strategy of cultural dominance resulting in a form of acculturation, as the taking possession of a given set of cultural values by charging them with the system of meanings, the symbolic codes, of the powerful. In the second sense, appropriation is a tactics of coping with reality, a way of cultural survival through a sometimes badly practicable, even frankly hostile social setting. It permits to achieve one's identity in spite of the structures of dominance. In this second sense, appropriation easily becomes a byway, the secret route of a poacher (this is the image used by Certeau himself), always on the edge of some form of perversion of the established order for his personal benefit, well-being or identity. Preferring the margins of the cultural system, this way of appropriation plays with the ambiguities of every form of social strategy, as a way of behaviour selected by others. It is very close to the concept of 'hidden transcripts', developed by J. C. Scott for alternative forms of collective action. Although Certeau's perspective was not at all directed towards minorities in history, one cannot deny that his theories may easily be picked up by victim groups who look for a theory legitimating their social inferiority or their cultural failures. Such a political misuse of his research perspective is however quite contrary to Certeau's own inspiration.

Certeau's bottom-up view of the tactics of appropriation has quickly become a major tool in cultural history. The French historian Roger Chartier made it operational in his seminal 1984 article on culture, entitled "Culture as appropriation", in which he defined culture as a context-oriented operation of appropriation of given sets of social practices (Chartier, "Culture"; Chartier, 1982 version of "Intellectual history", 37). For the historian, historical texts, acts or artefacts are not forcibly what they seem to be. We must deconstruct them in order to discover the sedimented cultural expressions to which they bear testimony, as Foucault has proposed, but we must also check the way they are used in the practice of life in order to discover the meaning with which they are actually charged. Chartier has applied these insights to the history of popular culture, by showing that the presumed 'popular' aspect of culture may be found on the side of the producer as well as on that of the receiver of cultural artefacts. Popular culture may be the 'other' culture perceived by a cultural elite at the opposite side of society, as well as a particular but familiar way of the powerless to appropriate the culture of the powerful other.

In fact, every receiver of culture is a new producer through his attribution of meaning, constitutive of a new cultural setting. This elegant solution of the problem of 'otherness' — the 'other' being a triumphant 'self' — may not conceal that culture in final analysis always remains a question of group policy and group acceptance. It involves the ability to persuade others that one's own attribution of meaning is equally meaningful for the group. Such a persuasion asks for new forms of social strategy. Which brings us back to the beginning of the process and to the tactics of everyday life described by Certeau.

6

Answering Foucault:
Notes on Modes of Order in the Cultural World and the Making of History

MARIO J. VALDÉS

Whatever judgement historians of philosophy may give the often brilliant and always provocative work of Michel Foucault, it is undeniable that his effect on late twentieth-century cultural history has been the equivalent of a major intellectual earthquake that has caused some contemporary cultural historiographical constructs to fracture and sometimes collapse. In this essay I want to describe this effect and subsequently to outline a post Foucault hermeneutics of history and especially of a history of literary culture.

Foucault's writings have consistently challenged established thinking on cultural history. His ideas often changed the ways we think about and write history, but without offering workable alternative historiographic paradigms that could hold up to his own critique. Let me expand on this point. In one of the most brilliant pages of the first volume of *The History of Sexuality 1* Foucault throws down the gauntlet to social historians and those of us who would later venture into cultural history:

> It seems to me that power must be understood in the first instance as the multiplicity of force relations immanent in the sphere in which they operate and which constitute their own organization; as the process which, through ceaseless struggles and confrontations, transforms, strengthens or reverses them; as the support which these force relations find in one another, thus forming a chain or a system, or on the contrary, the disjunctions and contradictions which isolate them from one another; and lastly, as the strategies in which they take effect, whose general design or institutional crystallization is embodied in the state apparatus, in the formulation of the law, in the various social hegemonies (92).

If we accept "force-relations" as an acceptable metaphor for institutional human relations, we must nevertheless question how it is that force-relations constitute their own organization? The metaphor could be expanded with geological terms that would augment the "ceaseless struggles and confrontations," the transformations that strengthen or reverse the formation. But the metaphor risks mystification when Foucault writes that these force-relations find support in one another and form chains or systems or, on the contrary, produce ruptures in the system. My contention is that since we must deal with human agents who participate in the development of state apparatus, the writing of the law and the rise and fall of social hegemonies, how do we examine their work without imposing a normative model of enquiry? In the aftermath to the Foucault phenomenon it has been the task of others to elaborate new directions and I count myself in this group. In responding to Foucault's deconstruction of history, I will draw on the work of philosophers and historians like Jacques Le Goff, Hayden White, David Carr and Paul Ricoeur.

I.

Let us consider the basis of Foucault's historiography. If, as Foucault often claims, historical interpretation of the archive is a violent and, at times, surreptitious appropriation of a system of rules, it has no meaning beyond its internal operations; it is an appropriation in which the historian can and does impose his own sense of direction and, in general, forces upon it a linear causal relationship, that is to say, the historian gives meaning to the past and history is, almost entirely, an ideological construct, one that attempts to perpetrate its domination as an ideological construct until it is displaced by a rival.

Let us hear Foucault on the making of history. I cite from "Nietzsche, Genealogy, History" (1971):

> The historian's history finds its support outside of time and pretends to base its judgments on an apocalyptic objectivity. This is only possible, however, because of its belief in eternal truth, the immortality of the soul, and the nature of consciousness as always identical to itself (152). 'Effective' history differs from traditional history in being without constants. Nothing in man — 'not even his body — is sufficiently stable to serve as the basis for self-recognition or for understanding other men. The traditional devices for constructing a comprehensive view of history and for retracing the past as a patient and continuous development must be systematically dismantled (153). The final trait of effective history is its affirmation of knowledge as perspective. Historians take unusual pains to erase the elements in their work which reveal their grounding in a particular time and place, their preferences in a controversy — the unavoidable obstacles of their passion (156–57).

Foucault never tires of showing the historical narrative to be at best the historian's attempt to analyse the mechanisms of power and reconsider events created by human agents as the immediate subject, but the historical narrative does much more than describe those events, it reconstructs them; in other words, it performs the same creative making of events as performed by the historical agents themselves. The event, therefore, as a temporal node in the past, is beyond apprehension, thus it is that the historian's reconstitution of it replaces the original as history but does not eliminate it as source. The original temporal node remains as an "absence" awaiting still another attempt at constructing a "presence" of the past, which is of course the task of other historians who will reconstitute the event in different ways.

The first of several major problems with Foucault's thinking emerges here. Once we accept my premise that the historical event is constructed and is given meaning through its construction, although not necessarily the same meaning both to the human agents who performed it and to the historian who has reconstituted the event, we must accept the conclusion *that history has meaning because human actions can be meaningful to the agents themselves and to those who observe them* and that these variable meanings are transmitted over the generations of observers of human action who remember, repeat and make history. Yet the Foucault of *La Volonté de Savoir* would have us think of history as a series of discontinuous *epistemes*.

The problem of continuity in historical representation is not unique to Foucault; indeed it is as old as the discipline itself, but it becomes a seriously acute crisis in Foucault's writing because of the radical nature of the disjunctures he postulates. The continuity of meaningfulness for human action is more than a supposition which must stand behind the event, it is also the inner current of history and of the human experience of time itself. Human time is not a mere serial consecution; it is organized into past, present and future and this consciousness of time is only possible because human agents as performers of events are *in* time and their performance as well as the historian's performance of reconstitution are performances of narrativity. To put it somewhat differently, to experience time as past, present or future rather than as a stream of instants in which every one has the same weight or significance as every other, is to experience action as meaningful, that is, human action has meaningfulness because the performers and the observers are *in* time. The entwined nature of human time and narrativity is the keystone to my counter-Foucault or, better, my post-Foucault concept of history. The experience of meaningful action can be represented symbolically in narrative discourse because such discourse is itself a result of the same figurational grasp of events as lives lived and human action consummated as an event.

A second problem that arises from Foucault's view of historical time is the impasse at which one soon arrives in trying to account for the quotidian that underlies the constituted event. If we attempt to work with the force-relations of the cited passage we are very soon confronted with the problem of the ordinary. Human action as purposeful behaviour cannot be merely assumed. How do we contextualize the stories of lives lived, the story of ordinary life, of work, of securing food, of seeking pleasure etc.; the account can only be built up into a functional context for the reconstituted event through empirical research, but in the end the quotidian is also a story on a different temporal scale. Quotidian time underlies the temporality of the event. The struggle through times of hunger or the survival of a severe winter is told on a different temporal scale than the scale of a battle or an election. The temporality of the quotidian is a blind-spot in Foucault's account of cultural history which is, in my view, unavoidable because of his concept of the social appropriation of discourse which is a gaining control of discourse and taking it out of the reach of the majority of the population (*L'ordre du discours* 45 – 7).

Our research has demonstrated that this is an unfounded assumption. There are multiple and differentiated levels of discourse in the social group. The response to Foucault is therefore to examine plural uses of discourse as well as multiple and diverse readings of texts which are not inscribed in the text, but which nevertheless enter the prefigurative. Perhaps the most useful counterpoint to Foucault on this issue is Roger Chartier's "The World Turned Upside-Down" in his *Cultural History* (115 – 26).

A third problem arising from Foucault's challenges is the assumption that the institutional record bespeaks the intellectual motivation behind the social construct. Foucault's concept of episteme ties discourse to a dominant scale of values of a period as if there were a number of specific modes of organizing knowledge. The uses of this organization is identified with the pursuit of domination and the exercise of power. The idea of the episteme has forced us to rethink social history in terms of ideological forces at war with each other for institutional control. But the problem here arises in the very nature of the episteme concept; it appears to be a self-contained zone into which the historian moves in and out of as so many distinct possible worlds. Foucault defined episteme in *The Archaeology of Knowledge* as follows: "The total set of relations that unite, at a given period, the discursive practices that give rise to epistemological figures, sciences, and possibly formalized systems . . . it is the totality of relations that can be discovered, for a given period between the sciences when one analyses them at the level of discursive regularities" (191). The fundamental problem here is that Foucault's inquiring mind can " discover" and move into and out of the episteme; yet we can ask, is this inquiring mind not subject to the episteme of his time and is he not also locked into it? There is of course no archival evidence to support this succession of radical disjunctures. The passage from one episteme to another comes close to the analogy of a sedimentary rock formation of a geological past. Each layer is deposited over the underlying one until the lake dries up. But on close scrutiny we realize that the sedimentary rock analogy is not a particularly apt one because the dynamics of lives lived cannot begin to be taken as a lake bottom with its uninterrupted settling of deposits. We are in need of another metaphor that will stress the open-ended performative nature of human action as lived action, or as reconstituted action, we call history. Perhaps we should turn from the sedimentary rock formation to the ocean's surface variability and its currents of predictability. But Foucault was not only provocative, he was effective and this was so because of an inner logic.

Michel Foucault's historiography, in both its constitution and its operation, is best characterized as an axiomatic system of explanation. Axiomatic systems have a rigorous internal mode of operation. First, there is a selection of statements which are designated as *axioms*; these are inserted into the system without proof. Second, *rules of inference* are laid down which are applied to all operations in the system; third, it is by means of these rules of inference that *derived statements* are deduced according to the axioms. Fourth, at each step of the process of explanation there is a precise specification of which axioms and which rules of derivation are pertinent to the case at hand. The conclusion is that in an axiomatic system the demonstration is completely determined by the axioms and the rules of inference. An axiomatic system like Foucault's is based on two basic operations: *(a)* Both the axioms and the derived statements of explanation belong to an abstract metalanguage, and *(b)* the rules of derivation that make the system work belong to a system's language of internal operations and are strictly heuristic.

For an axiomatic system to be effective it must above all be consistent. This requirement is not only that there be no contradictions, but it must prove that there *can be no contradiction*. This point may perhaps help to explain why Foucault moved from a system of *archaeology* which reinvented the past, to a subsequent system of *genealogy* and its interpretive analysis or, in Foucault's terms, critical history that traced discourse to social sources. The axiomatic injunction of eliminating the possibility of contradiction and proving this to be so could not be met in the earlier system of archaeology for its implicit nihilism would eventually lead it to undermine its own position. Genealogy meets the non-contradiction test better, but there is a second basic requirement of axiomatic systems and that is the requirement of *completeness* and the mutual independence of the axioms that have been established. *A system is called complete if all truth-claims in its field of operation have been derived and can be derived from the axioms. The axioms are considered independent if none of them is derivable from the others.* Foucault's genealogy is an interpretive analytic construct of our current situation which approaches discourses as so many clues of social practices. But Foucault is trapped in his own system. If he goes beyond his axioms he breaks the ring of completeness and if he stays within there is no way to account for the continuity of cultural practices both in stable tradition-bound societies and in revolutionary ones. If, for example, we consider social practices concerning race relations in Western Europe from the sixteenth to the nineteenth century we find economic factors that prompted the slave trade to be conceptualized into wide sweeping generalizations about the inequality of human races by the leading thinkers of eighteenth and nineteenth centuries like Hegel and Ernest Renan, who both held firmly to the superiority of the Indo-European, a term borrowed from linguistics to identify the superior Nordic race.

In order to demonstrate an axiomatic system developed by Foucault, it is instructive for us to consider the course description of Foucault's first year at the Collège de France in 1970–71 ("History of Systems of Thought") as cited by Donald F. Bouchard in *Language, Counter Memory, Practice* (199–204). The course hypothesis on discursive practices announced here is the principal aim argued in *L'Archéologie du savoir* published in 1969 to define a method of historical analysis freed from the anthropological theme.

Axiom one: Foucault argues that *discursive practices are history* and are characterized by: *a) the delimitation of a field of objects, b) the definition of a legitimate perspective for the agent of knowledge,* and *c) the fixing of norms for the elaborating of concepts and theories.* All three, *field of objects, fixing a perspective* and *fixing norms,* are the rules of derivation of the axiom of the *discursive practice as history.* Thus, each discursive practice implies a play of redescription that eventually designates both exclusions and selections.

Axiom two: these discursive regularities cannot be ascribed to specific texts or be identified with individual authors. *Discursive practices* are the ways of producing discourse and practices are thus *embodied in technical processes of production,* in institutions of governance, in the perceived patterns for general behaviour, in the forms of transmission and diffusion of discourse and finally in the pedagogical forms which both impose and maintain these practices. There is implicit in this axiom a logical doublet, i. e., that man is both the object and subject of knowledge, cf. *The Order of Things,* (309). These embodiments are the rules of derivation for the axiom of discursive regularities as the common ground of the social group.

Axiom three: Discursive practices possess specific modes of transformation. These transformations are not attributable to precise and individual positions taken on issues of the day. On the contrary, we cannot discern or characterize transformations of discursive practices as a change of outlook, state of mind, or attitude. The transformation of a discursive practice is linked to a range of modifications that come together *within* a discursive practice, *outside* its domain or *alongside* it in another discursive practice. Transformation is linked to these modifications not as linear cause and effect, but as a cause that remains a cause oblivious to any and all effects left in its wake, and effects that retain their identity, autonomy and full range of functions in relation to that which caused them. Thus, the rules of derivation here constitute Foucault's methodology for critical history which designates a will to knowledge that is anonymous, polymorphous, always susceptible to transformation and determined by the play of identifiable dependencies that the Foucault-inspired genealogist must follow as the detective follows clues and traces in what is purported to be a search into the social make-up of the will to power, but which, whether acknowledged or not, is primarily an inquiry *into the detective himself,* his sense of purpose, his constitution of self.

Foucault ends the course description with a quasi-admission of having entered a "cul-de-sac": "We are faced with the unavoidable fact that the tools that permit the analysis of the will to knowledge must be constructed and defined as we proceed, according to the needs and possibilities that arise from a series of concrete studies." This statement comes as close as is possible to movement from an axiomatic system to a dialectical hermeneutics which always responds to the problems of concrete studies rather than attempting to engage these problems through a series of a priori axioms. This closing statement, I contend, anticipates the fuller disclosure he makes in *The Use of Pleasure* (1984) where he states: "Considered from the standpoint of their [historical studies] pragmatics, they are the record of a long and tentative exercise that needed to be revised and corrected again and again" (9). In order to sum up this axiomatic system of historical study, I would say that the only interpretive propositions about the past that can be verified, which is to say proved true, are those concerned with closed systems which are themselves constructs. The performance of the event as well as the historian's performance of reconstitution are natural systems and are therefore open. Our knowledge of them is partial and, at best, approximate. Foucault worked his way through at least two major closed systems and would have undoubtedly developed another had he lived longer, but at each step of the way he made us rethink how we make history.

II.

If we accept Foucault's challenge as I outlined in the quote from *The History of Sexuality*, we must rethink historiography in terms of an open system. The idea of a historical memory of the quotidian must be dialectically countered with the idea of the specific action of performance that constitutes an event. An open hermeneutics of history joins together performance and memory and thereby displays the dialectic of human experience with its abstractions taken from the movement to and fro between the sense of tradition and the discrete event. This dialectic is an open system, a constant mode of contemporary redefinition and re-situation. The hermeneutic reinterpretation of the past can lead to opening up forgotten possibilities or reviving abandoned potentialities from the past that were left out because of the historical paradigm of selection that had governed historical writing. Furthermore, the making of new historical meaning for the past liberates the present as a history yet to be made.

Let us make no mistake about it, there are also rules in the development of an open system. A *system* is any conglomerate of interaction that can be discerned and an *open system* is one that cannot be predicted in terms of its directions and alterations. History as an open system extends beyond human agents and the events resulting from interaction. In history, as an open system, not only does the relationship to the natural world have to be considered, but also the historian's own role as the mediator between human agents, events, and the forces of the material world.

I would now like to turn to a brief consideration of the problems in literary history. I do not intend to disparage the procedures of literary history as we know it today nor to minimize some undeniably great achievements of scholars like Pedro Henríquez Ureña or Ernst Curtius. My purpose in responding to Foucault is to rethink the way we write literary history and to propose alternatives. Let us consider the idea of tradition in literary history. David Perkins sums it up well:

> Wordsworth's view of tradition and its function is shared by many literary historians, and it is explicitly set forth and defended by Hans-Georg Gadamer in *Truth and Method*. It applies, *mutis mutandi*, not only to national traditions but to those that form the consciousness of any social group. In this view, a history of literature, whether it be the literature of a nation, class, region, race of gender, would help instruct us who we are individually and as a community. It displays the tradition in which we stand whether we will or no, for this tradition has formed us (180–181).

Literary history stands astride intellectual history and cultural history, since literature embodies ideas but also represents communities; there is however the further consideration, often overlooked in literary histories of the past, that literature, its production and reception, also interacts with the conditions of life in communities where it is produced and received and, especially, with those that are represented. The social effect of the poetic imagination can be considered a *random event* but not one of chance, and this is so because a chance occurrence is a variable that can assume any number of values. Literary input is unpredictable for it is, above all, an imaginative provocation. But poetic expression and its reception are events, and the poetic imagination builds on temporally marked usage for both the poet and the reader. The social consequence of the poetic imagination may more properly be called a random event since it is a complex fluctuating phenomena determined by time and circumstance and this is so for both producers and receivers.

Contrary to both Foucault's disjunctive series of epistemes or David Perkins' sense of tradition, I propose that we consider literary history to be analogous to a non-linear equation insofar as it characterizes phenomena for which mutually related properties do not vary proportionally. A priori selections in the mode of canonical chronologies cannot be superimposed on the historical record. The impasse of literary history that confronts us has been in part brought about by an inability to examine the literary phenomena as one that changes with time. Literature is a dynamic system and literary history has been a fixed one. A literary text is a changing source of commentary and ideas in time and space; therefore, its representation in a fixed system will necessarily be a deformation and, at best, a limited abstraction. When one multiplies the number of literary texts and the wide range of contextual space in which they operate, David Perkins' open question, "Is literary history possible?" takes on new significance. A Foucault-inspired approach to literary history is attractive in its initial stress on the contextualization of the will to knowledge, but in the longer view it becomes a negative sense of order since it turns the consideration of the transmission and reappropriation of literary texts into a series of beginnings. If, however, contrary to Foucault's genealogy, we consider literature to be in a spiral of time in which each reading pulls together a configuration of poetic sense from the multiple variables possible, we have passed the threshold of static signification into dynamic open systems.

Literary history cannot be merely deconstructive of past authority or reconstructive of an ideological paradigm of the present. The hermeneutic foundation of literary history is both interactive with the assemblage of constituted events of the past and dialogically engaged in the present. In effect, the literary history we propose is a dialectic of two historicities – the constituted past event and the historian's performance that has reconstituted the event, and a second dialectic engagement with other historians, past, present and future. Thus, we can propose that historical truth should not be made relative to the knowing subject, but rather to the intersubjective status of the discussion which can be reopened for consideration at any time.

Literary texts acquire meaning in a social, historical context of both production and reception. Consequently, literary history can be the study of the rise and fall of diverse discursive contexts in which literature has been produced and reproduced. In so doing, we can trace the discursive elements from the past that have been carried by literary texts from one context to another. Foucault, building on Heidegger and Wittgenstein, stressed the commonality of language to shift the consideration of discourse as social environment, from the individual perspective to the general condition of the will to knowledge, that is, the epistemic. But if our primary historical concern is to account for the fact that the contextualized literary text is a self-generating source of imaginative power in the community of reception, we must move beyond Foucault and turn to other forms of historical writing.

A response to Michel Foucault that is worthy of him must be an alternative to his sense of critical history. In my case it will be one that is a focused history of literary culture. The philosophical basis for my open literary history is Paul Ricoeur's conceptual framework for linguistic interaction: the cyclical spiral of prefiguration, configuration and refiguration.

III. A Theory of Literary History

1. Defining the Terms

The *Prefigurative dimension* is the proto-historical reservoir of communal memory; it changes but at a pace that is generational rather than individual and its archive, which once was limited to human memory, is today expanded through mechanical records of sight and sound to more than a century of direct access and several thousand years of indirect access through the written record.

The Configurative dimension is the ontological point of entry. It is the reader's (or listener's) encounter with otherness through participation in the creative event of representation by reading or auditive presence. It is at this juncture of the experience of alterity that there is communication at different levels of immediacy. The reader of the novel, the spectator of a film, the audience at a poetry reading, all engage in the act of configuration as they respond to and make sense of the textual provocations and injunctions.

The Refigurative dimension is the reflective process which ensues from the configuration of the author's text. The reflective process can be relatively private receptivity or it can be public as is the case with the drama critic. In any case the reflective process is a means of self-understanding of what has been experienced as well as an explanation to others through a shared discourse about the originary experience. The refiguration of human textual interaction moves into the prefigurational dimension to the extent that the reflective response is shared with others.

In mapping the dynamic systems of configuration and refiguration as parts of a larger system of communication that transcends limitations of time and space, we must keep in mind that the configurative and refigurative dimensions interact not only among themselves, but also with the system as a whole which in turn affects and makes possible communicative exchange. The common linguistic and social values shared by the community in all of its multiple expressions constitutes the system as a whole. Thus, we can say that whatever gain is achieved in configuration, and is shared in refiguration, is only possible because of the system as a whole.

In an open literary history we will aim at contextualizing both the event of composition, and the performance of criticism and history about the event.

2. Historical Paradigm

An open literary history is a history of the related events of composition and recomposition of those texts that have the capacity to provoke reflection and engender a redescription of the rich diversity of life as we encounter it. Three initial questions are asked as we look at the literary event: where did it take place?; why did it take place in this site? and, how did it take place? Our task is to build up the documentary means to make accessible the configurative encounter as the primary historical event and the refigurative development as the secondary historical event. Obviously the prefigurative repertoire is what makes these connections possible. The prefigurative is contextualized lived language or, in other words, in our argument, literary history is about to join forces with the social sciences.

By putting literary history into direct contact with the social sciences — geography, demography, political economy, linguistics, anthropology, and sociology — open literary history aims to do more than seek the enrichment of multiple perspectives. Each of these highly developed disciplines cannot simply be ransacked for ideas; each has its own premises and methods. No single writer would obviously be capable of mastering all these disciplines, but as a group, the Latin American scholars who are working with me on a comparative literary history of Latin America have accepted the challenge and the responsibility of entering into dialogue with these fields in order to enlarge, synergetically, the frame of intellectual possibilities. Resisting the lure of what Braudel (and Michelet before him) called "total history," this literary history seeks to open up the disciplinary base of literary studies to the different interests of the social sciences and the other humanities. The aim is multiplicity, not totality — perspectival insight, not empyrean oversight similar to Foucault's sense of history but with the crucial difference that the present is always dialectically part of the past that is examined. We therefore account for both continuity and change.

As a comparative history of literary culture, this project will examine the empirical or material framework, of territories, peoples, languages, and their institutions, as well as their urban centers as places of the production and reception of various literary cultures. Societies produce space as "territory," as a manifestation of culture. In seeking to map such territory, the team is aware of the less than innocent nature of cartography and, indeed, of geography. Mapping has always been a way to make something exist for imperial eyes. And, geography has been called "the imposition of knowledge on experience in a specified landscape." Yet, mapping centers can tell us much about the important questions of access to literature and about the relation of cultural to economic power. Cities exist as expressions of cultural aspirations and values, but in complex ways. In examining the past of a literary culture from these multiple perspectives, this team of literary historians could well be faced with considerations of data and paradigms that have received scant attention in literary history before, whether in its national or comparative form.

Some might fear that, as a result of this broader focus on cultural formations and dynamic cultural processes, the more familiar literary historical narrative of authors and literary works might become a general history of all who write or are written about, or all who read and are read about — without giving due attention to those significant works of literature that are felt to make up a cultural identity. But, as the tentative table of contents reproduced here in the appendix will show, such is not the result of a historiographic interest in the long-term mapping of the past and present of literary culture. The framework of empirical data and the conceptual mapping that this history employs will contextualize those important works, but it will also, and most significantly, reveal the lines of development, the perceiving of highlights and surprising repetitions which are evidence of a living, shared heritage that is usually hidden behind the debris of yesterday's fashion. What these methodological procedures aim to do, then, is to reveal what is held in common as well as what is not, and thus to offer the reader various ways into the record of the lived time and space of literary culture. There can be no literary history in the momentary instants of lived experience; in that sense, for the literary historian, there is only what Fernand Braudel called the "longue durée."

In historical terms, the history of Latin America I will describe deals with an extended period of time (more than five centuries), a specific geographical area, as well as the diverse peoples who share the land, their institutions and communities. These are the dimensions of time and space that determine the history of this literary culture, but from these have been drawn multiple comparisons among ideas, images, textual forms and, of course, the representations of humanity that Latin Americans have produced. These comparisons operate across time and space, illuminating continuities, trends, repetitions, and differences, while functioning like a retrospective probe into the processes of individual and collective self-creation. This is how the dialectic of literary imagination as human habitat and as narrative constellation emerges; a comparative literary history can, therefore, bring together different responses to similar conditions of existence and shared human aspirations. The present endeavor in literary history aims to represent the literary cultures of the diverse peoples who have lived on this continent, but, at the same time, I am well aware that our history "will stand for" a culture and indeed for an identity. The refigurative dialectic between "representation", that is our purpose, and "standing for", that may be our fate, is a powerful destabilizing force which situates us in an endless rectification of our configurations. This dialectic process of literary history has the possibility of giving us a better idea of the prefigurative past as an inexhaustible resource.

In the specific case of Latin America, the history will explore the literary culture of the diverse peoples who share this particular territorial space by asking questions derived from an interdisciplinary perspective. These are questions about the contextual specificities of that common environment that can then be brought to bear on the historical record of a literary culture, which (as with all cultures) is always in process. This approach, however, obviously depends on the extraordinary good will and collaboration of colleagues from many disciplines, and the generous pooling of accumulated knowledge gathered by these individual scholars who, though expert in a particular area, have agreed to think comparatively, across the boundaries of their expertise and, specialty, to seek common ground. So, while the three volumes may at times appear to cover some of the same material as other literary histories in the past, they will do so from very different perspectives and will, therefore, ask very different questions.

And, while some of the collaborators on this team may well focus on the same institutions, works, or authors, the concerns and issues brought to bear on these materials are obviously going to be quite different. In a problematic-based approach like this, as opposed to a chronological or thematic one, the results invariably reflect the questions asked and the problems foregrounded. Thus, an internal dialectic of the comparative perspective among the various parts of this history will be a significant dimension of such a collaborative effort.

Part of what differentiates this undertaking from previous efforts, then, is the fact that this historiographic model brings about a constant playing of the documentary evidence of a distant cultural past against the ideas of only yesterday; it postulates past significance but as a made-in-the-present meaning. Obviously, if the literary past is cut off from the present, there can be no historical perspective; likewise, what has come between the past text and its present readers cannot be ignored. In a history of literary culture, there must be a recounting of constant themes, of means of emplotment, of the repetition of ideas and images but not as an aggregate that segregates literature into desultory fragments of life; this bifurcation of life and literature is not only a falsification of the past but an impoverishment of the present. As Ricoeur has observed, "the past separated from the dialectic of future, past and present remains an abstraction" (*Time and Narrative*, 156).

A not uncommon illusion of static literary history is the notion that the "classics" of literature are works of genius that exist beyond time and rise above lived life to the point of separating authors from their community. Such an illusion overlooks the fact that a work of literature consists of language that, despite being deployed through the practices of literary convention, is, in the end, derived from daily life usage; likewise, literary culture is perpetuated in turn by the reabsorption of its discourse into the language of everyday life. Disregard of this mutual interchange has led to a separation of literature and popular culture that the work of Dante, Cervantes, Milton, Joyce, Borges, or Neruda would belie. It is in part this inseparability of literature from the realities of its (and our) culture that drives this project's desire to contextualize the works of the past as part of life — then and now. To this end, the literatures (in the plural) examined in this history include literatures both elite and popular, both oral/performative and written, both canonical and historically ignored. The term "literatures," in other words, means figurative verbal discourse. Let us recall here that is was Foucault in *The Archaeology of Knowledge* who first confronted us with the opposition between continuity as personified by individual or community memory and the specificity of the historical document; he writes: "The document is not the fortunate tool of a history that is primarily and fundamentally memory; history is one way in which a society recognizes and develops a mass of documentation with which it is inextricably linked" (7). Foucault's point is as valid for literary history as it is for social or political history. However, with

Ricoeur, we must say that the discontinuity of documentary history far from getting rid of collective memory contributes to its expansion and enrichment by imposing the criticism of specific texts. Le Goff commenting on Foucault's views adds the following observation which is directly applicable to our undertaking:

> The documentary revolution tends to promote a new unit of information. Instead of the fact that leads to the event and to a linear history, to a progressive memory, the privileged position passes to the datum, which leads to the series and to a discontinuous history. Collective memory reevaluates itself, organizing itself into a cultural patrimony. The new document is stored in data bases and dealt with by means of such structures. A new discipline has arisen, one that is still taking its first steps, and that must respond in contemporary terms to the requirement for calculations as well as the constantly increasing criticism of its influence on our collective memory (42, trans. mine)

Although Le Goff wrote these remarks twenty years ago and he was not at all concerned with literary history they are profoundly relevant to our work and the present history of comparative literary history.

IV. From Theory to Practice

In a number of ways, the literary history of Latin America is a history of pluralities joined together under the perennially contested designation of "Latin America." It will not be a straightforward record of books and authors from a determined place; it will offer a provisional dialectic grid of perspectives to challenge the "epistemological privilege of evidence." These will often be presented in the interrogative form. Thus, among the new questions the history seeks to address are: Why a plurality of literatures? What are the parameters of Latin America as spatial and as human geography? What is meant by a cultural formation and, most pertinent to the case, why should the pursuit of literary history entertain such notions as cultural formations? The idea is to construct a history without closure, one that can be entered through many points and can unfold through many coherent, informed, and focused narrative lines. This will be a history of hundreds of communities linked by language, history, or economic patterns. The material conditions of these communities will serve as the mapped background against which to examine the institutions and the literary culture they share. The value of cultural artifacts such as literature lies, in part, in the ways these artifacts are held in common — in other words, their exchange value, the measure of their use. A poem can become a song which can eventually become an identity marker for a community — without there being anything bought or sold. So the material value of literature as commodity, as market product, is relative and even, in absolute terms, perhaps rather insignificant.

The comparative history of cultural formations that I am describing involves first and foremost a conceptual break with the Latin American literary histories of the past. It recognizes, for example, a number of central problematics that have previously been downplayed or ignored. For instance, the Spanish and Portuguese sectors of the continent have experienced parallel (yet, differing) cultural development in terms of their European ties: for both, the links were more with Paris than with either Lisbon or Madrid. Or, to take another example, this time from the economic side, Latin America's participation in the world marketplace has been one of commodity boom and bust periods (of coffee, sugar cane, rubber, copper, bananas, precious metals and, today, cocaine) that have their parallel in the realm of cultural commodities in the Latin American novel of the suggestively-named "boom" period of the 1960s and 1970s, and the "magical realisms" of the continent's imaginative products (whether fiction or film), that have been exoticized and commodified by the academic and publishing centers of the Anglo-American and European metropolitan markets. Beyond the acknowledged complex reality of a continent whose wealth, for the most part, is not shared amongst the population, there is also a largely unrecorded history of cultural formations that have generated *transnational* zones of cultural interaction, and these will provide the major focus of historical investigation. The transnational, however, is not here a simple synonym for the regional — with its frequent associations of ethnic purity and cultural authenticity. It is, instead, in Latin America, the human, geographical and demographical realm of the multi-ethnic and the multi-racial.

To say that Latin America is the creation of the peoples who inhabit it would be a problematic assertion, since the continent's culture and cartography have both been created in reaction to outside pressures and engendered in proactive as well as reactive ways. An arbitrary (and not a natural) entity, so named by the French for imperial purposes, Latin America is a discursive construct: it is contingent, heterogeneous, dynamic. Its different areas have different colonial histories, different creolization, different relations to modernity — and postmodernity. Figuratively and literally, the ground beneath the cultural construct called Latin America is, by definition, unstable; the processes of historical formation in the past have often been disrupted by small and large cataclysmic upheavals such as the Mexican Revolution of 1910, the wars of independence that swept Spanish America a century before, or the turbulent effects of changes in power in the Caribbean in the eighteenth century — to say nothing, of course, of the conquest itself. Its history has been punctuated with externally induced and internally self-inflicted turmoil that continues to alter the shape of the hemisphere's culture as much as the natural disasters of geological shifts alter its topography.

The cultural self-expression of peoples — speaking Amerindian languages, Spanish or Portuguese — must be read in this context today: such is the premise of this history. The specific texts designated at various times as literature are manifestations of this continuous process by which people recognize themselves, their shared myths, visions, ideals, as well as respond to the abuse of power in the relentless drive for wealth or political dominance. Therefore, Latin American literature will not be approached only through the individuated discourse of even its most well-known writers; instead, the focus will be on the situating of (plural) literatures in broader historical and cultural contexts. The obvious challenge is to write a history of cultural formations as a collaborative project, being faithful to the situational diversity of the contexts of both the literature and the scholars writing about it, while still maintaining a necessary consistency of focus.

Latin American Literary Cultures: A History of Cultural Formations will be divided into three structurally interdependent volumes entitled *Configurations of Literary Culture in Latin America, Institutional Modes and Cultural Modalities of Literature in Latin America,* and *Latin American Literature: Subject to History.* Rather than offering a mere chronological sequencing of information, the historiographical method deployed will at every step attempt to map out the material ground, examine the cultural/institutional formations that have direct bearing on literary production and its dissemination, and offer a self-consciously constructed, historical narrative situated within the framework of that cultural context. This should allow the reader to witness a complex network of cultural development over time.

Each collaborating scholar enters the project as an individual drawing on her or his expertise to narrate an account of specific aspects taken from a discrete number of texts, but this is merely the point of entry. The work is then passed on to the other members of the team who are working on the same subsection each adding another narrative layer until there is a complex integrated account of the issues of cultural formation under scrutiny. By means of the collaborative work of complementary perspectives we aim to both produce a narrative account and maintain an openness to its configuration. For example, let us ask the question of how a literary culture was produced in the sixteenth century in that part of the world we now call Latin America. The question has an initial response that demands a number of secondary questions. Literary culture is produced in urban centers, and a number were established in the continent, some on top of conquered urban centers notably in Mexico City and Lima. Others, like Quito and Bogotá, were established for strategic reasons of wealth and control. The subsequent questions continue the inquiry in terms of human geography, demography, economics, historical linguistics and sociology, but in all of these approaches the issue remains the development of literary cultures.

If we recall Ricoeur's paradigm we can recognize that configuration is the individual scholar's point of entry, refiguration is the collaborative refashioning of the initial interpretation, and prefiguration is the source of all the figuration in the archive of lives lived and stories told. At this point let me call Foucault back to the discussion, for he has one of the most remarkable descriptions of the prefigurative basis of the literary culture. He writes in *The Archaeology of Knowledge*:

> This repeatable materiality that characterizes the enunciative function reveals the statement as a specific and paradoxical object, but also as one of those objects that men produce, manipulate, use, transform, exchange, combine, decompose and recompose, and possibly destroy. Instead of being something said once and for all — and lost in the past like the result of a battle, a geological catastrophe, or the death of a king — the statement as it emerges in its materiality appears with a status, enters various networks and various fields of use, is subjected to transference or modifications, is integrated into operation and strategies in which its identity is maintained or effaced. Thus the statement circulates, is used, disappears, allows or prevents the realization of a desire, serves or resists various interests, participates in challenge and struggle, and becomes a theme of appropriation or rivalry (105).

The first volume of this history of literary cultures establishes the parameters — geographic, linguistic, and social — of the field of action. The second volume concentrates on cultural modalities, discursive modes, institutional sanctions, and the geographical centers that both attract and irradiate the writers and their works throughout wider and wider circles of distribution and influence. These centers make up the constellation of major and lesser concentrations of literary activity which are linked not only to each other but also to expatriate centers in places such as Paris and New York. The third volume focuses on modes of representation and the resultant narrative web that connects the cultural centers with each other and with European and (English-speaking) North American centers. These collective threads construct the fabric of the shared culture and identify the key role of certain individual writers whose works have become major cultural forces.

Authors such as Sor Juana, Rubén Darío, Pablo Neruda, Jorge Luis Borges, or Gabriel García Márquez, whose writings have been translated and transmitted far beyond their place of origin, become the major indicators of the cultural reality of Latin America. But when taken out of that local context, they create yet another Latin America which exists elsewhere — in the fabulations created by cultural distance. Like the first two, the third volume has its own specific structure and logic. The first section approaches Latin American literary history through specific complementary voices of the conquered and the conquerors that permit the building of a Latin American perspective on literary culture that hopes to resist localisms and regionalisms. The second section narrates the history of cultural encounters: these are tales of syncretism, hybridity, and adaptation. The central focus is on the specificities of the phenomenon of transculturation as it pertains to the special cases within Latin America. Finally, in the third section, the self-reflexive focus is on this, our century as the temporal moment from which the entire history is being configured and narrated.

In closing I want to recognize that the radical rethinking of literary history that I have sketched out begins with Foucault's challenge to the pious claims of objective history. The significant role that literary history has played in developing the ideology of nation has gone hand in hand with a system of exclusions and marginalizations of sectors of the community from cultural participation. These exclusions from literary history were determined on the basis of race, ethnic background, gender, sexual orientation, social class, ideology and languages other than the official language. These exclusions have long been accepted as normal discrimination of inferior cultural expression without recognizing that the norm was nothing more than the exercise of power. It is evident that we have questioned this construct and rejected the fun-house mirror of literature because Foucault made us look at cultural practice rather than its distorted reflection.

APPENDIX

LATIN AMERICAN LITERARY CULTURES:
A COMPARATIVE HISTORY OF CULTURAL FORMATIONS

VOLUME ONE: Configurations of Literary Culture in Latin America

1.   Material Framework: Parameters of Literary Culture
     1.1   Geographic factors and the formation of cultural terrain for literary production
     1.2   Demographics and the formation of cultural centers
     1.3   Socioeconomic factors in the production of cultural discourses
     1.4   Access and participation in the literary cultures of Latin America
     1.5   The linguistic diversity of Latin American literatures

2.   Ideological Framework: On the Margins of Literary History
     2.1   Configurations of racial and ethnic alterity in literary history
     2.2   Issues of gender and sexual orientation in the historical formation of the cultural imaginary
     2.3   Cultural constructions of poverty in literary history
     2.4   Exile, censorship and the formation of the historical archive
     2.5   Linguistic exclusion

3.   Quotidian Framework: Discursive Plurality of Latin American Culture
     3.1   Religious, scientific, and political discourses
     3.2   Orality and literature
     3.3   Theatrical discourses: the appropriation of codes
     3.4   Transformations in popular culture
     3.5   Cinema: cultural dialogue and the processes of Modernity

VOLUME TWO: Institutional Modes and Cultural Modalities in Latin America

1. Cultural Institutions: Social Structures
    1.1 History of the book, its production and imports in Latin America
    1.2 Patronage, censorship, and state institutions
    1.3 Schools, colleges, universities, museums, cultural associations, libraries and academies
    1.4 Media literary criticism: cultural journalism
    1.5 Translation as cultural institution

2. Textual Models and their Transformations in Latin America: Cultural Hybridity
    2.1 Novel and journalism: Strategic interchanges
    2.2 The performance of poetry: Public and private vocations
    2.3 Topography of narratives and the novelistic imagination
    2.4 The testimonial as genre and cultural chronicle
    2.5 Spaces of the essay: Schooling the national self

3. The Cultural Centers of Latin America
    3.1 Northern Mexico and the northern borderland (includes Mexico and U. S. A.)
    3.2 Mesoamerica (includes Mexico and Central America)
    3.3 The Caribbean and the Caribbean basin (includes Colombia, Cuba, Puerto Rico, Dominican Republic, Venezuela)
    3.4 Andean America (includes Bolivia, Chile, Colombia, Ecuador, Peru, Venezuela)
    3.5 Amazonian America and Amazonian borderland (includes Bolivia, Brazil, Colombia, Guyanas, Peru, Venezuela)
    3.6 Eastern Brazil (includes Northeast and Southeast)
    3.7 Rio de la Plata, the Pampas and southern borderlands (includes Argentina, Brazil, Paraguay, Uruguay)
    3.8 Southern Cone (includes Argentina, Chile)
    3.9 Latin American culture in New York
    3.10 Latin American culture in Paris

VOLUME THREE: Latin American Literature: Subject to History

1. Sites of Representation in the Literary Culture of Latin America: Foundations and Losses (16th – 18th centuries)
    1.1 Epic voices: Encounters and foundations
    1.2 The discourse of melancholy: A culture of loss
    1.3 Narratives of legitimation, the discourse of hegemony and the hermeneutics of globalization
    1.4 National installments: The Erotics of modernity

2. Transculturation and State Discourse
    2.1 Lettered Mediations
    2.2 Peoples, Communities and Nation Building
    2.3 The Inversion of Social Darwinism
    2.4 Modernization and the Formation of Cultural Identities
    2.5 The Crisis of Transculturation
3. The Literary Culture of Latin America in the Twentieth Century
    3.1 Presence of Amerindian literary cultures
    3.2 Latino literary culture in the United States
    3.3 Immigrations, exile and displacements
    3.4 Modernity, modernisms and their (Post-) avatars
    3.5 Ideologies and the imaginary

[Working plan May 25, 1997]

7

Foucault's Shells, Freud's Symptoms:
Towards a Psychoanalytic Conception of Cultural History

SARAH ROFF

I.

To move beyond Foucault, cultural history needs not so much to abandon what he wrote as to break with the interpretive paradigms that have been established by institutional Foucauldianism. This means seeking out opportunities missed or overlooked in the reception of his work. One of the richest of these is his inaugural dissertation, *Folie et déraison. Histoire de la folie à l'âge classique.*

Foucault's own objections to the work's metaphysical concept of discourse have encouraged his followers to dismiss it out of hand. Hubert L. Dreyfus and Paul Rabinow, for instance, protest *Folie et déraison*'s "flirtation with hermeneutic depth," remarking that the work "would have been strengthened by eliminating the recourse to ontology," an assessment that echoes Foucault's 1967 observation that, in order to avoid the kind of institutional history previously dominant in the history of science, he had "accorded far too great a place, and a very enigmatic one too, to what [he] called an 'experiment,' thus showing to what extent one was still close to admitting an anonymous and general subject of history" (Dreyfus and Rabinow 12; Foucault, *Archeology* 16).[1]

In fact, it is precisely because *Folie et déraison* forces us to confront the conditions of possibility of the collective historical subject, a problem it is currently more fashionable to ignore, that this book has so much to offer cultural history, particularly any psychoanalytically-oriented cultural history.[2]

Although Maurice Blanchot remarks that "Foucault, who was never fascinated by psychoanalysis, is even less prepared to take into account a collective

---

[1] Dreyfus and Rabinow are heavily influenced by Foucault's own critique of *Folie et déraison* in *The Archeology of Knowledge*. The same is true of Blanchot, who sometimes imbeds entire passages from the latter into his essay. Foucault's own assessment of his dissertation evolves in the course of his career, however, most notably in his 1972 response to Derrida, "My Body, This Paper, This Fire."

[2] On *Folie et déraison*'s complex publishing history, see Gordon. Throughout, we will refer to Foucault's dissertation by the original title rather than *Histoire de la folie*, the title the author himself gave the work in the 1963 abridgment (and which has since become standard). Citations are, however, from the English translation.

unconscious" (Blanchot 73), the recognition that Foucault's distaste for Freud masked a complex relation to psychoanalysis has played a prominent role in recent reassessments of his work. In a recent paper, Jacques-Alain Miller argues that whereas *The History of Sexuality* "exposes" psychoanalysis in the larger episteme Foucault terms "the apparatus of sexuality," an earlier work such as *The Order of Things* "is entirely and explicitly ordered around psychoanalysis" (Miller 58). Psychoanalysis, for Miller, is in the one instance "the object of inquiry," in the other "the guiding principle," a relation he characterizes as "symmetrical and inverse." He thus discerns "a shift in Foucault's work between 1966 and 1976," suggesting:

> Tomorrow, or the day after tomorrow, when the fundamental layout of knowledge has been changed, perhaps this shift [...] will appear to the future archeologist as the privileged indicator of the moment when the practice of psychoanalysis fell definitely into disuse. (Miller 58)

The shift from Foucault's use to abuse of psychoanalysis retroactively marks the rupture of the entire knowledge system to which it belongs. Since psychoanalysis always forecasts its own end, a dispassion in which it takes some pride, the prediction only draws Foucault's exposé of psychoanalysis further into its orbit. It is not the end of psychoanalysis that Foucault's work announces, but the "end of the cure."

A recent essay by Jacques Derrida similarly characterizes psychoanalysis as the "hinge" around which *Folie et déraison* turns (Derrida, Freud 234).[3] While the book concludes with a famous denunciation of psychoanalysis as a renewal rather than a repudiation of nineteenth-century psychiatry, Foucault portrays Freud as the evil genius, the figure of madness' eternal return he accuses Derrida of neutralizing in his response to the latter's 1964 critique. For Foucault, psychoanalysis performs a "genial short-circuit" of the structures of nineteenth-century psychiatry onto the person of the analyst (Derrida 248). Concerned to establish Foucault's "debt" to Freud, Derrida demonstrates how the cure can never end on account of psychoanalysis' "perpetual threat," which interrupts the logic of Foucault's foreclosure. Psychoanalysis is interminable. The source of its own resistance, it keeps coming back.

Foucault himself gives an intimation of the formative role of psychoanalysis in *Folie et déraison* in his 1967 auto-critique, remarking that he is

> no longer trying to reconstitute what madness itself might be, in the form in which it first presented itself [...] [or] in the form in which it was later organized ([...] *perhaps even repressed*) by discourses, and the oblique, often twisted play of their operations. (*Archeology* 47; italics mine)

---

[3] Derrida also points out the objectification to which Miller alludes: "Foucault regularly attempts to objectify psychoanalysis and to reduce it to that of which he speaks rather than to that from out of which he speaks" (Derrida 232, 242). He similarly sees "the project of this book" poised at the end of the cure: it "does and does not belong to the age of psychoanalysis: it already belongs to it and already no longer belongs to it" (251).

Echoing Derrida's 1964 critique of *Folie et déraison*'s pathos of silence, Foucault condemns his dissertation for its naive conception of signification, in which discourse is reduced to a distortionary operation. Rather than "twisting" and thus "organizing" its antecedent, madness, discursive practice should be liberated from any desire to "pierce through its density [...] to reach what remains silently anterior to it," allowing it to "emerge [instead] in its own complexity," embracing the self-enclosure of the empty signifier (Derrida, "Cogito" 37; Foucault, *Archeology* 47). The name Foucault gives to the model of signification he rejects is *repression*.[4]

As it turns out, it is psychoanalysis which reminds us of the merits of Foucault's early work, for *Folie et déraison* makes use of the concept of repression in a manner that is far more subtle than Foucault's account here allows. Although critics of *Folie et déraison* (both the Foucauldian and the non-Foucauldian) have failed adequately to appreciate as much, repression is the very critical tool Foucault employs to unfold the relations between madness, reason, and unreason. For Foucault, the concept of repression is the digging implement of his "archeology" of madness. At the same time, it is psychoanalysis which can show us the limitations of *Folie et déraison*.

II.

In his 1915 essay on "Repression," Freud remarks:

> We have dealt with the repression of an instinctual representative, and by the latter we have understood the idea or group of ideas which is cathected with a definite quota of psychic energy [...] coming from a [drive]. Clinical observation now obliges us to divide up what we have hitherto regarded as a single entity; for it shows us that besides the idea, some other element representing the [drive] has to be taken into account, and that this other element undergoes vicissitudes of repression which may be quite different from those undergone by the idea [...] From this point on, in describing a case of repression, we shall have to follow up separately what, as the result of repression, becomes of the idea, and what becomes of the [drive] energy attached to it. (Freud SE XIV: 152; translation modified)

Describing the phenomenon of decathexis, this passage marks a significant moment in the evolution of Freud's drive theory. For Freud, the demand for representation results from the drive's failure to enter the psychic system. An "entity" is formed he terms the "ideational" (sometimes also the "drive") representative.[5]

---

4 This critique of the hermeneutics of suspicion is most familiar from *The Order of Things*, although it first appears in Foucault's presentation to the Royaumont Nietzsche colloquium entitled "Nietzsche, Freud, Marx."

5 Freud's metapsychological essays are not always terminologically consistent, which creates some difficulties in the presentation of his conception of the drive, a term located on the border between psyche and soma. At certain moments, he characterizes the drive as a somatic impulse that requires representation by a delegate, at others, the drive is itself the delegate of somatic

The act of repression begins with the divorce of the two elements that make up this entity, the idea (or group of ideas) and a sum of libidinal energy attached to them. While the psychic atom is created by the investment or occupation (*Besetzung*) of idea by energy, their separation is characterized as a divestiture or *decathexis*. A somewhat ponderous creation of Freud's English translator, James Strachey, the latter term renders the more plain-spoken German *Entziehung der Besetzung*, a withdrawal, literally a "pulling-away" or regression of investment. For Freud, such a withdrawal is the minimal condition of an act of repression (Freud SE XIV: 154–5).

What is new in Freud's theory in 1915 is the proposition that the second element, the sum of psychic energy, also constitutes a mode of representation. As a result, representation ceases to be simply ideational, now also taking place in the form of the energy that both "stems from" the drive and "represents" it. In fact Freud's new account only adds to the complications attached to his theory of the symbol. For him, the idea is an eidetic form to be occupied by mobile cathexes, rather than a content.[6] As well as designating the relation of the unit of two elements to the drive, the term representation now characterizes the drive relation of each of them taken alone. At the same time, the relation of those elements to one another is termed an "occupation."

III.

One of *Folie et déraison*'s picaresque features is that it begins with the conclusion of an episode, the end of the Middle Ages and the disappearance of leprosy. For Foucault, it is the *withdrawal* (he also calls it a *regression*) of leprosy that brought the Middle Ages to a close. "The leper," he observes, "disappeared from the Western world":

> In the margins of the community, at the gates of cities, there stretched wastelands which sickness had ceased to haunt but had left sterile and long uninhabitable. For centuries, these reaches [...] would wait, soliciting with strange incantations a new incarnation of disease, another grimace of terror, renewed rites of purification and exclusion. (3)

During the Middle Ages, leprosy had become so widespread that the leprosariums had multiplied. Sites of a ritual sacralization through exclusion, these institu-

---

stimulus. Freud also sometimes treats the term "drive representative" as synonymous with the ideational representative, the portion of the delegate that takes the form of an idea, whereas at other times he uses that term to refer to the entire presentation of the drive by both idea and quota of affect.

[6] Although Laplanche and Pontalis remark on Freud's alteration of the conventional sense of the term *Vorstellung*, they focus on his abandonment in the concept of an unconscious idea of the sense of a "subjective presentation of an object to consciousness," rather than of the Aristotelian conception of the idea as an intermediary term between the word and the thing. (Laplanche and Pontalis 200).

tions were located in liminal spaces which symbolized the leper's eternal passage. The disappearance of leprosy was less "the effect of obscure medical practices" that had been devised to treat it, Foucault proposes, than "the spontaneous result of segregation and also the consequence, after the Crusades, of the break with Eastern sources of infection" (5, 6). What remained once it was gone were the "structures" that had been attached to it, which now stood empty and abandoned (7). In addition to the lazar houses themselves, what also outlasted leprosy were "the values and images attached to the figure of the leper, as well as the meaning of his exclusion" (6).

Once leprosy was gone, the "immense fortune represented by the endowments of the lazar houses" was suddenly freed up. The task of reallocating these "excess revenues," dividends of peace, fell to royal authority. By decree, they were diverted to the "sustenance of poor noblemen and crippled soldiers" and to the care of the poor (4). The lazar houses' fate took longer to resolve. A problem of sufficient "economic importance [to] provoke more than one conflict," the houses would be left uninhabited for several centuries. They would exert a certain pull, Foucault informs us, "soliciting [...] a new incarnation [...] with strange incantations." Still, it would not be until the Great Confinement that the "games of exclusion" would begin again, "often in the same places" (3). Then, a new set of occupants would be found (the poor, vagabonds, criminals, the mad) to fill what would now become the Hôpital Général.

With the end of leprosy, Foucault begins (as an act of repression does for Freud) with the withdrawal of energetic investments from ideas. As for Freud, there are three terms in play: the lazar houses, their inhabitants, and the revenues required for their upkeep. Once separated from one another, these elements undergo varying vicissitudes. The lazar houses, "shells" or ideas, cease to be "in use" and are pushed into the unconscious as the idea is in an act of repression. There they exert the attraction attributed to unconscious ideas, for Freud a necessary economic component of repression (Freud SE XIV: 148).

Foucault's account of the construction of madness by reason relies on a shifting identification of the energy that cathects ideas, sometimes as revenues (which find an immediate conversion outside of unconscious processes), sometimes as the changing inhabitants of the hospitals. What he creates is an astute reduplication of Freud's presentation of the drive sometimes outside, sometimes within the psychic system.

Arguably, the strongest indication of the Freudian character of Foucault's concept of madness is the association of the symbolic *value* of leprosy with its *sites*. Where Freud treats the "idea," locus of what Foucault terms "value," as a form rather than a content, Foucault regards the lazar houses (which he calls "shells") as outer casings of mobile social investments. Meanings inhabited instead of inhabiting, the "values and images attached" to the leper are inseparable from the places to which the disease is banned. While Foucault later critiques Freud for his ontological conception of the symptom, *Folie et déraison*'s theory of history, based on Freud's account of repression, relies not so much on a depth psychology, as on a conception of historical materiality embodied in the shells of the leprosariums.

IV.

If repression is the basis for Foucault's conception of history, this means that reason must soon be faced with the return of the madness it has repressed. Another passage from the "Repression" essay offers an intimation of what to expect:

> Psychoanalysis shows us that the instinctual representative develops with less interference and more profusely if it is withdrawn by repression from conscious influence. It prolifer-ates in the dark, as it were, and takes on extreme forms of expression which, when they are translated and presented to the neurotic, are not only bound to seem alien to him, but frighten him by giving him the picture of an extraordinary and dangerous strength of instinct. (Freud SE XIV: 149)

For Freud, repression has a contradictory outcome. While it is designed to exclude ideas deemed inappropriate from consciousness in order to avoid the distress attached to them, in fact it serves to provide a breeding ground for new forms of those ideas. Far from resolving matters, the idea's liberation from the censorship associated with the secondary process results in its unfettered development in the unconscious. Attracted to and grouped around a nucleus of other ideas, the repressed idea will "proliferate," taking on "extreme forms" as a result of the metonymic logic of the primary process. At the same time, the distortion to which such ideas are submitted, only possible because of the re-moval of secondary censorship, serves to make them more palatable to con-sciousness. As soon as they are disguised to a point where they are no longer recognizable, the pcs.-cs. (preconscious-conscious) barrier will be dropped, if only momentarily, and ideas are again "presented" to consciousness.

Consciousness is now confronted with a new problem. While it fails to recog-nize the returning idea as a derivative of the one it originally excluded, the idea's very strangeness, which is what makes possible its re-presentation, now becomes frightening, creating a perception of danger which will be registered as neurotic anxiety. This, Freud intimates, is the "true significance" of repression. It is the affect's vicissitudes, he proposes, which are more important to the success or failure of an act of repression than those of the idea.[7]

---

[7] Affect (of which anxiety is in Freud's thought the primary example) occupies an interesting position in recent psychoanalytic debates. French psychoanalysis has devoted considerable atten-tion to the problem. André Green argues, for instance, that Freud's work is characterized by a shift from a symbolic conception of the drive, in which the ideational representative takes center stage, to a theory of representation in which affect becomes the more important theoretical concept. According to Green, psychoanalytic theory refuses to theorize affect after Freud, begin-ning with Klein's emphasis on object relations and culminating in Lacan's insistence that affect

This passage should be compared to Foucault's account of the "Second Panic" which precedes the birth of the asylum:

> What the classical period had confined was not only an abstract unreason [...] but an enormous reservoir of the fantastic [...]. One might say that the fortresses of confinement added to their social role of segregation and purification a quite opposite cultural function. Even as they separated reason from unreason on society's surface, they preserved in depth the images, where they mingled and exchanged properties. The fortresses of confinement functioned as a great long, silent memory [...] created by the classical order, they preserved against it and against time. (Foucault 209)

Like Freud, Foucault calls attention to the conflict between repression's original aim, the elimination of distress, and its outcome, the exacerbation of anxiety. In *Folie et déraison* that contradiction is transformed into a distinction between the asylum's social and cultural functions.[8] While classical reason confines, separates, and purifies unreason, giving rise to social segregation, it creates a cultural reservoir in whose depths unreason flourishes. It is the insistence of Foucault's water metaphor (first used in the discussion of the *Ship of Fools*) which transforms Freud's "darkness" into "depth," so that *Verdrängung* now implies oppression (a vertical term) rather than marginalization (a horizontal one). Foucault's account of unreason's proliferation as a "mingling" and "exchange" of properties is remarkably similar, however, to Freud's depiction of the primary process. Following Freud, Foucault characterizes the primary process as a suspension of time. Initially reason's creation, in the end the asylum protects madness against reason.

Foucault emphasizes the alteration undergone by unconscious ideas, calling attention to the fear which results from the distortion facilitating the return of the repressed. While he speaks of the asylum as an "abolished time," he insists that "something had happened, in the darkness [...] the images liberated at the end of the eighteenth century were not identical at all points with those the seventeenth century had tried to eliminate" (209). A propaedeutic for the birth of the asylum, what occurs at the end of the eighteenth century is the rediscovery of "figures familiar at the end of the Middle Ages, deformed and endowed with new meaning" (210). It seems to the sane as if "evil began to ferment in the closed spaces of confinement," so that when it "reappeared, to the horror of the public," it is "in a fantastic guise" (203). Intended to protect reason against madness, the Great Confinement exacerbates the fear that gives rise to exclusion, transforming it into an even more profound social anxiety. It represents the triumph of structure over intention.

---

is not a conceptual category. On the significance of this account of affect in the second typology for Freud's political theory, see Lacoue-Labarthe and Nancy.

8 Dreyfus and Rabinow consider the account of social causation in *Folie et déraison* primitive in comparison to Foucault's later works (Dreyfus and Rabinow 5–6). The problem may be more that his distinction between social and cultural functions serves to lessen the contradiction Freud stresses between repression's aim and its outcome.

V.

For Freud, repression is a constant process, characteristic of normal as well as abnormal psychologies, as well as a transformative one which generates mental organization. It is only one of a number of vicissitudes an instinct may undergo, all subsumed under the more general rubric of defense. At the same time Freud places the modes of defense in a sequence, observing that "repression is not present from the beginning" and speculating that it "post-dates" other methods such as "reversal onto the opposite" and "turning onto the subject's own self" (Freud SE XIV: 147).

Repression, which "cannot arise until a sharp cleavage has occurred between conscious and unconscious activity," proves to be responsible, in its primal form, for bringing about that cleavage in the first place (Freud SE XIV: 147). It is preceded by defensive reversals and followed by a more complex form of mental organization to which Freud refers as "rejection based on judgment (condemnation)" (Freud SE XIV: 146). Repression is not the first or the last stage of mental life, but it remains exemplary of mental differentiation. It is the mechanism that generates the unconscious.[9]

It is possible to speak of *Folie et déraison*'s psychoanalytic conception of history on the basis of the similar tension it displays. The book's picaresque features are a product, we have shown, of repression's serial character, leading always to a return of the repressed and the need for fresh repressions. As in Freud, this does not prevent Foucault from providing unreason with a teleology, however, most evidently in the passage from the crude repression of the Great Confinement to the asylum's perpetual judgment. For Foucault, the Great Confinement is followed by the asylum's supposedly more "humane" form of social control, a progress celebrated by the Whig historians whose violence he exposes and condemns. Clearly, it is Freud, who sometimes argued for the replacement of repression by the judgment of condemnation as the only possible, if by no means satisfactory, goal of analysis, who is implicated here. It is also Freud, however, who maintains that repression is condemnation's "preliminary stage," and who insists, in opposition to the programs for sexual liberation espoused by many of his progressive disciples, that it would never be possible to eliminate repression (Freud SE XIV: 146). The internalization of violence in the super-ego is a profoundly Freudian idea.

As it turns out, such tensions are apparent from the opening sequence of *Folie et déraison*. While the disappearance of leprosy is presented as a withdrawal

[9] In the book he wrote prior to *Folie et déraison*, *Mental Illness and Psychology*, Foucault applauds Freud's liberation from Jackson's evolutionary theory of neurosis, at the same time as he recognizes the Oedipus complex and the theory of libidinal stages as teleological concepts (Foucault, *Mental Illness* 31). This may be regarded as another formulation of the same problem.

which meets the minimal condition for an act of repression, the repression of the Great Confinement (which Freud terms repression proper) is preceded, for Foucault, by a mode of defense that splits – in literature and painting – into the methods Freud describes as reversal onto the opposite (satire) and turning onto the subject's self (farce) (Foucault 24–34). Although it is the consequence of the withdrawal of cathexis, the Renaissance conception of madness both post-dates and precedes repression. This is a complication that has never adequately been attended to by those who have condemned the naive nostalgia of Foucault's "champ libre" (see Midelfort).

For the assessment of *Folie et déraison*'s relevance for a psychoanalytic conception of cultural history, this means two things. Firstly, it suggests that Foucault's controversial "structuralism" does not preclude him from producing a model of historical change. His historiography is serial and episodic, submitting madness to the metonymic alteration of the primary process. Repressed ideas never return in the same form. This is why Foucault can speak, in the Preface, of "a structure" that is both "eternal" and "forming" (Foucault xii). Foucault imitates Freud's tension, moreover, between repression's exemplary status and its place within a teleological development. As for Freud, repression is, for Foucault, a model of historical repetition.

Secondly, this means that Foucault's own fear that he had succumbed in *Folie et déraison* to a trans-historical account of madness may be too hasty. While what Foucault terms "déraison" is the unconscious repository of repressed ideas, it is not, as Dreyfus and Rabinow propose, an ontological concept. The unconscious is developed, for Freud, through individual acts of repression. One is not born with one. The unconscious, as Foucault concurs (suggesting that the hospitals preserve images "against time"), is timeless. Famously, it knows no negation. In it, we are called upon to conceive something generated historically as the other of reason, even as it is itself the generator of historical events. The unconscious presents us with a history that takes place in abolished time. It creates a history that transpires not trans-historically, but beyond temporality.

VI.

In his 1972 response to Derrida, Foucault characterizes the stakes of their conflict in terms of the "anxiety of philosophy." The question, he suggests, is whether anything precedes repression:

> Could there be anything anterior or exterior to philosophical discourse? Can its condition reside in an exclusion, a refusal, a risk avoided, *and why not, a fear*? Derrida rejects this suspicion passionately. (Foucault, "My Body" 10; italics mine)

Derrida insists that madness cannot be anterior to philosophy, that it is always included in it as its negation. Smacking of denial, what Derrida refuses to recognize, for Foucault, is the fear that reason experiences in the face of madness, a fear that gives rise to defense. Such fear is the "condition" of philosophical discourse, both the state in which it perpetually finds itself, always subject to the return of the repressed, and the principle that precedes it as its condition of possibility. In a passage whose viciousness is indeed remarkable, Foucault condemns Derrida's "little pedagogy," claiming that the latter's refusal to confront this fear "elides the events that occur in texts," transforming them into "marks for a reading" that reify textual interiority as the search for an origin that is under erasure (27).

As we have shown, the term "fear" appears at several crucial junctures in *Folie et déraison*. When leprosy has withdrawn, the lazar houses lie in wait for "another grimace of fear." They find such a grimace in the Great Confinement, and then again when reason is faced in the Second Panic with the return of the repressed. In *Folie et déraison*, fear is assumed from the outset, at the same time as it is discovered in repression proper, a process that sets in train the events which lead to its exacerbation in the return of the repressed. As we have seen, this tension is motivated by Foucault's presentation of the "champ libre" as both preceding and post-dating repression.

A similar difficulty is characteristic of Freud's concept of anxiety. Whether as one possible transformation of affect once withdrawn from the idea or as the effect of an alienation brought about by the return of the repressed, the founder of psycho-analysis frequently treated anxiety as the upshot of repression. Towards the end of his career, Freud began to entertain a more radical conception of anxiety, however, in which it could no longer be localized as an effect and became the source rather than the outcome of repression.

Foucault's response to Derrida, which treats fear as a consequence of repression as well as its condition of possibility, suggests that he adopted both views. *Folie et déraison* itself tells a slightly different story, however. For all the book has been condemned for its primordial nostalgia, the fact that it begins with the withdrawal of cathexis must be understood as a refusal to reach back to anything more primordial than repression itself. Gliding along the surface of symbolic formations, Foucault's picaresque is motivated by a curious ban on images of the *arche*. Ironically, it is precisely this refusal for which Derrida critiques the book in 1964, insisting that Foucault fails to confront the Greek origins of the *logos*. Had he done so, Derrida implies, Foucault would have been unable to accord the classical age "either specificity or privilege." Instead, exclusion would have proved "essential to the entirety of the history of philosophy and of reason" (Derrida, "Cogito" 39–40). As Derrida observes, "all the signs assembled by Foucault under the chapter heading *Stultifera navis* would [then] only play themselves out on the surface of a chronic dissension." In fact this may be precisely Foucault's point. If *Folie et déraison* slides resolutely along the chain of a mobile series of repressions, each one a metonymic repetition of the last, it may not rely on the concept of primordial exclusion for which Foucault applauds the book in 1972 — a foreclosure rather than a repression. Instead, its beginning would circulate in an oscillating spiral between repression and primal repression. For such a history, the privileged position of the "classical age" of repression would become at best profoundly ironic.

What would this mean for Foucault's conception of cultural history? Philippe Lacoue-Labarthe and Jean Luc Nancy have proposed that Freud's second concept of affect "invokes a [...] 'withdrawal' whose origin is more archaic than that of any repression," demonstrating the extent to which psychoanalysis should be understood as a sociology rather than a psychology in which affect becomes the basis for a primordial sociality prior to any symbolic field (198, 199). This would suggest that psychoanalysis does not allow for any simple "application" of individual psychology to the theory of culture, a point that Freud himself made. A compelling example of what it would mean to treat Freud's metapsychology as a model of the collective sphere, this book demonstrates that the psychoanalytic conception of history need not be based on the idea of a pre-symbolic affect which transcends discourse.

8

Reading/Writing/Killing:
Foucault, Cultural History and the French Revolution

WILLIAM SCOTT

> "One small inkwell more and the idol is overthrown!"
>
> (Marat)

One of the many voices of Foucault allows us to address productively important aspects of Cultural History in relation to interpretations of the Enlightenment and French Revolution. We here use the "political-historical" Foucault to comment on the weaknesses of some prominent cultural-historical approaches before suggesting how some of his concerns may help us to understand more deeply crucial dimensions of the Revolution. This is not to take Foucault as an authority, especially since we concentrate on his more occasional writings (articles, lecture courses, newspaper extracts, interviews) for we also note some of his blind spots. However, Foucault's concerns and preoccupations − especially his view that the intellectual's main task is to problematise existing assumptions, often by exposing submerged, subversive discourses − are directly relevant to a period of history which (the Enlightenment) he has confronted directly and which (the French Revolution) is a shadowy but significant presence behind much of his writing. Foucault's concern with apparatuses of power/knowledge, his concept of discursive events, his preoccupation with struggle (and his hunch that war might be the dominant model of political relationships through most of historical time)[1] are of obvious relevance to the "age of revolution". Some of Foucault's often-alleged weaknesses − his lack of interest in constitutions and rights, his downplaying of liberty and liberation, his failure (some say) to provide an analysis of, or a justification for, "resistance" to oppressive regimes − pose acute problems in analysing both the Enlightenment and the Revolution. Also of relevance are Foucault's rather ambivalent statements regarding the relationship of politics to economics and his neglect of the religious dimension of

---

[1] A theme explored especially in Foucault's *"Il faut défendre la société"* (=IFDS). In addition, the following abbreviations of Foucault's works will be used in the text: FL=*Foucault Live*; PPC=*Politics, Philosophy, Culture*; PK=*Power/Knowledge*; RM=*Remarks on Marx*; TS=*Technologies of the Self*; FL=*Foucault Live*; PPC=*Politics, Philosophy, Culture*; PK=*Power/Knowledge*; RM=*Remarks on Marx*; TS=*Technologies of the Self*.

modern history. Questions of power are obviously central to consideration of
the French Revolution. Foucault can contribute to the problematisation of existing interpretations — though these are hardly stable, unless one believes that a
coherent revisionist consensus has definitively buried the "Marxist" interpretation. Bringing Foucault and the Revolution more closely together provides an
opportunity to criticise some of his approaches — and supplement or confirm
others.

Already Roger Chartier ("Chimera") and Keith Baker ("French Revolution")
have explored the theme of a Foucauldian view of the French Revolution: but
their approach, pitched at the level of explicit ideas and aiming at conceptual
coherence, will not directly influence us here. Rather, we use Foucault's work as
he suggested using Nietzsche: that is, accepting a degree of distortion, an element of tactical unscrupulousness (PK 53−4). This allows criticism of would-
be comprehensive approaches to the Revolution, such as Chartier's or Baker's
— which over-concentrate on "print culture" within the context of the "linguistic turn" in history writing. In particular, Roger Chartier's *The Cultural Origins of
the French Revolution* meticulously analyses forms of print culture, and aspects of
its interaction with oral culture, in an ingenious but rather formalised fashion.[2]
Chartier's approach might, positively, be said to provide ways to engage with
the great fertility of eighteenth-century and revolutionary discourse-production:
however, it also seems to be rather mechanical, somewhat inert and disembod-
ied, and thus an inadequate entry into the issues involved in such a passionate
event as the French Revolution (or, indeed, into the issues at stake in the struggles of the Enlightenment). Of course approaches focusing on print culture
have yielded extremely valuable insights and have successfully problematised but
also illuminated areas of practice and discourse which had previously perhaps
been overlooked or ignored. However, such approaches tend to accord themselves excessive explanatory power by, for example, re-ifying "representation",
at the expense of what is, presumably, represented. Also they do not really
consider the intense emotional — sometimes affective, often vindictive — investment which representation involved, in such a period of conflict, struggle and
war. Little sense is given of how discourses and texts, how writing, reading and
hearing them, were imbued with acutely powerful emotional, as well as rational,
charges, in struggles involving issues wider than the rather abstractly defined re-
arrangement of political institutions and ideas, struggles in which people, and
peoples, competed for power across all levels of social activity (mass physical
force, military strength, national spirit, economic power, religious and anti-reli-
gious convictions, symbolic mobilisation). These struggles involved not only
disqualifying opponents' discourses (sometimes by the burning as well as the
banning of texts) but also attempting to destroy their institutions (the Catholic

---

[2] See also Keith M Baker, *Inventing the French Revolution.*

Church for example) and by killing their spokespersons (sometimes specifically targeted as producers and/or consumers of texts). In this extremely complex and ever-changing situation, often bewildering to those living through events and trying desperately to make sense of them, the sheer variety of texts – and their hybridity – makes too formalistic an approach especially inadequate.

To say this is not, of course, to make an absolute distinction between "print culture" and non-print culture. However, we do suggest that the Revolution, especially, cannot be fully integrated into cultural history without demonstrating, as well as a command of print culture, a deep knowledge of texts which did not, for whatever reason, reach print. While the Revolution saw an unprecedented explosion of printed material, many of its struggles were most graphically expressed in documents which possess the immediacy of written texts, with their clumsy style or, sometimes, handwriting too elegant for the moment, their uncorrected mistakes or crossings-out, their frequently quasi-phonetic spelling. While the study of such texts hardly ensures direct access to revolutionary "reality" at grass-roots level, or to people's real or true experience of an often murderous politics, one can be certain that lack of such study – often producing, too, a very timid selection of *printed* documentation – impoverishes our understanding and narrows our focus. Denunciations, the *procès-verbaux* of municipalities, clubs, committees of surveillance, cross-examinations before revolutionary tribunals, petitions from prisoners, the painful abjuration of priests, the hearing of witnesses to or participants in riots and disturbances – these were rarely printed, yet, at the very least, allow obscure voices to be heard, voices of struggle, sometimes of resistance.

Foucault, whatever the sources *he* used in his historical-political works, urged us to listen out for such voices. He, more than most academic cultural historians, regarded politics and history as being often dangerous and risky, even if this, and his praise of the physical commitment of those animating struggles, is sometimes criticised as being more "rhetorical" and "romantic" than soundly based. Foucault's engagement with 1968, his references to his Tunisian experience and to Iran certainly do not always inspire confidence in his judgement – and these can be supplemented by his rather alarming endorsement of "people's justice" in relation to the September Massacres of 1792.[3] However, and here perhaps unscrupulousness emerges, *any* attention to so crucial and controversial an episode of the French Revolution is symptomatically more "honest" (more truthful) than completely to ignore it, or to offer no insight as to how such an event could have occurred. In the context of today's "end of history" (when major struggles between world-views and values have, allegedly, ceased); in a period

---

[3] For 1968, see *RM*, 134–6, 140 etc.; for Tunisia, 135–6, (and note that Foucault invokes "capitalism, colonialism and neo-colonialism"); for Iran, Michiel Leezenberg's paper in this volume; for the September Massacres, *PK*, opening chapter on "people's justice".

when "culture" is often seen as a panacea against dissension and conflict, a comforting balm upon society's wounds (with heritage, *patrimoine*, memory carefully cultivated to soothe away tensions), the political-historical analysis of culture needs a sharper edge. At a time when culture is hailed as a lucrative factor of production in the creation of the New Europe; or when extremist groups like the French National Front see "culture" as the arena for present and future decisive battles, the darker areas of culture, and culture's complicity with barbarism need exposure and exploration: "Révolution *et* barbarie", remarks Foucault in a posthumously published work (IFDS 176). It may then be seen that the issues so deeply involved in the Enlightenment and French Revolution are not "finished" or "dead", as the late François Furet proclaimed two decades ago (Furet, *Penser*). Questions of rights, for example, − including the discursive rights championed in the Enlightenment and proclaimed in 1789 − are essential elements in need not only of extension but of vigilant defence.

In this perhaps slightly melodramatic context, it would seem that the cultural-historical approaches here criticised tend to advantage form over content (or content is sometimes treated in terms of arranging ideas or strands and currents of ideas in too regular and tidy a fashion, even as they conflict with each other). Thus the nature of the ideas expressed, their political implications and ramifications, their mobilising and illuminating power, their involvement in and incitement to struggles, are underplayed. Of course form and content are interdependent − in problematic and varying relationships to be evoked here later − but some influential treatments of discourse (for example, that of Hayden White) tip the balance too far towards form, analysed in an over-formalistic, pattern-making manner (White, *Metahistory*). While the rhetorical aspects of historical texts, whether primary or secondary, are often of decisive importance in situations of struggle − Michelet being an acutely powerful and poignant example − Hayden White hardly explores this problem. The means of communicating ideas, and the ideas themselves, together with the attitudes they presume, are to be analysed together, and in the widest, though still relevant contexts − with economic factors, too, sometimes of key importance. In situations of conflict and crisis, as in 1789 or 1848 − and Michelet and Marx deal imaginatively with the interaction between these years − Foucault's notion of problematisation is especially valuable (though the converse process of "naturalisation" is also often at work in revolutions, to stabilise new arrangements, so that they might endure). By definition, problematisation breaks down boundaries, tests and transgresses existing limits, with the whole notion of "representation" itself stretched, stressed and strained to breaking point and beyond, to the confusion or exhilaration of actors of the time and to the fruitful advantage of the subsequent historian. And if the prefixing of "history" by the word "cultural" expands the concerns of the practitioner (rather than confining him or her to a certain sector, as with "political", "economic", "military", or "diplomatic") then the cultural historian, especially "after Foucault", should be well placed to dissolve boundaries which have outlived any analytic usefulness which they might once have had.

In situations of conflict, questions of attitude, and of quick, quasi-instinctual response, are crucial. These require attention to more than rationally-explicit ideas and programmes – as aspirations and anxieties break through the carefully-crafted categories devised by cultural historians unwilling or unable to deal with the ignorant and the irrational, the affective and the vindictive, the fearful and the terrifying, the confused and the bewildered. Foucault suggests that "truth" may be more vividly disclosed in situations of violence than in the more ordered realm of rationality and debate, government and administration.

It is problems like these which suggest that Roger Chartier – whose total *oeuvre* is so impressive – is disarmed when attempting to deal with the hardly-new problem of relating "the Enlightenment" to "the French Revolution". A failure to relate reason, as well as unreason, to violence – or, more pointedly, to explore a violence of reason, which traversed the porous but key limit-date of 1789 – is debilitating. It underestimates the explosive charge of both the Enlightenment and the Revolution. Chartier recommends all the right interpretative strategies. But while constantly emphasising change and interaction, flexibility and openness of approach, he in fact tends to manipulate in a rather mechanistic manner inert distinctions and lifeless identities. He certainly here fails to show the dramatic and dynamic potential of contradictions and controversies, especially when bound up with struggles between socio-economic groups, in the often ruthless process of formation, within a challenging global context of increasing commercialisation, leading towards capitalism. Here Marx may be of more use than Foucault.

There is no question of presumptuously suggesting that Chartier lacks a theoretically sophisticated concept of representation (quite the reverse). However Chartier, who provides a "thin" rather than "thick" description, singularly fails to enliven and illuminate either the "cultural origins" of the French Revolution or the Revolution itself.[11] Partly this is because he gives little attention to contemporaries' own debates on representation, their own attempts at self-reflexivity where, for example, language was at stake – or their own debates on "the social history of ideas", – their own realisation, however partial we might see it now, that they were living in a period of change which was "problematising" all accepted practices and values. François-Jean de Chastellux appealed to his readers in the 1770s as "we moderns" (*De la félicité publique* 473). Pierre-Louis Lacretelle, in 1792, evoked the "modern spirit", stemming from the invention of printing, the rise of commerce and the eclipse of those noble-military values championed, as Foucault reminds us at length, (IFDS) by Boulainvilliers. This spirit produced the (bourgeois?) philosophy which, combined with the force of the people, was, in Lacretelle's striking phrase to "change the world" (*Discours*).

In such exciting – but risky and dangerous – times, the role of writing and reading in bringing about radical change, or even revolution, in inciting or containing popular violence, or in justifying state-organised killing, was seen as crucially important. Questions of access to written and spoken texts were discussed. The intense debates on education for example linked Enlightenment and revolutionary worries and concerns. Clearly, in the Revolution, with the explosion of texts, the proliferation of assemblies and meetings, such questions attained unprecedented intensity.

Too-narrow a concentration on "print-culture" fails to engage with what might be taken to be other types of history and history-writing: not just political thought and political culture, but social and economic history, scientific and medical history, gender history, religious and military history – all deeply involved in the Enlightenment and Revolution. The close engagement of cultural history with other types of history may, in fact, be more productive than more exotic but often disappointing encounters with "other" disciplines such as anthropology – though such encounters should obviously be sought out and made rewarding. Perhaps one might add that, in thus engaging with "different" histories, as well as with different disciplines, we might be brought into closer contact with a wider range of material objects. Certainly, historians of print culture, with superb pioneering contributions from Chartier, have treated "the book" as a material object, together with the pamphlet and, especially valuable, the newspaper (the religious press, the military press, an emerging economic press, a press directed towards women or the peasantry …) – all to be seen, of course, in a market context, involving advertising and consumption, the creation of new tastes, new needs, the pandering to new cravings or fostering of new aspirations, the alleviation of new or not so new anxieties in an atmosphere of increasing rivalry and competition in which some prospered and others went to the wall.

Despite much good work in this area, cultural historians, at one here with the "revisionist" view of the Revolution, tend to downplay the socio-economic dimensions of both Enlightenment and Revolution, despite the pervasiveness of metaphors of exchange. They scorn interpretations which invoke a global context or general framework of commercialisation and, even more decisively rejected, of "capitalism". Some say that Foucault shares this distaste. Or they suggest that any reference by Foucault to capitalism or any evocation of "the bourgeoisie" is an unfortunate throwback to an earlier, rather disreputably Marxist period of his intellectual trajectory. However, Foucault has fairly consistently referred to capitalism, or at least to economic needs and imperatives, and has spoken of the need to anchor (political) power relations to their economic infrastructures (FL 221). Certainly, he has always argued that other discourses and practices cannot be unproblematically aligned with a determining "economic" dimension, structure or base, suggesting links rather than anything more binding: he notes, for example, that just about anything can be *deduced* from the domination of the bourgeoisie (PK 100). Yet some of Foucault's explanations for the rise of disciplinary society are remarkably historically-specific (owing, no doubt, much to Annales histories). And, accused of being "too local", and thus masking general trends, Foucault maintains that local practices and discourses can often be integrated into global frameworks and strategies (PK 142). Foucault's recently published *"Il faut défendre la société"* operates on a *longue durée* – in which currents of thought change, are transformed or transform themselves, are appropriated by different groups for different, often mutually hostile, purposes in variations on a few basic themes, including a few interlinked notions of history, usable by antagonistic classes. *Discipline and Punish* covers much the same time-scale and likewise traverses different dimensions of social life, relating the discursive to the "non-discursive", very material, aspects of life (such as, obviously, prison buildings), speculating on their possibly functional purposes, within a wider economy of power.

Sometimes accused of being too empirical, with little explanation of his *implicit* theoretical framework, Foucault reverses the negativity of the charge, recognising empirical work as a key aspect of the historian's craft: "I do nothing *but* history …"; "I'm an empiricist. I don't try to advance things without seeing whether they are applicable …"; "I am speaking as a historian of culture …" (RM 129; PPC 106; FL 99). While criticising the uncritical use of global concepts like "society" and explanatory models imported into history (economic mechanisms; demographic trends; anthropological structures), Foucault nevertheless argues that, at around the time of the French Revolution, government discovered "society" and, by its destruction of corporate obstacles – what Marx termed the removal of "medieval rubbish" to create a nation-state and national market – prepared the ground for disciplinary and normalising powers, disguised to be sure by talk of constitutions and rights (FL 285; 279; PPC 186 ff; FL 337; PK 105). Foucault's emphasis on "police", as at least attempting to embrace and supervise all elements of society, likewise has a global potential – as do notions of normalisation, however imperfectly attained (from the most intimate concerns of the body, to policies – for example, medical – enmeshing all society).

Foucault acclaims Marx's most historical, least overtly theoretical texts for emphasising the complexities of the 1848 revolutionary struggles, texts which accord much importance to contingency, to differential time-scales, and to the deconstruction of unitary classes, ideologies, and so on. More generally, Foucault says that his class-struggle emphasises struggle rather than class (FL 224). Clearly, Foucault's appropriation of elements of Marx – and his accusation that the French Marxists of the 1970s knew very little history – is itself extremely problematic or provocative, as in his pronouncement: "One might even wonder what difference there could ultimately be between being a historian and being a Marxist ..."(FL 131; PK 53). Foucault regarded the bourgeoisie as a very conscious actor in history, especially from the time of the French Revolution: "it was perfectly aware that a new legislation or constitution wouldn't be enough to guarantee its hegemony". He also insisted that the nineteenth-century bourgeoisie constantly *said* what they were doing, and did not hide their disciplinary and normalising projects (FL 233 & 149). These strong statements suggest that what Chartier describes as "borrowings from the most rudimentary sort of Marxism" (Chartier, "Chimera" 180) were aimed to provide broad yet not infinitely flexible frameworks within which discourses and discursive practices struggled, while retaining certain basic characteristics in common.

The proliferation of disciplinary discourses in nineteenth-century Europe, argues Foucault, testifies to the precariousness of bourgeois domination (FL 237 & 258) – not a wholly un-Marxist idea given the continued power of the reactionary aristocracy overlapping with the threat "from below" exemplified by the sans-culottes of the Year II, the insurgents of the June Days of 1848 and the Commune. Of course this also may be "rudimentary Marxism" and is clearly far too general to be revealing. To relate the general and the particular, the secure and the insecure, the spiritual, the ideological and the material, we take a striking remark by Foucault: the economy of the eighteenth century, that is, capitalism in process of formation, needed a form of power whose meshes were fine enough to protect property from pilfering (FL 193 & 230 ff). We know, of course, that workers who went home with raw materials and tools did indeed provide a reason for installing measures of surveillance and discipline: but a very vivid illustration of this occurs in P. L. Bérenger's revealingly entitled book *Le peuple instruit de ses propres vertus*, published in 1787, a substantial collection of homilies and moral tales. The time and labour of workers belonged to the man who hired them. Total honesty was essential. The temptation to take advantage of an employer's absence (we are dealing with a France of small workshops) had to be resisted, out of "loyalty" certainly, but also because to deprive him of time and effort was "a real theft", a violation of the contract ("les conditions du marché"). One real theft envisaged was the stealing of raw materials behind the employer's back. But God was always present, the ultimate agent of surveillance, never inattentive. All Bérenger's stories inculcated an ideal of self-control and self-discipline but with a "long-stop" to catch the errant. However, not only moral but psychological benefits would follow from internalising honesty – "la paix de coeur" and almost a "volupté". The honest worker would receive material benefits too: he would never lack a job. But work was moral too ...

Bérenger's two volumes, full of vivid instances of a fairly commonplace morality (owing much to Benjamin Franklin) reveal an anxiety about the possible subversion of the social order, reflecting an urgent need to facilitate a transition between a natural, static, aristocratic order and one likely to be more fluid and precarious (one of the most common tropes is the honest artisan or peasant –

not rich but obviously not desperately poor either – coming to the aid of an honest but down-on-his-luck aristocrat). Foucault captures, better than many cultural historians who deal at length with the eighteenth century, feelings of precariousness and anxiety, partly because of his own uniquely disturbing sense of strain and struggle.

Also, Foucault's concept of writing as a passionate intervention in politics, his anxious search for the possibility of a historical truth which could have a political effect, is particularly appropriate for those who wrote, read (and spoke) in eighteenth-century France, both before and after 1789. Foucault's project of "excavating our own culture", finding subjugated, submerged, disqualified voices sometimes desperately seeking expression, likewise has a particular relevance (PK 82–3), with 1789 seeing the tumultuous emergence of many such voices, 1789 being a discursive event, or constellation of such events, of explosive intensity and force – perhaps, indeed, the greatest discursive event in western history. To view the French Revolution, not just as a linguistic event, but as a fantastic apparatus of which every component was productive of an amazing variety of texts is certainly to seize an important dimension of its history and legacy.

If texts need to be related to practices, language likewise needs to be contextualised. It would naturally be desirable to see the insights afforded by the linguistic turn extended and developed by historians with a real knowledge of, and feeling for, language, in period and in context – a concern for language (or languages and "idioms") as a resource or resources to be used and abused, adopted or rejected, according to the needs, fears and desires of people and groups in specific situations, and bent to different and often antagonistic purposes. Moreover, this would involve showing how the revolutionaries (and counter-revolutionaries) *themselves* engaged in passionate debates on language – on, for example, the problems of devising (or first importing from the Anglo-Americans) a specifically "political" language, in conditions of bitter struggle – some wanting such a language (of clarity, simplicity and energy) for the common man – if not woman – others decrying or deploring its very possibility, wishing to preserve distance and mystification, to obscure and protect the workings of power.

Of course, the Revolution professed "transparency" which meant, in political and economic terms, accountability – a disclosure of power to surveillance from below, on the part of citizens as voters, taxpayers and state creditors. The Enlightenment, too, aspired to demystify and to problematise relationships deemed natural, therefore eternal. It is now fashionable to scoff at the idea that risk or danger might have been involved in such an undertaking: this, besides being condescending, is unhistorical (ask de Sade). Anyway, in the process of challenging existing values, the Enlightenment was loquacious, sociable, largely discursively constructed, and always in danger of deconstruction. Meeting resistance from vested interests, recalcitrant by definition to "problematisation", and long having used the resources of language to embed, encrust and enshrine themselves as permanent features of the landscape, the Enlightenment itself was fissured — riven with rivalries and tensions, resentments and dislikes, with military metaphors not always directed against "external" enemies. Whether subsumed under the Enlightenment or not, some of the most basic concerns of the pre-1789 period can be explored, with the help of Marx as well as Foucault, through submerged discourses circulating through France (via its impressive post roads), discourses often in manuscript form, which arguably "prepared" 1789 from below the level usually studied by historians of print culture, yet which were neither clandestine still less the pornographic material which has so captured the attention of historians recently. Such texts add to what we know from Farge, Arasse, Hunt and others who, perhaps influenced by Foucault, have brilliantly exposed the less literate and less "rational" aspects of Enlightenment and Revolution, though sometimes giving the impression of treating the exceptional and the exotic. This is perhaps justifiable when focusing on the Terror, but it had important dimensions which are not as exciting as "the imaginary of the guillotine".[4]

Here, to draw attention to the importance of "submerged discourses", I take something as banal and as (allegedly) tedious as the essay competitions organised by the provincial academies of eighteenth-century France.[5] Such bodies were an integral part of the corporate, hierarchical structures of power/knowledge. Patronised and supervised by the authorities, forbidden by statute to discuss matters of government and religion, their publications subject to censorship, academies produced high-profile "discursive events", annual public sessions of pomp and ceremonial mise en scène, involving the reading of extracts from prize-winning essays. However they were also highly self-conscious agents in the international Republic of Letters and, though restrictive in some ways, professed to be interested in the wide diffusion of knowledge. Their essay competitions made famous, or notorious, by Rousseau, covered a vast range of subjects and, collectively, were surely part of that "discovery of society", this opening-out of society to various "gazes", to which Foucault and others have drawn our

---

[4] Works such as Arlette Farge, *Fragile Lives* and *Dire et mal dire*; Daniel Arasse, *La guillotine*; Lynn Hunt, *Politics, Culture and Class in the French Revolution*; *Eroticism and the Body Politic*, and *The Family Romance of the French Revolution*.

[5] Based on personal research in the archives of French provincial Academies with a view to publishing a monograph on the formation of modern French political culture in the pre-revolutionary and revolutionary periods. The Academies which have proved most fruitful have been those of Marseille, Metz, Dijon, Besançon and Bordeaux. I have studied the whole corpus of works submitted for a variety of essay competitions, the "losing" essays ("submerged" ever since the 1780s) sometimes being more interesting than those that were "crowned". In the context of the present rather general essay, however, I have not thought it necessary to multiply references to material from French archives.

attention: indeed, they were part of the *creation* of society. Topics traversed the boundaries which we might customarily impose on knowledge: from the "economic" through the "moral" to the "political" – the Lyon silk industry and its crises of unemployment and the demoralisation of the work-force; problems of food and water supply; the impact of commerce on the mind and *moeurs* of nations, involving, of course, the notion of "luxury"; ways to improve the conditions of the peasantry (a vast question this, as posed by Châlons-sur-Marne, but elsewhere broken down into numerous more detailed, even technical questions: such as, how to prevent peasant cottages catching fire so often?). Other competitions discussed problems of population and depopulation, involving the role of the Church and the institutions of marriage and the family. Numerous essays treated poverty and vagabondage. Some were devoted to aspects of taxation – one of the areas where society was probed, as it were, most exhaustively; to problems of medicine and hygiene in town and countryside; to education – with much attention being given to that of girls. Some tackled the comparative merits of monarchical and republican patriotism, or the reform of provincial administration. Through such competitions, many anonymous would-be authors sought entry into the public sphere of discourse, ardently concerned with contributing to the better governance of France and to the prosperity and happiness of her people. Thus, however stuffy and stifling the official face of the Academy, their essay questions were often bold (and sometimes got them into trouble) and covered almost every conceivable area of socio-economic life. Though there was criticism of the Church, and though the inadequacies of government were exposed regarding education, for example, specifically "political" debate tended to be muffled. Few writers were bold enough to *demand* a representative assembly accountable to the Nation.

A sincere desire to help the *patrie*, a *passionate* patriotism, did not eliminate darker feelings, often quite the reverse. Recently both Foucault and Marx have been taken to task by Gareth Stedman Jones ("The Deterministic Fix") for being too harsh on Enlightenment ideals, for emphasising a dark side of the Enlightenment, aiming at mastery and control, complicit with discipline and surveillance, rather than aspiring towards freedom and liberation. Yet, in the academic essays, a "dark side" can be seen emerging, as it were, into the light. Humanitarian penal and legal reform *did* involve control, discipline, surveillance – as well as a sometimes grotesque legibility, as when one reformer wished to brand the body of a recidivist with details of all his crimes, till – theoretically – there would be no skin undedicated to writing, unamenable to reading. (Some reports on such proposals did wonder if a lingering death in prison was not worse than a quick exit from life itself.)

Light and dark were indeed inextricably bound together. The academic plans for school reform for Marseille in the 1780s included, certainly, the Greek ideal – and Marseille was, or had been, Greek – the lycée on the hill, airy, open to free, even perambulating discussion, liberated from autocratic attitudes.[6] But, also, more generally, colourful and airy classrooms were to be provided for *all* schools. Discipline was to be mild, even enforced by forms of pupil self-govern-ment. But surveillance was to be all-pervasive. If boys' dormitories were always to be lit this was for ceaseless nocturnal supervision. Dressage and discipline of mind and body were to be intense during the daytime. So too was the surveil-lance of boys coming and going from school – the bustling streets a danger zone of freedom and escape, liberty and licence, pickpockets and prostitutes. There were to be no real holidays, for fairly obvious reasons. Surveillance was to extend to parents' family life (never good, clean, hygienic or sober enough) – and therefore to apply to the period before birth, with particular attention to maintaining respectability and decorum at the moment of conception. There was a dismal distrust of sexuality, a deep distrust of women and a depressing reliance on sport to dampen or delay pubertal sexual feelings: wrestling, cer-tainly, but boys' shorts were to be securely fastened at the waist! (Hardly a Greek touch, this?)

Thus the writers struggling to enter the public sphere frequently exposed neurotic, suspicious, paranoid anxieties. They were particularly anxious at the impossibility of imposing secure classifications, of assigning things to clear cate-gories, putting them into sealed compartments, fixing "les mots" irrevocably to "les choses". Often their proposals aimed at alleviating the effects of existing, worrying changes – usually economic in nature – rather than proposing "radi-cal" solutions to society's problems. Moreover, stylistically they revealed in their writings Pierre Bourdieu's "hypercorrection of the petty bourgeoisie" (*Parler* 7). Over-anxious to master classical style and language, they clumsily tried to repress subjectivity but often ineptly exposed raw nerves in their desperate desire for acceptance by the guardians of the norms and standards of *écriture* and morality. The generous aspirations of such men, their sincere hopes for *their* future and *their* country's future were accompanied (and indeed reinforced) by bitter resent-ment at the rich and powerful of the old regime. From the corpus of academic – i. e. "bloodless" – writing, one can fairly clearly discern those categories which, missing their chance to rally in the euphoria of 1789, were to be targeted in the Terror. Certainly, social stereotyping's villains – ruthless nobles, "fat-cat" clerics, unscrupulous financiers, speculators and hoarders – have a life of *longue durée* – at least from medieval preachers onwards: the "successful", in an unjust world.

---

[6] On "a system of public education suitable for a port city", launched in 1782 by the Municipality, backed by the Chamber of Commerce, the Academy's *concours* attracted 28 essays, some of them very substantial. No prize was offered, however. An article based on these essays has been accepted for publication by *Studies on Voltaire*. Archives of the Academy of Marseille, Manuscrits en portefeuille, IV, Sciences philosophiques, tome 2, Education.

What constituted success, even disregarding what might have justified it, was debatable. It seemed, increasingly, to depend on money. In relation to "reading" and "writing", it is noticeable that Habermas's "bourgeois public sphere", though frequently invoked, is often divested of its "bourgeoisie". Having rashly jettisoned Marx, as well as having eviscerated Foucault, cultural historians such as Chartier make few references to the market, and certainly give very little sense of the market's ruthless struggles, involving actual socio-economic groups and interests in the difficult process of formation, of forming, indeed, *the* market. Moreover Foucault in *"Il faut défendre la société"*, in his concentration on aristocratic discourse, neglects – and goes close to denying (186) – the formation of a bourgeois historical meta-narrative to counter that of Boulainvilliers. This counter-discourse, centred round the rise of the communes and the discoveries of printing and of America, related the growth of commerce and the exchange of goods and ideas to questions of power and knowledge. Though France had been much less successful than Britain in consolidating such a relationship, this account became hegemonic to the point of cliché in certain circles, underpinning Sieyès's crucial contribution to 1789. His pamphlet, *What is the Third Estate?*, is highlighted by Foucault for its emphasis on "capacités" (knowledge and competence as entitlement to success and power), though Foucault might have noted Sieyès's likening of government to the chief shareholding interests of a commercial company.[7] What may need stressing, for it has hardly been integrated into "main-line" accounts of the cultural origins of the French Revolution, is that these "economic" groups and their members invariably produced texts, which sometimes did not cross the threshold of print culture till they burst out into the open in the political (and economic) struggles of 1789. However, here too, earlier writings in print and manuscript do exist (among academic essays, for example) which prefigured alignments which we can summarily, crudely divide as *for* and *against* commercialism, favourable to or fearful of accompanying change.[8] We may add that Foucault might have noticed that in his own work the concept of *needs* is undertheorised, as is the concept of *interests*, which he sometimes rejects and sometimes uses. There is no reason to see either of these as necessarily preformulated and imported from "outside". Indeed attempts to define needs and interests, to attach these to specific social, political and economic groupings, were an integral part of most revolutionary struggles, and involved texts from the lowest to the highest level of elaboration. Closer attention to such processes – troublesome then as now – might have

---

[7] Yet the Bicentenary produced numerous works on economic, or political-economic, discourse: for example, G. Faccarello's and P. Steiner's *La pensée économique*. See also, Morilhat and Larrère.

[8] For example, in an essay competition held by Marseille Academy in the 1770s, on the influence of commerce on the mind and *moeurs* of peoples.

helped Foucault articulate more clearly the various discursive and non-discursive elements which float around his texts.

In 1789, of course, all levels of discourse were represented, in this "mise en insurrection des savoirs". (IFDS 13) The Metz magistrate, Pierre-Louis Roederer, passionately involved in political struggles, theorised political economy and wrestled with the question of "interests" while managing — or at least owning — a glassworks. Cahiers — lists of grievances from localities or socio-economic groups — varied from the badly-written ink-smudged single grievance from a Pyrenean village to the most eloquent and erudite printed exposition of enlightened constitutional principles (with transparency and accountability in the nation's bookkeeping demanded by merchants accustomed to the good ordering of their own). The very process of consulting the Nation, of holding nationwide, remarkably democratic elections, in conditions of the absolute freedom of the press and of meetings, helped to discover, and to constitute, society. The making of the Constitution (as much as the end-result) was not just of superficial importance here, as Foucault should have noted. The Declaration of the Rights of Man and the Citizen consecrated vital "discursive" rights (sometimes only grudgingly or apprehensively, perhaps appropriately so, as with freedom of religious expression, soon to be a disaster-area for the Revolution). So the *struggle* over rights (to be extended to women? to include rights, or entitlements, to work, to welfare, to education?) became a key stake in this and subsequent revolutions: a new, more social and egalitarian Declaration was formulated in 1793. All this is, or should be, commonplace. (Let us add that the Bicentenary's choice of "rights" for celebration was not, of course, politically innocent, but at least led to a thorough academic analysis of the whole concept.) Foucault is not here being examined, even judged, as a professional historian, and found wanting, even guilty, but his neglect of rights weakens some of his arguments.

Especially in 1789, then, entry into the patriotic public sphere involved struggles between groups often bent upon disqualifying (silencing, or if they persisted, eliminating) their political rivals and economic competitors — these being sometimes the same persons. Foucault's emphasis on struggle can illuminate these processes. (A point, incidentally, reinforced by Patrice Leconte's brilliant, passionate film *Ridicule*: a "petty" nobleman, poor and powerless, but with engineering knowledge, struggles to get through the barrier of scoffing, cynical Court society, to interest the king in drainage schemes for his remote, unhealthy province — schemes realised by the Revolution). However, here we use our local research on Marseille to indicate briefly the complexity and acrimony of such struggles as reflected partly at least in a remarkable variety of discursive practices. Take, for example, the masonic lodges. In theory devoted to high and bright ideals, and therefore philanthropically all-embracing, they were in reality socially — and culturally — segregated discursive *dispositifs*. In the 1780s, lodges at Marseille, and elsewhere, engaged in the most disreputable and scurrilous squabbling, mostly clandestine, involving purges and character assassinations which sometimes emerged ignobly into the public sphere via the law court. The lodges exhausted themselves tearing each other apart but members continued their quarrels (often of amour-propre) in an open politics which they did much to embitter and fragment, thus pushing towards extreme solutions and murderous factions (the lover of all men frequently became a killer of many of his fellows).[9]

At Marseille, artisans of the guilds (themselves divided and squabbling) and merchants of the Chamber of Commerce rarely shared the same masonic lodge. *Their* struggles both constructed and deconstructed the Revolution. The Chamber of Commerce, by a self-interested doctrine of virtual representation – whereby merchants represented Commerce and were therefore heroes of a meta-narrative of achievement and enlightenment (of power/knowledge and the money often accompanying them) – claimed to represent their workers and dependents to whom they "gave" a livelihood. They thus tried to disqualify guildsmen from writing and speaking. Equating economic and political representation (and power) merchants tried to silence, and disenfranchise, their "ignorant" inferiors and used naked economic power to sack those who signed, or put a cross at the bottom of, patriotic petitions. However, perhaps going against both Marx and Foucault, as it were, and heeding instead the "local intellectuals" – the patriots of the writing/reading classes – these artisans regarded *rights* as important weapons, especially perhaps the *discursive* rights enshrined in the Declaration.[10] These rights they saw as empowering, with their by no means negligible notions of justice, dignity, recognition and participation. The concept of rights was important in helping to mobilise a mixture of discursive energy and physical force: rights, attached more or less securely to real socio-economic groups in the process of defining themselves, enabled them to find a voice with which to assert their interests, and gave individuals a feeling of solidarity and fraternity, but also an exhilarating, elevating sense of individual worth – as they addressed their fellows and a wider audience in writing or from the hustings, in a mood of physical, mental and moral elation. The lower commercial and industrial classes at Marseille destroyed the Chamber of Commerce. In the Terror, men who in 1789 had been proud to be recognised as "négociants" (merchants) were executed for "négociantisme" – a new, and ugly, word for a new crime.

Words, in this fervid, treacherous atmosphere, could be crucial. In the Revolution, as one pamphleteer observed, "les mots sont les choses" – in extreme situations, words could have the effect of things themselves. In a world of

---

[9] Papers of the lodges of Marseille, Bibliothèque nationale, FM²282–292.

[10] Marx no doubt had a complex view of rights. If these, in 1789, were rights to become bourgeois, they were perhaps necessary but certainly not sufficient steps on the way to a more general emancipation. Foucault does not seem to have recognised this potential.

expanding but precarious commerce, in which some aspired to be winners but more feared losing out, the word "bankruptcy" had made many nervous before 1789. In 1789 the State's bankruptcy betokened massive financial incompetence − of book-keeping, of calculation and tabulation, of rationality − a failure of both knowledge and power, discipline and surveillance on the part of the "absolute" State. The successful merchant, master of *his* books, judged this failure severely, in the name of accountability and transparency and a discipline and surveillance now to be exercised from below − with the punishment demanded of those responsible (or, hitherto, irresponsible). But in the context of the struggles already outlined, the rich *merchant* who did not pay his accounts for work done or goods supplied by the artisan, forced this honest man into bankruptcy. If the merchant himself declared a "fraudulent" bankruptcy to escape such modest creditors, these might go to the wall this way too. This involved questions of shame and honour, feelings of personal worth and subjectivity − or a lack of these which might lead to suicide, or a desire for vengeance (source of more than one subsequent denunciation). Perhaps, however, bankruptcy can be objectified and measured. A devastating commercial crisis of 1774 at Marseille was both quoted in 1789 as proof of the *moral* bankruptcy of the rich *and* has been thoroughly analysed by modern economic historians as an early but classic crisis of what *they* are not afraid to call capitalism (see Carrière and Emmanuelli). France's 1789 bankruptcy produced a discursive explosion of economic and financial texts − and more or less accurate statistics − texts aspiring to the level of scientific knowledge but helping rather, or also, to boost a fiscal bureaucracy whose capillary power and thirst for knowledge was formidable, an aspect of governmentality unduly neglected by Foucault. But bankruptcy also became a particularly bourgeois pretext for disqualifying men from political existence, a political death sentence, a brand of infamy and impotence − a form of permanent legal terror and an anxiety-inducing means of discipline.

What perhaps might be emphasised here is the discursive hybridity of so many texts, even on what might first appear to be utilitarian subjects such as tax reform (though, in Britain, the poll tax − and its riots − have recently shown how many issues are bound up with fiscality). If we look for elements of continuity before and after 1789, the academic essay writer Claude Eymar who, first writing on "the severity of laws" as a deterrent, or not, to crime, then turned his literary attention to a tax plan for the city of Marseille need not surprise us, perhaps, by citing classical authors, Persian examples, French disasters, or by combining attempts to quantify the city's wealth in a quadrillage of space, (*quartier* by *quartier*, street by street, type of house by type of house) with moralistic penalisation of "luxury", gambling and celibacy. A rival scheme by Mathieu Blanc-Gilly coupled declamations against the "aristocracy of wealth" with lamentations of decadence and an obsession with prostitution (to be taxed − and relegated to certain areas, amenable to discipline and surveillance ...).

All this was mingled with *récits* of the author's own upbringing, his simplicity, frugality and concern for the unfortunate but, also, his distaste for the growing insubordination of the city's working population, concluding with the view that tax policy must (as well as protect the food of the poor) encourage economic progress via inward industrial investment (and docile, low-cost labour). Tax questions gave much opportunity for revenge, resentment and vindictiveness to be portrayed as social justice (though we would not deny the reality of such loftier motivation). Tax questions also aroused strong passions, as well as "rational" reactions. Taking examples of *reading,* I would like merely to cite two glimpses of responses to texts. Individual, as when the rich, educated and surprisingly honest merchant Jacques Seimandy admitted in print that Blanc-Gilly's pamphlet had been a revelation, in problematising an age-old tax-system hitherto blindly accepted as natural and just to the people: or, collectively, as when the authorities, sending armed men to arrest Blanc-Gilly, were confronted and driven back by an irate army of his readers ... A reader response for which he thanked them in his next hand-grenade of a pamphlet.

One might, also, of course, spatialise reading and writing (and speaking and singing) during these debates of early 1789: in the café, the theatre, the artisan's workshop, in markets, in the street – where *placards* and *affiches*, lists of denunciation, false royal orders to *kill all nobles* were put up, torn down, defaced, pasted over or, sometimes, reproduced in oral or scribbled form in the language of the people, the "jargon" of the fish wives. One might *gender* discourse, though this is difficult when male writers sometimes purported to be women and women claimed to be men, in a world momentarily turned upside down. Public and private utterances might be confronted, especially revealing if these tried to assess the relative importance of "philosophy" and physical violence, of the discursive and the non-discursive, the intentional and the unintentional, in bringing about the triumph of justice, or tried to evaluate the role of reading and writing in "preparing" a Revolution which few had ever thought likely to be one of sweetness and light, the conversion of bad to good, by mere virtue, or magic, of the *word.*

Anyone who made a socially useful contribution was embraced with open arms, with enthusiasm, gratitude. Feelings of fraternity and a longing for community were strong. However, offers of fraternity, if rejected, spurned and denied, might provoke an immense upwelling of bitterness, an upsurge of vindictiveness, a sharp sense of wrongs and humiliations suffered in silence. The desire emerged to destroy what had been idolised – God as loving father above, the king as caring father on this earth, leaders recently applauded: even when some of these could not be physically eliminated, their written traces should be annihilated: "all books dealing with God" might be burned, all emblems of monarchy, the journals of Hébert and Desmoulins. Once-esteemed "friendly" peoples were regarded as "cannibals" – as war, real war, was pursued against Britain (no prisoners were to be taken). Not surprisingly, therefore, in the struggles of the Revolution, even in 1789 which knew moments of euphoria, darker aspects of recent controversies (over religious intolerance especially) were not forgotten. Against Breton nobles boasting of their charity to the poor, Volney quoted the academician Thomas's caustic comment: "L'histoire des bienfaiteurs est un chapitre de plus à joindre à l'histoire des tyrans" (*Sentinelle* 5 Dec. 1789). Earlier writings – highly inflammatory extracts from Raynal – were resurrected (sometimes, embarrassingly, their author, or purported author, still lived). Writers quoted themselves, having been persecuted and derided as troublemakers, republicans, visionaries, and now cited their evocations of the virtues of republican Rome. They now published essays rejected by academies as too radical – too scathing in their criticism of Court, nobility and Church, too outspoken in their defence of the people over questions of taxation, penal laws or seigneurial oppression. Many now claimed that in the old regime all the frivolous arts had been encouraged: over the "science of politics and morality" (linked incessantly) a veil of obscurity had been deliberately preserved. Even worse, enforced frivolity, and moral-political ignorance, was blamed for the "excesses" of a Revolution which might otherwise have been peaceful.

Forms of rationality were questioned. Clearly, "divine reason" was troublesome and disruptive, as interpreted by priests, but elevating and reassuring as revealed in celebrations of Nature and the Supreme Being in gothic cathedrals, like Laon's, converted into Temples of Reason and Truth. In desperate struggles, in war, it became obvious that "military reason" and "civil reason" might part company. As Reason as an all-embracing ideal came under pressure, in a situation where *salut public* was primordial, raison d'état, earlier branded the duplicity of the old regime, might assume new virtues. Or the moralisation of politics, so obsessively called for by reformers of the 1770s and 1780s and so central to the Revolution, might demand the deployment of "la politique" (though still rather frowned upon as "Machiavellian") to defeat Reason's enemies. But if reason and virtue were to be indissolubly married – an idealised "people" bearing witness to this much-desired union – then all enemies had to be eliminated. Their duplicity, argued Saint-Just, could be defeated only by revolutionary policies taking their tactics from ruse and crime. Robespierre's criticism of the intellectuals of the old regime – the philosophes, the academies, the materialists, the atheists – while hardly discriminating, revived Rousseau's themes: they had preferred corrupt "civilisation", in their life-style and their writings, to the defence of the people's rights. Flattering the aristocracy, they had valued pleasure above truth. Dislike of upper-class enjoyment became part of the Terror, incorporating a philistine dismissal of "useless" and self-indulgent knowledge and science, pushing for the guillotining of Lavoisier and Condorcet and imposing a cultural nihilism of vandalism and iconoclasm. Or, more creditably perhaps, it might lead to the awkward question: why, despite all our – or "your" – reason and philosophy, arts and sciences, has Henri IV's wish, that all peasant families should enjoy a "poule au pot" each Sunday (old style) not been fulfilled?

Strife and struggle, the perpetual war of aristocrats versus people, priests versus reason and truth, rich versus poor — "on est forcément l'adversaire de quelqu'un", remarks Foucault (IFDS 44) — meant that, by mid 1793, great hope was vested in a new Constitution, to end strife, bring happiness, fulfil the promises of Philosophy. Yet the Constitution, as a text, needed explanation — a possible infinity of other texts — and, as an "edifice", needed buttressing by, for example, the education of the people. But, to make education work, would one not need to undertake the immense task of closing the enormous gap between rich and poor? Foucault's statement that the bourgeoisie could not rely on constitutions to consolidate their hegemony may perhaps draw attention to the wide range of strategies needed, across different fields. After all, in 1793, one pamphleteer, arguing for the involvement of the people in public affairs, to be facilitated by a democratic Constitution, noted that, in the old regime, the strategy had been to divide "la classe indigente" and "la classe riche". The rich, out of vanity as well as interest, had been persuaded that the people should be "separated" from them and had accomplished this by force and by "supplice" (the spectacular punishments described so graphically by Foucault). A heavy legacy of distrust and enmity had to be overcome. This proved impossible. But the shelving of the Constitution of the Year II, and with it the much-discussed new Declaration of Rights (with its right of resistance to oppression), should not totally justify cynicism: it provided a flag for future resistance to a disciplinary bourgeois domination. Whether this Constitution, and subsequent ones, served, as Foucault suggests, as a mask for the introduction of disciplinary power is debatable and doubtless worth pursuing, possibly bearing in mind Foucault's chilling reference to "le sang qui a séché dans les codes" (IFDS 242). Clearly conditions of war and revolution are unfavourable to liberal and democratic constitutions, and conducive to control, surveillance and discipline — no strikes in the munition factories, or in the printing presses putting the government's message across. Any troublesome resistance or dissent is easily branded as treason.

That justice should come to seem a bogus ideal, as the ever-widening hunt for "suspects" dispelled dreams of reconciliation; that, far from the death penalty being abolished, killing became routine and normalised; that far from prisons being exemplary sites of moralisation, and rehabilitation, they descended further into realms of squalor, disease, promiscuity and despair — or scenes of a savage "people's justice" which Foucault comes dangerously near to praising — all this formed aspects and episodes of a "Franco-French War". This involved the punishment of whole populations or "races" (in the Vendée); the apocalyptic punishment of whole towns ("Lyon n'est plus"), the destruction of its buildings, to return the site to sylvan Nature, with peasants pastorally dwelling in scattered

cottages; the humiliation of disgraced Marseille (Ville Sans Nom); the killing of
God and the soul ("Death is an Eternal Sleep"). In a "mortal politics" of sacral-
ised killing and martyrdom, the true Friend of the People could only demand
the extermination of its enemies, in ever more lurid language... But others than
Marat were verbally violent. Priests, it was alleged, "built their altars on human
skulls"; kings were "devourers of men". Death was to be "put on the agenda";
local revolutionaries boasted that they would drink blood from the skulls of
their enemies, before playing *boules* with them. Tyrannicide was praised, with
proposals to form bands of such assassins. Local atrocities excelled in barbarism
− the *noyades* of Nantes, for example, where priests and young women, stripped
naked, bound together on barges, consummated "republican marriages" in the
dark, swirling waters of the Loire. All this, and more, reveals the workings of
"Power" in extreme situations, even − or especially − when in the service of
high ideals (and metaphors of elevation occur obsessively in writings of the
Terror). Little wonder that Reason was questioned from within the Revolution.[11]

Little wonder that observations were made regarding "Power" too (some of
the most notable in the period after the shock of the Terror − but we do not
go beyond the Year II). The Terror has been portrayed, by Marx and/or Engels,
as the work of frightened men, aware of their precarious hold on power. Just as
the earlier (1789−92) proliferation of texts and laws testified to deep-rooted
anxiety and insecurity, so the constant redoubling of measures of Terror, and
the voluminous textual justifications for these, together with the multiplication
of occasions when the people would read them or have them read out to them,
suggest a fear that some historians have branded as paranoid. Power, and a fear
of power, had, after all, been a key issue throughout the Revolution. The 1789
Declaration enshrined the separation of powers as essential to any regular government. The Constituent Assembly had "unlimited power", perhaps a contradiction in terms in a Foucauldian perspective − a contradiction which helps to
explain many of the Revolution's difficulties. Distrust of governmental power,
of the executive branch, had allowed the breakdown of law and order, the emergence of rival powers (clubs whose power was based on "opinion"). To reassert
central authority, the Revolutionary Government again resumed unlimited powers, or delegated such powers to deputies on mission who, ever more belea-
guered in an often hostile environment, frequently resorted to bloodthirsty measures, as at Nantes. "Unlimited powers", they lamented, "but no power". Power,
some said, would not tolerate an absence of power, so distrust of power, excessive "jealousy" of power, was counter-productive. Another writer observed that
there could be no government without power, as some seemed to hope, and

---

[11] Needless to say, the "counter-revolution", which was *part* of the Revolution, had a radical critique
of "reason". This deserves separate analysis elsewhere.

there could be no power without danger. The "illusions" of power were perhaps the greatest danger.

On the theme of power and reason, one obscure but perceptive writer, Jean-Louis Seconds, warned of "an imaginary optimism which exceeds our strength". He noted how difficult it was to distinguish between "réalités" and "chimères", especially given men's disposition to take illusions as real, especially since they were usually more agreeable. Such wishful thinking was all the more easy since reality could not be perceived directly: man's thought "moved continually in a vicious circle", always affirming "the same of the same", whether this be fictive or real. Nothing could be proved (nor, using a Foucauldian phrase, was there any "meilleur ordre primitif" to be recovered or liberated). Reason was not "the art of seeing, directly and immediately, each thing in itself". So Reason was vague, indeterminate, uncertain. In such a situation, "public reason" was the opinion of the greatest number on matters of general concern. Using a military metaphor, Seconds posited the existence of an informed avant-garde leading reason against error but this avant-garde was not necessarily followed: and even the most ignorant could *claim* to speak for reason. There was thus a need to appeal to "la raison présumée" – formed by good books, enlightened men, experience, history and public opinion, as democratically constituted as possible: this, though not infallible, might inform a rational art of politics, based on the knowledge of men (sic), their situation and needs. Criticising many who saw reason as an eagle, soaring to seize its prey, Seconds preferred a tortoise – or a slow and timid snail, leaving a shining trace behind her.

To trace, in our turn, such reflective comments might detect interesting patterns. Studies of the intrusion of revolutionary power into hitherto isolated communities have already provided not only intensely vivid local histories, but important insights into the dynamics of power relations. Foucault's comment that power is best known by its effects can be tested in such case studies. Via frequent purges, power circulated, though within politically fairly narrow channels, but covering the whole of France in a formidable variety of *appareils*. At least some degree of surveillance was to be exercised against those in power, through a capillary network of clubs and committees of surveillance themselves staffed by a minority of militants. At least ideas were floated regarding the recall of deputies and control of their enrichment, to prevent the formation of a new corporation of politicians. Foucault's argument that revolutionary power destroyed the corporate obstacles to the generalisation of disciplinary power can be further explored, though it is hardly a novel suggestion, except in so far as it seems to deny or ignore individual empowerment (perhaps this reflects the weakness of French liberalism) (PK 105). What needs stressing here is that though, in some ways, the Terror attempted a *closure* of discourse – certainly via censorship, the execution of orators and journalists, the persecution of the Church – it was in fact, despite the laconicism of Saint-Just, for whom each sentence was an act – extremely garrulous. The writing emanating profusely from the Committee of Public Safety was amazingly metaphorical – what a proliferation of venomous reptiles, or even vampires, to combat! (Not to mention "sacerdotal caterpillars" to destroy). The sheer diversity of writing in the Terror has hardly been surveyed.

To be dispelled here is a too-easy identification of Jacobinism and "totalitarianism". Despite common features, no doubt, we would argue that even in the Terror, the French Revolution retained a creative, liberating potential, that it was not totally destructive (and this not just because it lacked the technological means for mass killing). Some of the murderous policies mentioned above were local – disavowed or ended by the central government. Death was not "put on the agenda": "We are not cannibals", protested the indignant president of the Convention. "The French Republic believes in the immortality of the soul", France, led by Robespierre, proclaimed to the world and beyond. Heeding Foucault's contention that there is no power without resistance, we should surely seek for discordant or at least independent voices in the Year II. Certainly some, like the Enragés, wished to push the social war further and faster; others wished to eradicate religion. But the voices of women, though soon silenced, demand attention. Perhaps all those who "resisted" by pursuing "non-political" interests – of business, work, family, daily life – were championing the "modern liberty" of Benjamin Constant or the "negative liberty" of Isaiah Berlin, rather than just speculating lucratively in expropriated property and depreciated paper currency. The "muscadins", condemned for flaunting their own foppish dress, gestures, bodily postures (languid) and language, likewise, however unedifyingly, resisted after a fashion.

While George Mosse claimed that Robespierre might well have been at home in a Nazi Rally ("Fascism", 11), revolutionary festivals – if we read the texts which plan, prepare and then describe or sketch them, if we find in archives the letters which give personal reactions – reveal (besides the occasional frustration at not being able to hear the speeches) enormous enthusiasm, especially for the Fête of the Supreme Being. More importantly, there was often a genuinely joyous mixture or "confusion" of deputies and guardsmen, men and women, young and old, in a fraternal mêlée which gives way to ordered union, certainly, but not to a ruthless regimentation. At a lower level, the popular traditions of carnival were not entirely stifled. If republican rectitude curbed such derisive displays (or turned them against priests and nobles), it also urged dignity upon the people – they now hated the familiar *tutoiement* from condescending superiors – to instill a sense of citizenship, which Foucault sometimes seems to envy (FL, 463; RM, 12), with the dignity of participating in the formation of the national will. As one revolutionary stated: "The word citizen signifies nothing if it does not contain the idea of having political influence". Language was to embody these ideas, as was dress. Educational plans – speeches but also veritable treatises –

were not uniformly dogmatic and doctrinaire, though some critics alleged that they were: schooling for what we might term clones, plans far too "systematic", giving no opportunity for spontaneity or individual choice, all too likely to render the people "inert".

The revolutionaries did not wish to be regarded as barbarians. While they might consider themselves and not the aristocrats – who might have been compulsive killers of game but were now poor warriors – as the true descendants of the freedom-loving Franks, who feature so prominently in Foucault's "*Il faut défendre la société*", they equated barbarism with all that was inhuman. Much writing warned the sans-culottes not to act, and look, as if a republican had to be "ferocious". The politicians' concern with education ("manly" certainly) responded to an intense *popular* aspiration: "The Constitution and Education" was one slogan from the grass roots. Not all civilisation was effete, not all cultured people were "hermaphrodites", unwilling to make a clear choice for the Revolution. Energy and vigour were indeed republican qualities but ignorance was no virtue. The Committee of Public Safety and the Committee of Public Instruction tried – and obviously needed to try – to preserve the cultural heritage of France, partly because they did not wish to appear to fellow Europeans as vandals. Hence long and detailed texts on how to preserve historical manuscripts and art works, sometimes including scornful comments on revolutionary zealots who had destroyed mythical, classical, medieval or even modern images (a statue of Linnaeus, demolished by those who thought he was a despot). Hence the discussion of the setting up of public libraries. Hence the instructions on the principles and techniques of bibliography and cataloguing: at Amiens, cataloguers were even exempted from service in the national guard. Hence the architectural competitions, not only for "elevating" official buildings but also for "salubrious" cottages for the peasants: official (and actually rather intimidating) buildings with constitutional texts, peasant houses with homilies for each room, the Declaration of Rights figuring prominently and a wife's duty to her husband gracing the female quarters. Hence, also, competitions for elementary text books and for hymns to Nature or the Supreme Being and forlorn appeals for plays worthy of the new-won dignity of the French people.

There were many who regarded the Revolution as brought about by books – as a culmination of a modernity that had begun with printing. And printing, hitherto enchained, was now released. (Volney, in 1789, urged the people to go on strike against the upper classes – but in the next number of his paper beseeched the printers not to). Soon the explosion of writing was one factor in producing a shortage of paper: desperate appeals for old rags, draconian penalties for exporting such raw materials, became part and parcel of the Terror. For, now, writing and reading were to be democratised. Even books were to be liberated, especially those sans-culottes of the book world who had championed the rights of the people, Milton representing the English. The flesh-and-blood sans-culottes were not "phraseurs" but, in the new democracy, Vox populi, vox Dei. The new republicans were strict and severe. To call for a strong and frank language; to appreciate a proud and passionate, not cold and calculating style; to distrust metaphors, complex sentences and brilliant effects; to expect the Revolution's "beautiful and heroic actions" to be narrated soberly and simply; to deplore indecent raillery, sarcastic "persiflage" at the expense of their elected officials; to combat "profane and sacriligeous pens" − all this might lead to the outright condemnation, and even burning, of offending writings. Few revolutionaries wanted much theology in their libraries, public or private. Old legal texts had lost their pernicious usefulness. Almanacs and the *bibliothèque bleue* were thought by some to have prolonged the people's credulity, gullibility and superstitiousness. One hardly imagines sans-culottes having much time for romantic novels. Pro-royalist plays could be pelted and booed off the stage. Plays portraying the "sublime" Festival of the Supreme Being were banned because they reduced it to ridicule. Conversely plays such as *Brutus* should make the spectator leave the theatre wishing to stab the first despot he encountered. Religion was the bitterest battle-ground, between the extremist who wished to burn all books which mentioned God and the ex-bishop of Tréguier, for whom revolutionary writing emanated from "infernal nothingness". At times, written words seemed all-important. One word added when taking the clerical oath − to recognise the Constitution only in *temporal* matters − might, when read later, lead a priest to deportation or to death. The whole problem of press freedom was extremely fraught. On 30 October 1792, the Convention debated, precisely, the case of writings inciting to murder, deciding that no law was practicable.

To speak was also risky. Speech was, of course, at a greater or lesser distance from writing: one could write speeches both before and after giving them (very few famous orators, with Danton the exception, extemporised). Speech was more authentic than writing, which might more easily harbour ruse and deceit. At Lille, it was suggested that the best way to spread the good news of the Revolution to foreign countries was not by manifestos but by the more intimate and persuasive means of friendly conversations with Dutch and British p.o.w.s, who would be allowed to return home enthusing about the rights of man. But, speech − or speechifying: the "harangues" so often referred to − might also excite passions, especially when delivered to a large, excited and unsophisticated audience. At worst, such speakers might incite to violence and to murder. *Ecriture* allowed time for calm reflection. On the other hand − and there was no risk-less solution − patriotic sentiments were more likely to be expressed in open assembly than in the more restrictive spheres characteristic of the old regime. Speaking before a large, attentive audience increased confidence and self-esteem. The rhetorical arts of oratory might be taught to foster restrained and dignified delivery.

Writing and speaking might come nearest to each other in the "familiar conversations", the "agreeable chats", which were to follow more formal sessions of instruction, and which were reproduced, often as dialogues or in verse, in brochures or newspapers aimed at the peasants and artisans, full of the adages and proverbs which testified to their own good sense. Singing might provide real enjoyment, even "volupté". But enthusiasm could go too far: the man who gesticulated through the sheer joy of singing the Marseillaise was accused of parodying the sacred song.[12] Sometimes silence was advisable. Garrulousness was frowned on in many clubs: should not speeches (and in the National Assembly too) be limited in length? While "un citoyen demande la parole", in club minutes, testifies to a real determination to let the common man, and the occasional woman, speak, the person who made too many interventions was censured. Clubs which were full of "squawkers" ("piaillarts") often found membership dropping fast.

Particularly interesting — and we now revert to drawing examples from the whole revolutionary period, not just the Terror — are those instances where writing, speaking, reading and hearing seem to come closest. For example: a long *récit* by a "Poor Devil" (*Pauvre Diable*) which attained the status of a comic *conte*, as he, son of a peasant, had tried to advance himself in old-regime society by first becoming a soldier (see Royez). "From the cloisters to the barracks, I found the distance very short", he tells us. A frequent visitor to a convent in his youth, he now found that the day, in each place, was rigorously divided and regulated. Discipline was much the same (if punishment was worse in the army): in fact, "discipline" was invading all services, all administrations, depriving people of spirit and initiative. The net of discipline and the "régime monacho-militaire" extended the length and breadth of Europe. For a time, he served as valet to an unusually well-off priest. Waiting at table, he had overheard many an interesting conversation on clerical concerns (mostly very material ones, accompanying the good food and fine wines). He now (1789) passed on details of these conversations to his readers, as well as the fruits of his attempts to become a lawyer and a doctor. Thus, in a Revolution which some attributed to, or blamed on, the reading of books, and which one writer equated with *seeing* ("the cataract of slavery fell from our eyes"[13]) reading was obviously important, and sometimes even entertaining.

Certainly, the ideal was of an already-existing inner conviction which preceded reading or hearing, which instinctively understood laws, and the need for these laws, before they were formulated in words. Many writers and orators, especially when addressing the peasantry or urban lower classes, felt that their words were merely expressing what was already in the hearts and minds of

12 Archives départementales of the Aisne, Laon, L2117, Club of Chauny, 19 May and 6 June 1794.
13 Archives départementales of the Aisne, L1686, District of Chauny, 3 December 1793.

their enthralled but tongue-tied and illiterate audience. Evidence can be obtained regarding the interaction of orator, writer and audience, though often only as an account of a rhetorical triumph. The popular leader Varlet added to a draft declaration of rights a "note historique" in which he thanked the "Peuple sans-culotte", who had taught him in four years of encounters in public places more than all the "timid savants". In general, reading, literacy and education would reduce what the new revolutionary bourgeoisie tended to regard as the rather mindless violence of the people. The numerous catechisms – political, military or addressed to women and children – inculcated obedience to the laws, as well as both public and private morality. A woman reading "with pleasure" to fellow clubists Robespierre's speech on the Supreme Being, or young children, at Laon, reciting the articles of the Declaration of Rights which their elders were to comment on as the most didactic part of a festival, before music, harmony and dance swept them off their feet – these were scenes of calm in a world of strife, still moments of closeness to nature and to the creator (how many accounts of festivals note that the sky was "serene", the breezes "gentle"?). Why, then, so many quarrels over words when, said some, there was already, or might so easily be, agreement on things? Words were not of course the source of all misunderstanding and clearly not all incited to violence. However, we have tried to show how, in the French Revolution, texts, discourses, certain discursive prac-tices and events, the superabundance of *appareils* and *dispositifs* of one sort or another, were closely bound up in struggles of life and death. Such struggles sometimes seem, and often seemed, "senseless", or without pattern, certainly without reason. It is suggested here that some of Michel Foucault's concepts – and concerns – can illuminate important aspects of the Revolution, though other aspects are neglected (the Revolution's intense nationalism; military matters – despite Foucault's military metaphors – and religious questions, in-cluding the Church as an apparatus of discipline, immensely fertile in discourse-production, adept at techniques of surveillance and with a wide and effective armoury of punishments ...). However Foucault does not have to treat these questions specifically in order to provide us with illuminating insights.

The texts of Foucault most used here make no claim to comprehensiveness or, indeed, to complete consistency. In this, they are refreshing and inspirational: for the historian, Foucault makes entering the archive(s) more exciting. In fact the indeterminacy, or open-ness, of many of his formulations seems to *expand* the archives, by the pertinent problems they pose – leading from an excessively "culturalist" approach to wider and perhaps "sharper" concerns. A new work by Ken Alder, on arms and Enlightenment, deplores that "recent historical 'revisionists' have divorced eighteenth-century material conditions from con-comitant political struggles" (jacket blurb). John A. Lynn's recent study of the armies of the French Revolution has a fascinating cultural dimension, looking at songs written to fire soldiers' enthusiasm for the Republic. Both integrate the problematic of war into cultural history: empirically and conceptually they expand the archive. This is in the spirit of Foucault's determination to listen to the widest possible range of "voices", a democratisation of discourse, not without problems, but which is particularly appropriate for the revolutionary period. It also accords well with the eighteenth-century practice of treating problems "philosophically", that is, searching for links between different phenomena across different fields — intense interest in, even impassioned promotion of, "principles", certainly, but also meticulous attention to the empirical practices which were almost inextricably bound up with them.

To repeat: the sheer diversity of the printed and written archives of the French Revolution, and particularly those of the Terror, has hardly been surveyed — the tableau of the *maximum* of prices throughout France, including all material artefacts, all trades, making society more "legible" than hitherto, advancing the "science" of political economy while republicanising and moralising commerce. Also the ethnographic writing of representatives *en mission* in darkest France, among an illiterate and fanaticised peasantry, encountering strange *moeurs* sustained by alien languages ... The pathetic "last letters", on the eve of the guillotine ... Letters of poor persecuted priests, hounded to abjure or marry, revealing age, infirmity, bewilderment, sometimes despair, but often faith and fortitude ... Remarkable writings of hope — Condorcet's *Esquisse* envisaging collective life projected into a happier future, the individual's life-span healthily extended ... Writings which *surprise*, de Sade advocating clemency, not killing ... Of course, writing itself could be a death sentence — or a virtual suicide as for Desmoulins, touchingly portrayed in Wajda's *Danton*. So too could reading — one's life might depend on the journals one subscribed to.

But the iconic representation of Reading/Writing/Killing is Marat, killed after reading Charlotte Corday's hand-written letter (reproduced by David, but how accurately?) — a text appealing to the right to Marat's goodwill. But did she also *speak*, less charitably, even more deceitfully — offering vital secrets from Caen, which themselves might have led to more killing? The *other* letter, from Marat's pen, generously offered a perhaps bloody assignat "to that mother of five children whose husband died in the defence of his country" (see Kadish and Bonnet). An obscure text, emerging into immortality, it evoked war, women and the people, thus opening out into an almost infinite context of struggle ...[14]

---

[14] I wish to thank Mrs Jill Davey, Cultural History Group, Aberdeen, for her help in completing this article.

III

Modes of Conceptualizing Cultural History

9

The Process of Intellectual Change:
A Post-Foucauldian Hypothesis

IAN MACLEAN

The manner in which thought evolves has been a matter of great interest to cultural historians and theorists of history throughout the century, and has been investigated in a wide range of ways, nearly all of them addressing some or all of the following questions: does thought evolve independently of the broad cultural context in which it occurs? If it is inseparable from such a context, is it an epiphenomenon of other forces, or an ingredient of the context itself, interacting with other forces and acting upon them? What accounts for the relative stability and length of the periods in which a given conceptual scheme (let us call it a paradigm) dominates? What brings these periods of relative stability to an end? It would of course be possible to investigate the history of thought (as some have done) as though paradigms of thought consisted purely of unhistorical idealities, accessible to some sort of overarching rationality and recordable in some sort of universal notation in an unproblematic way; or to assume that thought is in constant evolution, and that there are no such things as epistemological breaks. But these two views are no longer popular, and much of the credit for their unpopularity must go to Gaston Bachelard, Georges Canguilhem, and latterly to Michel Foucault, who carried forward and popularised their ideas. In their wake, most historians of thought, in acknowledging that paradigms are authoritative for periods of time and are replaced by other paradigms, accept also, if only implicitly, that the history of thought is not a history of continual progress, in the way some nineteenth-century intellectual historians assumed it to be. They also accept that the question of the nature of paradigms must be settled before one can determine how they change or are replaced; and that whether or not this change is theorised, the right way of going about a historical account of conceptual schemes is to present them in chronological order.

One example of such a chronology is Michel Foucault's *Les mots et les choses*. Since its publication in 1966, this has been accused of all of the following deficiencies: of citing insufficient evidence, or the wrong evidence, in support of its theses; of being wrong in its determination of epistemological breaks; of being wrong in its characterisation of linguistic and philosophical issues; of being excessively anti-humanist in its claim that those who inhabit the successive epistemes which it describes did not master them, but were the victims of them; of being misguided in its methodology and theoretical assumptions; but as far as I know, no-one has accused Foucault of being indifferent to the problems of writing intellectual history. He devoted at least one full-length study to them (*L'archéologie du savoir* of 1969), and evinced a willingness later in his career to develop other models of historical analysis. He conceded that *L'archéologie* was a sort of heroic failure; but I should like here to pay tribute to it as an ingenious attempt to set down a methodology for the study of the history of thought which has forced a considerable degree of sophistication on subsequent writers in the same area. However, it seems to me that one of its major weaknesses as theory lies in its failure to look beyond a very French context for ideas about the history of thought: Max Weber, Edmund Husserl, R. G. Collingwood and Thomas Kuhn had already struggled with problems similar to those of Foucault, but had done so from different intellectual backgrounds. One of the purposes of this paper is to see whether some of their insights can be brought to bear on the question of paradigms and paradigms shifts in a profitable way. Moreover, Foucault himself never offered a theoretical explanation of change in intellectual life, whereas all of the above did. My intention therefore is to begin with an account of the paradigm as this is conceived by Foucault, before turning to the thinkers I have mentioned, and suggesting a consequential modification of Foucault's episteme. I shall then take the example of Foucault's episteme for the Renaissance and sketch an alternative account of it and its relationship with the alleged epistemological break of the seventeenth century in the light of this modification.

Foucault produced his "theoretical work" *L'archéologie du savoir* as the explanatory frame to his earlier historical writings: *L'histoire de la folie à l'âge classique* (1961), *La naissance de la clinique* (1963), and *Les mots et les choses* (1966). It was written at least partly in a polemical spirit: not only the various traditions in the history of ideas, but also the products of the Annales school are in Foucault's sights. One mark of this spirit is his refusal to use the terminology elaborated by such historical schools to describe the successive states of the human sciences: words such as tradition, influence, source, idea, discipline, science, system, ideology, rationality, cause, and the more precise lexicon of the Annales school – "outillage mental", "représentation collective", "structure et conjoncture", "mentalité" – are all eschewed. But Foucault's subversion of accepted procedures, it will be remembered, goes much further than that. At various points in the text he rejects all of the following: the unicity of the voice of the historian – part of *L'archéologie du savoir* is written in dialogue (28), and in his 1970 inaugural lecture *L'ordre du discours* he expresses the wish to do away with voice altogether (81) – structural analysis (the postulation of a stable corpus of material whose minimal units can be identified and combined); psychologism (either in the sense of the recourse to norms of human mental behaviour, or that of the location of the objects of human cognition in the mind); idealism (the independent existence of concepts); hermeneutics (the extraction of meaning from texts of the past: for Foucault there is nothing but surface; there is no depth or hidden sense). All forms of totality or totalising discourses of a Marxist kind are spurned. Man is described as a modern self-invention, fashioned from a particular configuration of knowledge, destined soon to disappear; Foucault's history of man is a story about the way he constituted himself as a subject, and then made his body, his behaviour, his reason and his consciousness the object of his study, and a field to be controlled, regulated, trained and coerced. In this analysis, man's "rationality" becomes not a faculty, but an authoritarian straitjacket.

What Foucault sets out to investigate is a very fundamental form of ontology, but not one associated with profound knowledge; it is a superficial, finite, if largely invisible, field, which is discontinuous, not defined by the agenda of the modern state of any associated discipline, and is peopled by "utterances" which are only graspable in their differences and their dispersion. If coagulations of these "utterances" occur at all − which Foucault calls "discursive formations" − they appear only in the form of consistent relations: the objects to which they "refer" are no more than objectifications, whose scientific status cannot be established, and whose meaning cannot be recovered by semantic or rhetorical analysis. In calling his previous book *Les mots et les choses*, he was being explicitly ironic, for neither the words nor the things of the title have any substance to them: they are not presences, but absences. The description made by the historian is remote from his object, indirect, incomplete; it describes a "preconceptual field" in which the "preconcepts" are no more than organizing operators or functions revealing relationships of dependence, processes of validation, contingent theories of truth. The "utterances" which these "preconcepts" inform come together in "discourses" which are neither systems nor mere aggregations of knowledge; archaeological history as practised by Foucault uncovers not a "mentalité" but an "episteme" which he defines as the total set of relations that unite, at a given period, the discursive practices that give rise to epistemological figures, sciences, possibly formalised systems. The episteme is not a form of knowledge or type of rationality which manifests the sovereign unity of a subject, a spirit, or a period; it is the group ("ensemble") of relations that can be discovered, for a given period, between the sciences when one analyses them at the level of discursive regularities (*L'archéologie* 250). The notion of "episteme" offers access to the past, but an untotalisable past characterised by regularities, not rules, and by modes of discourse in which truth, knowledge and power somehow cohabit, but which are not mastered by the human subjects who inhabit them rather than use them; an episteme is an "ensemble", not even a structure, and like its "formations discursives", it has no interior and no depth, nor is it a finite set of organising principles.

Foucault therefore avoids the implicit positivism of the Annales school, the totalising tendency of Marxist thought, the scientificity of structuralism, the striving after significance of Diltheyan hermeneutics; but I do not believe he avoids a quasi-Kantian categorialism; the episteme which he describes seems to me and others (Dreyfus and Rabinow 25–30, 92) to set down conditions of possibility or occurrence which constrain the production of discourse absolutely. It is also clear why Foucault could not elaborate a theory of intellectual change: his episteme has no agents through which to bring about such a change, for he effectively removes the human element from his episteme; one critic, Otto (74), compared his Renaissance intellectual scene to a laboratory without a scientist in it; whatever is being experimented on or done is devoid of any form of agency. He also avoids (at least in this early stage of his work) causal explanation of any kind.

These features of the episteme emerge clearly when it is compared to similar models such as Weber's ideal type, Husserl's notion of disciplinary sedimentation, Collingwood's constellations of absolute presuppositions and Kuhn's paradigm. All of these grapple not only with the question of change, but do so in the context of the distinction between understanding and explanation, made famous by Wilhelm Dilthey in his essay on hermeneutics published in 1910, and brilliantly elucidated more recently in Georg Hendrik von Wright's book on the subject, which appeared in 1971. I shall examine the models produced by these thinkers in turn.

Max Weber's ideal type, as this is set out in the introductory essay to the *Archiv für Sozialwissenschaft und Sozialpolitik* of 1904, is an alternative methodology to that available at the time through the writings of Dilthey, Marx, and German historians in the wake of Ranke and Droysen. It addresses directly the historiographical problems encountered by sociologists and political historians, but can be readily applied to the sphere of intellectual history, as was shown in *Politics, Language and Time* (1973) by J. G. A. Pocock. It is informed by the following premises: that value-free historiography is not possible (which is not to say, however, that all history is a victim of its own biases); that history is not entirely determined by the human will and by human actions; and that individual events (or, for our purposes, individual theories or conceptual schemes) of the past are unique. But for all this, explanation (as opposed to understanding) does have a role to play in historical writing, and the "ideal type" is the form which such explanation takes. Weber does not deny the value of understanding ("einfühlen" as much as "verstehen") in historiography, but claims that ideal-typical accounts of the past, unlike those of narrative history or hermeneutic exposition, are subject to logical presentation and analysis, and can be predictive. An ideal type (later called a "pure type") can be a category ("Renaissance", "city state") or a trend or process ("protestant ethic", "civilisation"); it is postulated not to fit cultural phenomena into categories but to obtain knowledge of particular events of the past whose specificity can be gauged by subtracting their individual features from the generic description of the ideal type. It is therefore a heuristic device, making no claims to normativity or correct representation of reality; it is perspectival, and not complete, although a semblance of completion can be achieved by interlocking a number of ideal types into a structure; it incorporates values at the theoretical level, but it is not used to evaluate its object. It is thus not a hypothesis, nor an approximation, nor a deductive average type, nor a description reached inductively, but a means of subjecting the past to a rigorous analysis which does not reduce the specificity of individual events, and which recognises that a complete account of the past is impossible.

An ideal type can be used to describe a paradigm; but it is also able to describe progressive change and epistemological breaks. To explain such changes Weber asked himself, in his essay on the logic of historical explanation written in 1906, the following question: "through what logical operations do we arrive at and demonstratively support that a causal relationship exists between the 'essential' constituents of [a given] effect and certain constituents selected from the infinity of determining factors?" (*Selections* 117). Part of his answer lies in his theory of rationality, which he set out in *Wirtschaft und Gesellschaft*, published in 1921; there he distinguishes four kinds of substantive rationality (affective, traditional, value-rationality and instrumental rationality) from formal rationality, the non-human logic inherent in systems. Foucault's own notion of the inhuman logic inherent in epistemes closely resembles this formal rationality, without there ever being in Foucault's work acknowledgement of this proximity. Weber's method thus reintroduces both the individuality of acts of consciousness and the factor of voluntary action by human beings into intellectual history, yet without falling into an unreflective positivist approach to data or a purely hermeneutic approach to historical understanding.

Edmund Husserl's essay "Die Frage nach dem Ursprung der Geometrie als intentional-historisches Problem" of 1939 is a phenomenological study of a narrower issue which is particularly problematic to phenomenologists, namely: how do the abstract sciences arise? how are they related to the Lebenswelt and to the historically located individuals who first enunciate them? how do omnitemporal truths permit of future development (i. e. in what form is infinity present in apodictic truths whose apodicticity is grounded in a finite demonstration of truth)? All truth claims, according to Husserl, come in three forms: at the first and lowest level, these are propositions which we understand but to which we neither accord nor refuse belief ; secondly, truth-claims which we justify to ourselves by acquiring the corresponding evidence; finally, truth-claims which we assent to without the corresponding evidence. In the case of geometry, the first kind does not arise; but Husserl wishes to argue that both of the other kinds do arise. For him, geometry is a linguistic entity, i. e. one founded in a communicable sign system; part of its truths is tested and justified by geometers to themselves and others, but another part is simply assented in. This latter consists in the accumulated truths of the discipline. It is conceivable, but in fact impractical, for every geometer to begin from first principles (i. e. the premiss that contingent spatiality can be generalised and abstracted) and work up to the present state of the science, but in fact impractical: what he does in fact is to accept that geometry is the result of social and historical "sedimentation" (a metaphor which Foucault was to exploit in turn). This is an insight of very limited application, as there are many sciences whose successive states are discontinuous; it cannot account for developments in a science which threaten its axiomatic base (for example, Gödel's incompleteness theorems); it establishes no link between a science and its institutional manifestations; and it fails also to answer the fundamental question about the origin of science, namely how did the first person communicate his insight to others when he came to realize that space could be represented in an abstract form? But I believe that the metaphor of sedimentation and the parallel of a system of thought with language are of interest to us here, because the first draws attention to the role of notation in conceptual change, and the second offers the possibility that certain presuppositions can be recovered by those who are informed by them, whereas Foucault's episteme denies human beings all access to these.

Such presuppositions are discussed by Husserl's contemporary R. G. Collingwood in his *Essay on Metaphysics* (1940). His "absolute presuppositions" are found in all thinkers of a given generation; they are *ex hypothesi* inaccessible to them and cannot be validated by them; but they can be mutually inconsistent, and hence subject to eventual explicitation and relativisation. As we shall see, this means that Collingwood is able to offer a theory of intellectual change; he is also able to accommodate absolute presuppositions in his own more famous "logic of question and answer" ' by which historians are able to "re-enact past thought" (*Autobiography* 29 – 43). According to Collingwood, there is no sense in a proposition unless we discover the question or problem which a thinker of the past was posing himself in order to produce the proposition; and when we discover the question, we will uncover also the absolute presuppositions which subtend it. We may reasonably expect thinkers in the same generation or age to share the same set of absolute presuppositions, but this does not have to be the case; so this procedure can permit the localisation of the context of a thought in such a way as to avoid many of the problems which historians face when they set out to describe the thought of a whole age or generation. Nor does the set of presuppositions imprison that age or generation in a categorial straitjacket of a Foucauldian kind, since it does not disable human reflective ability. Collingwood argues furthermore that his "logic of question and answer", which leads to the re-enactment of past thought in the historian, is both explanatory (since it is causal) and descriptive; it both records the event of thought, and explains it at the same time. In this, it can be seen to be the ancestor of the use of speech act theory by Skinner and others as a rule by which to determine the sense of texts of the past (see Tully and Skinner).

Collingwood's theory can also accommodate the process of discontinuous change. In a manuscript addition to the *Essay on Metaphysics*, Collingwood wrote:

> [Conceptual systems] change because the absolute presuppositions of any given society at any given phase in its history, form a structure which is subject to "strains" of greater or less intensity, which are "taken up" in various ways, but never annihilated. If the strains are too great, the structure collapses and is replaced by another, which will be a modification not consciously devised but created by a process of unconscious thought (quoted by Toulmin in Krausz 210).

This claim is consistent with his earlier description of thought in his *Essay on Philosophical Method* (1933) as a dialectical series which is connective, cumulative, asymmetrical and non-deterministic (terms do not determine their successors: but later terms absolutely presuppose earlier terms). But it poses a number of problems: what could unconscious ratiocinative thought be? What is the origin of the "strain" on the system? Is it internal or external to it? What sorts of reasons, principles and procedures can we appeal to, in order to justify the intellectual step of abandoning one constellation of fundamental concepts for another? Can there possibly be a system of thought that is not in some way or other, and to some extent or other, determined by the notation in which it is couched? Some of these problems Collingwood shares with Foucault (the latter's "preconcepts" and "non-discursive sets of rules", for example sound rather like unconscious ratiocinative thought); but he addresses a number of issues which are not addressed by Foucault, notably the motivation of truth-claims and the importance of human reflective activity, which I shall try to take account of in my modification of the notion of paradigm.

Thomas Kuhn's notion of paradigm as this is set out in his *Structure of Scientific Revolutions* of 1962 and the subsequent revisions to this work is even less grandiose in its claims, and even less like a set of Kantian categories. His version of paradigm can be modified; it includes its own validating procedures; it does not have to set out to describe all of nature, but must be successful at solving problems in the area in which it is applied; it can coexist with other paradigms (although because it is described in terms of a Gestalt, it cannot be espoused simultaneously with another paradigm by the same thinker); its authority is vested in the community of scientists who espouse it, but that does not make its basis irrational, even if it introduces into it the human element of social consensus. Kuhn believes also that he can explain both the persistence of past thought patterns and why they change, which Foucault does not attempt to do. Paradigms persist because they satisfy the need of the communities who use them successfully to solve problems; they are abandoned when they can no longer satisfy this need, and also fail the test of elegance (i. e. the requirement of achieving minimum complexity). Armed with these criteria, Kuhn does not have to claim that he has explained everything about the paradigm or the process of change it undergoes; his explanation needs to be no more than sufficient.

Where his theory was most vigorously attacked was on the issue of Gestalt switch and the concomitant claim that paradigms are incommensurable with each other. In 1965, at a conference on Thomas Kuhn's work held in London at which Kuhn himself was present, Karl Popper launched a sharp and clearly formulated attack on what he saw as Kuhn's irrationalism and historicism, which argues against Kuhn's alleged view that we are prisoners of a given paradigm, and are unable to engage in a critical discussion of it. Kuhn had claimed that there is no overarching rationality, neutral language or notation by which different configurations of knowledge can be compared, and had introduced the analogy with natural languages and the fact that it was impossible to produce perfect translations from one to another to illustrate this. Against such a view Popper declared that it was a dangerous dogma to propose that the different frameworks are like mutually untranslatable languages. For Popper, even totally different languages (like English, or Chinese) are not untranslatable one into the other ("Normal Science" 51–8). To be fair to Kuhn, one should point out that he never claimed that translation was impossible, only impure, just as he never accepted that he was the "irrationalist" Popper accused him of being, only a "selectivist", that is, someone who believes that different paradigms or frameworks are not distortions of reality but selections from it, and that this selection is grounded not in the superiority of a given set of logical procedures but in the agreement of a professional community of scholars or scientists as to what constitutes a field of study and what means are most suitable to engage in problem-solving within it (Kuhn "Reflections on my Critics"). Where Kuhn's paradigm seems to me to be most successful is in its claim to provide an explanation for both gradual and discontinuous change in intellectual life, even if it does not address the problem of understanding the past in a Collingwoodian sense. (A more recent model which is yet, to my knowledge, to be applied to historical continuity and change, but which has been successfully used in zoology, is catastrophe theory: see Deakin). Kuhn also draws attention to the role of institutions in the persistence and eventual abandonment of paradigms, although he describes these in terms of communities of scholars, without looking into their precise nature.

I should now like to draw the threads of this paper together, and sketch out a few claims relating to my proposed modification of Foucault's episteme. I shall try to do this without recourse to Popper's universal yardstick of rationality and his implicit belief, through the doctrine of falsification (*Framework* 82–111), that there is some sort of objectively verifiable progress in human affairs. But my first claim is drawn from his critique of Kuhn, namely that frameworks, or paradigms, or mind-sets, contain within them the means of self-critique; more-over, that these means, which imply the existence of a metalanguage or a mental space beyond the framework, are supplied by the ability of language to refer to itself, and are related to the specific feature of human consciousness which is to be aware of itself and of its operations; and finally, that thinkers are thereby enabled to discuss both the presuppositions of their systems which are accessible to them and the point at which they break down, or fall into paradox. To me (and to Louis Mink, who makes this point elegantly in *Historical Understanding* 205) thinkers within paradigms seem to be able to think *with* concepts *about* other concepts *by means of* yet other concepts, but that this does not imply a hierarchy of abstraction: the concepts thought *about* can become the concepts thought *with*, or the concepts *by means of which* this is done; these three functions are interchangeable. This does not mean that a given thinker was capable of making explicit all the ideological investments in his work, nor that he was free from the constraints of academic institutions, politics and religion of his day, nor that he mastered the framework in which he lived to such a degree that he was as capable as we are from a different standpoint to expose its limitations. I owe my suspicion of past thought and indeed my own to Foucault's exposure of such limitations on conceptualisation. But I should wish to claim (with Col-lingwood, and with Graham Priest) both that at any given moment thinkers are both enabled and constrained by the intellectual framework in which they oper-ate; and (more controversially) that they are not even absolutely limited by the notation and terminology which they inherit or evolve. Moreover, conceptual schemes are potentially both pluralist and polyphonic; they contain different discourses which interact with each other both methodologically and termino-logically, and are not closed or finite in the sense suggested by Foucault.

I should furthermore wish to include in any model of a paradigm both the pedagogical process by which it is propagated and the relationship of the institu-tions which support it to the various media of publicity through which it comes to be known. This is implicit in Kuhn's model, although absent from Foucault's, Collingwood's and Husserl's. Ideas are sustained and spread through human institutions; the speed with which they change, and whether they change at all, are factors dependent on the means available to teach them to others, to publi-cize and circulate them, and the willingness of sponsors to pay for such diffu-sion. In doing so such sponsors may be serving a variety of interests beyond the purely intellectual (if there is such a thing as a purely intellectual interest); and they may be engaging in a process which they do not fully control (indeed, which no-one may fully control, for it is not possible fully to predict the uptake by others of texts which are widely circulated). The ideas thus diffused may not be perfectly or completely comprehended, or may be taken up in contexts quite different from that in which they were first conceived. But the uptake of the ideas has in turn to be public in some way; I do not believe that a history of ideas which restricts itself to private reactions to conceptual systems is either possible or desirable. This would imply that the sedimentation metaphor of Husserl, valuable though it is as a means of explaining the recovery of presuppositions by an individual scientist and the subsequent possibility of radical critique of those presuppositions, needs to be modified in some way to accommodate the more confused pattern of uptake which I am trying to describe, and the need for this to achieve public expression.

It follows from the more generous space which I allow to independence of thought (or, if one prefers, from the less precise limits I would set to a given paradigm) that if discontinuous change is to occur, then it will need to be distinguished from the limited self-critique which I suggest can occur within any broad conceptual system; and for it to impose itself, it will need the support of institutional and other modes of publicity. This meshes well with Kuhn's description of scientific revolutions, and can accommodate some aspects of Collingwood's notion of change, especially the emergence into the consciousness of a generation of thinkers of contradictions in their own system of thought. It is inconsistent with Foucault's bald juxtaposition of epistemes, but can accommodate his own use of formal rationality (which is akin to Weber's) to explain the inability of thinkers to prevent conceptual change; or rather, the ability of the logic of a system to impose itself on its human operators. It would clearly be necessary at this point to take into account the question of notation, and to ask to what degree human beings are constrained by the various languages which they employ. Some very interesting work has been done in this respect on Babylonian mathematics by Eleanor Robson (*Mesopotamian Mathematics*), which shows the importance of distinguishing between operative knowledge and theoretical knowledge; and I believe similar points can be made in respect of the prehistory of the modern notion of probability, which seems only to be able to be couched in notations developed in the seventeenth century.

It may be helpful to exemplify these claims by sketching out (in a far too cursory manner) part of my own version of a Renaissance episteme as a rival to that of Foucault. It will be remembered that Foucault describes the preconceptual episteme of the sixteenth century as an all-constraining system of interlocking categories of similitudes which condemned thinkers to tautology by collapsing together semiology and hermeneutics (*Les mots et les choses* 32–59). I shall not give an extensive account of it here; instead, I should like to make a number of points about the paradigm of this period based on a different range of texts to those referred to by Foucault. Where his are mainly drawn from the hermetic tradition and the sphere of natural philosophy, my sample comes from the standard teaching materials used for the senior disciplines of law and medicine, and from the university arts course which served as a propedeutic to both. They can be shown to be widely diffused throughout Europe, both in printed form and through the diaspora of students from influential centres such as Padua (in the case of medicine); together with other pedagogical materials, they had an established place in academic institutions and their publication served a number of interest groups, not least that of the international publishers who made money out of them. To demonstrate the claims I have made about paradigms and paradigm shifts, I shall cite some of the logical procedures taught in the arts course, and show how they were adapted in the ways I have suggested. My choice — of diairesis, theories of opposition, causality and circumstantial description — is dictated by the need to show how Foucault has egregiously set aside evidence for the flexibility and vitality of Renaissance thought in areas such as scientific taxonomy.

The basis of predication is, in law and medicine, diairesis or the technique of division, best known through the tree of Porphyry; this appears to yield necessary relationships between genera, genera subalterna and species, but in fact is employed in law as a nominal way to generate working definitions which allow the law to be applied to real situations. Thus, a definition of "human being" according to Porphyry's tree is a mortal, rational, sentient, animate, corporeal, substance; but the law needs a definition of "human being" in order to determine whether a murderer who has, let us say, six fingers on each hand or two heads is in fact punishable by the law which condemns human murderers to death, or is exempt because his or her deformities exclude him or her from the relevant legal category ; in the same way, a person of ambiguous sex has to be determined to be male or female for practical purposes of inheritance; in both cases, it is not a scientific definition which is authoritative, but a stipulative one (see Maclean, *Interpretation* 104–14). In medicine and in natural philosophy, division is used to create taxonomies of natural species and illnesses, but these also are not claimed to be apodictic, but rather working categorisations. The art of law and medicine is, as the ancient philosopher Pophyry himself put it, the finite knowledge of infinite things: and the art leaves residues of a totally unKantian kind which cannot be accommodated within the loose division that generates its working categories. Another striking example of the same feature of Renaissance thought is afforded by those grammarians who write ingenious and well-ordered grammars of Latin, and then include a section at the end entitled "latinitas"; namely, all those usages, aberrant examples, small classes and idioms which fall outside the explanatory grid (see Jensen 51–90).

In a similar way, the practice of establishing contraries through complex grids of opposition, which in logical terms is a necessary and apodictic science, is adapted in the higher disciplines to accommodate the imperfect nature of realist opposites. In medicine, for example, all contraries are said not to be terms having the *greatest* difference as in Aristotelian metaphysics, but simply having a great difference (Campilongo f. 42v); and all oppositions are in the mode of mediate contraries, which allow for a spectrum of possibilities (including more and less; now and then; and contrary terms which in fact overlap: Dubois,

Methodus 25ff; Maclean, *Renaissance Notion* 28ff.). Causes, in logic, are found in the form of the four Aristotelian kinds (material, formal, efficient, final); in law these are reduced to two ("impulsive" and "final"; what in common law are called mischief and remedy); in medicine they are increased to eight (the four Aristotelian kinds, together with "subjective", "instrumental", "necessary" and "enabling": i. e. a catalyst), to accommodate explanations of the working of remedies (Maclean, *Interpretation* 124−5; Argenterio col. 1493). The fact that one discipline reduces the number of causes, and another increases it, indicates the vigour and flexibility of competing discourses at this time.

There is no accommodation at all of individual beings or events in syllogistic; but both law and medicine have to deal with them, which they do by having recourse to circumstantial description. In law, all cases coming before a magistrate are unique: but a set of questions can bring this unique case under specific laws: through the questions "who", "what", "where", "when", "why", "with whose help" (Maclean, *Interpretation* 81). In medicine, the range of questions varies from those asked in posology, which concern temperament, age, quantity, timing, place, and method of application (Hasler) to the much longer set applicable to diagnosis (the nature of the patient, his or her age, present and past constitution, strength, mode of life, habits, pulse, state of mind, and physical mobility; the season of the year and geographical location; the nature of the illness, its cause, location, and symptoms, and its similarities to other illnesses; indications of factors which may be beneficial or nefarious: see Santori). Both law and medicine make use of similarity and dissimilarity, but in highly sophisticated ways which demonstrate that practitioners are not the dupes of this mode of argument as Foucault claims them to be. One of the definitions of equity, for example, is "the equivalence of things, which requires the same laws to be applied in the same cases": this is acknowledged to be an act of judgment, not a logical procedure, because "similarities are found in dissimilar things", and what is needed is the establishment of *significant* similarity (Maclean, *Interpretation* 78−80, 175−7). In medicine also, the use of inductive processes and the elimination of error by methodical use of syndromes of signs evince the same awareness of the imperfection of the cognitive tools at hand, and their adaptation to real circumstances (see Santori).

It is of course well known that seventeenth-century thinkers such as Bacon, Descartes and Galileo engage in a campaign to discredit their sixteenth-century forbears; Foucault acknowledges this to be one of the sources of his chapter on the Renaissance ("La prose" 20). I wonder myself to what degree he is a victim of their highly effective polemic. It is clear that the mathematicisation of the sciences, the abandoning of complex causation, the adoption of controlled experimental procedures and negative induction are all features of a quite different mind-set from that of the legal and medical arts of the previous age; but it is not clear to me that this makes the earlier age a victim of its own thought patterns. Kuhn's principle of elegance does indeed offer a criterion by which a group of scientists could be led to prefer the mechanical philosophy of the seventeenth century, but his criterion of improved problem-solving does not work, for it was some time before the Copernican system was made to predict the movement of the heavens as well as the Ptolemaic one, or chemical medicine to save more people than it apparently killed. Without looking to the institutions of science at this time, and to the patronage, material support and publicity given to figures such as Descartes, a sufficient explanation of the paradigm shift cannot be given. It is also the case that the shift was not effected without some loss (a loss which figures prominently in Kuhn's theory of revolutions): Renaissance lawyers, for example, had a theory of speech acts which disappeared from view until Austin's *How to do Things with Words* reinvented it; and the benefits of humoral medicine in its determination of the idiosyncrasy of each living organism have only just been rediscovered by practitioners of holistic medicine. Finally, it is also true that seventeenth-century scholars were able to draw on the resources of Aristotelianism in a piecemeal way, just as that same Aristotelianism had contained its own pluralism in its assemblage of competing discourses; so Foucault's claim that "the classical ages gave prior thought [about resemblance] its marching orders" ("La prose" 20) seems to me to be demonstrably false .

I should wish therefore to suggest that it is possible to construct a working hypothesis of a paradigm and a paradigm shift which is not constrained by Kantian categorialism. It would take the form of an ideal type (that is, it would set out to do no more than to offer a heuristic model by which to determine, as it were by subtraction, the individuality of any given theory or thinker); it would retain, from Weber or from Foucault himself, a role for formal rationality in the inherent logic of systems; it would assume, as does Husserl, that sedimented knowledge can be reactivated and subjected to radical critique, without however suggesting that any mode of thought is apodictic in his sense of the word; it would extend Kuhn's sociological insights into the area of the teaching, publication and institutionalisation of learning; and it would look to notation itself as a source of information about conceptual change and conceptual stasis, without, however, presupposing that notation or its lack constitute an insuperable barrier to conceptual change. It would finally develop Collingwood's reflective ability into an exploration of thought at the margins and limits of discourses.

In making these claims, I have an ally in the later Foucault himself: not only the writer of the stirring coda to *Surveiller et punir* of 1975, but also the author of a post-Kantian essay entitled "What is enlightenment?". There Foucault famously declares:

> If the Kantian question was that of knowing the limits knowledge has to renounce transgressing, it seems to me that the critical question today has to be turned back into a positive one: in what is given to us as universal, necessary, obligatory, what place is occupied

by whatever is singular, contingent, and the product of arbitrary constraint? The point, in brief, is to transform the critique conducted in the form of necessary limitation into a practical critique that takes the form of possible transgression ... (Rabinow 45–46)

Nothing could better illustrate the dangers of selective quotation than this passage: or rather, nothing could make clearer that there is more than one Foucault, and that his multiple receptions reflect the *Vielschichtigkeit* of his oeuvre in Nies's sense of the term (*Gattungspoetik* 228); a *Vielschichtigkeit* which will probably ensure its survival long after his name has ceased to be used as a fashionable shibboleth in cultural analysis and history.

10

Periodization as a Technique of Cultural Identification

VLADIMIR BITI

Periodization would appear to be a mite of an anachronistic subject in an age turning its past into a postmodern museum. Nowadays we seem to inhabit a kind of global space which has denied succession in favor of simultaneity and it should be obvious that there is no periodization without succession. To be sure, it would be difficult to trace back to its "roots" the contemporary inclination toward simultaneity and I shall scarcely attempt here to undertake this task. Let me therefore start with the simple remark that in the framework of our century periods of the formerly limited time-span underwent a considerable expansion, as early as with the practice of the theorists of the revolutionary sixties.

This might have been connected primarily to the transformed concept of history introduced approximately at the same time by the school of *la nouvelle histoire*. As is known, the members of this school distinguished three temporal series of different historical speed by diverting the attention of historians from the accelerated history of human events to the slow-motion history of nature. The latter was regarded to be the enabling condition of the former in a similar way as, for instance, the deep structure of the sentence conditioned its surface structure within the conceptual frame of transformational-generative grammar. There is however an important difference between these two claims inasmuch as historians are in the final analysis obliged to demarcate the temporal limits of their deep period structures i. e. to explain in which way, under which circumstances and for what reasons an earlier structure is replaced by a later one.

No wonder, it was exactly in addressing this demand that historians confronted serious difficulties. Consider the case of Foucault the archeologist. In *The Order of Things* he delimited three large periods of modern European history: the Renaissance until 1660, Classicism until 1775, and Modernism obviously up to the "age of Foucault". All of them were determined by an a priori epistemological "order of things" i. e. by similarity during the Renaissance, by representation during Classicism, and by historical dialectics during Modernism. But no continuity was established between these three different enabling set of discursive relations. Foucault carefully avoided introducing it since if he had done so, he could not have pretended of dispensing with the historical dialectics of the modernist humanistic episteme i. e. with its idea of man whose death he declares at the threshold of his own antihumanistic age. To be sure, if discontinuity reigns within the framework of Foucault's archeology, this is for good reasons since the logocentric and eurocentric totalizations, the two tacit assumptions of the former principle of historical continuity, were already laid bare at that time.

Nevertheless, some difficulties with the established contrastive principle of periodization remain. For instance, how to capture the outstanding thinkers into the set of discursive rules of their age although they anticipate and sometimes even shape the discussion of the following age? Take the case of Descartes for example. First of all, Foucault tries to implant him into the representational episteme of Classicism though he died ten years before the end of the Renaissance episteme (placed by Foucault in 1660). Does this not entail a kind of interference between the epistemes in the sense that the Classicist principle had already been initiated during the Renaissance? Further on, Foucault unconvincingly attempts to deny the well known Cartesian character of Husserl's phenomenology only in order to separate the modernist idea of man from the Classicist idea of *cogito*. Finally, how to explain the obvious Cartesian shape of the French intellectual and philosophical scene at the time Foucault was entering it — if Descartes belongs only to Classicism (Séan Burke)?

The case of Nietzsche is the second serious obstacle to Foucault's line of argument. If Nietzsche belongs to Kant's age of transcendental anthropology, how could he then subvert the idea of man inherent to it? On the other hand, if he indeed was able to do this, then Foucault would not be in a position to open the antihumanistic episteme by himself. A continuity with Marx, Freud and Nietzsche would be undeniable — but then the principle of discontinuity would not hold any more. If on the contrary it holds, how to explain Foucault's famous and openly admitted debt to Nietzsche's thinking (Séan Burke)?

Hence the interferences between the epistemes appear to contradict the idea of historical discontinuity with its insistence on radical contrasts. Foucault neglected the involvement of the present with the past probably for the reason that this concept of periodization based on breaks and upheavals was developed during the revolutionary sixties. Besides, we should recall that its forebears among the Russian formalists had also been contemporaries of an important social and artistic revolution. The idea of discontinuity rests on an insight into the contingency, if not the "complete randomness" of history: later periods do not necessarily follow from former ones, they are regarded to be the sheer products of chance or conjuncture. Therefore the present is by no means indebted to its past, it is announced free to chose and shape the past of a kind it likes or needs.

One of the problems with this recognizably emancipatory ideology is that if a revolution does not necessarily follow from the past, then it has no means to prove its own legitimity. Or to put it otherwise, how would Foucault refuse the objection that his thresholds between Renaissance, Classicism and Modernism have been established arbitrarily — despite all the demonstrated evidence — if his hypothesis claims no logical or methodological advantage over older different hypotheses underpinned by different evidence? On the other hand, if it does claim such a preference, it is not as discontinuous with them as it declares.

As a very consistent and self-reflective thinker, Foucault of course became aware of these problems and it was apparently because of them that in the course of the seventies his archeology was replaced by genealogy. The latter gets rid of the former breaks and thresholds between the epistemes in favor of a united and all-pervasive field of power. Placed within this complex battlefield of forces, practices and mechanisms, the archeologist discovers the conditioned or limited character of his historical insight. He therefore turns into a genealogist raising some of the following important questions: What makes me think in precisely this and not in another way? Of what consists my own "regime of truth", what are the enabling conditions of my own *problématique*? In a word, power is now defined as a productive net traversing the entire social entity i. e. the body, sexuality, kinship relations, the family, knowledge, labor, identity, technology etc., which means that it can be neither occupied nor contested by anyone. On the contrary, all the roles and positions including that of its critic are produced and distributed by the maneuvers of anonymous power itself.

It has been rarely, if ever, noticed how similar this re-union of the historical field under the heading of power appears in comparison with Derrida's concept of metaphysical closure, especially if we pay attention to the always-already-involved position of the critic willing to step out. Derrida introduced this concept toward the end of the sixties by heavily drawing on Heidegger's idea about "the end of philosophy and the task of thinking." If I may risk a summary on this perplexing point, let me start with the contention that actually neither of the two thinkers announced the conclusion (*das Ende*) but rather the completion (*die Vollendung*) of metaphysics. Although all the essential possibilities of metaphysics are exhausted with Nietzsche's reversal of it, this does not mean for Heidegger that metaphysics will disappear. On the contrary, disguised as the technology of science, "it will last longer than the previous history of metaphysics." Derrida remains faithful to this point precisely by introducing the concept of closure (*clôture*) which he carefully distinguishes from the concept of the end. A closure is in-finite, in-definite, implying that metaphysics permits no transgression without simultaneous restoration of itself. Moreover, inasmuch as closure (in a sense of *Vollendung* or *Verendung*) denies any enclosed epochal totality, it even disrupts and fissures the concept of metaphysics as a unified and homogeneous epoch (Critchley).

To point this out, Derrida seems to position himself at a certain distance from Heidegger's analysis of the history of metaphysics by overcoming his *onto-logical* difference between Being and beings through the *logocentric* difference between speech and writing. Whereas Being (*das Sein*) endures for Heidegger in a spatial and temporal transcendence underlying no identification, beings (*das Seiende*) are on the contrary both spatially and temporally identifiable; hence the distinction between the ever-presentness of the former and the finitude of the latter (*das Sein-zum-Tode*). Inasmuch as they are finite by maintaining an unavoidable relationship to death, beings can only presence (*gegenwärtigen*) by opening themselves toward the promise of Being but they can never be self-present in the way Being is. It is exactly this distinction between the presencing of beings and the presence of Being that, according to Heidegger's claim, has been forgotten through the onto-theological history of Western metaphysics which from Plato onward mistakenly conceives being as a self-present origin and ground (Séan Burke).

Derrida now replaces the Heideggerian onto-theological with the logocentric metaphysics based on the oblivion of the difference between speech and writing. He asserts that the metaphysical determination of being as presence could only have been produced as the outcome of the repression of writing i. e. that the former should be regarded as an effect of the latter. According to him, "there may be a difference still more unthought than the difference between Being and beings", and this is of course the *différance* "without presence and without absence, without history, without cause, without *archia*, without *telos*, a writing that absolutely upsets all dialectics, all theology, all teleology, all ontology" (Margins 66–7). It is this *différance* that cannot be contained within the concepts of epoch and epochality, the latter being suggested by a certain unilateralism of Heidegger's claim that there is a sending (*Schickung*) of Being from the Greeks through the epochs of increased oblivion to the destiny of Being (*das Seins-Geschick*) at the end of philosophy. The *différance* of writing subverts the "postal idea" of such an epoch of the history of Being. Since writing has no assured destination but always only plural sendings (*envois*), it cannot be gathered into a unitary history (*grande époque*) of Being. Sendings are a self-deferring, differing web of traces that do not originate in the self; they actually do not originate at all but arise from the other (*renvoi*), from others, thereby producing the so called general textuality.

The question is whether Derrida, by dissolving the postal idea of the epoch of the oblivion of Being on the one hand, did not produce a new kind of vast, unified, and all-inclusive *episteme of writing* on the other hand. This would by no means appear as a miracle but only as a repetition of the ambiguity of the Heideggerian situation with regard to the metaphysics of presence. To put the point in Derrida's own words, "the very movement of transgression sometimes retains it (i. e. metaphysics or logocentrism) on this side of the limit" (Grammatology 22). That is to say: Derrida does not only eliminate the problem of epoch, he restores it at the same time. He does this precisely by dismissing the logocentric epoch of epochality i. e. by positing a threshold between a phonocentrically unaware past and a much more sensitive and insightful present (represented by Derrida himself). The advantage of the present thinker over the past ones comes to the fore, for instance, in the insight into the provisional i. e. logocentrically repressive character of all the authors, works, movements, periods and even the concepts that have been introduced be it in order to designate or to question them. As regional instances of the overall network of logocentric determination, as mere effects of this all-pervasive infrastructure, they have no substantial but only indicative value; and this reminds us again of Foucault's concept of power. In order to demonstrate his advantage over the former thinkers, Derrida even goes so far (similarly as Foucault does) to call into question his own concepts as well. He writes: "*All concepts hitherto proposed in order to think the articulation of a discourse and of an historical totality are caught within the metaphysical closure that I question here*" (Grammatology 99; emphasis in the original). This high degree of self-reflection is substantially different not only from all the authors with whom Derrida is extensively dealing (Rousseau, Lévi-Strauss, De Saussure) by demonstrating that they never say what they intend to say but also from Heidegger who is held to be insufficiently radical in effectuating his project. If the reasoning of other thinkers blindly presupposes the necessity of the logocentric *episteme* for which Derrida, on the contrary, is able to forward an appropriate account, then it becomes clear what he is actually constructing: a history of his own philosophical endeavor. According to Séan Burke: "everything proceeds as though this history were given, and the deconstructor bringing a decisive moment in its articulation into the sharpest focus. [...] For Derrida [...] logocentrism, as the privileging of speech, must be the first condition of two-and-a-half thousand years of metaphysical thought if the thought of writing as *différance* is to have the power to force some sort of breach in the metaphysical enclosure" (136). Insofar as logocentrism is, despite all the contrary assertions, composed as a history, it *has* an addressee, be it even a provisional and temporary one: Derrida himself. And it is this postal character that turns it, maybe unwillingly but unmistakably, into an epoch.

If Derrida's subversion of the concept of epoch fails, this is because he does not succeed in the attempt he makes to dissolve the privileged site of historiographic discourse. This privilege continues persisting in his alleged insight into the single origin (*epoché*) of the apparent variety of the past — an origin amounting in Derrida and Foucault to a never-ending process of displacement from difference to difference, a powerful stream that supposedly cannot be overruled by any framing, at least not definitely. To be sure, they both contend the necessity of framing, but this necessity seems to pertain more to other authors, not to them themselves, since they chose to identify their site of discourse with dispersion, deferment and postponement i. e. to make it as evasive and ungraspable as possible. In the final analysis, this literary dissolution of their theoretical site of discourse aims at the devaluation of the same criteria that they have applied in denouncing the phallogocentric character of other authors and texts. To put it in a phrase of Hayden White: "Foucault's 'discourse about discourse' seeks to effect the dissolution of the Discourse itself" in order to liberate the "space of a deep freedom"(115). But the principle of this freedom reads: Stay uninvolved with any of the recognizable historical frames so as to be able to make everyone else involved with them! And here is a short comment by Michael Holquist on Jacques Derrida's discourse which can serve as an appropriate description of the effect of this freedom: "No one can be quite as self-conscious as he, so all the striving of his various explicators to suspect their own words as radically as he does his seems foredoomed to failure. Explicators despair of ever fixing this constantly self-decentering figure, who even signs his works with different names" (Holquist 137).

So there is nevertheless a lot of power involved with the self-destructive techniques of periodization engaged by Foucault and Derrida, a power stemming from the institutional frame of their discourses. Someone deprived of a proper institutional shelter would scarcely be able to risk the incommunicability in a way the French master-thinkers (evidently including Lacan) do. This reminds us of the situation of avant-garde literature striving to transgress the institutional borders of literature in favor of "life itself" – but only after these same borders had already produced a sufficient degree of literary autonomy to permit this totalizing movement. The same is the case with the totalizing movement of *theory*, put since the sixties progressively in the service of the so called "excluded enabling domain" in order to transgress its own professional limits – but only after these institutional limits had first of all enabled such a movement at all. This might have been the point made by Stanley Fish when behind the ideology of anti-professionalism – i. e. of theory disguised as literature in order to be able to save the lost totality – he actually denounced the ideology of profession taking itself extremely seriously. Thus the anti-professionalism of the discourse constantly "put under erasure" amounts to a triumph of the biased appeal tacitly acquiring such an institutional force that it appears independent. But in reality it only occupies the position of independence thanks to the power that it has gained and that it continues exerting and enlarging (126).

If one would like to prove this claim, one ought only compare the theory of history with the practice of it which takes place at a completely different social and institutional site within an entire cultural network. As Michel de Certeau remarks in *The Writing of History*: "the making of history is buttressed by a political power which creates a space proper (a walled city, a nation, etc.) where a will can and must write (construct) a system (a reason articulating practices)" (6). Therefore, "the historians are not the agents of the operation for which they are technicians. [...] They are solely 'around' power. [...] They reflect on the power that they lack". Therefore they "must act *as if* effective power fell under the jurisdiction of [their] teaching even while, against all probability, [their] teaching expects the prince to insert [themselves] into a democratic organization" (8). So the site of modern historiographical production seems to be determined by multiple containments and dependencies, be it on political or institutional power, on professional objectives, on the particular historical environment, on the traditionally established standards of its genre, or on the commercial publisher's claims adapted to the current taste of the audience. "The real which is written in historiographical discourse originates from the determinations of a place." (De Certeau, History 10)

Inasmuch as the "network places" of historical theory and practice are entirely different, one should not be surprised by the discrepancy between them. According to the German theorist of literary history Uwe Japp there are few disciplines so obviously disconnected one from the other as are literary historiography and its theory (32). According to another recent German theorist Jörg Schönert, "possible *revisions of literary-historical practice* are already rejected before scholars have even began to elaborate them" (305). Whereas theory seems to be obliged by the "excluded enabling domain" of the existing period patterns, practice, on the contrary, sticks to them insistently as if obliged by the "generic memory" of its own tradition. This astonishingly "conservative" aspect has been stressed by a couple of recent investigators (Rosenberg 1987, 1992; Fohrmann 1988; 1993; Ort; Johnstone; Perkins). If the pressure of the traditional period schemes holds the upper hand over the frequent and enforced demands of theory and the transformations of literature itself (which would eventually ask for the displacement of the established thresholds between periods), this entails an unavoidable inference about the *autoreferentiality* of the periodization procedures. They appear to belong to a closed "discourse region" provided with particular and resistant rules of its self-reproduction — at least similarly as the denaturalizing procedures of contemporary theory do. Both disciplinary fields are characterized by a set of specific claims, standards and norms, by a division of roles, capacities and responsibilities, and finally by distinctive rules of communication and competition dependent on their distinctive place within the framework of a social system. The theory of literary historiography attempts to defamiliarize enrooted classificational fictions while its practice strives to make them natural and familiar. In a certain sense, both tendencies may be regarded as necessary techniques of cultural identification insofar as there is no homogeneous and unified body of "cultural memory," as any cultural memory is fissured by discontinuities between its national, ethnic, racial, religious, social, gender, and professional zones. And in as much as any culture appears within itself heterogeneous and multifaceted, there is no technique of periodization which could be taken to "serve its interests." Of course, this does not mean that they are all equipped with equal power, status, influence, and perspective at one and the same historical and social moment. But just because they are not — be it within the framework of a single national culture or within the global framework of different world cultures — we have always to ask, instead of taking any "periodizational grid" for granted, who undertook it, for which purposes, faced with which problems, under which historical, situational, institutional and inter-textual circumstances, and followed by which particular consequences. In other words, techniques of periodization are by all means necessary, but by no means unproblematic social practices. They should be measured one against another in order not to be petrified or sanctified.

11

The Suppression of the Negative Moment in Foucault's *History of Sexuality*[1]

PAUL ALLEN MILLER

> An entire historical tradition (theological or rationalistic) aims at dissolving the singular event into an ideal continuity — as a teleological movement or a natural process. "Effective" history, however, deals with events in terms of their most unique characteristics, their most acute manifestations.
>
> (Foucault, "Nietzsche, Genealogy, History" 154)[2]

In volume three of the *History of Sexuality*, Michel Foucault outlines a new form of the subject's relation to himself (and in the texts Foucault examines, the subjects *are* men) characteristic of the Roman imperial period. This new model of subjectivation, which he terms "care of the self," 'le souci de soi,' possesses certain clear continuities with the classical period's ethic of self-mastery, but is not characterized by the same set of isomorphic relations between personal, domestic and political structures of power that Foucault claims is found in fourth-century Greece.[3] The texts on which he bases his depiction are primarily medical, philosophical, and prescriptive texts from the first and second centuries C. E.[4]

It has long been recognized that the structures governing the subject's relation to both itself and the community at large had altered in some fundamental way during the late Hellenistic period in Greece and the early imperial period in Rome. In general, this change has been taken to represent a heightened individualism among the upper classes as the increasingly monarchical structure of both Rome and the Hellenistic kingdoms shut off access to the traditional

---

[1] The first two sections of this article are substantially based on my essay, "Catullan Consciousness, the 'Care of the Self,' and the Force of the Negative in History" in *Rethinking Sexuality: Foucault and Classical Antiquity*, eds. David H. J. Larmour, Paul Allen Miller, and Charles Platter (Princeton: Princeton UP, 1998).

[2] Original published as "Nietzsche, Généalogie, Histoire," in *Hommage à Jean Hyppolite* (161). Hereafter, the first set of number refers to Foucault's French texts and the second to English translations.

[3] Foucault, *Le souci de soi* (English = *The Care of the Self*), 84–85/67–68, 116/94–95, and 175/148–49, hereafter cited as *LSDS*.

[4] On the generic restrictions guiding his investigation, see *L'usage des plaisirs*, (English = *The Use of Pleasure*), hereafter cited as *LUDP* 18/12–13; and Goldhill xii, 44–45.

public arenas of self-valorization for the ruling elite of the Mediterranean world: individual military glory and city-state politics. This growth in individualism is often said to represent also the articulation of a new heightened sense of interiority that is seen as laying the groundwork for Christianity's concern with the salvation of the individual soul (Foucault, *LSDS* 55/41, 57/43 and 103/83; *LUDP* 74/63).[5] Foucault, while not rejecting outright this common narrative, radically questions its teleological construction of a growth in individualism, which is depicted as a mere epiphenomenon of underlying political change.

What I propose in this paper is to perform a similarly critical reading of Foucault's own narrative. I want to save those elements that represent clear improvements over his predecessors: the anti-teleological thrust of his argument; the problematization of the concept of individualism (which throws into question the notion that a society could ever in any simple sense become more or less individualistic); and the position that the "care of the self" as a form of ethical self-relation can never be understood as a mere reflection of an ontologically prior socio-political infrastructure, but must be perceived as an original response to a complex and overdetermined practical and discursive situation (*LSDS* 89/71). The importance of these contributions to our understanding of the processes of subject formation in the ancient world and to contemporary debates about the value of "individualism" in competing socio-economic systems should not be underestimated. At the same time, I wish to show that the model of self-relation constructed by Foucault under the rubric of the "care of the self" is not adequate to understand the full panoply of forms of subjectivity that achieved discursive visibility in the Roman world, once the period of classical self-mastery, that he centers in fourth-century Greece, had passed. My chief exhibit in this case will be the poetry of Catullus, which presents a clearly articulated image of a subject with a complex and clearly delineated relation both to itself and the world around it.[6] Similar results could also be found in a sustained reading of the poetry of Propertius, Tibullus, Ovid, Juvenal and other Latin poets.[7] As is the case in Foucault's own examination of the processes of subjectivation delineated in the medical and philosophical texts he interrogates, I am not making a claim about the actual nature of the subjectivities of these poets, rather I am concerned with the way in which subjectivity is represented in their highly formalized discourses (*LSDS* 175/149, 215/184–85).

The problem I am describing is more than a simple lacuna that could be remedied by adding more information and a few conceptual epicycles to Fou-

---

[5] For an example of the kind of historiography Foucault is talking about, see Auerbach 247–48. For a more nuanced version of this same narrative, see Syme 490, 507–08, and 516–18; Peters 185–87; and Anderson 51.

[6] On the poverty of Foucauldian theories of the subject with particular regard to Catullus and the problems of erotic poetry, see Janan 154–55, n. 84.

[7] See Richlin, "Zeus and Metis" 171; "Not Before Homosexuality" 541–55; Hallett 48.

cault's Ptolemaic model. At its heart is the fundamental question whether one can examine the history of the individual's constitution as an ethical subject by restricting oneself to prescriptive, scientific, and philosophical forms of discourse.[8] Indeed I would argue that this generic selection also selects the forms of subjectivity that can be recognized as existing at a given moment, that different genres of discourse represent subjectivity in fundamentally different ways, in short that different material practices (including discursive practices) produce different effects. Hence, by restricting himself to a set of genres that generally portray subjects as positive normative models, Foucault ignores that other genres may present alternative models within the same society.[9] He thus underestimates the multivalent and often conflicting effects of different positive discursive practices in a single community.[10] Finally, by flattening out the discursive field and privileging those practices which present positive normative models, as opposed to complex, contradictory, and conflicted representations of the subject's relation to itself, Foucault ultimately privileges a static vision of history that precedes from one steady-state model to the next without any substantial transitional stages. The history of the constitution of the subject in Foucault remains paradoxically synchronic.[11] We are given detailed snapshots of fourth-century Greece and of the first two centuries of imperial Rome with only the barest outline of what comes between. The inability of Foucault's history to account for Catullan consciousness thus points to an exclusion of the negative moment from Foucault's positive account that ultimately makes any accounting of historical change problematic if not impossible (Adorno 53, 140–43; Jameson, *Political Unconscious* 91, 95, 97–98; *Prison-house* 193–94; Rose 218).

This paper will examine the following points. First it will look at both Foucault's construction of the ethic of the "care of the self" and its relation to that of self-mastery in order to show better how the former is unable to account for certain specific elements that play a determining role in the Catullan corpus. Then it will show how the problem noted at our first level of analysis is not only one of neglecting the thematics of Catullus' representation of subjectivity but also of failing to account for the force of different genres of composition on that representation. I shall argue that the lyric collection, whether consisting in the form we currently have of Catullus' corpus or in some other form of

---

[8] On the goal of Foucault's project as studying the history of that constitution of the individual's self-relation that aims to produce a "moral subject," see *LUDP* 12/6 and 35–36/28–29; and Davidson 118.

[9] Catharine Edwards has recently questioned "the extent to which" Foucault's texts "represent the views of most members of the Roman upper classes" (56–57), to say nothing of those who fall outside this narrow social category.

[10] Thus as early as 1967 Foucault's work was criticized for creating "an isolated totality" out of certain cultural structures, while leaving aside other "entire sectors," Jeannette Colombel, *La nouvelle critique* May (1967): 9, cited by Kremer-Marietti 49.

[11] See Ignatieff (1071), "His historical work lacked a theory of historical change."

imaginative reconstruction, necessarily presents a model of subjectivity that cannot be homologized with that found in Foucault's prescriptive texts. Thus I argue that choices made on the level of form necessarily have a determining effect on the level of content or signification (Jameson, *Political Unconscious* 99). Next I shall examine how Foucault's privileging of a single genre or small group of related genres of discourse necessarily flattens out the picture of the period's discursive practices and makes history consist in a succession of neat synchronic systems rather than in a simultaneous co-existence of divergent and often antagonistic forces. In short, I shall argue that Foucault's totalizing vision has no room in it for those negative counterforces within a society whose presence as a potential positive alternative to the *status quo* — as opposed to a mere inert resistance — is necessary if historical change is to be accounted for as something other than an inexplicable catastrophe, or the product of some kind of transcendental *deus ex machina*.[12] This part of the argument also examines the concept of transgression that Foucault advances as an alternative to that of dialectical negation, and proposes that it is inadequate to the task at hand. I conclude by suggesting that one way the power of the negative can be restored, without returning to a teleological vision of history, is through Lacan's concept of the Real.

I.

Foucault begins his discussion of the "care of the self" by explaining how this new process of subject formation differs from the classical ethic of self-mastery. His challenge is to make this distinction without falling into the trap of envisioning some type of pseudo-Hegelian progress of the concept of the individual, whose perfection would be reached in the modern, bourgeois west, and where, presumably, each historical alteration in the constitution of the subject would be revealed as a necessary step in the manifestation of its ultimate essence. He starts his investigation of antiquity's changing modes of subjectivation by arguing that the word *individualiste* frequently conceals beneath it such divergent meanings as: valorization of the individual in his singularity, separate from whatever groups to which he might belong; increased recognition of the value of domestic and family life as opposed to public achievement; and an increased emphasis on the self as both an object of knowledge and a field of action and correction (*LSDS* 55−56/41−42). Clearly it is possible for one of these meanings to be true for a given society while the others may not, and as Foucault aptly demonstrates in the texts he examines, what we are talking about in the Hellenistic and Roman imperial periods is more a complex restructuring of what it means to

---

[12] On the potentially paralyzing effects of Foucault's total explanatory system, see Jameson (*Postmodernism* 5−6, 405−06). On the necessity of an always-already-existing internal articulation that makes a reputedly external cause or adhesion possible, see Derrida (*Of Grammatology* 144−45).

be a subject than a simple process that can be analyzed under the opposed rubrics of individual and collectivity.[13]

The complicating factors which require this more differentiated analysis are several. First, while political life on the grand scale in the imperial period was excluded from the reach of the traditional aristocracy, there remained a substantial degree of local autonomy in individual municipalities that allowed well-placed citizens to continue to seek political office. Likewise, the options of entering the Senate and becoming a provincial governor remained open, even if the power of those offices was now substantially circumscribed.

> Civic and political activity may have, to some degree, changed its form; it nonetheless remained an important part of life for the upper classes. Broadly speaking, the ancient societies remained societies of promiscuity, where existence was led 'in public.' They were also societies in which everyone was situated within strong systems of local relationships, family ties, economic dependencies, and relations of patronage and friendship. (*LSDS* 56/41–42, see also 103/83)

What we see in the early imperial period, then, is not a complete dissolution of the isomorphic structures of power over the self, the members of one's household, and other members of the community, that characterized the ethic of self-mastery, but a problematization of those relations as they are inserted into a new more complex set of determinations, in which local power remains a viable option, but always within limits imposed by a larger structure that is itself discontinuous with the power relations of daily life.[14]

One of the clearest examples of this new relationship is the way in which marriage simultaneously gains in institutional status, achieving both legal recognition and encouragement from the state, and at the same time restructures its own internal power relations around a new emphasis on the affective bond between the two partners and their reciprocal obligations. The function of the *paterfamilias* as head of the household is not directly put into question, but the

---

13 *LSDS* 117/95, "A growth of public constraints and prohibitions? An individualistic withdrawal accompanying the valorization of private life? We need instead to think in terms of a difficulty in the manner in which the individual could form himself as the ethical subject of his actions, and efforts to find in devotion to self that which could enable him to submit to rules and give a purpose to his existence."

14 *LSDS* 104–07/84–87, especially ". . . if one wishes to understand the interest that was directed in these elites to personal ethics, to the morality of everyday conduct, it is not at all pertinent to speak of decadence, frustration, and sullen retreat. Instead one should see in this interest the search for a new way of conceiving the relationship that one ought to have with one's status, one's functions, one's activities, and one's obligations. Whereas formerly ethics implied a connection between power over oneself and power over others, and therefore had to refer to an aesthetics of life that accorded with one's status, the new rules of the political game made it more difficult to define the relations between what one was, what one could do, and what one was expected to accomplish. The formation of oneself as the ethical subject of one's own actions became more problematic." See also, *LUDP* 82–83/70–71, 88/75, 96/82–83, 237/215; Konstan 121; Edwards 195.

relations between husbands and wives are no longer exactly modeled on those of the larger economic and political power relations in which the household finds itself enmeshed. The couple as a unit gains in relative autonomy, as it becomes more widely recognized by institutions and discourses outside of it (*LSDS* 93–96/74–77, 116/94–95, and 174–75/148–49). It is at once more and less implicated in external structures of power.

Thus the complication of the power relations governing the constitution of the individual as a moral subject, which occurs as a response to the same social and political changes giving rise to the empire, does not in any simple fashion result in a heightened sense of individualism. For, as in the example of marriage, the greater personal autonomy with which the married couple is endowed is part and parcel of that same couple's greater institutionalization. Indeed this double response seems to be characteristic of Foucault's portrait of the emergence of the ethic of the "care of the self." Thus he observes that the increased problematization of the subject's insertion into power relations gave rise to two possible antithetical responses, namely an increased emphasis on the externally recognizable marks of status, and a concentration on one's relation to oneself, so as to become as independent as possible from external pressures beyond one's control. Both of these phenomena can be observed in the period in question (*LSDS* 82/65,105–06/85). Likewise, even in the practice of the "care of the self" we are not dealing with a simple withdrawal from society. Indeed this very process can be read as an intensification of social relations rather than their abrogation. The search for internal independence often involved a guide of conscience, such as Seneca was to Lucilius or Cornutus to Persius, in which a series of reciprocal obligations governed their mutual interactions. As Foucault notes after a reading of Seneca's thirty-fifth letter to Lucilius, "The care of the self seems therefore intrinsically linked to a 'service of the soul,' which includes the possibility of a round of exchanges with the other and a system of reciprocal obligations" (*LSDS* 66–69/51–54, translation altered). The "care of the self," then, can be seen as an increased level of social integration rather than an individualistic retreat.

One of the prime examples Foucault offers of the kind of subject produced by this ethic is Pliny the Younger. Without being the adherent of any dogma, he devotes great care to both his married life and his individual self, yet this in no way implies a withdrawal from the duties and obligations of public and political life (*LSDS* 63/48, 97–98/78–79, and 188–89/160–61). Pliny experiences an increased disjunction between internal and external power relations compared to that of the classical era, but no opposition between those realms. He does not posit himself in an antagonistic relation to the social world of political power and honors, but tries to preserve his tranquillity. Thus we picture Pliny easily moving between the realms of light poetic composition, the pondering of his own ethical obligations, professing passionate love for his wife, and fulfilling his duties as a provincial governor by writing to the emperor for advice on handling those troublesome Christians. The worlds in which he lives are not mirror images of one another, but neither are they antagonistic.

Can the same be said of Catullus? Certainly most critics would say no. In poem 5, he explicitly tells his beloved, who is married to a respectable ex-consul, to ignore the grumblings of stern old moralists. In 7 he celebrates a numberless passion to the point of madness. In 16, he humorously threatens with oral and anal rape those who question his manhood because of the sensuality of his verse, and in poem 50 he celebrates the virtues of *otium*, the opposite of *negotium*, the traditional devotion to public, legal and monetary affairs. This same *otium* in the following poem is credited with the past destruction of great kings and wealthy cities.[15] Thus on the surface Catullus clearly seems to establish an opposition between his passionate subjectivity—devoted to illicit love and verse, and disdainful of traditional values—and the normative public world that constituted the individual's primary arena of self-valorization. As Charles Segal writes, "This defiance of Roman busyness for a life of love and poetry is implicit in much (though not all) of the Catullan corpus and helps prepare the way for the private world of the Augustan elegists" (28). Likewise Paul Veyne notes, "Catullus turns quickly to telling us what public opinion thinks about passion, just as in Ovid's elegy. Love is objectively a flail, the fruit of too much spare time (of being apolitical, we might say), and its tenderness kills civic spirit and ruins the most solid of cities" (*Roman Erotic Elegy* 56).[16] It would seem then that only with a great deal of violence could Catullus be assimilated to the moral and discursive ideal incarnated by the younger Pliny. For Catullus there was not merely discontinuity between the public and private, but often open antagonism.

To the objection that Catullus is from an earlier historical period than Pliny and so cannot be considered to have participated in the same discursive structures as those which produced the ethic of the "care of the self," I would respond that neither can he be assimilated to the ethic of self-mastery and its assumed homology of power relations between one's public and private self. Hence, either one of Foucault's two constructions is deficient, or Catullus belongs to a transitional stage which falls between them. Yet such a transitional stage is nowhere mentioned in Foucault, and since such a concept would be in complicity with a kind of idealist Hegelian teleology (since *transition* often implies a directed movement from one stage to another), it is doubtful that he would have had much sympathy with the idea.

---

15 See Rankin 74, "Catullus' revolutionary contribution to the development of Roman poetry did not simply consist in a new frankness and sincerity about personal feelings; it introduced as a novel and significant element the poet's sense of preoccupation with his individual and private feelings in opposition to public commitment, indeed to the virtual exclusion of public duty"; Rubino 293, "In poems such as 5, 7, and 16 Catullus openly repudiates the Roman world in which he lives"; Ross 5; Lyne, 12, 65–68; Johnson 117.

16 Veyne is one of the few influences Foucault acknowledges at the beginning of *LUDP* 14/18.

Another important source and model for Foucault in his elaboration of the ethic of the "care of the self" is the younger Seneca. Philosopher, poet, tutor and advisor to the emperor Nero, and spiritual guide to his friend Lucilius, he too, like Pliny, appeared to move between the various, discontinuous realms of personal and discursive practice with relative ease, at least on the conceptual level. Foucault highlights one activity in particular advocated by Seneca, the daily examination of conscience. The self-relation implicit in this exercise is not an agonistic or accusatory one, such as would characterize later Christian practice, but more one of quality control. At the end of each day, the philosopher makes an inventory of action and words and decides what things he did well and what things he could do better. It is an exercise in self-improvement, a kind of attention to oneself which has Stoic *tranquillitas* as its goal. It is not a struggle against one's innermost thoughts and feelings nor a methodical effort to ferret out evil (*LSDS* 78/61 – 62).[17]

Catullus' interior monologues are of a very different character. They are definitively agonistic. In W. R. Johnson's words, they represent attempts "to write about inner conflicts and divisions, about fragmentations of the self that could be barely glimpsed," attempts "to grasp . . . opaque inward alienations" (4, 122). Thus poem 8 represents the poet reviewing the course of his relationship with Lesbia. Rather than presenting a calm inventory of words and deeds, the poet is trying to gather the resolve to break off a failed and now tortured relationship:

> Miser Catulle, *desinas* ineptire,
> et quod vides perisse, perditum *ducas.*
> fulsere quondam candidi tibi soles,
> cum ventitabas quo puella ducebat
> 5 amata nobis quantum amabitur nulla
> ibi illa multa cum iocosa fiebant,
> quae tu volebas nec puella nolebat
> fulsere vere candidi tibi soles.
> nunc iam illa non volt: tu quoque, inpote⟨ns, *noli*⟩
> 10 nec quae fugit *sectare,* nec miser *vive,*
> sed obstinata mente *perfer, obdura.*
> vale, puella. iam Catullus obdurat,
> nec te requiret nec rogabit invitam.
> at tu dolebis, cum rogaberis nulla.
> 15 scelesta, vae te, quae tibi manet vita?
> quis nunc te adibit? cui videberis bella?
> quis nunc amabis? cuius esse diceris?
> quem basiabis? cui labella mordebis?
> at tu, Catulle, destinatus *obdura.*

Wretched Catullus, *stop* acting like a fool, and *consider* lost what you know to be lost. Once bright suns shown for you, when you were always following where the girl was leading, a girl loved by us as none will ever be loved. In the past, when many happy games were played, which you desired and she did not refuse, truly bright suns shown

---

[17] On *tranquillitas*, see Seneca, *De Tranquillitate Animi*, 2.1 – 5.

for you. Now she does not want those things, you also, madman, *refuse* them and *do not pursue* her if she flees, nor *live* miserably. But *press on* with a resolute mind, *endure*. Good-bye, girl. Now Catullus endures. He does not seek you, nor will he ask after you if you are unwilling. But you will regret it when you will not be asked for: wretch, misery for you! What life now remains for you? Who now will come to you? To whom will you seem beautiful? Whom now will you love? Whose will you be said to be? Whom will you kiss? Whose lips will you bite. But you, Catullus, having cast your lot, *endure*.[18]

Certainly, this poem does represent the poet in the process of caring for himself, trying to effect a cure from the disease of love, but the repeated use of the imperative and the jussive subjunctive also attests to the struggle required to summon up the necessary resolution. This is no calm inventory, but a subject split against itself.[19] Moreover, once Catullus musters the courage to tell her good-bye (8.12), he immediately suffers a relapse as he goes through an enumeration of all those things she (but also he) will miss with his leaving (8.14−18). By the end of the poem, the ultimate issue of this exercise in internal agonistics is left in doubt and in poem 11 we see the poet once again trying to say good-bye.

Poem 76 offers an even more tortured example of this same phenomenon. In it the poet examines the affair as a whole and strives to come terms with his own internal contradictions by appropriating the language and reasoning of traditional morality.[20] He begins by explaining why he should be rewarded by the gods for the *pietas* he has shown in his relationship with Lesbia.[21]

> Si qua recordanti benefacta priora voluptas
>   est homini, cum se cogitat esse pium
> nec sanctam violasse fidem nec foedere nullo
>   divum ad fallendos numine abusum homines:
> 5 multa parata manent in longa aetate, Catulle,
>   ex hoc ingrato gaudia amore tibi.
> nam quaecumque homines bene cuiquam aut dicere possunt
>   aut facere, haec a te dictaque factaque sunt.

> If there is any pleasure to a man recalling previous good deeds, when he knows that he has done his duty and has neither violated a sacred trust nor misused the power of the gods to deceive others in any compact, many joys await you in old age, Catullus, on account of this thankless love. For whatever good things men are able to say or do, these things have been said and done by you.

This argument for Catullus' *bona fides* and the reward he expects for it would be perfectly sensible in terms of the traditional Roman ideology of reciprocal obligations between actors of the same status except for two crucial problems

---

18 All translations of Catullus are my own.
19 The non-coincidence of the speaking subject with itself in Catullus has been well studied by Janan, who argues for the superiority of the Lacanian over the Foucauldian model for articulating the kind of internal complexity and division characteristic of the Catullan lyric consciousness, x and 19.
20 On 76 as a summary of the affair as a whole, see Rubino 289, and Commager 97−98.
21 For a good definition of *pietas* see Johnson 121.

(Wiseman, *Catullus and His World* 105). One, Lesbia as a woman would not normally be granted such status. Thus Catullus in this poem and others shows considerable eccentricity in placing such a high value on his relationship with her, and in so doing reveals himself to be in conflict with those very social values he invokes here for his own benefit (Rankin 71–72; Lilja 43–44, 100–09; Veyne, *Roman Erotic Elegy* 56; Pomeroy 116; Shelton 37–44; and Wilkinson 116–18).[22] Indeed, traditional Roman ideology regarded love as a dangerous mental illness which kept men from the serious business of making money and defending the state. Two, Lesbia was a married woman when the affair began, so that Catullus' actions are violations of the rights and prerogatives of her husband, his peer. Catullus' *pietas* to Lesbia is thus an act of *iniuria* to her husband, Metellus. Yet Metellus, as a man, has a better claim to Catullus' good faith. Hence Catullus' claims to virtue are founded on an original act of vice. This implicit contradiction leads to explicit self-conflict (Rubino 291):

> Omnia quae ingratae perierunt credita menti.
> 10   quare iam te cur amplius excrucies?
> quin tu animo offirmas atque istinc teque reducis,
>   et dis invitis desinis esse miser?
> difficile est longum subito deponere amorem,
>   difficile est, verum hoc qua lubet efficias:
> 15 una salus haec est, hoc est tibi pervincendum,
>   hoc facias, sive id non pote sive pote.
> O di, si vestrum est misereri, aut si quibus umquam
>   extremam iam ipsa in morte tulistis opem,
> me miserum aspicite et, si vitam puriter egi,
> 20   eripite hanc pestem perniciemque mihi,
> quae mihi subrepens imos ut torpor in artus
>   expulit ex omni pectore laetitias.

Everything you entrusted to her ungrateful mind has perished. Why then do you torture yourself even more now? Why not strengthen your spirit, pull out, and cease to be miserable against the gods' will? It's hard suddenly to put aside a long love, it's hard, but you must do this through any means available: this alone is healthy; this must be overcome by you; you must do this whether it is possible or not. Oh gods, if there is any pity in you, or if ever you brought urgent aid to those then on the verge of death itself, behold me in my misery and, if I have lived my life rightly, rip out this plague and ruin from me, this disease which, like a numbness crawling deep inside my limbs, drives joy from all my breast.

We are clearly far removed from Seneca's calm, rational inventory of the day's events. The imagery of disease and morbidity is vividly called forth (see also 77.3–6), and it is difficult not to wonder if this evocation does not represent

---

[22] As in the ethic of self-mastery, the Roman republican aristocracy essentially recognized no difference between public and private life so that the exaltation of private pleasure was considered a direct assault on public virtue. See Cicero, *In Pisonem*, 10.22–11.26, 16.37, 18.41–19–45, 20.46–47, 21.48–50, and 27.66–29.72; Nicolet 721; Veyne, "The Roman Empire" 95; *Roman Erotic Elegy* 104–05.

Catullus' consciousness of having breached the very *pietas* he invokes. The poet, as in poem 8, seeks to care for himself, yet the obstacle is not Lesbia or any other external circumstance but the poet's own intractable desire, *difficile est longum subito deponere amorem,/ difficile est* ["It's hard suddenly to put aside a long love, it's hard"]. Poem 76, thus, presents the image of a consciousness at once at war with society's expectations and with itself. It must seek to do the impossible, having already done the unspeakable.

The final discrepancy that should be noted between Foucault's model of the subject's relation to itself and that found in Catullus' poetry, concerns what might be termed the unity of love and lust. In some ways, Foucault's position is limited from the start by his failure to deal with affective relations between men and women except in the context of marriage. An adulterous relationship, such as that of Catullus and Lesbia, never rises to the level of theoretical visibility in his discourse. Citing the Stoic Musonius Rufus, Foucault argues that in the ethic of the "care of the self" affective relations between partners in marriage assume a greater role because of a new thesis proposing a natural attraction between men and women that is at once sexual and emotional. These two elements are not conceived of as separate entities that ideally should both be present in a marriage, but as two aspects of a single undifferentiated phenomenon.[23] In Catullus, however, it is precisely the incommensurability of these two states of feeling, whether inside or outside of marriage, that causes so much agony. Thus in 72.8 he says that Lesbia's infidelity has forced him to love her more, but to wish her well less ("amare magis, sed bene velle minus"), a formula that is repeated in 75.3−4 ("ut iam nec bene velle queat tibi, si optima fias,/ nec desistere amare, omnia si facias" ["so that it would not be possible to wish you well if you became the best of all women/ nor to stop loving you, no matter what you might do"]) and prepares the way for the conflicted monologue which we just examined in 76. This contradictory duality in turn reaches it final crystallization in 85.1's anguished "odi et amo" ["I hate and I love"].

Moreover, the way in which this contradictory set of feelings is embodied in this sequence of poems, not only shows the presence of a radical antagonism within the Catullan consciousness that cannot be encompassed by Musonius' doctrine or Seneca's rational self-analysis, but also shows this subject's self-relation to be inhabited by a temporal complexity nowhere present in Foucault's prescriptive texts. As I have argued elsewhere, one of the fundamental generic characteristics separating Catullus' lyric subjectivity from that of his Greek predecessors of the archaic and classical periods, is the demonstrable evidence that

---

23 *LSDS* 179−80/152, "For Musonius, then, what founds marriage is not that it is situated at the point of intersection of two heterogeneous predilections, one of which is physical, the other rational and social. It is rooted in a single, primitive tendency that aims directly toward it as an essential goal and hence, through it, towards its two intrinsic effects, the formation of a common progeny and companionship in life." On the typicality of Musonius' positions, see Goldhill 134.

Catullus' work was meant to be read as a collection.[24] For Catullus the poem not only gains its meaning from its relation to its audience, but also from its relation to other poems in the corpus. They provide the primary context in which the individual poem is to be understood. Our vision of Catullus' self-relation in any one poem is modified by our knowledge of these other poems, and thus the poem itself is in constant dialogue not only with its readers, but with the other poems of the collection. Rereading is in fact programmed into the repetitive nature of the corpus as the same themes and images recur again and again (Janan 90). It is, in fact, this intratextual quality of Catullus' work that gives it that sense of intimacy which all readers perceive. We seem ever to be eavesdropping on the poet in dialogue with himself, but that dialogue is infinite because it is always being reshaped and remodeled by our reading of the other poems in the corpus.[25] Thus, as we have seen, poems 72, 75, 76, and 85 form part of a progressive sequence in which Catullus analyzes the dissociation of feelings he is experiencing between love and lust that finally crystallizes in the explicit contradiction of love and hate. This work of self-analysis, as we have seen in poem 76, is not carried out in a calm or rational fashion, but in the form of an internal struggle to find a resolution to a potentially devastating intellectual and emotional pain.

By the same token, however, this sequence is hardly self-contained. Poem 70 clearly anticipates poem 72 on the level of both theme and diction. Thus in poem 70 the poet writes:

Nulli se dicit mulier mea nubere malle
    quam mihi, non si se Iuppiter ipse petat.
dicit: sed mulier cupido quod dicit amanti,
    in vento et rapida scribere oportet aqua.

My woman says she'd rather marry no one more than me, even if Jupiter himself should ask her. She says: but what a woman says to a desirous lover ought to be written on the wind and rapid water.

The triple repetition of the verb *dicit,* "she says," in 70 is answered by the beginning of 72:

Dicebas quondam solum te nosse Catullum,
    Lesbia, nec prae me velle tenere Iovem.
dilexi tum te non tantum ut vulgus amicam,
    sed pater ut gnatos diligit et generos. (72.1–4)

You used to say once that you knew only Catullus, Lesbia, and that you did not wish to hold Jupiter before me. I loved you then not as the common man does his mistress but as a father does his sons and sons-in-law.

---

[24] See Miller chapters 4, 6, and 7. The next few pages are based on the fuller analysis given there.
[25] There remains disagreement over how much of Catullus' corpus was arranged by the author himself. My argument does not depend upon accepting any one schema of arrangement, but rather on the notion that we read the poems in terms of one another, and that the numerous cross-references between the poems and the use of repeated motifs show that they were meant to be read as a group, whether they were originally placed in the order we now have them or not.

The switch from the present *dicit* in 70 to the imperfect *dicebas*, "you said," in 72, which is paralleled by the switch from the perfect *dilexi* to the present *diligit* in the second couplet of 72 itself, shows that we are dealing with two poems examining one phenomenon from two separate temporal perspectives, adding the oppositional categories of before and after to the already existing ones of love and lust, and love and hate, that are structuring this discourse. At the same time, between 70 and 72 is poem 71 on a certain Rufus whose amorous adventures are thwarted by both a rival and a smelly goat said to inhabit his armpits. This same Rufus is also discussed in 69. Thus the pair 70, 72 is paralleled by that of 69 and 71 (Wiseman, *Catullus and His World* 166–67; *Catullan Questions* 28). Moreover, in each case the second poem in the pair is concerned with infidelity, although in 69 and 71 the tone is obviously lighter.

What we see then is the poet analyzing the same set of problems over and over again from disparate angles. Thus poems 70 and 72, which focus on the problem of whether Lesbia's declarations of love can be believed, are paralleled by 107 and 109, in which Catullus first celebrates Lesbia's return after a breakup, and then prays that when she vows eternal love "she can promise truly and speak [*dicat*] from the heart" (109.3–4). Once again we see the same essential set of problems (how to evaluate Lesbia's speech) examined from two perspectives (107 appears to be both spatially and temporally prior to 109), whose relation to the pairs examined in the earlier sequence is never clearly defined.[26] Are 107 and 109 supposed to have taken place before or after 70 and 72, and at what point does the pair 69 and 71 intersect with either of these two?

Yet even within the sequence defined by poems 70, 72, 75, 76, and 85 we find moments of specifically articulated contrast. Thus in poem 83, immediately before 85's "odi et amo," Catullus tells us that Lesbia always speaks ill of him before her husband. "The ass," he says contemptuously, takes great pleasure in her abuse, without understanding that Lesbia's actions mean she cannot stop thinking of Catullus. Hence what seems to be abuse is really love. Whether Catullus is deluding himself here or not, 83's stubborn optimism clearly represents a radically different moment from 85. Moreover, 83 anticipates poem 92, where Catullus returns to the topic of Lesbia's speaking ill of him and reveals that he does the same to her, but since he is madly in love with her even so, he assumes that her speaking ill of him must therefore mean that she too is madly in love with him. This statement is highly problematic. It underlines the opacities of both self and other to the observing consciousness of the poet. It also throws any notion of the logical, or even emotional, consistency of the poet into radical disorder. For if, as he states here, protests of hatred and distaste are in fact veiled declarations of love, how then are we to read his earlier statements of agony and internal conflict? Is 85 mere rhetorical posturing? Is the agony ex-

---

[26] On the connection between 70 and 109, see Quinn 102–03.

pressed there a mask for love? It is hard to believe that such is the case, both because of the poem's radical concision and its tonal consistency with poems 70, 72, 75, and 76. Yet any attempt to square the apparent contradiction between these two moments in the representation of Catullan consciousness educed by poems 83 and 92 on the one hand, and 70, 72, 75, 76, and 85 on the other, would necessarily involve reducing the collection's inherent complexity by imposing on it a linear, univocal narrative to which the poems do not obviously lend themselves. Instead, the logically impossible solution the collection invites us to consider is that both these states of thought and feeling exist simultaneously at different levels or in different places in that complex synthetic unity – put into motion by our own act of reading – which we call Catullan consciousness.[27]

What we are left with, in the end, is the vertiginous flux of a complex multi-leveled and multi-temporal subjectivity whose relation to itself can never be reduced to the rational normative model implicit in the discourse of Seneca, Pliny, and Musonius Rufus. This image of a subject constantly turning in upon itself, analyzing and re-analyzing past events, struggling with its own contradictions, is not merely a thematic feature of Catullus' poetry but is implicit in the very form itself. The content of that form implies a self-relation, which if not antagonistic to that outlined in the model of the "care of the self," is at least nowhere articulated within its bounds. Nor could it be, because the form that makes the representation of such a self-relation possible, the lyric collection, is generically proscribed from Foucault's archive of prescriptive texts.

II.

> Not all people exist in the same Now.
> (Bloch 22)
>
> Hegel again, always ....
> (Derrida, "Cogito" 43)

What the flattening out of the discursive field by this generic selection ultimately implies is the failure to examine fully the possibility of oppositional discourses, to articulate the potentiality for antagonisms within a given culture that are not simply variations on an underlying unity.[28] This is a problem which has haunted

---

[27] Compare Janan ix, 23, 38, 40, 78, 83.

[28] For two important efforts to work out what Bloch terms a "polyphonous" and "multi-spatial dialectics" that would be adequate to the multiple temporalities and perspectives contained in any cultural moment, see his "Nonsynchronism and the Obligation to Its Dialectics," 22–38, and Williams' notions of "dominant," "residual," and "emergent" cultural elements 3–16. For an application of their work to the problems posed by Foucault's notion of the *épistémè* see Reed 41–56.

Foucault's work from the beginning. For example, in his landmark *Les mots et les choses*, he advances the assertion that at any given moment, "in any given culture," there is only one *épistémè* that functions as the precondition for the production of all positive knowledge. Differences of opinion within that *épistémè* are of interest only on the sociological level, not in terms of the production of new knowledge that might fundamentally alter the primary structures of discursive production.[29] Thus at a given point and time such oppositions as do exist would appear to be overridden by a more fundamental unity that reveals difference to be, if not illusory, at least without concrete effects on the history of discursive formations.[30] Yet if this is the case, if there is no negative moment of real difference within the discursive and intellectual positivities of a given era, then the change from one *épistémè* to another becomes inexplicable, except as the arbitrary intervention of an external force.[31] In Foucault's later work the term *dispositif* is often used in place of *épistémè*. It is a broader term that includes material as well as discursive practices. Nonetheless, it does not alter the fundamental unity that characterizes the *épistémè*, it simply expands its reach to cover a wider domain. As Dreyfus and Rabinow acknowledge, "*Dispositif* is distinguished from *episteme* primarily because it encompasses the non-discursive practices as well as the discursive" (121). Foucault's later genealogical work thus examines a wider range of social phenomena than did his earlier archaeological studies, but it does not alter his basic methodological assumptions.[32]

---

29 See *Les mots et les choses* (English = *The Order of Things*) hereafter cited as *LMC*, 179/168, "In any given culture, at any given moment, there is always only one *episteme* that defines the possibility of all knowledge"; 89/75 "One must reconstitute the general system of thought whose network, in its positivity, renders an interplay of simultaneous and apparently contradictory opinions possible"; and 77/63, 88/74, 103/89, and 171/157–58. Compare *L'archéologie du savoir* (English = *The Archeology of Knowledge*), hereafter cited as *AS*, 166–73/126–31; Dreyfus and Rabinow 27; Macey 163; and Laqueur 21. On *LMC* presenting an impoverished and oversimplified image of the periods in question, see Bannet 145; and Waswo 69.

30 Thus, for example, as Macey notes in his account of *LMC*, for Foucault the differences between the classical economic theories of Smith, Ricardo, and Marx "are no more than ripples in a children's paddling pool" since all three see value "as the result of a productive process which implies a temporal dimension" (168). See also 163.

31 On Foucault's refusal to examine the causes of the historical changes recorded in *LMC* until the archeology of knowledge is complete (an impossibly large task), see *LMC* 64–65/50–51; on archeology as strictly the description of empirical events, see *LMC* 230/218. Thus Bannet writes (108), "in *L'archéologie du savoir* he tried to defend himself against the charge that archeology seems to freeze history . [...] But Foucault's defense is not very convincing, because it consists of admitting that temporal successions have to be suspended to a large extent, first because the rules do not change with every statement, and secondly because they make visible the relations within a discursive formation." See also Dreyfus and Rabinow 56 and 83. Derrida notes that the *Histoire de la folie* runs the risk of a "structuralist totalitarianism" incompatible with "history," "Cogito," (44, 57). On historical change presuming opposition and struggle, see Rose 218.

32 See Macey, "The *épistémè* was no more than a specifically discursive *dispositif*." On the relation between archeology and genealogy, see Dreyfus and Rabinow 103–177. For the notion that

This predilection for examining empirical unities without reference to their causes, however overdetermined, or the forces that might lead to their transformation over time has led some commentators to see Foucault as flirting with positivism,[33] a charge that he ironically accepted when he described his method of examination as "un postivisme heureux" ["a happy positivism"].[34] In doing so, he was no doubt responding to critics such as Sartre and Sylvie Le Bon who in their reactions to *Les mots et les choses* accused Foucault of practicing a "despairing positivism."[35] Nonetheless, the fact remains that however active Foucault may have been in his personal political practice and however active he may have inspired others to be,[36] in ways hardly characteristic of positivist research as generally understood, his theoretical project seeks to describe positive totalities that are in essence frozen in time and hence offer no concrete articulation either of how change has occurred in the past or of how it might come to pass in the future. As Joseph Rouse has noted, his aim was not to explain the shifts between epistemic paradigms, but "to display their structural differences" (39). In short, his theoretical structures often either fail to do justice to, or to authorize, his political practice.

Thus while Foucault speaks of resistance to power in volume one of the *History of Sexuality*, and indeed argues that it is inherent in the very differential ratios out of which power is constituted, resistance in his sense is always conceived of as reactive force "co-constituted" with power.[37] It is not a self-determining oppositional movement, but a reaction. The metaphor of resistance is one that envisions a static blocking action rather than a dynamic counterforce. As Jameson notes in a formulation that captures not only the progressive political aspects of Foucault's thought but also the theoretical positivism to which it and much other postmodern thought succumbs, "The new or postmodern

---

the differences between these two phases of Foucault's career have been exaggerated by some writers, see Stoekl 192; and Bannet 96–97.

[33] See, for example, Frow 79; Poster 23–24; Descombes 110–11; Flynn 30. Dreyfus and Rabinow refer to his early work's "phenomenological positivism" and note that he "proposes to begin like a pure empiricist" (52 and 59).

[34] See Foucault's inaugural lecture at the Collège de France, *L'ordre du discours* (English = "Discourse on Language"), 72/234, hereafter cited as *OD* (I have preferred my own translation, but include the page numbers of Swyer's rendering for reference purposes). Deleuze, at one point, refers to "le positivisme romantique de Foucault" (cited in Kremer-Marietti, 119 n. 60).

[35] For a good summary of the critical reaction to *LMC*, see Macey 175–76.

[36] For Foucault's personal activism, see Macey 203–31, 257–352, 378–414, 436–56; and J. Miller 165–207; and Jameson, *Postmodernism* 203. For Foucault's response to the charge that *LMC* does not leave any theoretical space for political action, see Macey 194–95. The galvanizing force of volume 1 of the *History of Sexuality* on the political activism of gays in the United States is eloquently described by Halperin 15–27.

[37] Foucault, *La volonté de savoir* (English = *History of sexuality vol. 1*), 125–27/95–96; Rouse 108–09; Sawicki 294, 296, 303–04.

development, indeed, remains progressive to the degree to which it dispels any last illusions as to the autonomy of thought, even though the dissipation of those illusions may reveal a wholly positivist landscape from which the negative has evaporated altogether" (*Postmodernism* 323; see also Sawicki 293). This evaporation of the negative, this search to describe pure positivities, offers no space from which the negation of the present might be seen to emerge, no real possibility for the material passage of time, except as the repetition of the always already given. And while it is true that the *History of Sexuality* makes a greater effort to accommodate diversity and conflict than did *Les mots et les choses*, and that volume three includes a brief narrative where Foucault rightly contrasts his understanding of the effects brought about by the transition from the republic to the empire with that of traditional history, nonetheless we are left with a major historical lacuna between fourth century BCE Greece and first century CE Rome; and in that lacuna we find Catullus whose representation of the subject's self-relation can be accounted for neither by the ethic of self-mastery nor by that of the "care of the self" (*LUDP* 28/21; *LSDS* 93−107/74−86; Richlin, "Zeus and Metis" 170−71; Dean-Jones 73). In short, despite all of Foucault's theoretical rigor, "self-mastery" and "the care of the self" are presented as virtual monoliths whose possible negations are nowhere in sight.

Still, it will be objected that while Foucault has no explicit theorization of the negative, this seeming lacuna is hardly a vice but rather a virtue. For what Foucault's eschewing of the negative represents is precisely an attempt to revive French philosophical and historical thought from its long ideological slumber in the shadow of Hegel and the dialectic,[38] whether in its original idealist form or in its later Marxist, materialist renderings. Such a dialectic is necessarily teleological in the conventional view, and so ultimately recuperates all moments of real difference or discontinuity into the long march of historical progress and final self-identity (Poster 10−11; Roberts 101−02).[39] Thus in place of a negation which will always be recuperated, Foucault proposes the concept of "transgression" ("PT" 765−68/48−51; Stoekl 179−80; Roberts 103):

> At the root of sexuality, of the movement that nothing can ever limit [...] and at the root of this discourse on God which Western culture has maintained for so long [...] a singular experience is shaped: that of transgression. Perhaps one day it will seem as decisive for our culture, as much a part of its soil, as the experience of contradiction was at an earlier time for dialectical thought. ("PT" 754/33)

---

[38] "I know very well that our whole epoch, whether through logic or epistemology, whether through Marx or Nietzsche, is trying to escape Hegel, and what I was saying earlier about discourse is not at all faithful to the Hegelian logos" (*OD* 74/235, my translation).

[39] For Foucault's often conflicted and ambivalent relation to Marxism and Hegel, and his eventual acceptance of the *Nouveaux Philosophes*' contention that there is direct connection between Hegel and the Gulag, see his "Préface à la transgression" (English = "Preface to Transgression") 757−61/38−43, hereafter cited as "PT"; *Remarks on Marx passim*; Macey 105−06, 149−50, 243, 387−89; J. Miller 171, 296; and Sakolsky 115, 118.

Yet, as we shall see, transgression is itself incapable of accounting for historical change, because it leaves that which it transgresses untouched. Thus it too ultimately reproduces the same problem of idealist identity that Foucault finds characteristic of dialectics. Negation itself, I would argue, when properly understood, is the only concept that allows real historical difference to be thought. For history without a logic of transformation or change is, in fact, nothing more than a series of synchronically juxtaposed presents.[40]

Foucault himself rigorously distinguishes between transgression and negation by observing that transgression's function is not to overcome limits, but to affirm them by crossing them. It creates nothing new in its wake because it makes no positive affirmation:

> Transgression contains nothing negative, but affirms limited being −affirms the limitlessness into which it leaps as it opens this zone to existence for the first time. But correspondingly, this affirmation contains nothing positive: no content can bind it, since by definition, no limit can possibly restrict it ("PT" 756/35−36)[41]

Transgression, however, by crossing limits without overcoming them, also necessarily leaves them unchanged. It is a static act that leaves everything as it was before: "transgression incessantly crosses and recrosses a line which closes up behind it in a wave of extremely short duration" ("PT" 754−55/34). It is for this reason that a philosophical position that attempts to replace dialectical negation with the transgression of limits ends by denying history itself. For transgression in its insistent emptiness, in its refusal to affirm anything but the limit it momentarily crosses, offers no logic of transformation, no motive for change, but rather constantly reaffirms the existence of the boundary itself.

Negation, on the other hand, is by definition a form of determination (Jameson, *Postmodernism* 385). It makes a difference. It leaves a mark. From this perspective, the opposite of Foucault's discursive positivities is not absence, transgression, or a mere breaking of the rules that leaves the rules in place. "The opposite of a positive force is [...] *another* force which possesses its own positive ontological actuality." Negation implies an intervention in the reigning positive order that possesses the potential to transform that order. It represents a clash between two opposed moments whose outcome produces difference, not serial replication. Thus all moments of purest negation are themselves also pure positivities (Zizek, *Negative* 22−24, 109, italics his).[42] Indeed, the most radical negativity of all would be the absolute lack of any relation to anything, an absolute refusal of all reigning positivities. Yet such an absolute lack of relation would,

---

[40] Stoekl describes Foucault's notion of historical temporality as that of "a relentless seriality," (180). One might refer to this as the Henry Ford school of historicity, "one damned thing after another." On synchrony as an idealist construct, see Voloshinov 66.

[41] See also Stoekl 176; J. Miller 88; Macey 138; Boyne 82.

[42] See also Jameson, *Postmodernism* 332; and Hegel 119.

by definition, be unspeakable, meaningless. And this absolute meaninglessness, this pristine irrelevance, would consequently cease to be negative at all, since the total lack of relation required of it would result in there being no object to negate. As Derrida notes, "Negativity cannot be spoken of, nor has it ever been except in [a] fabric of meaning" ("From Restricted to General Economy" 259–60). The most absolute negativity is thus always already its own positive negation. But to see this moment of transformation, to recognize this process whereby opposed valences metamorphose into their opposites, is already to be thinking dialectically. The rejection of dialectics and the adoption of a logic of identity closes off the possibility of thinking through this kind of multidimensional, temporal process. If dialectics are rejected, transgression can only be transgression, positivity can only be positivity, and the possibility of their determined conflict and mutual transformation cannot be envisioned. It is this moment of clash, of structured opposition, as opposed to simple resistance, that is lacking from Foucault's account of these single unified *épistémès* or *dispositifs*. This is true whether we are speaking of eighteenth-century political economy in *Les mots et les choses* or Roman regimes of the self in *Le souci de soi*.

In this light, Catullus' lyric subjectivity does not simply fail to conform to the epistemic constraints of the model put forward in the *Care of the Self*, it offers an alternative model of the subject whose complex temporal structure, internal agonistics, and dissociation of the identity of love and lust are radically opposed to the normative model Foucault constructs from Pliny, Seneca, Musonius and others. Through his continued influence in the early empire, as attested by the imitations of writers such as Ovid and Martial, Catullus offers an alternative to the hegemonic model of subjectivity found in the philosophical and medical writers cited by Foucault. Through the content of its generic form, his collection demonstrates the dependence of Foucault's hegemonic model on a relatively restricted range of discourses in a society whose rich literary and rhetorical heritage offered numerous alternative models from which to choose. Finally, by offering a model of lyric subjectivity that is assimilable neither to the classical ethic of "self-mastery" nor to the imperial and Alexandrian model of "care of the self," the Catullan collection demonstrates the inability of any historical methodology founded on the description of pure positivities to account for the transition from one dominant cultural system to the next without also taking into account those moments of radical otherness that make the negation of the present and the passage to the future possible. For if the present or past is seen as essentially homogeneous, then the otherness necessary for historical change remains rigorously unthinkable. The negation offered by the Catullan lyric collection shows that historiography in the form of a series of juxtaposed synchronic presents can never account for the alterity essential to any meaningful concept of change.

204 Paul Allen Miller

The return to a concept of dialectical negation that I am advocating as an alternative to the Foucauldian concept of transgression may to some seem a step backward. But there is also the perspective from which it can be said to be truer to Foucault's understanding of the importance and position of Hegel, than Foucault was himself. For, as he acknowledged in his praise of Jean Hyppolite at the end of his inaugural address at the *Collège de France*:

> To really escape from Hegel assumes an appreciation of exactly what it costs to detach yourself from him. It assumes that you know how far Hegel, insidiously perhaps, has approached us. It supposes that we know how much of what allows us to think against Hegel is still Hegelian, and in what measure our recourse against him is perhaps only a ruse that he deploys against us, at the end of which he awaits, unmoving and elsewhere. (*OD* 74–75/235, my translation)[43]

Here Foucault seems to imply that the only way to go beyond Hegel is through Hegel, and on one level this is exactly what he has done. For the very idea of transgression is derived from Bataille, who as Allan Stoekl notes "considered himself a Kojèvian-Hegelian." Hence the concept of transgression can be said, from a genealogical perspective to be Hegelian. In this light, Stoekl argues that "it is time to reinterpret Foucault's own reinterpretation of Hegelianism – against him but also with him." For any concept of transgression that would supersede negation itself implies a negation. Hence this attempt to go beyond Hegel is an "eminently Hegelian gesture" (180–82).[44]

All the same, to be true to Foucault's intention of transcending Hegel through Hegel, the moment of transgression must not be recuperated into the limit it supposedly crosses, rather its negativity, its lasting difference from what constitutes the limit must be preserved. To return to our opening quotation, from Foucault's own "Nietzsche, Genealogy, History," a form of historical writing that seeks to go beyond all idealist teleologies and deal "with events in terms of their most unique characteristics, their most acute manifestations," cannot be one which denies the negative moment by reducing the variety of discursive forms or themes present at a given historical moment to a single dominant epistemic model.[45] It cannot be one that reduces the Catullan lyric subjectivity

---

[43] This passage can also be read as an implicit concession to Derrida's charge in "Cogito and the History of Madness" that Foucault in his *L'Histoire de la folie dans l'age classique* had inadvertently reproduced the classic Hegelian story of reason's self-division rather than chronicled the history of reason's confrontation with its other: "As always, the dissension is internal. The exterior (is) the interior, is the fission that produces and divides it along the lines of the Hegelian *Entzweiung*" (39). On Foucault's implicit concession to Derrida on this point, see Boyne 76, 118.

[44] Stoekl cites extensively from Derrida's "From Restricted to General Economy." See especially 251 and 274–75. Thus Kremer-Marietti poses the question, "mais ce langage est-il non dialectique, comme le pense Foucault?" ("but this language [of transgression] is it nondialectical, as Foucault thinks it to be"), 99, my translation.

[45] Thus Derrida, in "Cogito," describes *Histoire de la Folie* as "a powerful gesture of protection and confinement. A Cartesian gesture for the twentieth century. A recuperation of negativity" (55;

to a model homologous to that of Seneca and Pliny without recognizing its real difference. Indeed, as one of Foucault's more lyrical French commentators, Angèle Kremer-Marietti, argues, the purpose of Foucauldian genealogy is "to refuse the parody of the identical and instead to restore the plurality of souls," in short, to demonstrate that we do not all live in the same Now (Kremer-Marietti 101, my translation). Hence, I would argue, the only way to be true to Foucault's intentions as announced in this programmatic essay is to read him against himself by restoring the full power of the negative.

The final question, then, becomes: Does not the dialectic itself recuperate the negative in the gesture of synthesis, so that it too is ultimately ahistorical since every moment of rupture or difference is eventually restored to a primal unity in which all difference is ultimately sublated and annulled? History in this reading of the dialectic is reduced to nothing more than the unfolding of an identity that was always already present. Consequently, nothing ever really changes. Certainly this is a standard depiction of the dialectic in both its most idealist and its most vulgar materialist forms. Here, teleology replaces real historical change in a gesture that unites the seeming opposites of absolute idealism and mechanical materialism (Poster 62−64; Flynn 42). But such an understanding of dialectics is not the only, or even necessarily the truest, one. It too annihilates that very moment of negation that is the dialectic's distinguishing characteristic. As Slavoj Zizek in his Lacanian inspired reading of Hegel has argued:

> "Synthesis" does not affirm the identity of the extremes, their common ground [...] but on the contrary *their difference as such*: what "links up" the elements of a signifying network is their very difference. Within a differential order, the identity of each of the elements consists in the bundle of differential features which discern it from all other elements. The "synthesis" thus delivers the difference from the "compulsion to identify": the contradiction is resolved when we acknowledge the primacy of difference. [...] The idea that the concluding moment of a dialectical process ("synthesis") consists of the advent of an Identity which encompasses the difference [...] is thus totally misleading: *it is only with "synthesis" that the difference is acknowledged as such*. (*Negative*, 98, 122−24, italics his)

Paradoxically, then, the true specificity of the ethic of the care of the self that Foucault outlines with admirable rigor can only really be understood in relation to its own negative counter-moment, be it that of the Catullan lyric consciousness, of the slaves whose labor made the Roman empire possible, of women who are excluded from its normative model except in their role as the wives of those whose selves are being cared for, or of the conquered or marginalized peoples whose continued pressure on the Roman state and its culture would eventually be the immediate cause of its collapse. The moment of synthesis is not that which obliterates those differences, but rather that which allows us to think those differences in their complex relations to one another. It does not

cited by Macey, 144, in his own slightly altered translation). See also 35−36 in Derrida's "Cogito".

reduce everything to some posited common identity, but examines the conflicts and interaction between opposed positivities and tries to understand the transformations this manifold of differences produces. Each negation thus ceases to exist in a simple static relation with that which it opposes, but enters a larger, more complex series of relations in which its own identity is determined by its self-positioning within a tissue of differential relations. What is termed synthesis, then—a word never employed by Hegel himself (Zizek, *Negative* 263)—is, in fact, the negation of the negation, the process by which a simple oppositional moment is sublated into a larger complex of such moments, so that its very being, its very identity, becomes a function of its interiorization of that initial principle of negation which at first seemed merely to denote its external opposition to a single positive moment. The challenge for cultural history after Foucault, then, is not to elide the difference between Catullan lyric subjectivity and the ethic of the care of the self, but to try to articulate the differences that bring them together in that complex, self-transforming and open-ended totality we call Roman culture, both in terms of the synchronic unity of that culture and of its diachronic changes.

III.

[I]t is not terribly difficult to say what is meant by the Real in Lacan. It is simply History itself.

(Jameson, "Imaginary and Symbolic" 104)

The Real is History, Jameson says, that which has already happened. But I would add that inasmuch as history is distorted, interpreted, and reconstructed, it is no longer the Real.

(Ragland-Sullivan 194)

I would like to close by suggesting that this moment of absolute negation, which Foucault forecloses, can be positively envisioned in terms of what Lacan designates the emergence of the Real: for the Real is that which is unassimilable to the structures of explanation available to any given cultural formation. It is the absolute alterity that makes the historical succession of cultural, linguistic, and political forms and institutions thinkable as something other than an inexplicable series of random transformations.[46] For the Real marks the point at which the Symbolic, and hence any given epistemic formation, meets its own systemic negation (Copjec 9, 121), its principle of finitude or limit. This moment of

---

[46] See Lacan (32–33) on Marx's insight that history is the possibility of completely subverting the function of discourse, hence history is that which demonstrates the contingency of a given Symbolic system and its consequent inadequacy vis-à-vis the Real.

negation, as we have argued, is necessary to any meaningful concept of historical change, since it is precisely that which figures the possibility of otherness within the reigning positive system (Adorno 53, 140–43; Jameson, *Prison-house* 193–94; *Political Unconscious* 91, 95, 97–98; *Postmodernism* 5–6; Zizek, *Negation* 23, 109). Without the negation of the Real, without this conception of the beyond of the norms and systems of meaning that constitute the Symbolic, epistemic forma-tions would absolutize themselves in a way that would allow no room to con-ceive of the radically other (Jameson, *Political Unconscious*, 90–91; *Postmodernism* 405–06; Copjec 17, 23–24). As Derrida has written, the concept of the future, of the yet-to-come (*a-venir*), depends on an opening within the Symbolic that cannot be reduced to the categories of either knowledge or ignorance, but must be seen as a systematic heterogeneity, an absolute otherness that cannot be reduced to the reigning positive system (*Spectres* 68).

Yet it is precisely this gesture of the reduction of the Symbolic to a pure positivity removed from the vicissitudes of the Real that characterizes what we have objected to in Foucault's method of historical description. As Eve Bannet observes, Foucauldian "archeology seems to freeze history, describing discursive formations and seeking general rules which are valid for all points of time but neglecting the temporal series within these formations and reducing chronology to the point of rupture when one discursive formation is substituted for an-other" (108–09). From Foucault's perspective, this neglect is the price we have to pay for preserving, real historical difference, for not falling into a teleological vision of history that annihilates difference. The Lacanian position, however, by founding the possibility of the Symbolic in its own inherent limitation, its sever-ance and hence inability to account for the Real (Eagleton 168), makes the negation of the Symbolic a constitutive part of any given discursive formation. Thus where Foucault must homogenize a given period's *épistémè* in the name of preserving historical difference (*LMC* 77, 103, 171; Bannet 157; Sedgwick 46–47; Macey 163), and so cut that *épistémè* off from any narrative that would explain its position in the larger historical sequence (Kremer-Marietti 49), Lacan sees the Law of the Symbolic as always opposed to and constituted by its own principle of generation and succession, a principle that escapes the Symbolic itself (Copjec 122).

Difference, for Lacan as opposed to Foucault, is not an external relation between regimes of power and knowledge, but internal to them (Copjec 9–10, 60). In this sense, the generative principle of any given discursive formation, its relation to that which exceeds it, also contains that formation's negation, the moment which escapes the dominant ideology's grasp and so makes change possible. Every form of hegemony is always haunted by the moment of repres-sion through which it is constituted, and is thus always already internally split (Derrida, *Spectres* 69). This internal fissure is precisely the point at which we witness the emergence of the Real, of History. It is the space of difference that this fissure implies, the space between the Symbolic and the Real, that prevents epistemic totalization and thus makes historicization possible (Zizek, *Sublime Object* 135).

IV.

In sum, Foucault's *History of Sexuality* is a monumental achievement in its demonstration of the constructed nature of sexual norms, its revelation of the intricate power games that inhabit those norms, and its demolition of the west's teleological myth of evolution through time toward greater individuality. This is no minor achievement and none of my preceding remarks should be seen as in any way diminishing its quality. At the same time, Foucault's wider goal as announced in the "Introduction" of volume 2 was to write a history of the individual constituting itself as a subject of ethical action through the figure of "one who desires." On this level, his work is at least incomplete. We have shown in this paper that the ethic of the "care of the self" is not able to include the model of subjectivity presented by the Catullan corpus on either a thematic or a formal level. This represents not only an important gap in Foucault's project, but also points to an underestimation on his part of the role of different discursive genres in creating different models of subjectivity. If the representation of subjectivity can be fundamentally altered by the use of different discursive practices, then any account that does not take this into consideration will necessarily undervalue the effect of competing and antagonistic models of subjectivity that can be present in single culture at a single time or in rapid succession to one another. This devaluation of contradiction, of the force of the negative, ultimately results in a theory of history that moves from one static formation to another without being able to account for change itself. On that level of analysis, Foucault's *History of Sexuality* has yet to articulate the relation between competing discursive systems in a given social formation, their inability to assimilate and consequent negation of one another and their final positioning vis-a-vis that ultimate negation, the unutterable Real.

12

Foucault in Gay America:
Sexuality at Plymouth Plantation

DAVID VAN LEER

Academic gay studies, in the United States at least, inevitably begins with the first volume of Michel Foucault's *Histoire de la sexualité*, and in particular with a paragraph early in the analysis of homosexuality in the nineteenth century. According to Foucault:

> This new hunting after peripheral sexualities entails an *embodiment of perversions* and a new *specification of individuals*. The "sodomy" of ancient civil or canonical laws was a type of forbidden act; the perpetrator was merely their juridical subject. The nineteenth-century homosexual became a personage: a past, a history and childhood, a character-type, a life form; also a morphology, with an indiscreet/undifferentiated anatomy and possibly a mysterious physiology. Nothing that goes into his totality escapes his sexuality. It is everywhere present in him: rooted in all his actions because it is their insidious and indefinitely active principle; written immodestly on his face and on his body because it is a secret that always gives itself away. It is consubstantial with him, less as a habitual sin than as a singularizing nature. We must not forget that the psychological, psychiatric, medical category of homosexuality was constituted on the day it was characterized – Westphal's famous article of 1870 on "contrary sexual sensations" can stand as its date of birth – less by a type of sexual relations than by a certain quality of sexual sensibility, a certain way of inverting in oneself the masculine and the feminine. Homosexuality appeared as one of the faces of sexuality when it was discounted from the practice of sodomy onto a kind of interior androgyny, a hermaphrodism of the soul. The sodomite was a regression; the homosexual is now a species.[1]

---

[1] "Cette chasse nouvelle aux sexualités périphériques entraîne une *incorporation des perversions* et une *spécification nouvelle des individus*. La sodomie – celle des anciens droits civil ou canonique – était un type d'actes interdits; leur auteur n'en était que le sujet juridique. L'homosexuel du XIXe siècle est devenu un personnage: un passé, une histoire et une enfance, un caractère, une forme de vie; une morphologie aussi, avec une anatomie indiscrète et peut-être une physiologie mystérieuse. Rien de ce qu'il est au total n'échappe à sa sexualité. Partout en lui, elle est présente: sous-jacente à toutes ses conduites parce qu'elle en est le principe insidieux et indéfiniment actif; inscrite sans pudeur sur son visage et sur son corps parce qu'elle est un secret qui se trahit toujours. Elle lui est consubstantielle, moins comme un péché d'habitude que comme une nature singulière. Il ne faut pas oublier que la catégorie psychologique, psychiatrique, médicale de l'homosexualité s'est constituée du jour où on l'a caractérisée – le fameux article de Westphal en 1870, sur les 'sensations sexuelles contraires' peut valoir comme date de naissance – moins par un type de relations sexuelles que par une certaine qualité de la sensibilité sexuelle, une certaine manière d'intervertir en soi-même le masculin et le féminin. L'homosexualité est ap-

With its final ringing aphorism, the passage ably exemplifies Foucault's prose wit. His references to "types," "characters," "figures," and "forms" emphasize how biomedical terminology blurred the distinction between individuals and ideas. An explicit pun points to the covert moralism which saw sexuality as both indiscrete and indiscreet; while an implicit one (on the slang meaning of *espèce*) underscores the ways in which this species is a damnable one.

Less clear, however, are the historiographic implications of Foucault's definition of sexuality as a "*dispositif*" (usually rendered in English a "construction").[2] Most simply, Foucault's paragraph makes the fairly uncontroversial point that any sexual category has itself a history. As always Foucault slyly inverts the traditional liberal assumption that abnormality grows out of and in response to normalcy. His *History of Sexuality* repeatedly implies that the concept of "heterosexuality" (and probably of "sexuality" itself) emerges only after "homosexuality" has been defined as a problem. And Foucault takes his customary sideswipes at Freud and Marx as unwitting apologists for such newly deployed heterosexism.

But on the more important issue of the relation between historical constructions and something we might wish to call reality or truth Foucault remains conspicuously silent. To explore this silence, American Foucauldians have mounted a wholesale attack on the notion of "underlying realities," usually stigmatized as "essences."[3] In queer theory, the debate focuses on the pre-history of sexuality — how we are to speak of events before the linguistic invention of "homosexuality." Three conclusions are customarily drawn from Foucault's paragraph. First, that there can be no homosexuality before the term "homosexuality," and that any attempt to delineate a proto-history for same-sex desire is to be rejected out of hand as "transhistorical." Second, since the concept of homosexuality is a politically-prejudiced construction, even after the coinage of the term we cannot profitably speak of something called homosexuality but only of the word "homosexuality," always accompanied by scare quotations. Finally, since the false construction of "homosexuality" is roughly comparable to other prejudicial labels for social difference — for example, "female" or "black" — it is useful to see how these minority categories are similarly hidden, especially in early modern history, before the terminologies of minority differences are fully articulated.

I do not wish to challenge the usefulness of these conclusions — or their desire to find a place for minority identity within academic scholarship. Yet the

---

parue comme une des figures de la sexualité lorsqu-elle a été rabattue de la practique de la sodomie sur une sorte d'androgynie intérieure, un hermaphrodisme de l'âme. Le sodomite était un relaps, l'homosexual est maintenant une espèce" (Foucault, *Histoire* 58–59, *History* 42–43). As I suggest in my analysis, my idiosyncratic revision of Hurley's translation emphasizes Foucault's verbal playfulness.

[2] For sexuality as "*dispositif*," see *Histoire* 139, *History* 105.

[3] For overviews of the social construction debate, see Fuss, Stein, and Halperin 41–53.

same assumptions that have opened up discussion in some directions have closed it down in others. To review some limitations of these assumptions, then, I wish to re-consider one celebrated debate in the recent historiography of sexuality. Near the end of William Bradford's history *Of Plymouth Plantation*, arguably the most canonical of early American texts, the youth Thomas Granger is put to death for "unnatural" sexual activities with numerous barnyard animals and a turkey.[4] This incident of bestiality at Plymouth, the first and most famous of Puritan settlements in seventeenth-century America, at first received little attention from traditional Americanist scholars. In the last decade, however, post-Foucauldian theory has transformed the passage into a test case not only for pre-nineteenth-century discourse of sexuality but for the convergences of sexuality with other minority discourses of gender, ethnicity, and race.[5]

Part of the difficulty (and fascination) of the Granger episode involves the larger setting in which Bradford places it. Although presented simply as an overview of the year 1642, the chapter is preoccupied with "sundry notorious sins" that plagued New England in that year (and "other[s]") (316). By conflating a number of events, Bradford implicitly suggests how Puritans grouped together, as "unnatural," acts that we today view as distinct. Yet at the same time, Bradford's ordering is so vague that it is often difficult to determine which event any given analysis means to explain. Most of the chapter reprints the responses of three Pilgrim ministers to a set of questions sent to Plymouth by the governor of Massachusetts Bay, Richard Bellingham. In his questions Bellingham is trying to adjudicate a difficult case of alleged child abuse. He wants to know whether the act comes under the statutes governing "sodomy," and particularly which acts are punishable by death and what might be the role of witnesses and force in gathering evidence.[6]

---

4 Bradford's text was written in two parts – the first probably sometime around 1630, and the second (from yearly notes) sometime after 1646. Though unpublished, the manuscript was known by historians until shortly before the American Revolution, when it disappeared. Sections of the text were available indirectly in histories by Thomas Morton and Thomas Prince. References to the manuscript's presence in the library of the Bishop of London began to appear in the 1840s, along with partial quotations from the text. Bradford's complete manuscript was printed in 1856 and returned to the United States in 1897. The standard modern edition is Morison; all references will cite this edition parenthetically. Murphy's useful paperback reissue entirely omits crucial passages that Morison (somewhat prejudicially) had relocated to the appendices.

5 See, for example, Katz 20–22, Bray 17, 25–26, D'Emilio and Freedman 16–18, Warner, and especially Goldberg 223–49.

6 Our knowledge of the episode derives from Winthrop's *Journal*. Bradford only mentions "the abuse of those two children" to contextualize the letters he reprints (320); and in fact the episode is edited out of the standard modern edition of Winthrop. For the fullest reading of the episode, see Oaks, "Sodomy." For readings of the incident in the broader context of Puritan responses to sodomy, see Oaks, "Fearful," and Crompton, "Homosexuals."

Although the ministers respond in general to Bellingham's questions, they pay little attention to the specific heterosexual circumstances his questions mean to address. Instead they foreground male homosexual activity, both in their quotations from the Old Testament, and in their phallic preoccupation with the potential difference between *penetratio* and *fricatio usque ad effusionem seminis* (frottage or what contemporary gay slang calls the "Princeton rub") (404). Only one of the three respondents suggests that child abuse might be sufficiently like sodomy to merit death. The most lenient decides that without penetration child abuse cannot count as sodomy; furthermore even *fricatio* between men is not a capital offense (407). The third feels that homosexual penetration and friction are equally punishable by death. It insists, however, that heterosexual child abuse is less sinful. Not only is homosexuality more unclean than other acts in "sinning against family and posterity." It requires more strict legal enforcement – because "it might be committed with more secrecy and less suspicion" (405).

We should not overread the ministers' conflation of homosexuality and child abuse. Since we do not know exactly what questions they were asked – or how fully they understood the context of Bellingham's questions – we cannot assume that they knew they were changing his emphasis. Moreover, their definition of sodomy in terms of homosexuality may not mark a general conceptual framework; cases of homosexual sodomy in Plymouth that year may merely have led them to formulate their responses in terms of issues more immediate than Bellingham's problems in Boston.[7]

At the same time, the responses do suggest some characteristics of Puritan sexual discourse. As Foucault might have predicted, the ministers' analysis is focused entirely on sexual *acts*, without any reference to the later expansion of the concept of sexuality to include an individual's psychology – thoughts, desires, motives. And in confirmation of Foucault's famous formulation, the ministers show no sense of homosexuals as a "species" with a distinct sensibility. On the other hand, however, it is equally true that while homosexuals do not for the ministers constitute a category, "homosexuality" does. Their desire to penalize same-sex acts more than other forms of sodomy suggests a qualitative difference between those acts and other forms of "unnaturalness."

It is imprecise to call the ministers' prohibitions homophobic. In their very attempt to define the nature of homosexual sinfulness, the ministers grant it a kind of authority.[8] Not only does their debate all but consume the chapter of

---

[7] Bellingham's own relation to these events may not be neutral: the year before these events Bellingham was himself implicitly accused of adultery. For a discussion of these sexual irregularities, see Colacurcio and, for a more theoretical reading of the same documents, Berlant, 57–95.

[8] This irony, too, is predicted by Foucault, in his observation that what is from one angle sexual "repression" is from another a "discursive explosion." Quite simply prohibitions require careful delineation; it takes a lot of talk to enact a silencing. See Foucault, *Histoire* 25–49, *History* 17–35.

Bradford in which it appears. Their very rhetoric of containment gives homosexuality a broader influence than it might have otherwise felt. In labeling as sinful the "voluntary effusion of seed *per modum concubitu* of man with man" (407), one minister unwittingly suggests the potential universality of such perverse emotions – the possibility that sinless men might still experience comparable effusions "*in*voluntarily." Paradoxically the most censorious of the ministers is in some senses the most modern. Charles Chauncy, later president of Harvard, undeniably writes the toughest of the three responses. He extends the death penalty not only to rape, incest, and bestiality, but by analogy to abortion and child abuse (411). In extracting confessions he invites the magistrates to employ "bodily torments, as racks, hot irons, etc" (413). And he finds *fricatio* as culpable as penetration. Yet in his eagerness to expose the evils of sodomy, Chauncy begins to consider personal psychology as a contributing factor in determining the heinousness of the act. He distinguishes not only between sudden temptations and habitual practices, but also between the acts of the unconverted and those of saints (412). And his dismissal of the phallic emphasis on penetration permits him to make – for the masculinist seventeenth century – a startlingly explicit reference to the possibility of female same-sex desire (411).[9]

It is in light of the ambiguities of the ministers' accounts that we must consider Bradford's own treatment of Granger. Again the ordering of his chapter somewhat obscures the nature of his references. But Bradford makes no specific mention of the male homosexual activities in Plymouth which probably inform the ministers' responses.[10] And in his own letter to Bellingham, which introduces the ministers' analyses, he councils even greater leniency than the most tolerant of the three.[11]

---

[9] The general wisdom is that the public discourse of homosexuality was more concerned with male activity than with female. It is at least true that Foucault's account of the nineteenth-century invention of the "homosexual" makes no reference to lesbianism, and that the historical references in seventeenth-century America were almost exclusively male. For qualifications of the more general silence concerning women, see Brown and Crompton, "Myth" 11–25.

[10] His early distinction between "sodomy" and "buggery" suggests that the first term probably for him denotes homosexuality (316). Similarly the discussion of how Granger and others learned their practices may mention acts between men – though, as often in Bradford, it is uncertain exactly to which nouns his pronouns refer (321). Although the exact relation between all the events is unclear, the sequence is plain enough: Bellingham writes in March and is answered in May. Plymouth's trial for male homosexuality takes place in March (and results only in public whippings); the Granger case ends with his execution in September.

[11] Bradford defends his leniency with a comparison to cases of murder (119). His simple point is that murderous assaults that do not result in death are not capital; just so with sodomy (or adultery or) without penetration. Yet even this simple comparison is vague about the teleology of sex. While death is clearly the goal of murder, is the goal of sex penetration or procreation? If merely the former, Bradford implicitly acknowledges the non-procreation, purely pleasurable aspects of intercourse. If the latter, he effectively pardons all homosexuals (and many adulterers), whose acts do not result in offspring. Whatever Bradford's intentions, it is at least important to realize that the Puritan laws against homosexuality – which forbade self-incrimination and

A similar circumspection informs his discussion of Plymouth's problems. Most strikingly his explanations of both Granger's misdeeds and the year's more general wickedness lack any sense of moral outrage. His conjectures about the "causes" of Granger's unnaturalness are not theological but economic. He is, of course, eager to insist that these practices are imported from "old England" – foreign, and not native to the plantation (321). But otherwise his explanations focus on problems of generating a labor force in the new world. Not only did unscrupulous captains deliver to the colony anyone who could pay the transport fee; the pool of able-bodied workers was sufficiently limited that the Pilgrims could not be particularly choosy in selecting employees (321).

Equally nonjudgmental are his explanations of the more widespread sins – where the list extends explicitly to "even sodomy and buggery (things fearful to name)" (316). He makes a hollow gesture towards blaming the wickedness on the intensity of the Devil's spite against an otherwise pure community. But his more convincing answers bracket the question of sin. He is most "persuaded" that the problem is one not of evil but of visibility: Plymouth does not have an especially high concentration of unnatural activity, but merely prosecutes its relatively rare infractions more publicly than do libertine societies (317). Such an explanation not only grants too quickly the inevitability of evil in a colony striving for purity. It does so in terms of a distinction between appearance and reality that inverts the way visibility usually functions within a Puritan context: if evil in Plymouth is not truly greater but merely more visible, what does that "mere" visibility do for the notion of visible sanctity?

Even more surprising is Bradford's remaining and most metaphorical explanation. "Another reason may be, that it may be in this case as it is with waters when their streams are stopped or dammed up. When they get passage they flow with more violence and make more noise and disturbance than when they are suffered to run quietly in their own channels" (316). Far from theological, this explanation might pass as proto-psychological.[12] In drawing an analogy with the natural world, Bradford conflates the predictability of evil with its inevitability: in explaining why something might happen he appears to say that it must happen. And his image of the dammed river anticipates modern debunkings of Puritan piety as just a form of sexual repression.

None of Bradford's explanations is especially convincing. Yet their failure underscores the oddity of Bradford's tone in this chapter. Unlike the ministers, who see male homosexuality as different from other indiscretions, Bradford treats all sexual sins as comparable. Such non-differentiation not only un-

---

required the testimony of two witnesses – made convictions almost impossible. Only one man (and no women) was executed for the crime in seventeenth-century New England. See Oaks 1978 and 1985.

[12] See, for example, the use of the stream image for repression in *Dora*; Freud 68.

dermines the difference between venial and mortal sins; it closes the very gap between good and evil, saint and sinner. Discussions of how evil can exist among us shade over into considerations of how evil comes from within us. Such moral ambiguities make impossible the confidence of Bradford's earlier readings of divine providence — his ability, for example, in crossing the Atlantic to distinguish between the unregenerate sailor who taunts the Puritans and dies and the saved young man who almost drowns but lives to become a pillar of the community. In the Granger chapter, written over fifteen years later, the only lesson of sodomy is the universal corruption of all human nature; and he concludes worrying "whether the greater part be not grown the worser" (316, 322).

It is in light of Bradford's moral uncertainty that we must read his description of the Granger incident. And here, to attend to the specifics of his formulations, I will have to quote all of this familiar passage.

> There was a youth whose name was Thomas Granger. He was servant to an honest man of Duxbury, being about 16 or 17 years of age. (His father and mother lived at the same time at Scituate.) He was this year detected of buggery, and indicted for the same, with a mare, a cow, two goats, five sheep, two calves and a turkey. Horrible it is to mention, but the truth of the history requires it. He was first discovered by one that accidentally saw his lewd practice toward the mare. (I forebear particulars.) Being upon it examined and committed, in the end he not only confessed the fact with that beast at that time, but sundry times before and at several times with all the rest of the forenamed in his indictment. And this his free confession was not only in private to the magistrates (though at first he strived to deny it) but to sundry, both minister and others; and afterwards, upon his indictment, to the whole Court and jury; and confirmed it at his execution. And whereas some of the sheep could not so well be known by his description of them, others with them were brought before him and he declared which were they and which were not. And accordingly he was cast by the jury and condemned, and after executed about the 8th of September, 1642. A very sad spectacle it was. For first the mare and then the cow and the rest of the lesser cattle were killed before his face, according to the law, Leviticus xx.15; and then he himself was executed. The cattle were all cast into a great large pit that was digged of purpose for them, and no use made of any part of them. (320–21)

The passage's power derives from the tension between Bradford's need to specify and his desire to repress — the irony of his parenthetic disclaimer to "forbear particulars." Despite this aside, and similarly parenthetic "fears" about "naming" earlier in the chapter, the passage is most remarkable for its detail, epitomized by the almost comic cadences of the list of victims — a mare, a cow, two goats, five sheep, two calves and a turkey. Some of the details — the multiple confessions, the repeated infractions — establish the legality of the plantation's proceedings. Yet others are not necessary to justify the action. Moreover, though Bradford implies that his forbearance largely concerns the exact nature of Granger's relations with animals, in fact those are present in more detail than most readers wish. The specifics forborne are not those of sexuality but those of the legal process itself — any description of the accusation, examination, trials, sentencing, or even of Granger's own execution.

Bradford's silence about the trial may mean to obscure the authoritarianism of Puritan discipline. But it has as well the opposite effect. For in the absence of representations of Puritan authority, Granger himself becomes an authority figure in the final lines of the passage. The lengthy description of the cattle's execution invites us to extend our sympathy from the beasts to Granger, with whom they are "cast." In seeing the cattle "before his face," we experience the "sad spectacle" of the executions through Granger's eyes. It is probably over-reading to attribute the "sadness" of the moment to Granger's loss of loved ones. But Bradford could not have missed the unstated typological reference of this final section — its relation to another kind of judgment scene. Just as in Genesis 2.19 God parades the animals before Adam to be named, so the Puritans bring the sheep and lesser cattle before Granger to be identified. Bradford's account is in fact so convincing as typology that it seems implausible as reportage. It is difficult for the literal-minded reader not to wonder how Granger actually identified which was *his* turkey. Yet whatever his relation to the parade of livestock, in the absence of the Puritan judges in Bradford's account, Granger himself functions as both judge and namer-poet — a figure of Adamic innocence and creativity.

Earlier in *Of Plymouth Plantation*, the narrative vivacity and linguistic playfulness with which Bradford describes the Puritan assault on the non-conformist (Anglican) community at Merrymount make Thomas Morton, the putative villain of this famous episode, into a spokesperson for imagination and ethnic toleration. So in the bestiality passage, the metaphoric language converts Thomas Granger into a figure of considerable symbolic power, and Bradford's description of him seems torn between moral disapproval and linguistic richness. Neo-Foucauldian readings of the passage as "merciless" or the characterization as "scapegoating" seem insensitive to Bradford's language and narrative strategies (Goldberg 225, Warner 25). At this point I think we have to reconsider how the passages complicates our understanding of the three assumptions of American Foucauldianism. It is true that, in the absence of vocabulary, categories do get jumbled together. In that confusion various minorities — especially women, Indians, children, and homosexuals — are treated as if they were the same. But the question remains how to read that indiscriminate jumbling.

First it seems a kind of false precision to insist that there is no way to talk about homosexuality before 1870. Although there is no consistent vocabulary for distinguishing among various forms of sexual difference, it is still clear that Puritans saw some kind of difference. Most obviously, the Puritans treated differently sexual acts involving women, children, same-sex partners and animals. It is true that same-sex activities were defined differently across centuries. Yet to reject as "transhistorical" all attempts to read these cross-century differences overemphasizes these differences. Delineations of a homosexual "tradition" do not have a strong definition of the adjective "homosexual." But this problem derives less from the nature of sexuality than from the limits of language — our difficulties in understanding how any abstract noun hooks up with the individual members of the category it defines.

"Homosexual," "female" and "black" are sloppy, shifty terms. But so is "poet." In using the noun "poet," we usually refer to a Romantic notion of the artist as an isolated (and probably countercultural) voice. While such Romanticism may accurately describe writers like Wordsworth, Baudelaire, and Wallace Stevens, it does not tell us much about Geoffrey Chaucer, William Shakespeare, or Alexander Pope — all of whom had a different relation to society than that implied in the traditional definition of "poet." As philosophy since Wittgenstein has taken pains to remind us, naming is a complicated linguistic process. We do not really have a convincing explanation for any noun — for what, say, unites a physically diverse body of furniture under the sign of "chair." Yet it would seem overscrupulous for that reason to reject customary uses of that noun as "transhistorical"; and in fact no one ever does.

Foucault's *Histoire* argues explicitly that "homosexuality," as a biomedical concept invented in response to specific conditions of nineteenth-century culture, cannot be reapplied to earlier cultures without misrepresentation. In a similar fashion, it suggests by extension that a neologism like "gay" cannot usefully describe earlier persons who, whatever their sexual object-choices, could not by definition share in the late-twentieth-century political and aesthetic presuppositions of that term. Yet such arguments do not entail the atomistic nominalism of the most rigorous forms of American constructionism. It is unclear whether Foucault would have denounced "chairs" as transhistorical. He does not at least show, in the Classical second and third volumes of the *Histoire*, any qualms about provisionally stringing together different conceptualizations of same-sex desire. More important, extreme constructionism in gay theory tends to lose track of Foucault's crucial point about the genealogy of sexual terminology. As culture began to perceive same-sex desire as a problem, it ostracized it as "homosexuality." This disciplinary action required the subsequent postulation of two related categories — "sexuality" and "heterosexuality." In ignoring the central irony of this progression — that there is no such thing as "sexuality" without a prior "homosexuality" — gay theorists tend to perpetuate the invisible heterosexism that the *Histoire* exists to expose.

The charge of transhistoricism, then, can prevent scholars from affording to minority traditions the same free-and-easy sense of continuity that seems unproblematic when discussing hegemonic concepts like "poet," "family," or "imagination." Nervousness about the transhistorical potential of concepts like "homosexuality" is further complicated by the suspicion that sexuality has a special relation to the notion of "secrecy." In this error Foucault himself might seem complicit in his reference to homosexuality as "a secret that always gave itself away." Here I think the problem is simply a misreading of tone, a tendency to accept unironically what is in Foucault a highly skeptical paraphrase of bio-medical discourse. In the famous paragraph Foucault does not claim that same-sex desire was an open secret, but that such a prejudicial representation was one of the techniques used to discipline "the homosexual." Here again, Granger offers a useful corrective. There is no closet rhetoric in Bradford. Puritan culture had specific laws designed to address what they saw as an identifiable activity. Nor is Granger himself an invisible figure – hidden from history. In delineating a homosexuality "hidden from history," what we primarily mean to correct is the way in which sexuality does not figure significantly in the kinds of documentation once favored by historians. Like other aspects of social history – especially the experiences of disempowered classes, genders, and ethnic minorities – the traces of homosexuality frequently appear only indirectly, in forgotten court records or unpublished private writings.[13] Yet Bradford's account was never "hidden" in this sense. Far from forgotten, it is one of the foundational texts of the traditional Americanist canon. Nor is the Granger episode exactly new territory. The episode was popularized in the 1950s in Charles Olson's poem "There Was a Youth whose Name Was Thomas Granger," and has been anthologized since the '80s in the most popular textbook of American literature.[14]

To applaud gay scholarship's recovery of the hidden may do more than misrepresent the cultural status of Bradford and Granger. The very metaphor of a hidden history is implicated in a discourse of secrecy and discovery that has traditionally served to oppress homosexuals. It is exhilarating to declare, with Eve Kosofsky Sedgwick, that "an understanding of virtually any aspect of modern Western culture must be, not merely incomplete, but damaged in its central substance to the degree that it does not incorporate a critical analysis of modern homo-heterosexual definition" (Sedgwick 1). Yet Granger seems a poor place to start such a critique. Founding one's history on a turkey bugger not only conflates bestiality, buggery, sodomy, and homosexuality more quickly than did any seventeenth-century writer. As Sedgwick's own metaphors of damage and centrality warn, the critical processes of displacement and re-centering run the risk of recovering the gay hero only as victim.[15]

---

[13] It is in fact from such sources that we deduce the occurrence of male-male sodomy, only alluded to in Bradford's history.

[14] My chronology here is prejudicial. Granger's appearance in the third edition of the Norton (1989) comes long after his recovery by gay historian Katz. Yet the passage was on undergraduate shelves a good three years before the analyses of Warner and Goldberg. It is interesting that the passage is not, however, included in the most politically correct of recent Americanist anthologies, the Heath. See Baym 73–75, Lauter 245–66. For the Olson poem, first collected in *The Distance* (1960), see Creeley 179–81.

[15] For a fuller exploration of relation between minority status and "damage," see JanMohamed and Lloyd. JanMohamed's critique of the political implications of Homi Bhabha's theories is similar to my own reservations about Sedgwick's deconstructions, Van Leer 99–131.

Our rediscovery of Granger has not rescued him from the dustbin of history, but recast a readily available narrative in terms of theoretical paradigms congenial to modern sensibilities. There is of course nothing wrong with addressing people in terms of vocabulary and concepts they can understand. Yet in situating the passage with respect to racism, misogyny, and homophobia, we have to ask whether we are using modern tools to illuminate Bradford, or exploiting the voyeuristic potential of a passage to validate our critical methodologies. While not hidden from Americanist historiography, Puritan literature is not universally cherished. In critiquing texts easily sacrificed for audiences eager to sacrifice them, we not only collapse categories the Puritans kept tantalizingly distinct. We invite ourselves to conflate oppositional politics, liberal guilt, and academic advancement. At this point talking about duplicity in the seventeenth century can begin to seem like a way of not talking about complicity in the twentieth.

I do not mean to minimize the achievement of those who explore the sexual diversity of narrative thematics. Nor am I calling for a return to the days when sex was banished from polite conversation. Yet in exploding a politically problematic history of sexual discourse, one would not want to reinvent an equally suspect tradition of Puritan-bashing. It is intellectually prodigal to kill Puritan fathers only to resurrect H. L. Mencken. If Puritanism once silenced Thomas and his turkey, it forever after afforded them the means to speak. For delineating sexual difference, the language of sin may actually be a more supple vehicle than that of victimization. Despite the obvious limitations of his moral and legal universe, Bradford's depiction of Granger's unnaturalness respects sexual nuances more fully than does Olson's celebration of Granger's anti-authoritarian individualism.[16] The most interesting reading will not merely flatter modern sensibilities by rehearsing Granger's martyrdom. It will see in the interdependence of author and incident a challenge to our historiography and a reprimand to our amnesia.

---

[16] While Olson's poem quotes almost every passage to which I refer (including the ministers' *fricatio*) in naming Bradford's "fears" it omits the key words — "sodomy" and "buggery." Olson's omissions may mark a sympathetic desire not to reproduce problematic vocabulary; they, however, situate Puritan sexual anxiety wholly within heterosexuality. Although himself straight-identified, Olson was also one of the century's most vocal admirers of the gay novelist Herman Melville. As a result, about Olson's sexuality the usual rumors exist.

13

Philosophy in the Filigree of Power: The Limits of an Immanent Critique[1]

SAUL TOBIAS

The question of whether or to what extent the work of Michel Foucault constitutes philosophy, though a familiar subject of academic dispute, would not strike many as having immediate consequences for the evaluation of Foucault's writings in general and for his analysis of power, in particular. At a time when much contemporary cultural theory defines itself on the basis of its release from the "tutelage" of Enlightenment philosophy, on its awakening from a metaphysical dogmatic slumber, the question of the philosophical status of Foucault's work seems hardly relevant when philosophy's own status and, indeed, very possibility, is open to question. No one has done more to encourage this scepticism than Foucault himself, who wrote that "contemporary philosophy is [...] the politics immanent in history and the history indispensable to politics" (Power 159). Such radical historicisation and politicisation of philosophy has subordinated philosophy's self-conception to the analysis of discourse and power in the shape of a will to knowledge.

Yet the question of the relation of Foucault's methodology to the philosophical tradition does have important implications for the conception of power which dominates Foucault's work. The exclusion of certain philosophical categories in Foucault's analytic of power, though methodologically consistent, leads to an impasse which Foucault recognised but could not resolve. One possible approach to this problem, hinted at by Foucault but never pursued in his work, would consist in locating within Foucault's analysis of power, a space for philosophy, or for a particular notion of philosophy, which despite its interrogation and deflation (most notably by deconstruction) still bears the hallmark of the classical Kantian formulation of philosophy as the enquiry into the transcendental conditions of phenomena. In focusing on the phenomenon of power in this way, Foucault's later thought is shown to open itself, arguably even call for, a more formally philosophical analysis, one which cultural history and theory to-

[1] I am indebted to Ulrike Kistner and Andreas Bertoldi for bringing Foucault's "War in the Filigree of Peace" to my attention and for the numerous discussions we have had around this and related articles.

day should not ignore in attempting to overcome the limitations to which Foucault's own analysis of power is subject. In order to demonstrate the necessity of such an analysis, one must recall Foucault's conception of the relation between power, philosophy and the state. In "The Subject and Power" Foucault writes:

> It is certain that in contemporary societies the state is not simply one of the forms or specific situations of the exercise of power[...]but that in a certain way all other forms of power relation must refer to it[...].One could say that power relations have been progressively governmentalised, that is to say, elaborated, rationalised, and centralised in the form of, or under the auspices of, state institutions.(Subject 793)

This prioritising of the role of the state is one which readers of Foucault sometimes neglect. But it should not be forgotten that all the intricacies of biopower, the proliferation of techniques of discipline and subjectivisation which Foucault uncovers in the semi-autonomous domains of the school, the university, the prison, the clinic and the asylum, all refer in a direct and specific way to the state. According to Foucault, with the emergence of the modern state through the centralisation of sovereignty and the integration of social and economic life into an hierarchical structure, state power maintains and extends itself *precisely through* the deployment of the empirical knowledge and technologies which the Enlightenment made available as a means to organise social relations and regulate populations. Painstaking historical and sociological research, techniques of quantification, categorisation, specialisation and diagnosis thus come to form part of the state's disciplinary armoury. Therefore, in modernity, power can no longer be thought as brute force or repression, exposed by and opposed by knowledge. In modernity, where there is power there is knowledge, where there is knowledge, power. It is precisely because of this new articulation of power-knowledge that Foucault casts doubt on the usefulness of Enlightenment philosophy as a basis for analysing power in modernity. Again, in "The Subject and Power", Foucault writes:

> Since Kant, the role of philosophy is to prevent reason from going beyond the limits of what is given in experience: but from the same moment − that is since the development of the modern state and the political management of society − the role of philosophy is also to keep watch over the excessive powers of political rationality, which is a rather high expectation. (Subject 779)

It is in fact, according to Foucault, an expectation which philosophy cannot hope to meet. The reasons for the demotion of philosophy as a means of analysing power result, paradoxically, from the Enlightenment's own scientific production. Enlightenment political philosophy failed to recognise the changes in the deployment of power which its own empiricisation and rationalisation of knowledge and its scientific and technological advances had made possible. Rather, it viewed power in terms of a metaphysics of the state. Such a theory of the state did not proceed from empirical, historical evidence, but drew its form and features, one might say, from philosophy's own backyard, from the domain of abstract concepts such as reason and right. It was a theory of the state which proceeded from ideal juridical forms and upheld the opposition between knowledge and power. But for Foucault, such political philosophy, as the elucidation and application of metaphysical concepts of law, legitimacy, sovereignty and justice, as these pertained to the nature and role of the state, fail to encapsulate, in fact serve only to disguise, the workings of power in modernity. It is thus around this question of the state and its deployment of power that Foucault makes his break with philosophy. "In order to conduct a *concrete* analysis of the relations of power," Foucault writes, "we must abandon the juridical model of sovereignty. This model [...] sets out to account for the genesis, in *ideal* terms, of the State [...]. It makes law the fundamental manifestation of power" (War 15, emphasis mine).

Therefore, for Foucault, the concrete, empirical and immanent articulation of power and knowledge in modernity demands an analysis of power conducted along these same concrete and immanent terms, an approach "which is more empirical, more directly related to our present situation, and which implies more relations between theory and practice" (Subject 780). Foucault's position is therefore fascinatingly paradoxical: it states that the increasing role of the state, its pervasion, via the technologies of bio-power, of greater areas of social life, is accompanied by a decreasing relevance of theories of the state as such. Put another way, the rationalisation, technologisation, and secularisation of knowledge which Enlightenment science provided to an increasingly powerful and effective state apparatus disposes, in Foucault's view, of the usefulness of the Enlightenment's other great accomplishment, the philosophical elaboration of universal theories of society and the state.

However, in proposing an analysis of power immanent to the institutions and discourses of the state Foucault faces a problem, and it is simply this: if the proliferation of scientific, empirical knowledge and technologies of power, the heritage of the Enlightenment, is precisely the means by which the state orders, individualises, and rationalises the deployment of power in society and thus exerts itself all the more effectively, what kind of knowledge production is not complicit with precisely this power/knowledge regime? If the deployment of biopower makes redundant metaphysical accounts of the state as effective means to analyse power in modernity, what exactly is the critical value of an analysis of the relations of power in terms of the technologies and disciplines of bio-power when the modalities and strategies of that analysis are no less constitutive of and may reinforce and reduplicate the interests of the civil order?

Foucault is certainly not unaware of this problem. At various points in his work, he questions the real efficacy of discourses of resistance which oppose the existing articulation of power-knowledge relations but in fact only reproduce the form of such relations by reinforcing further individualisation, by embracing "rights talk", or by generally adding to the proliferation of instrumental knowledges. The celebration of insanity, sexual deviance, criminality, in resisting the norm, only reinforce the categories by which the state masters the social domain, providing further fodder for an army of jurists, psychiatrists and social policy makers to hone their skills and test their theories. As we have seen, that this should be the case follows from Foucault's rejection of the power-knowledge opposition: in so far as knowledge and power are caught in a relation of mutual implication, manifesting concretely only as an admixture of the two, our own knowledge of power-knowledge, to the extent that it proceeds along the lines of empirical or historical investigation, in terms immanent to the state's array of knowledge regimes, remains data for the state's own knowledge crunching machine.

How then do we resolve this dilemma? In a course summary entitled "War in the Filigree of Peace" Foucault raises again the problem outlined above and proposes a line of thought as a possible solution to the problem. In this course outline, Foucault writes,

> If we have to avoid collapsing the analysis of power back onto the schema proposed by the juridical constitution of sovereignty and conceive power in terms of relations of force, must we then decipher it following the general form of war? (War 15)

Foucault's proposal, put plainly, is this: "can war act as the operator of analysis of the relations of power?"(War 15) Concern with war and warfare is not a dominant feature of Foucault's work. This is surprising, considering the fact that war obviously has some relation to power, to the state, and to questions of authority and sovereignty, all issues that are of interest to Foucault. The reason for this omission, I would contend, is not accidental. It is not merely because warfare takes place largely between states or social formations, whereas Foucault's analysis has been concerned with power relations internal to the state. The reason for Foucault's avoidance of the problem of warfare until so late in his career relates rather to the fact that Foucault's entire methodology, having foresworn all transcendental or metaphysical forms of argument, is reliant on the positive forms of knowledge production internal, immanent and proper to the state itself. The documentation of archives, libraries and museums, the statistics and record keeping of institutions and organisations, the maps, the architectural blueprints, the textbooks, pamphlets and manuals, the entire body of empirical, historical and scientific knowledge which in their positivity constitute the resources of the state's rearticulation and redeployment of power in modernity are also what constitute the resources and indeed horizon of Foucault's mode of analysis. In pointing to war as the sign of a notion of force irreducible to power in its concrete and legible civic manifestations, Foucault is pointing beyond the state, to its condition of possibility or to what the state, in its positivity, disavows or represses, and in so doing, is pointing beyond the resources and methodology which have characterised his own empirical and immanent mode of analysis. Indeed, if we look at the way Foucault poses this question of war in "War in the Filigree of Peace", the suggestion of a transcendental or noumenal notion of power, something that constitutes an essence or absolute condition of possibility beyond the positivity of empirical structures and legible discourses, is clearly apparent:

> Must we regard war as a *primary and fundamental state of things* [the Kantian *ding an sich* clearly resonates here] in relation to which all the phenomena of social domination, differentiation and hierarchisation are merely derivative?
> [...]. Are the[...]. war-making institutions[...] the *nucleus* of political institutions (either closely or remotely, directly or indirectly)?
> [...][Is the] civil order[...] *fundamentally* a battle order? (War 16, emphasis mine)

What is being suggested here is a notion of power which lies at the limit of what is given in the experience of the state's empirical knowledge regimes. It is as if Foucault is proposing the methodological necessity of a quasi-Nietzschean, transcendental notion of power which is at the furthest remove from both an idealistic juridical notion of power *and* from an empirical model of micro- or biopower as the visible and measurable relation of imminent forces. Yet, despite the opening to a transcendental argument implied by the above questions, Foucault's further discussion of power as war remains firmly entrenched within a discursive and historical regime. He recognises the potential for the theorisation of power as war to undermine the Enlightenment tradition of metaphysical and ideal discourses of state power, but he does not recognise its potential to undermine the analysis of power as biopower, which is no less the fruit of the Enlightenment. Two remarks by Foucault indicate the extent to which his conceptualisation of power as war remains within the framework of his own empirico-discursive methodology:

> What we have here is thus a political and historical discourse which lays claim to truth and right, but excludes itself specifically from juridico-philosophical universality. (War 17)

Here Foucault's concern is with war as a theme identified in the writings of various thinkers throughout history, among them Coke, Lilburne and Boulainvilliers. In their writings, the principle of decipherment of power is no longer a universal concept, but the contingency and specificity of local and historical battles, chance victories, defeats, struggles and betrayals. In examining the question of power as war in this way, Foucault limits his investigation of the question to discourses of war as empirical and historical phenomena, colouring debates around sovereignty, power and law, and competing with other discourses on a terrain of knowledge production internal to the state. No concern is shown with the structure of the argument or the mode of enquiry to which such a notion of power as war would give rise. At another point Foucault writes:

> all in all, by opposition to the philosophico-juridical discourse, which is ordered by the problem of sovereignty and the law, this discourse is an essentially historico-political one, which deciphers the permanence of war in society.(War 18)

Besides here again reinforcing the historico-discursive approach to the question, Foucault also indicates how he views war as a positive phenomenon internal to the social, in so doing, refusing the possibility that war in fact marks the limit of the social. Foucault makes this assumption elsewhere when he writes, "A society entirely permeated by war relations was gradually replaced by a State equipped by military institutions."(War 16) That Foucault makes this assumption regarding the internality of war to the social, follows from his, dare I call it, positivist methodology. What is thinkable is only that of which we can have positive knowledge, what is visible, empirical or historical, and thereby amenable to description. It is the social, viewed as a visible and concrete domain of institutions and discourses which is primary in Foucault's analysis. War is a deriv-ative phenomenon viewed through these empirical and positivist spectacles. From this it follows that war may change its form with the emergence of the state, may become technicised and professionalised, but remains none-the-less a component internal to and coextensive with the social fabric. From first pro-posing that war may be the "secret motor of institutions, laws and order" Fou-cault's methodology strips this secret of its secrecy, reducing it to the status of a visible relation within the social order, knowable and describable. Such a con-ception of war may overturn the premises of a idealist juridical political philoso-phy, but it does not exceed the terms or escape the appropriating capacities of historical and social scientific analysis.

By limiting the investigation of power to a positivist historical methodology, the opportunity contained in the notion of war to provide a condition of state power which exceeds the state's own mechanism's for the theorisation, recupera-tion and disarming of such a notion is lost. Furthermore, due to his rejection of any non-empirical non-historical propositions regarding the conditions of state power, Foucault cannot perceive the degree to which such a conception also may constitute the conditions and limits of his own empirical-imminent analysis of power.[2]

What would it mean then to take Foucault at his word, if by "war being the secret motor of institutions, laws and order" we take him to mean not the hitherto unrecognised but now visible and knowable secret, but truly the secret, the mystery, the noumenon, the unconscious of history and knowledge? If the promise contained in such a proposal were to be realised, then Foucault scholars would have to take up the task of renewing the project which such a proposal presages, but which Foucault's methodology would not allow him to carry out,

---

[2] The work of Jacques Derrida would provide another important source for the proposals that I have been making. Much of Derrida's work on the relation between theory and politics, between constative and performative discourses, and particularly on the notion of "founding" (of univer-sities, of states etc.) argues for the inherent deconstructibility of pure notions of truth and power (and therefore for their inevitable mutual interpenetration and "contamination"), but also for the impossibility of dispensing with these notions and for their irreducibility to crude empiricisation. See for example Derrida's "Mochlos" and "Force of Law," and for a more detailed elucidation of Derrida's argument, Hent de Vries's *Philosophy and the Turn to Religion.*

the task of elaborating the structure of a transcendental analysis of power. While retaining a guarded suspicion of the reductionism of universal theories of the state and of power, such a transcendental analysis would nevertheless begin from an appreciation of both the methodological and political necessity of maintaining a notion of pure power, above and beyond its concrete adulteration by (and of) knowledge.[3] Furthermore, it would not take the state as its horizon and field of enquiry, but posit a notion of power against which the modalities of state power would be relativised and qualified. Some indication of the irreducibility of power as war to any modality of state power has been given in the work of two of Foucault's contemporaries, Gilles Deleuze and Felix Guattari, for whom the notion of the war machine or nomad constitutes the condition of possibility of the state. Whereas Foucault writes, "With the emergence of states from the middle ages, the practices and institutions of war became the preserve of the state (or monarch) alone. Along with this, war became increasingly technicised and professionalised," Deleuze and Guattari would hold that either the state has violence without war – the police, jails etc. – or it appropriates a war machine from the outside and institutionalises it. Essentially however, the war machine is incompatible with the state, and even when appropriated by the state as the military, always threatens to seep out of the state's control, to betray any contract it may appear to have entered into. As Deleuze and Guattari write, "the war machine is of another species, another nature, another origin than the State apparatus." (Plateaus 353) For Deleuze then, the relation between the state and the war machine is one of perpetual externality. The state, in its positivity and institutional concreteness, constitutes itself on the repression and denial of the war machine, which was present at its birth and hangs over it like a shadow. The war machine thus functions as a quasi-transcendental limit of the state and all its modalities of knowledge, it is the secret motor of history in the strongest sense of the word secret, and in describing it as such, Deleuze invokes explicitly the Kantian terminology of transcendental philosophy when he writes, "there is no history from the point of view of the nomads (even though everything happens through them,) to that extent they are like the "noumena", the unknowables of history" (Line 104).

---

3 Here Kant's critical thinking could be utilised to theorise the transcendental conditions of the state and its concrete deployment of knowledge-power. In *The Conflict of the Faculties*, in his discussion of the relation between the State and the faculty of philosophy, Kant asserts the purity of the two opposing poles of absolute power and pure knowledge while recognising the necessity of their constant negotiation and indeed mutual interpenetration within the realm of concrete action. It is in the monarch's right to declare war that Kant sees a notion of power which is incommensurate not only with the modalities of power internal to the state, but with the capacities of reason, including empirical or instrumental reason, to grasp its nature. Such a notion of power exceeds and indeed provides the condition of the state, as well as suggesting a notion of pure materiality or activity which functions as a transcendental limit to theory itself. See Kant's *The Conflict of the Faculties*, Part 1:1 and 163n

The tradition of transcendental philosophy offers only a few tantalising hints as to how a transcendental critique of power might proceed. But at the very least, it would suggest a conceptualisation of war which pits it against the state and does so in a form that follows from a philosophical investigation into the transcendental limits of knowledge. The work of philosophers such as Kant, Derrida and Deleuze offers clues to a reassessment of Foucault's slim and unimplemented proposals in "War In The Filigree of Peace" and should inspire in cultural history not only a renewed respect for what is so opaque and unthematisable in war, what escapes conceptualisation, reason and explanation, but also renewed attention to the limits of empirical and immanent modes of analysis. For we should never forget, and Foucault makes this explicit, that both technological knowledge and the social sciences, whatever their other conditions of emergence, sustain and are sustained by the nexus of power knowledge configurations which are contemporaneous with and cannot be disengaged from the state. Therefore, if a cultural history of power is to fulfil its task of uncovering beneath ideological and political dogma the real conditions of power, if, in other words, its project is to be truly critical, then it cannot brake before the apparent positivity of the state as its self-evident terrain and horizon. A critical cultural history calls for the articulation of conditions which are not reducible to visible structures or legible discourses, it calls for the thinking of transcendental limits to what can be articulated in empirical, scientific or rational language. In thus calling for the investigation into the transcendental or quasi-transcendental conditions of phenomena, cultural history calls, perhaps, for philosophy.

Bibliography

Abrahamian, Ervand. *Khomeinism: Essays on the Islamic Republic.* London: I. B. Tauris, 1993.

Adorno, Theodor. *Negative Dialectics.* Trans. E. B. Ashton. NY: Continuum, 1983.

Ahearne, Jeremy, Luce Giard, Dominique Julia, et al. "Feux persistants. Entretien sur Michel de Certeau. *Études* 3 (March 1996): 131–154.

Ahearne, Jeremy. *Michel de Certeau: Interpretation and its Other.* Cambridge: Polity P, 1995.

Alder, Ken. *Engineering the Revolution. Arms and Enlightenment in France, 1763–1815,* Princeton: Princeton UP, 1997.

Altman, Dennis. *The Homosexualization of America.* Boston: Beacon, 1982.

Anderson, Perry. *Passages From Antiquity to Feudalism.* London: New Left, 1978.

Ankersmit, Frank R. *De spiegel van het verleden: Exploraties I: geschiedtheorie.* Kampen/Kapellen: Kok Agora/Pelckmans, 1996.

Anon. *Onania.* London, 1730.

Arasse, Daniel. *La guillotine et l'imaginaire de la Terreur.* Paris: Flammarion, 1987.

Arendt, Hannah. *The Human Condition.* NY: Doubleday, 1958.

—. *Between Past and Future.* Harmondsworth: Penguin, 1968.

Argenterio, Giovanni. *Opera.* Hanau, 1610.

Auerbach, Erich. *Literary Language and Its Public in Latin Antiquity and in the Middle Ages.* Trans. Ralph Manheim. Bollingen Series 74. NY: Pantheon, 1965.

Austin, J. L. *How to do Things with Words.* Oxford: Oxford UP, 1962.

Backhauss, A. S. *De amore insano.* Geneva, 1686.

Baker, Keith Michael. *Inventing the French Revolution.* Cambridge: Cambridge UP, 1990.

—. "A Foucauldian French Revolution." Goldstein, *Writing of History.* 188–205.

Bakhash, Shaul. *The Reign of the Ayatollahs: Iran and the Islamic Revolution.* Rev. ed. London: Unwin, 1986.

Bal, Mieke. *Double Exposures: The Subject of Cultural Analysis.* London: Routledge, 1996.

Bannet, Eve Tavor. *Structuralism and the Logic of Dissent.* Urbana: U of Illinois P, 1989.

Barbin, Herculine. *Herculine Barbin: Being the Recently Discovered Memoirs of a Nineteenth-Century French Hermaphrodite.* Intr. Michel Foucault. Trans. Richard McDougall. Brighton: Harvester, 1980.

Barrett,W. *Death of the Soul: From Descartes to the Computer.* NY: Doubleday, 1986.

Barthes, Roland. *Incidents.* Trans. Richard Howard. Berkeley: U of California P, 1992.

Baudrillard, Jean. *Forget Foucault: and Forget Baudrillard.* NY: Semiotext(e), 1987.

—. *America.* London: Verso, 1989.

—. *L'Illusion de la fin.* Paris: Galilée, 1992.

Baym, Nina, et al., ed. *The Norton Anthology of American Literature.* Third ed. NY: Norton, 1989.

Bercovitch, Sacvan. *The Puritan Origins of the American Self.* New Haven: Yale UP, 1975.

Bérenger, P. L. *Le peuple instruit de ses propres vertus.* Paris, 1787.

Berlant, Lauren. *The Anatomy of National Fantasy: Hawthorne, Utopia, and Everyday Life.* Chicago: U of Chicago P, 1991.

Bertels, Kees. *Geschiedenis tussen struktuur en evenement. Een metodologies en wijsgerig onderzoek.* Amsterdam: Wetenschappelijke Uitgeverij, 1973.

Bienville, M. D. T. *Nymphomania or a Dissertation concerning the Furor Uterinus.* Trans. E. Sloane Wilmot. London, 1775.

Blackmer, Corinne E., and Pat Smith, eds. *En Travesti: Women, Gender Subversion, Opera.* NY: Columbia UP, 1995.

Blanc-Gilly, Mathieu. *Plan de révolution concernant les finances.* Marseille, 1789. Vol. 1 of Fonds de Provence, 4717, Impositions, Bibliothèque municipale, Marseille.

Blanchot, Maurice. "Michel Foucault As I Imagine Him." Trans. Jeffrey Mehlman. *Foucault-Blanchot.* NY: Zone Books, 1987. 63–109.

Bloch, Ernst. "Nonsynchronism and the Obligation to Its Dialectics." Orig. German 1935. *New German Critique* 11 (1977): 22–38.

Bloch, Ivan. *Sexual Life in England.* 1938. Royston: Oracle, 1996.

Bloom, Harold. *Omens of Millennium: the Gnosis of Angels, Dreams, and Resurrection.* London: Fourth Estate, 1996.

Bolgar, R. R. "Victor Cousin and Nineteenth-Century Education." *Cambridge Journal* 2 (1949): 357–68.

Bonnet, Jean-Claude, ed. *La Mort de Marat.* Paris: Flammarion, 1986.

Bourdé, Guy, and Hervé Martin. *Les écoles historiques.* Paris: Seuil, 1983.

Bourdieu, Pierre. *Ce que parler veut dire.* Paris: Seuil, 1982.

Boureau, Alain. "De la croyance comme compétence. Une nouvelle histoire des mentalités." *Critique* 529–530 (1991): 512–26.

Boutier, Jean, and Dominique Julia. "Ouverture: A quoi pensent les historiens? *Passés recomposés. Champs et chantiers de l'histoire.* Ed. Jean Boutier and Dominique Julia. Paris: Autrement, 1995. 13–53.

Boyne, Roy. *Foucault and Derrida: The Other Side of Reason.* London: Unwin, 1990.

Bradford, William. *Of Plymouth Plantation, 1620–1647.* Ed. Samuel Eliot Morison. NY: Modern Library, 1952.

–. *Of Plymouth Plantation.* Ed. Francis Murphy. NY: Modern Library, 1981.

Bray, Alan. *Homosexuality in Renaissance England.* London: Gay Men's P, 1982.

Brett, Philip, et al., eds. *Queering the Pitch: The New Gay and Lesbian Musicology.* London: Routledge, 1994.

Brown, Judith C. *Immodest Acts: The Life of a Lesbian Nun in Renaissance Italy.* NY: Oxford UP, 1986.

Bruner, Jerome S. *Acts of Meaning.* Cambridge, MA: Harvard UP, 1990.

Buren, W. H. Van. *A Practical Treatise on the Surgical Diseases of the Genito-urinary Organs, including Syphilis.* London: Churchill, 1874.

Burke, Peter. *Popular Culture in Early Modern Europe.* London: Temple Smith, 1978.

–. *History and Social Theory.* Cambridge: Polity P, 1992.

Burke, Séan. *The Death and Return of the Author: Criticism and Subjectivity in Barthes, Foucault and Derrida.* Edinburgh: Edinburgh UP, 1992.

Campilongo, Emilio. *Semeiotike seu nova cognoscendi morbos methodus.* Wittenberg, 1601.

Canguilhem, Georges, ed. *Michel Foucault Filósofo.* Barcelona: Gedisa, 1989.

—. *The Normal and the Pathological.* 1943. Trans. Carolyn R. Fawcett with Robert S. Cohen. NY: Zone Books, 1989.

Carrière, Charles. *Négociants marseillais au XVIIIe siècle.* 2 vols. Marseille: Institut historique de Provence, 1973.

Carruthers, Mary. *The Book of Memory: A Study of Memory in Medieval Culture.* Cambridge: Cambridge UP, 1990.

Certeau, Michel de. "Les sciences humaines et la mort de l'homme." *Études* 326 (March 1967): 344–360; repr. "Le noir soleil du langage: Michel Foucault." *L'absent de l'histoire.* N.p.: Mame, 1973. 115–32; *Heterologies. Discourse on the Other.* Trans. Brian Massumi. Minneapolis: U of Minnesota P, 1986, chapter 12.

—. "L'opération historique." Jacques Le Goff and Pierre Nora 3–41. Repr. de Certeau *L'Écriture de l'histoire.* 63–120.

—. *L'Écriture de l'histoire.* Paris: Gallimard, 1975.

—. *L'Invention du quotidien. I. Arts de faire.* Paris: UGE, 1980. Second ed. Paris: Gallimard, 1990.

—. *The Writing of History.* Trans. Tom Conley. NY: Columbia UP, 1988.

Chartier, Roger. "Intellectual History or Sociocultural History? The French Trajectories." *Modern European Intellectual History. Reappraisals and New Perspectives.* Ed. Dominick LaCapra and Steven L. Kaplan. Ithaca: Cornell UP, 1982. 13–46. Rev. ed. "Intellectual History and the History of *mentalités*: a dual Re-evaluation." Chartier *Cultural History* 19–52.

—. "Culture as Appropriation: Popular Culture Uses in Early Modern France." *Understanding Popular Culture. Europe from the Middle Ages to the Nineteenth Century.* Ed. Steven L. Kaplan. Berlin: Mouton, 1984. 229–53.

—. "L'histoire ou le savoir de l'autre." *Michel de Certeau.* Ed. Luce Giard. Paris: Centre Georges Pompidou, 1987. 155–67.

—. *Cultural History between Practices and Representations.* Trans. Lydia G. Cochrane. Ithaca: Cornell UP, 1988.

—. "Social Figuration and Habitus: Reading Elias." Chartier *Cultural History* 71–94.

—. "Trajectoires et tensions culturelles de l'Ancien Régime." *Histoire de la France.* Ed. André Burguière and Jacques Revel. 4 vols. Paris: Seuil, 1989–93. 4: 307–92.

—. *The Cultural Origins of the French Revolution.* Durham: Duke UP, 1991.

—. "The Chimera of the Origin : Archaeology, Cultural History and the French Revolution." Goldstein *Writing of History.* 167–87.

Chastellux, François-Jean de. *De la félicité publique.* 1776. Ed. Roger Basoni. Paris: Sorbonne, 1989.

Chomsky, Noam. *American Power and the New Mandarins.* NY: Pantheon, 1969.

Clark, Marcia. *Beyond a Doubt.* NY: Viking, 1997.

Clément, Catherine. *Opera, or the Undoing of Women.* London: Virago, 1989.

Cohen, Jean L., and Andrew Arato. *Civil Society and Political Theory.* Cambridge MA: MIT P, 1990.

Colacurcio Jr., Michael J. " 'The Woman's Own Choice': Sex, Metaphor, and the Puritan 'Sources' of 'The Scarlet Letter.' " *New Essays on The Scarlet Letter.* Ed. Michael J. Colacurcio Jr. Cambridge: Cambridge UP, 1985. 101–35.

Collingwood, R. J. *An Essay on Philosophical Method.* Oxford: Oxford UP, 1933.

—. *An Autobiography.* Oxford: Oxford UP, 1939.

—. *An Essay on Metaphysics.* Oxford: Oxford UP, 1940.

232 Bibliography

Commager, Steele. "Notes on Some Poems of Catullus." *Harvard Studies in Classical Philology* 70 (1965): 83–110.

Cooter, Roger. *The Cultural Meaning of Popular Science: Phrenology and the Organization of Consent in Nineteenth-Century Britain.* Cambridge: Cambridge UP, 1984.

Copjec, Joan. *Read My Desire: Lacan Against the Historicists.* Cambridge, MA: MIT P, 1994.

Corber, Robert J. *Homosexuality in Cold War America: Resistance and the Crisis of Masculinity.* Durham: Duke UP, 1997.

Corbin, Henry. *En islam iranien: Aspects spirituels et philosophiques.* 4 vols. Paris: Gallimard, 1971.

—. *Histoire de la philosophie islamique.* 1974. Paris: Gallimard, 1986.

Cornford, F. M. *Microcosmographia Academia.* Oxford: MainSail, 1993.

Cousin. Victor. *Introduction à l'histoire de philosophie.* Paris: Pichon and Didier, 1828.

Creeley, Robert, ed. *Selected Writings of Charles Olson.* NY: New Directions, 1966.

Critchley, Simon. *The Ethics of Deconstruction. Derrida and Levinas.* Oxford: Blackwell, 1992.

Crompton, Louis. "Homosexuals and the Death Penalty in Colonial America." *Journal of Homosexuality* 1.3 (1976): 277–93.

—. "The Myth of Lesbian Impunity: Capital Laws from 1270 to 1791." Licata and Petersen 11–25.

Culler, Jonathan. "In Defense of Overinterpretation". *Interpretation and Overinterpretation.* Ed. Stefan Collini. Cambridge: Cambridge UP, 1992. 109–24.

Davidson, Arnold I. "Ethics as Ascetics: Foucault, the History of Ethics, and Ancient Thought." Gutting 115–40.

Davis, Mike. *City of Quartz.* NY: Vintage, 1992.

Deakin, M. A. B. "Applied Catastrophe Theory in the Social and Biological Sciences." *Bulletin of Mathematical Biology* 42 (1980): 647–79.

Dean-Jones, Lesley. "Politics of Pleasure: Female Sexual Appetite in the Hippocratic Corpus." *Helios* 19 (1992): 72–91.

Deleuze, Gilles. *Foucault.* Trans. Seán Hand. Minneapolis: U of Minnesota P, 1988.

Deleuze, Gilles and Felix Guattari. *On the Line.* NY: Semiotext(e), 1983.

—. *A Thousand Plateaus.* Trans. Brian Massumi. London: Athlone, 1988.

D'Emilio, John, and Estelle Freedman. *Intimate Matters: A History of Sexuality in America.* NY: Harper, 1988.

Derrida, Jacques. "Cogito et histoire de la folie." *L'écriture et la différence.* Paris: Seuil, 1967. 51–97.

—. *Of Grammatology.* Trans. Gayatri Chakravorty Spivak. Baltimore: Johns Hopkins UP, 1976.

—. *Writing and Difference.* Trans. Alan Bass. Chicago: U of Chicago P, 1978.

—. "From Restricted to General Economy: A Hegelianism without Reserve." *Writing* 251–77.

—. "Cogito and the History of Madness." Derrida *Writing* 31–63.

—. *Margins of Philosophy.* Trans. Alan Bass. Chicago: U of Chicago P, 1982.

—. "Force of Law: The 'Mystical Foundation of Authority.'" Trans. Mary Quaintance. *Cardozo Law Review* 11 (1990): 919–1045.

—. "Mochlos." *Logomachia.* Ed. R. Rand. Lincoln: U of Nebraska P, 1992. 1–34.

—. *Spectres de Marx.* Paris: Galilée, 1993.

—. "To Do Justice To Freud: The History of Madness in the Age of Psychoanalysis." Trans. Pascale-Anne Brault and Michael Nass. *Critical Inquiry* 20 (1994): 227–66.

Descombes, Vincent. *Modern French Philosophy.* Trans. L. Scott-Fox and J. M. Harding. Cambridge: Cambridge UP, 1980.

Dinges, Martin. "Frühneuzeitliche Armenfürsorge als Sozialdisziplinierung? Probleme mit einem Konzept." *Geschichte und Gesellschaft* 17 (1991): 5–29.

—. "Michel Foucault, Justizphantasien und die Macht." *Mit den Waffen der Justiz. Zur Kriminalitätsgeschichte des Spätmittelalters und der frühen Neuzeit.* Ed. Andreas Blauert and Gerd Schwerhoff. Frankfurt/M: Fischer, 1993. 189–212.

Donzelot, Jacques. *The Policing of Families.* [Trans. *Le police des familles,* 1977]. Foreword Gilles Deleuze. Trans. Robert Hurley. NY: Pantheon, 1979.

Downey, James, and B. Jones, eds. *Fearful Joy: Papers from the Thomas Gray Bicentenary Conference.* Montréal: McGill-Queen's UP, 1974.

Dreyfus, Hubert L., and Paul Rabinow. *Michel Foucault: Beyond Structuralism and Hermeneutics.* Afterword by Michel Foucault. Chicago: U of Chicago P, 1982.

Duberman, Martin. *Cures: a Gay Man's Odyssey.* NY: Dutton, 1991.

Dubois, Jacques. *Methodus sex librorum Galeni in differentiis et causis morborum et symptomatorum in tabellas sex ordine suo coniecta.* Paris, 1537.

Dutton, Dennis and Patrick Henry. "Editorial: Truth Matters." *Philosophy and Literature* 20 (1996): 299–304.

Eagleton, Terry. *Literary Theory: An Introduction.* Minneapolis: U of Minnesota P, 1983.

Edwards, Catharine. *The Politics of Immorality in Ancient Rome.* Cambridge: Cambridge UP, 1993.

Ellis, Brett Easton. *Less than Zero.* Harmondsworth: Penguin, 1985.

Emmanuelli, François-Xavier. *La crise marseillaise de 1774.* Paris: CNRS, 1979.

Epstein, William. "Counter-Intelligence: Cold-War Criticism and Eighteenth-Century Studies." *ELH* 57 (1990): 63–99.

—. "Assumed Identities: Gray's Correspondence and the 'Intelligence Communities' of Eighteenth-Century Studies." *The Eighteenth Century: Theory and Interpretation* 32 (1991): 274–88.

Eribon, Didier. *Michel Foucault (1926–1984).* [Orig. French ed. 1989.] Trans. Betsy Wing. London: Faber, 1992.

Etlin, Richard. *In Defence of Humanism.* Cambridge: Cambridge UP, 1996.

Eymar, Claude. *Réflexions sur l'impôt.* Marseille, 1789. Vol. 2 of Fonds de Provence, 4717, Impositions, Bibliothèque municipale, Marseille.

Fabian, Johannes. *Language and Colonial Power. The Appropriation of Swahili in former Belgian Congo 1880–1938.* Berkeley: U of California P, 1986.

Faccarello, G., and P. Steiner, eds. *La pensée économique pendant la Révolution française.* Grenoble: Presses universitaires de Grenoble, 1990.

Farge, Arlette. *Dire et mal dire. L'opinion publique au XVIIIᵉ siècle.* Paris: Seuil, 1992.

—, Colin Jones, and Martin Dinges. "Michel Foucault und die Historiker." *Österreichische Zeitschrift für Geschichtswissenschaften* 4 (1993): 620–41.

—. *Fragile Lives: Violence, Power and Solidarity in Eighteenth-Century Paris.* Cambridge, MA: Harvard UP, 1993.

Ferrand, Jacques. *A Treatise on Lovesickness.* Trans. D. A. Beecher and M. Ciavolella. Syracuse, NY: Syracuse UP, 1989.

Fish, Stanley. "Resistance and Independence: A Reply to Gerald Graff." *New Literary History* 17 (1985): 119–27.

Flynn, Thomas. "Foucault's Mapping of History." Gutting 28–46.

Fohrmann, Jürgen. "Remarks towards a Theory of Literary Genres." *Poetics* 17 (1988): 273–85.

—. "Über das Schreiben von Literaturgeschichte." *Geist, Geld und Wissenschaft.* Ed. P. J. Brenner. Frankfurt/M.: Suhrkamp, 1993. 175–202.

Foucault, Michel. *Folie et déraison. Histoire de la folie à l'âge classique.* Paris: Plon, 1961.

—. *Histoire de la folie à l'âge classique* [shortened version of *Folie et déraison*]. Paris: Collection 10/18, 1961.

—. *Naissance de la clinique: une archéologie du regard médical.* Paris: PUF, 1963.

—. "Préface à la transgression." *Critique* 195–96 (1963): 751–69

—. *Madness and Civilization: A History of Insanity in the Age of Reason.* [Trans. *Histoire de la folie.* 1961.] Trans. Richard Howard. NY: Random House, 1965.

—. "La prose du monde." *Diogène,* (Jan–Mar 1966): 20–41.

—. *Les mots et les choses.* Paris: Gallimard, 1966.

—. *L'archéologie du savoir.* Paris: Gallimard, 1969.

—. "Nietzsche, Généalogie, Histoire." *Hommage à Jean Hyppolite.* Ed. Michel Foucault. Paris: PUF, 1971. 145–72.

—. *The Order of Things.* [Trans. *Les mots et les choses.* 1966.] Trans. Alan Sheridan. NY: Pantheon, 1971.

—. *L'ordre du discours.* Paris: Gallimard, 1971.

—. "The Discourse on Language." *The Archeology of Knowledge.* Trans. Rupert Swyer. 215–37.

—. *The Archaeology of Knowledge.* [Trans. *L'archéologie du savoir.* 1969.] Trans. A. M. Sheridan Smith. NY: Pantheon, 1972.

—, ed. *Moi, Pierre Rivière, ayant égorgé ma mère, ma soeur et mon frère …: un cas de parricide au XIXe siècle.* Paris: Gallimard/Julliard, 1973.

—. *Surveiller et Punir: Naissance de la prison.* Paris: Gallimard, 1975.

—. *Histoire de la sexualité, vol. 1: La volonté de savoir.* Paris: Gallimard, 1976.

—. *Language, Counter-Memory, Practice.* Ed. Donald F. Bouchard. Trans. F. Bouchard and Sherry Simon. Ithaca: Cornell UP, 1977.

—. "Preface to Transgression." *Language, Counter-Memory, Practice.* 29–52.

—. "Nietzsche, Genealogy, History." *Language, Counter-Memory, Practice.* 149–64.

—. *Discipline and Punish. The Birth of the Prison.* [Trans. *Surveiller et punir.* 1975.] Trans. Alan Sheridan. NY: Pantheon, 1977.

—. *Microfisica del potere: interventi politici.* Turin: Einaudi, 1977. German ed. *Mikrophysik der Macht: über Strafjustiz, Psychiatrie und Medizin.* Berlin: Merve, 1976.

—. "Power and Sex: An Interview with Michel Foucault." *Telos* No. 32, (Summer 1977): 152–61.

—. *The History of Sexuality.* [Trans. *La volonté de savoir.* 1976.] Trans. Robert Hurley. Vol. 1: *An Introduction.* NY: Random House, 1978.

—. "My Body, This Paper, This Fire." Trans. Geoff Bennington. *Oxford Literary Review* 4 (1979): 9–28.

—. *Power/Knowledge: Selected Interviews and Other Writings 1972–1977.* Ed. Colin Gordon. Trans. Leo Marshall et al. Brighton: Harvester, 1980.

—. "La poussière et le nuage." *L'Impossible prison: Recherches sur le système pénitentiaire au XIXe siècle.* Ed. Michelle Perrot. Paris: Seuil, 1980. 29–39.

—. "The Subject and Power." *Critical Inquiry* 8 (1982): 777–95; rpt. Dreyfus and Rabinow 208–26.

—. "War in the Filigree of Peace. Course Summary." Trans. Ian Mcleod. *Oxford Literary Review* 4/2 (1982): 15–19.

—. *Histoire de la sexualité, vol. 2: L'usage des plaisirs.* Paris: Gallimard, 1984.

—. *Histoire de la sexualité, vol. 3: Le souci de soi.* Paris: Gallimard, 1984.

—. "On the Genealogy of Ethics: An Overview of Work in Progress." Rabinow, *The Foucault Reader* 340–72.

—. *The History of Sexuality.* [Trans. *L'usage des plaisirs.* 1984.] Trans. Robert Hurley. Vol. 2: *The Use of Pleasure.* NY: Random House, 1985.

—. "Nietzsche, Freud, Marx." Trans. Jon Anderson and Gary Hentzi. *Critical Texts* 3 (1986): 1–5.

—. *The History of Sexuality.* [Trans. *Le souci de soi.* 1984.] Trans. Robert Hurley. Vol. 3: *The Care of the Self.* NY: Random House, 1986.

—. *Mental Illness and Psychology.* Trans. Alan Sheridan. Berkeley: U of California P, 1987.

—. *Politics, Philosophy, Culture. Interviews and other Writings, 1977–1984.* Ed. Lawrence D. Kritzman. London: Routledge, 1988.

—. *Résumé des cours, 1970–1982.* Paris: Julliard, 1988.

—. *Technologies of the Self. A Seminar with Michel Foucault.* Ed. L. H. Martin, H. Gutman, and P. H. Hutton. Amherst, MA: U of Massachusetts P, 1988.

—. *Foucault Live.* Ed. Sylvère Lotringer. Trans. John Johnston. NY: Semiotext(e), 1989.

—. *Remarks on Marx: Conversations with Duccio Trombadori.* Trans. R. James Goldstein and James Cascaito. NY: Semiotext(e), 1991.

—. *Dits et Écrits 1954–1988.* 4 vols. Paris: Gallimard, 1994.

—. *"Il faut défendre la société": Cours au Collège de France, 1975–1976.* Paris: Gallimard/Seuil, 1997.

Freud, Sigmund. "Repression." *The Standard Edition.* Trans. and ed. James Strachey and Anna Freud. London: Hogarth P, 1953. 14: 146–58.

—. *Dora: An Analysis of a Case of Hysteria.* NY: Collier, 1963.

Frijhoff, Willem. *Cultuur, mentaliteit: illusies van elites?* [inaugural lecture Rotterdam] Nijmegen: SUN, 1984; partial trans.: "Kultur und Mentalität: Illusion von Eliten?" *Österreichische Zeitschrift für Geschichtswissenschaften* 2/2 (1991): 7–33.

—. *Wegen van Evert Willemsz. Een Hollands weeskind op zoek naar zichzelf, 1607–1647.* Nijmegen: SUN, 1995.

—. "Toeëigening: van bezitsdrang naar betekenisgeving." *Trajecta* 6/2 (1997): 99–118.

—. *Volkskunde en cultuurwetenschap: de ups en downs van een dialoog.* Amsterdam: Edita, 1997.

Frow, John. *Marxism and Literary History.* Cambridge MA: Harvard UP, 1986.

Furet, François. "L'histoire quantitative et la construction du fait historique." *Annales ESC* 26/1 (1971): 63–75.

—. *Penser la Révolution française.* Paris: Gallimard, 1979.

Fuss, Diana. *Essentially Speaking: Feminism, Nature and Difference.* NY: Routledge, 1989.

Gates, Jr., Henry Louis. "The Naked Republic." *The New Yorker.* 25 Aug. 1997.

Gatien-Arnoult, A.-F. *Cours de lectures philosophiques.* Paris and Toulouse: J.-B. Paya, 1838.

Gay, Peter. *The Bourgeois Experience: Victoria to Freud.* Oxford: Oxford UP, 1984.

—. *Freud for Historians.* Oxford: Oxford UP, 1986.

Geertz, Clifford. "Stir Crazy." Rev. of *Discipline and Punish: The Birth of Prison*, by Michel Foucault. *NY Review of Books* 26 Jan. 1978: 3–6.

Giard, Luce, ed. *Michel Foucault – lire l'œuvre.* Grenoble: Jérôme Millon, 1992.

Gilman, Sander. *Seeing the Insane: a Cultural History of Madness and Art in the Western World.* NY: Wiley-Interscience, 1985.

Ginzburg, Carlo. *The Cheese and the Worms. The Cosmos of a Sixteenth-Century Miller.* [Trans. *Il formaggio e I vermi: il cosmo di un mugnaio del '500.* 1976.] Trans. John and Anne Tedeschi. London: Routledge, 1981.

—. *The Night Battles. Witchcraft and Agrarian Cults in the Sixteenth and Seventeenth Centuries.* [Trans. *I Benandanti: stregoneria e culti agrari tra Cinquencento e Seicento.* 1966.] Trans. John and Anne Tedeschi. London: Routledge, 1983.

—. *Ecstasies: Deciphering the Witches' Sabbath.* [Trans. *Storia notturna: una decifrazione del sabba.* 1989.] Trans. Raymond Rosenthal. London: Hutchinson Radius, 1990.

Gleckner, Robert F. *Gray Agonistes: Thomas Gray and Masculine Friendship.* Baltimore: Johns Hopkins UP, 1997.

Goldberg, Jonathan. *Sodometries: Renaissance Texts, Modern Sexualities.* Stanford: Stanford UP, 1992.

Goldhill, Simon. *Foucault's Virginity: Ancient Erotic Fiction and the History of Sexuality.* Cambridge: Cambridge UP, 1994.

Goldman, Lucien. "Introduction to the Problems of a Sociology of the Novel." *Telos* 18 (1973–74): 122–34.

Goldstein, Doris S. "'Official Philosophies' in Modern France: The Example of Victor Cousin." *Journal of Social History* (Spring 1968): 259–79.

Goldstein, Jan. "Foucault among the Sociologists: The 'Disciplines' and the History of the Professions." *History and Theory* 23 (1984): 170–92.

Goldstein, Jan, ed. *Foucault and the Writing of History.* Chicago: U of Chicago P, 1993.

—. Introduction. *Writing of History.* 1–15.

—. "Foucault and the Post-Revolutionary Self: The Uses of Cousinian Pedagogy in Nineteenth-Century France." *Writing of History.* 99–115, 276–80.

—. "Saying 'I': Victor Cousin, Caroline Angebert, and the Politics of Selfhood in Nineteenth-Century France." *Rediscovering History: Culture, Politics, and the Psyche.* Ed. Michael S. Roth. Stanford: Stanford UP, 1994. 321–35, 496–99.

—. "The Advent of Psychological Modernism in France: An Alternate Narrative." *Modernist Impulses in the Human Sciences.* Ed. Dorothy Ross. Baltimore: Johns Hopkins UP, 1994. 190–209, 342–46.

—. "Eclectic Subjectivity and the Impossibility of Female Beauty." *Picturing Science, Producing Art.* Ed. Peter Galison and Caroline Jones. London: Routledge, forthcoming.

Gordon, Colin. "'Histoire de la folie': An Unknown Book by Michel Foucault." *Rewriting the History of Madness: Studies in Foucault's 'Histoire de la folie'.* Eds. Arthur Still and Irving Velody. London: Routledge, 1992. 19–42.

Gould, Stephen Jay. *Wonderful Life: The Burgess Shale and the Nature of History.* 1989. Harmondsworth: Penguin, 1991.

—. *The Mismeasure of Man.* 1981. Harmondsworth: Penguin, 1992.

—. *Full House: The Spread of Excellence from Plato to Darwin.* NY: Harmony Books, 1996.

Green, André. *Le discours vivant. La conception psychanalytique de l'affect.* Paris: PUF, 1973.

Groot, Joanna de. "Sex and Race: The Construction of Language and Image in the Nineteenth Century." *Sexuality and Subordination: Interdisciplinary Studies of Gender in the Nineteenth Century.* Ed. Susan Mendus and Jane Rendall. London: Routledge, 1989. 89–130.

Gros, Frédéric. *Michel Foucault.* Paris: PUF, 1996.

Gross, Paul R. *Higher Superstition: the Academic Left and its Quarrels with Science.* Baltimore: Johns Hopkins UP, 1994.

Gutting, Gary, ed. *The Cambridge Companion to Foucault.* Cambridge: Cambridge UP, 1994.

Habermas, Jürgen. *The Structural Transformation of the Public Sphere: An Inquiry into a Category of Bourgeois Society.* Trans. Thomas Burger. Cambridge, MA: MIT P, 1989.

Haggerty, George E. "'O lachrymarum fons': Tears, Poetry, and Desire in Gray." *Eighteenth-Century Studies* 30 (1996): 81–95.

Hagstrum, Jean. "Gray's Sensibility." *Fearful Joy: Papers from the Thomas Gray Bicentenary Conference.* Ed. J. Downey and B. Jones. Montréal: McGill-Queen's UP, 1974. 77–94.

Hallett, Judith. "Feminist Theory, Historical Periods, Literary Canons, and the Study of Greco-Roman Antiquity." Rabinowitz and Richlin 44–72.

Halliday, Fred. *Iran: Dictatorship and Development.* Harmondsworth: Penguin, 1979.

Halperin, David M. *One Hundred Years of Homosexuality and Other Essays on Greek Love.* NY: Routledge, 1990.

–. *Saint Foucault: Towards a Gay Hagiography.* NY: Oxford UP, 1995.

Harvey, Gideon. *Morbus Anglicus.* London, 1672.

Hasler, Johannes. *De logistica medica.* Augsburg, 1578.

Hegel, G. F. *Encyclopedia of Philosophy.* Trans. Gustav Emil Mueller. NY: Philosophical Library, 1959.

Heilbut, Anthony. *Thomas Mann: Eros and Literature.* London: Macmillan, 1995.

Heintze, J. C. *De erotomania; von der Krankheit da man verliebt ist.* Rostock, 1719.

Hiro, Dilip. *Iran under the Ayatollahs.* London: Routledge, 1985.

Hofstadter, Richard. *Anti-intellectualism in American Life.* NY: Alfred Knopf, 1963.

Holquist, Michael. "The Surd Head: Bakhtin and Derrida." *Literature and History: Theoretical Problems and Russian Case Studies.* Ed. Gary Saul Morson. Stanford: Stanford UP, 1986.

Horton, Richard. "Is homosexuality inherited?" *The New York Review of Books* July 1995: 36.

Hoy, David Couzens. *Foucault: A Critical Reader.* London: Blackwell, 1986.

Hoyningen-Huene, Paul. *Reconstructing Scientific Revolutions: Thomas S. Kuhn's Philosophy of Science.* Chicago: Chicago UP, 1993.

Hsia, R. Po-chia. *Social Discipline in the Reformation. Central Europe 1550–1750.* London: Routledge, 1989.

Hunt, Lynn. *Politics, Culture and Class in the French Revolution.* Berkeley: U of California P, 1984.

––, ed. *The New Cultural History. Studies on the History of Society and Culture.* Berkeley: U of California P, 1989.

–. "Introduction: History, Culture and Text." *New Cultural History.* 1–22.

–. *Eroticism and the Body Politic.* Baltimore: Johns Hopkins UP, 1991.

–. *The Family Romance of the French Revolution.* London: Routledge, 1992.

Huppert, George. "Divinatio et erudition: Thoughts on Foucault." *History and Theory* 13 (1974): 191–207.

Husserl, Edmund. "Die Frage nach dem Ursprung der Geometrie als intentional-historisches Problem." *Revue internationale de philosophie* 1 (1939): 203–25.

—. "The origin of geometry." *The Crisis of European Sciences and Transcendental Philosophy.* Trans. D. Carr. Evanston: Northwestern UP, 1970. 255–70.

Hutcheon, Linda and Michael. *Opera: Desire, Disease, Death.* Lincoln: U of Nebraska P, 1996.

Hutton, Patrick R. "The Foucault Phenomenon and Contemporary French Historiography." *Historical Reflections* 17 (1991): 77–102.

Hyman, Anthony. *Charles Babbage: Pioneer of the Computer.* Oxford: Oxford UP, 1982.

Iggers, Georg G. "Zur 'linguistischen Wende' im Geschichtsdenken und in der Geschichtsschreibung." *Geschichte und Gesellschaft* 21 (1995): 557–70.

Ignatieff, Michael. "Anxiety and Asceticism." *Times Literary Supplement,* September 28 (1984): 1071–72.

—. *Scar Tissue.* London: Vantage, 1993.

Jambet, Christian. "The constitution of the subject and spiritual practice: Observations on L'Histoire de la sexualité." Trans. T. J. Armstrong. *Michel Foucault Philosopher.* Ed. T. J. Armstrong. NY: Harvester Wheatsheaf, 1992. 233–47.

Jameson, Fredric. *The Prison-House of Language: A Critical Account of Structuralism and Russian Formalism.* Princeton: Princeton UP, 1972.

—. *The Political Unconscious: Narrative as a Socially Symbolic Act.* Ithaca: Cornell UP, 1981.

—. "Imaginary and Symbolic in Lacan." *The Ideologies of Theory,* vol. 1. Minneapolis: U of Minnesota P, 1988. 75–115.

—. *Postmodernism, or the Cultural Logic of Late Capitalism.* London: Verso, 1991.

Janan, Micaela. '*When the Lamp is Shattered': Desire and Narrative in Catullus.* Carbondale: Southern Illinois UP, 1994.

JanMohamed, Abdul, and David Lloyd. "Introduction: Toward a Theory of Minority Discourse: What Is To Be Done?" *The Nature and Context of Minority Discourse.* Ed. JanMohamed and Lloyd. NY: Oxford UP, 1990. 1–16.

Japp, Uwe. *Beziehungssinn:* Ein Konzept der Literaturgeschichte. Frankfurt/M: Europa, 1980.

Jensen, Kristian. *Rhetorical Philosophy and Philosophical Grammar: Julius Caesar Scaliger's Theory of Language.* Munich: Fink, 1990.

Johnson, Barbara. *The Critical Difference: Essays in the Contemporary Rhetoric of Reading.* Baltimore: John Hopkins UP, 1980.

Johnson, W. R. *The Idea of Lyric.* Berkeley: U of California P, 1982.

Johnstone, Robert. "The Impossible Genre: Reading Comprehensive Literary History." *PMLA* 107 (1992): 26–37.

Jones, Gareth Stedman. "The Determinist Fix." *History Workshop Journal* 42 (1996): 19–35.

Jones, J. *Alfred C. Kinsey: A Public/Private Life.* NY: Norton, 1997.

Kadish, Doris Y. *Politicizing Gender. Narrative Strategies in the Aftermath of the French Revolution.* New Brunswick: Rutgers UP, 1991.

Kant, Immanuel. *The Conflict of the Faculties.* Trans. Mary Gregor. Lincoln: U of Nebraska P, 1979.

Katz, Jonathan Ned. *Gay American History: Lesbians and Gay Men in the U. S. A.; A Documentary History.* NY: Penguin, 1992.

Keller, Evelyn Fox. *Reflections on Gender and Science.* New Haven: Yale UP, 1985.

—-, and Elisabeth A. Lloyd, eds. *Keywords in Evolutionary Biology* Cambridge, MA: Harvard UP, 1992.

—. *Secrets of Life/Secrets of Death: Essays on Language, Gender and Science.* London: Routledge, 1992.

—. *Refiguring Life: Metaphors of Twentieth-Century Biology.* NY: Columbia UP, 1995.

Kellner, Hans. "'As Real as It Gets': Ricoeur and Narrativity." *Meanings in Texts and Actions: Questioning Paul Ricoeur.* Ed. David E. Klemm and William Schweiker. Charlottesville: U of Virginia P, 1993. 49–66.

Ketton-Cremer, R. W. *Thomas Gray: A Biography.* Cambridge: Cambridge UP, 1955.

Kinsey, Alfred C., Wardell B. Pomeroy, and Clyde E. Martin. *Sexual Behavior in the Human Male.* London and Philadelphia: Saunders, 1948.

Koestenbaum, Wayne. *Double Talk: The Erotics of Male Literary Collaboration.* NY: Routledge, 1989.

—. *The Queen's Throat: Opera, Homosexuality and the Mystery of Desire.* Harmondsworth: Penguin, 1994.

Konstan, David. *Sexual Symmetry: Love in the Ancient Novel and Related Genres.* Princeton: Princeton UP, 1994.

Krausz, Michael, ed. *Critical Essays on the Philosophy of R. G. Collingwood.* Oxford: Clarendon, 1972.

Kremer-Marietti, Angèle. *Michel Foucault: Archéologie et Généalogie.* Second, rev. ed. Paris: Livre de Poche, 1985.

Krieger, Murray. *The Institution of Theory.* Baltimore: Johns Hopkins UP, 1994.

Kuhn, Thomas S. *The Structure of Scientific Revolutions.* Rev. 2nd ed. Chicago: U of Chicago P, 1970.

—. "Reflections on my Critics." Lakatos and Musgrave 231–78.

Kunadus, T. *Erotomania seu amoris insani, theoriam et praxis pertractatem submitit.* Wittenburg, 1681.

Lacan, Jacques. *Le séminaire livre XX: Encore.* Ed. Jacques-Alain Miller. Paris: Seuil, 1975.

Lacoue-Labarthe, Phillippe and Jean Luc Nancy. "The Unconscious Is Destructured Like an Affect." (Part I of "The Jewish People Do Not Dream") Trans. Brian Holmes. *Stanford Literature Review* 6 (Fall 1989): 191–209.

Lacretelle, Pierre-Louis. *Discours sur l'état actuel de la Révolution française.* Paris, 1792.

Laermans, Rudi. "Geloven, handelen, weten. Michel de Certeau en de moderne cultuur." *Sluipwegen van het denken. Over Michel de Certeau.* Ed. Koenraad Geldof and Rudi Laermans. Nijmegen: SUN, 1996. 6–71.

Lakatos, Imre, and Alan Musgrave, eds. *Criticism and the Growth of Knowledge,* Cambridge: Cambridge UP, 1970.

Lake, Peter, and Michael C. Questier. "Agency, Appropriation and Rhetoric under the Gallows: Puritans, Romanists and the State in Early Modern England." *Past & Present* 153 (1996): 64–107.

Landow, George. "Hypertext in Literary Education, Criticism, and Scholarship." *Computers and the Humanities* 23 (1989): 173–98.

Laplanche, Jean, and J.-B. Pontalis. *The Language of Psychoanalysis*. Trans. Donald Nicholson. NY: Norton, 1974.

Laqueur, Thomas. *Making Sex: Body and Gender From the Greeks to Freud*. Cambridge, MA: Harvard UP, 1990.

Larrère, Catherine. *L'invention de l'économie au XVIIIe siècle*. Paris: PUF, 1992.

Latour, Bruno. *Science in Action: How to Follow Scientists and Engineers through Society*. Milton Keynes: Open UP, 1987.

Lauretis, Teresa De. *Alice Doesn't: Feminism, Semiotics, Cinema*. Bloomington: Indiana UP, 1984.

Lauter, Paul, et al., ed. *The Heath Anthology of American Literature*. Second edition. Lexington, MA: Heath, 1994.

Laycock, Thomas. *A treatise on the nervous diseases of women; comprising an inquiry into the nature, causes, and treatment of . . . hysterical disorders*. London: Longman, 1840.

Le Goff, Jacques and Pierre Nora, eds. *Faire de l'histoire. I: Nouveaux Problèmes*. Paris: Gallimard, 1974.

Le Goff, Jacques. "Documento/Monumento." *Enciclopedia Einaudi*. Turin: Einaudi, 1977. 5: 38–48.

—. "Présentation." *La nouvelle histoire*. Ed. Jacques Le Goff, Roger Chartier and Jacques Revel. Paris: CEPL, 1978. 11–20.

Leezenberg, Michiel. "From Freiburg to Isfahan: Heidegger and the 'Wisdom of the East'." Paper presented at the international conference on Heidegger's "Brief über den Humanismus," Amsterdam, April 1997.

Léonard, Jacques. "L'historien et le philosophe. A propos de: Surveiller et punir; naissance de la prison." *Annales historiques de la Révolution française* 1977/2. Repr. *L'impossible prison. Recherches sur le système pénitentiaire au XIXe siècle*. Ed. Michelle Perrot. Paris: Seuil, 1980. 9–28.

Levi, Giovanni. "On Microhistory." *New Perspectives on Historical Writing*. Ed. Peter Burke. Cambridge: Polity P, 1991. 93–113.

Levine, George, and Alan Rausch, eds. *One Culture: Essays in Science and Literature*. Madison: U of Wisconsin P, 1987.

Lévy, Bernard-Henry. *Les aventures de la liberté: Une histoire subjective des intellectuels*. Paris: Grasset, 1991.

Licata, Salvatore J., and Robert P. Petersen, eds. *The Gay Past: A Collection of Historical Essays*. NY: Harrington Park P, 1985.

Lilja, S. *The Roman Elegists' Attitude to Women*. Helsinki: Suomalainen Tiedekatemia, 1965.

List, Elisabeth. "Der Körper (in) der Geschichte. Theoretische Fragen an einem Paradigmenwandel." *Österreichische Zeitschrift für Geschichtswissenschaften* 8/2 (1997): 167–85.

Locke, David. *Science as Writing*. New Haven: Yale UP, 1992.

Luedtke, Luther S. *Making America: The Society and Culture of the United States*. Chapel Hill: U of North Carolina P, 1992.

Lyne, R. O. A. M. *The Latin Love Poets from Catullus to Horace*. Oxford: Oxford UP, 1980.

Lynn, John A. *The Bayonets of the Republic*. Boulder, CO: Westview, 1996.

MacDonald, M. *Mystical Bedlam: Madness, Anxiety, and Healing in Seventeenth-Century England*. Cambridge: Cambridge UP, 1981.

Macey, David. *The Lives of Michel Foucault*. NY: Pantheon, 1993.

Mack, Maynard. *Alexander Pope*. New Haven: Yale UP, 1985.

Maclean, Ian. *The Renaissance Notion of Woman: a Study in the Fortunes of Scholasticism and Medical Science in European Intellectual Life.* Cambridge: Cambridge UP, 1980.

—. *Interpretation and Meaning in the Renaissance: the Case of Law.* Cambridge: Cambridge UP, 1992.

Major-Poetzl, Pamela. *Michel Foucault's Archaeology of Western Culture: Toward a New Science of History.* Chapel Hill: U of North Carolina P, 1983.

Man, Paul De. "Semiology and Rhetoric." *Allegories of Reading: Figural Language in Rousseau, Nietzsche, Rilke and Proust.* New Haven: Yale UP, 1979. 3–19.

Matter, A.-Jacques. "Moi." *Dictionnaire de la conversation et de la lecture.* 52 vols. Paris: Belin-Mondar, 1832–39. 38: 259–61.

McGrane, Bernard. *Beyond Anthropology: Society and the Other.* NY: Columbia UP, 1989.

McKay, Elizabeth N. *Franz Schubert: a Biography.* Oxford: Oxford UP, 1996.

McNay, Lois. *Foucault. A Critical Introduction.* Cambridge: Polity P, 1994.

Mendus, Susan, and Jane Kendall, eds. *Sexuality and Subordination: Interdisciplinary Studies of Gender in the Nineteenth Century.* London: Routledge, 1989.

Merquior, J. G. *Foucault.* Berkeley: U of California P, 1985.

Midelfort, H. C. Erik. "Madness and Civilization in Early Modern Europe: A Reappraisal of Michel Foucault." *After the Reformation: Essays in Honor of J. H. Hexter.* Ed. B. C. Malament. Philadelphia: U of Pennsylvania P, 1980. 247–65.

Miguel-Alfonso, Ricardo, and Silvia Caporale-Bizzini, eds. *Reconstructing Foucault: Essays in the Wake of the 1980s.* Amsterdam: Rodopi, 1994.

Miller, Jacques-Alain. "Michel Foucault and Psychoanalysis." *Michel Foucault: Philosopher.* Ed. T. J. Armstrong. NY: Harvester Wheatsheaf, 1992. 58–64.

Miller, James. *The Passion of Michel Foucault.* NY: Simon and Schuster, 1993.

Miller, Paul Allen. *Lyric Texts and Lyric Consciousness: The Birth of a Genre from Archaic Greece to Augustan Rome.* London: Routledge, 1994.

Mink, Louis O. *Historical Understanding.* Ed. Brian Fay, Eugene O. Golob and Richard T. Vann. Ithaca: Cornell UP, 1987.

Minson, Jeffrey. *Genealogies of Morals: Nietzsche, Foucault, Donzelot and the Eccentricity of Ethics.* Basingstoke: MacMillan, 1985.

Morilhat, Claude. *La prise de conscience de capitalisme.* Paris: Méridiens Klincksieck, 1988.

Mosse, George. "Fascism and the French Revolution." *Journal of Contemporary History* 24 (1989): 5–26.

Mottahedeh, Roy. *The Mantle of the Prophet: Religion and Politics in Iran.* London: Chatto and Windus, 1985.

Muchembled, Robert. *Culture populaire et culture des élites dans la France moderne (XVe–XVIIIe siècles).* Paris: Flammarion, 1978.

—. *Popular Culture and Elite Culture in France, 1400–1750.* Trans. Lydia Cochrane. Baton Rouge: Louisiana State UP, 1985.

—. *L'invention de l'homme moderne: sensibilités, moeurs et comportements collectifs sous l'Ancien Régime.* Paris: Fayard, 1988.

Murray, Stephen O. *American Gay.* Chicago: U of Chicago P, 1996.

Neubauer, John. "Models for the History of Science and of Literature". *Bucknell Review* 2 (1983): 17–37.

Nies, Fritz. *Gattungspoetik und Publikumsstruktur: zur Geschichte der Sévignébriefe.* Munich: Fink, 1972.

Noiriel, Gérard. "Foucault and History: the Lessons of a Desillusion." *Journal of Modern History* 66 (1994): 547–68.

O'Hara, David T. "Why Foucault No Longer Matters." Miguel-Alfonso and Caporale-Bizzini 139–58.

Oaks, Robert F. "'Things Fearful to Name': Sodomy and Buggery in Seventeenth-Century New England." *Journal of Social History* 12 (1978): 268–81.

—. "Defining Sodomy in Seventeenth-Century Massachusetts." Licata and Petersen 79–83.

O'Brien, Patricia. "Michel Foucault's History of Culture." Hunt 25–46.

O'Farrell, Clare. *Foucault: Historian or Philosopher?* Basingstoke: MacMillan, 1993.

Oestreich, Gerhard. "Strukturprobleme des europäischen Absolutismus." *Geist und Gestalt des frühmodernen Staates. Ausgewählte Aufsätze.* Berlin: Duncker and Humblot, 1969. 179–97.

Olivier, Lawrence, and Sylvain Labbé. "Foucault et l'Iran: A propos du désir de révolution." *Canadian Journal of Political Science* 24 (1991): 219–36.

Ort, Claus-Michael. "Literarischer Wandel und sozialer Wandel: Theoretische Anmerkungen zum Verhältnis von Wissenssoziologie und Diskursgeschichte." *Modelle des literarischen Strukturwandelns.* Ed. M. Titzmann. Tübingen: Niemeyer, 1991. 367–94.

Otto, Stephan. *Das Wissen des Ähnlichen: Michel Foucault und die Renaissance.* Bern: Lang, 1992.

Pagden, Anthony. *The Fall of Natural Man.* Cambridge: Cambridge UP, 1986.

Peñalver, Patricio. "Archaeology, History, Deconstruction: Foucault's Thought and the Philosophical Experience." Miguel-Alfonso and Caporale Bizzini 3–33.

Perkins, David. *Is Literary History Possible?* Baltimore: Johns Hopkins UP, 1992.

Peters, F. E. *The Harvest of Hellenism.* NY: Simon and Schuster, 1970.

Platter, Charles. "*Officium* in Catullus and Propertius: A Foucauldian Reading." *Classical Philology* 90 (1995): 211–24.

Pleij, Herman. *De sneeuwpoppen van 1511. Literatuur en stadscultuur tussen middeleeuwen en moderne tijd.* Amsterdam: Meulenhoff / Leuven: Kritak, 1988.

—-, ed. *Op belofte van profijt. Stadsliteratuur en burgermoraal in de Nederlandse letterkunde van de middeleeuwen.* Amsterdam: Prometheus, 1991.

Pocock, J. G. A. *Politics, Language and Time.* London: Methuen, 1972.

Pomeroy, Sarah. B. *Goddesses, Whores, Wives, and Slaves.* London: Schocken, 1976.

Popper, Karl. "Normal Science and its Dangers." Lakatos and Musgrave 51–58.

—. *The Myth of the Framework.* London: Routledge, 1994.

Poster, Mark. *Foucault, Marxism and History.* Cambridge: Polity P, 1984.

Power, Henry, and Leonard W. Sedgwick. *The New Sydenham Society's Lexicon of Medicine and Allied Sciences.* 12 vols. London: The New Sydenham Society, 1881–99.

Prado, C. G. *Starting with Foucault: An Introduction to Genealogy.* Boulder, CO: Westview, 1995.

Priest, Graham. *Beyond the Limits of Thought.* Cambridge: Cambridge UP, 1995.

Privitera, Walter. *Problems of Style: Michel Foucault's Epistemology.* Albany: SUNY P, 1995.

"Procès-verbaux des délibérations du Conseil royal de l'instruction publique." Archives Nationales, Paris. F17*1795, Session of September 28, 1832.

Prochasson, Christophe. "L'histoire et Foucault." *Vingtième siècle. Revue d'histoire* 50 (1996): 123–25.

Quinn, Kenneth. *Catullus: An Interpretation.* London: Batsford, 1972.

Rabinow, Paul, ed. *The Foucault Reader.* NY: Pantheon, 1984.

Rabinowitz, Nancy Sorkin, and Amy Richlin, eds. *Feminist Theory and the Classics.* London: Routledge, 1993.

Ragland-Sullivan, Ellie. *Jacques Lacan and the Philosophy of Psychoanalysis.* Urbana: U of Illinois P, 1986.

Rankin, H. D. "Catullus and the Privacy of Love." *Wiener Studien* N. F. (1975): 67–74.

Reed, Joel. "Academically Speaking: Language and Nationalism in Seventeenth- and Eighteenth-Century England." Ph.D. Diss. U of California, Irvine 1991.

Rejali, Darius M. *Torture and Modernity: Self, Society, and State in Modern Iran.* Boulder, CO: Westview, 1994.

Richlin, Amy. "Not Before Homosexuality: The Materiality of the *Cinaedus* and the Roman Law against Love Between Men." *Journal of the History of Sexuality* 2 (1993): 523–73.

—. "Zeus and Metis: Foucault, Feminism, and Classics." *Helios* 18 (1991): 160–80.

Ricoeur, Paul. *Time and Narrative.* [Trans. *Temps et récit.* 1983–1985.] Trans. Kathleen McLaughlin (Blamey) and David Pellauer. 3 vols. Chicago: U of Chicago P, 1984–88.

—. *Reflection and Imagination.* Ed. M. J. Valdés. Toronto: U of Toronto P, 1991.

Roberts, Michael. "Rereading Marx and Nietzsche." *Rethinking MARXISM* 8 (1996): 100–11.

Robson, Eleanor. *Mesopotamian mathematics,* Oxford: Oxford UP, forthcoming.

Rodinson, Maxime. *L'Islam: politique et croyance.* Paris: Fayard, 1993.

Rose, Mary Beth. *Women in the Middle Ages and the Renaissance.* Syracuse: Syracuse UP, 1986.

Rose, Peter. "The Case for Not Ignoring Marx in the Study of Women in Antiquity." Rabinowitz and Richlin 211–37.

Rosenberg, Rainer. "Epochen." *Literaturwissenschaft: Ein Grundkurs.* Ed. H. Brackert and J. Stückrath. Hamburg: Rohwolt, 1992. 269–80.

—. "Epochengliederung: Zur Geschichte des Periodisierungsproblems in der deutschen Literaturgeschichtsschreibung." *Von der gelehrten zur disziplinären Gemeinschaft.* Ed. J. Fohrmann and W. Voßkamp. Special issue of the *Deutsche Vierteljahrsschrift für Literaturwissenschaft und Geistesgeschichte.* 1987. 216–35.

Ross Jr., David O. *Backgrounds to Augustan Elegy.* Cambridge: Cambridge UP, 1975.

Roth, M. S. "Foucault's History of the Present." *History and Theory* 20 (1981): 32–46.

Rouse, Joseph. "Power / Knowledge." Gutting 92–114.

Rousseau, G. S. "The Death of Michel Foucault." *London Literary Review* 6 (1984): 13–15.

—. "Whose Enlightenment? Not Man's: The Case of Michel Foucault." *Eighteenth-Century Studies* 6 (1972): 238–56.

—. *Perilous Enlightenment.* Manchester: Manchester UP, 1991.

Royez (?). *La vie et les doléances d'un Pauvre diable.* Paris(?), 1789.

Rubino, Carl. "The Erotic World of Catullus." *Classical World* 68 (1975): 289–98.

Ryan, Michael. "Foucault's Fallacy." Miguel-Alfonso and Caporale-Bizzini 159–81.

Said, Edward. "Michel Foucault 1926–1984." *After Foucault: Humanistic Knowledge, Postmodern Challenges.* Ed. Jonathan Arac. New Brunswick: Rutgers UP, 1988.

Sakolsky, Ron. "'Disciplinary Power,' The Labor Process and the Constitution of the Laboring Subject." *Rethinking MARXISM* 5 (1992): 114–26.

Saleh, Hashim. *al-fikr al-islâmî: al-naqd wa'l-ijtihâd [Islamic Thought: Critique and Judgment]*. London: Dar al-Saqi, 1990.

Salle, Eusèbe de. *Lettre d'un médecin à un avocat*. Paris: Gabon, 1828.

Santori, Santori. *Methodi vitandorum errorum*. Venice, 1603.

Sartre, Jean-Paul. *Saint Genet: Actor and Martyr*. 1963. London: Heinemann, 1988.

Saslow, James M. *Ganymede in the Renaissance: Homosexuality in Art and Society*. New Haven: Yale UP, 1986.

Sawicki, Jana. "Foucault, Feminism and Questions of Identity." Gutting 286 – 313.

Schilling, Heinz, ed. *Kirchenzucht und Sozialdisziplinierung im frühneuzeitlichen Europa*. Berlin: Duncker and Humblot, 1994.

Schönert, Jörn . "The Social History of German Literature: On the Present State of Distress in the Social History of German Literature." *Poetics* 14 (1985): 303 – 19.

Scott, J. C. *Domination and the Art of Resistance: Hidden Transcripts*. New Haven: Yale UP, 1990.

Seconds, Jean-Louis. *De l'état social*. Paris, 1792.

Sedgwick, Eve Kosofsky. *The Epistemology of the Closet*. Berkeley: U of California P, 1990.

Segal, Charles. "Catullan *Otiosi*: The Lover and the Poet." *Greece and Rome* 17 (1970): 25 – 31.

Shariati, Ali. *Marxism and other Western Fallacies: An Islamic Critique*. Trans. R. Campbell. Berkeley: Mizan P, 1980.

Shelton, Jo-Ann. *As the Romans Did: Sourcebook in Roman Social History*. Oxford: Oxford UP, 1988.

Sheridan, Alan. *Michel Foucault: The Will to Power*. London: Tavistock, 1980.

Showalter, Elaine. "Representing Ophelia: Women, Madness, and the Responsibilities of Feminist Criticism." *Shakespeare and the Question of Theory*. Ed. Patricia Parker and Geoffrey Hartman. NY: Methuen, 1985. 77 – 94.

– . *The Female Malady: Women, Madness, and English Culture, 1830 – 1980*. London: Virago, 1985.

– . *Hystories: Hysterical Epidemics and Modern Culture*. London: Picador, 1996.

Shumway, David R. *Michel Foucault*. Charlottesville: U of Virginia P, 1989.

Skultans, Vieda. *English Madness: Ideas on Insanity, 1580 – 1890*. London: Routledge, 1979.

Sokal, Alan D. "Transgressing the Boundaries: An Afterword." *Philosophy and Literature* 20 (1996): 338 – 46.

Solomon, Maynard. "Franz Schubert and the Peacocks of Benvenuto Cellini." *Nineteenth-Century Music* 12 (1989): 193 – 206.

Sontag, Susan. "Camp." *Against Interpretation and other Essays*. NY: Delta, 1966. 275 – 92.

Spitzer, Alan B. *The French Generation of 1820*. Princeton: Princeton UP, 1987.

Stallybrass, Peter, and Allon White. *The Politics and Poetics of Transgression*. London: Methuen, 1986.

Stauth, Georg. *Revolution in Spiritless Times: An Essay on the Inquiries of Michel Foucault on the Iranian Revolution*. Singapore: National U of Singapore, Dept. of Sociology (Working papers no. 103), 1991.

Stein, Edward, ed. *Forms of Desire: Sexual Orientation and the Social Constructionist Controversy*. NY: Routledge, 1992.

Steinberg, Michael P. "Cultural History and Cultural Studies." *Disciplinarity and Dissent in Cultural Studies*. Ed. Cary Nelson and Dilip Parameshwar Gaonkar. London: Routledge, 1996. 103 – 29.

Stoekl, Allan. *Agonies of the Intellectual: Commitment, Subjectivity, and the Performative in the 20th Century French Tradition.* Lincoln: U of Nebraska P, 1992.

Stone, Lawrence. "The Revival of Narrative: Reflections on a New Old History. *Past and Present* 85 (November 1979): 3–24.

—. "Madness." *The New York Review of Books* 16 Dec. 1982.

Syme, Ronald. *The Roman Revolution.* 1939. Oxford: Oxford UP, 1983.

Tatum, James. "The Tales in Apuleius' *Metamorphoses.*" *Transactions of the American Philological Association* 100 (1969): 487–527.

Taylor, Charles. "Michel Foucault on Freedom and Truth." *Philosophy and the Human Sciences: Collected Papers.* Cambridge: Cambridge UP, 1985. 2: 152–84.

Thompson, E. P. *The Making of the English Working Class.* London: Gollancz, 1963. Rev. ed. Harmondsworth: Penguin, 1968.

Thomson, Damian. *The End of Time.* NY: Vintage, 1997.

Tomlinson, Gary. *Music in Renaissance Magic: Toward a Historiography of Others.* Chicago: U of Chicago P, 1993.

Toulmin, Stephen. "Conceptual Change and the Problem of Relativity." Krausz 201-20.

Tully, James, and Quentin Skinner, eds. *Meaning and Context: Quentin Skinner and his Critics.* Cambridge: Polity P, 1988.

Turkle, Sherry. *Life on the Screen: Identity in the Age of the Internet.* NY: Simon and Schuster, 1995.

Van Leer, David. *The Queening of America: Gay Culture in Straight Society.* NY: Routledge, 1995.

Varlet, Jean-François. *Déclaration solennelle.* Paris, 1793.

Vermeren, Patrice. *Victor Cousin: Le jeu de la philosophie et de l'état.* Paris: L'Harmattan, 1995.

Veyne, Paul. "Foucault révolutionne l'histoire!" *Comment on écrit l'histoire.* Ed. Paul Veyne. Paris: Seuil, 1978. 201–42.

—. "The Roman Empire." *From Pagan Rome to Byzantium.* Trans. Arthur Goldhammer. *A History of Private Life,* vol. 1. Ed. Philippe Ariès and Georges Duby. Cambridge, MA: Harvard UP, 1987. 6–234.

—. *Roman Erotic Elegy: Love, Poetry, and the West.* Trans. David Pellauer. Chicago: U of Chicago P, 1988.

Vilar, Pierre. "Histoire marxiste, histoire en construction." Le Goff and Nora 169–209.

Villa, Dana R. *Arendt and Heidegger: The Fate of the Political.* Princeton: Princeton UP, 1996.

Volney, C. F. *Sentinelle du peuple.* Rennes, 1789.

Voloshinov, V. N. *Marxism and the Philosophy of Language.* Trans. Ladislav Matejka and I. R. Titunik. Cambridge, MA: Harvard UP, 1973.

Vries, Hent de. *Philosophy and the Turn to Religion,* John Hopkins UP, forthcoming

Waldrop, M. M. *Complexity: The Emerging Science at the Edge of Order and Chaos.* NY: Simon and Schuster, 1992.

Warner, Michael. "New English Sodom." *American Literature* 64 (1992): 19–47. Rpt. *Queering the Renaissance.* Ed. Jonathan Goldberg. Durham: Duke UP, 1994. 330–58.

Waswo, Richard. *Language and Meaning in the Renaissance.* Princeton: Princeton UP, 1987.

Weber, Max. "Die 'Objektivität' sozialwissenschaftlicher und sozialpolitischer Erkenntnis." 1904. *Gesammelte Aufsätze zur Wissenschaftslehre.* Ed. J. Winckelmann. 3rd ed. Tübingen: Mohr, 1968. 146–214.

—. *Wirtschaft und Gesellschaft.* Tübingen: Mohr, 1976.

—. *Selection in Translation*. Ed. W. G. Runciman, trans. E. Matthews. Cambridge: Cambridge UP, 1978.

White, Hayden V. *Metahistory*. Baltimore: Johns Hopkins UP, 1973.

—. *The Content of the Form: Narrative Discourse and Historical Representation*. Baltimore: Johns Hopkins UP, 1987.

Wilkinson, L. P. *The Roman Experience*. Lanham, MD: UP of America, 1974.

Winick, Charles. *The Desexualization in American Life*. 1968. Rev. ed. New Brunswick: Transaction, 1995.

Winthrop, John. *The History of New England from 1630 to 1649*. Ed. James Savage. Boston: Phelps, 1825–26.

Wiseman, T. P. *Catullan Questions*. Leicester: Leicester UP, 1969.

—. *Catullus and His World*. Cambridge: Cambridge UP, 1985.

Wood, David. *On Paul Ricœur: Narrative and Interpretation*. London: Routledge, 1991.

Woodman, W. Bathurst, and Charles Meymott Tidy. *A Handy-Book of Forensic Medicine and Toxicology*. London: Churchill, 1877.

Wright, Georg Hendrik von. *Explanation and Understanding*. London: Routledge, 1971.

Wuthnow, Robert L. *Cultural Analysis: The Work of Peter L. Berger, Mary Douglas, Michel Foucault, and Jürgen Habermas*. London: Routledge, 1984.

Yates, Frances. *The Art of Memory*. Chicago: U of Chicago P, 1966.

Zeldin, Theodore. *France 1848–1945*. 2 vols. Oxford: Oxford UP, 1973–77.

Zizek, Slavoj. *The Sublime Object of Ideology*. London: Verso, 1989.

—. *Tarrying With the Negative: Kant, Hegel and the Critique of Ideology*. Durham: Duke UP, 1993.